LEARNING
FOR TOMORROW
The Role of the Future
in Education

LEARNING FOR TOMORROW

The Role of the Future
in Education

Edited by Alvin Toffler

Random House   New York

Library of Congress Cataloging in Publication Data

Toffler, Alvin.
Learning for tomorrow.

Bibliography: p.
1. Education—United States—1965-   2. Forecasting.
3. Civilization, Modern—1950-
I. Title.
LA209.2.T57   1974   370.19′0973   73-12914
ISBN 0-394-48313-8

Manufactured in the United States of America
24689753

For Karen

Table of Contents

PART TWO

The Place of the Future in the Curriculum

PART THREE
Directions and Resources

Acknowledgment

This book of original materials could not have been prepared without the assistance of the Ellis L. Phillips Foundation, whose support of the project through its various early transformations has been unwavering, even when it seemed at times that the long-range future would arrive well before a publishable manuscript was in hand. I must, however, go beyond the formalities to thank the real person behind the Foundation—Ellis L. Phillips, Jr., President of Ithaca College, whose gentle patience and good humor has been never failing. Because of him the Foundation has made a series of quiet, but significant contributions to educational change in the last decade.

Notes about the Authors

PAULINE B. BART is a sociologist teaching behavioral science to medical students at Abraham Lincoln Medical School at the University of Illinois. She is chairperson for the section on sex roles of the American Sociological Association and has been active in Sociologists for Women in Society. Trapped by the feminine mystique in the fifties, she returned to UCLA in 1961 after having added two children and dropped a husband. She obtained her Ph.D. studying depression in middle-aged women, *Portnoy's Mother's Complaint* (1967).

WENDELL BELL taught at Stanford University, Northwestern University, and UCLA before moving to Yale University as Professor of Sociology in 1963. He served as Chairman of the Department from 1965 to 1969 and now directs a training program in comparative sociology. His research has been in urban sociology and political sociology, including field work in the new nations of the Caribbean, where he became interested in futuristics. His publications include *Social Area Analysis* (1955), *Public Leadership* (1961), *Decisions of Nationhood* (1964), *Jamaican Leaders* (1964), *The Democratic Revolution in the West Indies* (1967), *The Sociology of the Future* (1971), and *Ethnicity and Nation-Building* (1973).

IRVING H. BUCHEN is Professor of English at Fairleigh Dickinson University, Madison, New Jersey, and the author of *Isaac Bashevis Singer and the Eternal Past* and *The Perverse Imagination,* as well as nearly thirty articles on literary and humanistic subjects, with emphasis on aesthetics and societal forms. Most recently he designed an intercollege program in futuristics which services students from all disciplines at both undergradute and graduate levels.

H. WENTWORTH ELDREDGE is Professor of Sociology at Dartmouth College, where he teaches "Futurism and Long-Range Planning." He has been involved in the educational futures movement from its inception, having taught "The Future of Urbanism and Cities" in 1967 at Berkeley. He has edited and written various books dealing with cities and the future.

NELL EURICH, Professor of English and Literature, is Provost, Dean of Faculty, and Director of Curriculum Development at Manhattanville College. Formerly Dean of Faculty at Vassar College, she is a trustee of New College, Sarasota, Florida, a member of the Visiting Committee, Harvard University, and a consultant to the National Endowment for the Humanities. In the late 1940s she organized the White House Conference on the Family. Married, with two children, she is the author of *Science in Utopia*.

PRISCILLA P. GRIFFITH has been teaching social studies at Melbourne High School near Cape Kennedy since 1961. She earned her A.B. degree at Florida State University and her M.A. in American Studies at Stetson University. She is a field consultant for the World Law Fund and has served as consultant to the Office of Education, Department of Health, Education and Welfare. She is coeditor with Betty Reardon and Jacob Dresden of the World Order Reader Series. A revised version of the "21st Century" course described in her chapter is now being taught by her at Melbourne.

HOWARD KIRSCHENBAUM is Director of the Adirondack Mt. Humanistic Education Center in Upper Jay, New York. He formerly taught at Temple University and the New School for Social Research and has led workshops for educators all over the country on values education and humanistic education. He has written numerous professional articles and books, including (with Sidney B. Simon) *Values Clarification: A Handbook of Practical Strategies*; *WAD-JA-GET? The Grading Game in American Education*; *Clarifying Values Through Subject Matter*; and *The Alternative Wedding*.

DENNIS LIVINGSTON received a Ph.D. in political science from Princeton University and has taught courses on international relations at the University of California in Davis, and on science and public policy at Case Western Reserve University. He has written widely on such diverse topics as pollution, science fiction, science policy and international law. Work in progress includes a book on international pollution problems for the World Law Fund and a paper on global arrangements for the control of ocean pollution for the Scripps Institution on Oceanography. Based in Cleveland Heights, Ohio, he is a consultant on education for alternative world futures.

MICHAEL A. MCDANIELD was formerly Assistant Vice-President and Executive Editor of Social Science and English in the Educational Book Division, Prentice-Hall, Inc. In this position he designed and developed many innovative programs in social science and English.

Mr. McDanield has been involved in education for more than fifteen years, initially as a teacher and then in educational publishing. During this period he continued graduate study at the University of Maryland and in a special interdisciplinary graduate program at The Johns Hopkins University. His current work involves the use of models in social science curriculum and the development of programs at the interface of science and social science.

ALVIN F. POUSSAINT, a graduate of Columbia and Cornell Universities, is currently Associate Professor of Psychiatry and Associate Dean of Student Affairs at Harvard Medical School. He grew up in East Harlem's ghetto and has worked extensively in the field of civil rights. He is the author of numerous articles on the black struggle, which have appeared both in scientific and lay publications.

BILLY ROJAS was Director of the Futuristics Curriculum Project at Alice Lloyd College, where he designed and developed ten undergraduate futures courses. He has degrees from Roosevelt University and the University of Massachusetts. At the U. of M. School of Education in Amherst, Rojas created the Program for the Study of the Future in Education, making it the first graduate school to allow major concentration in futures research.

HAROLD G. SHANE is University Professor of Education at Indiana University, where he served for a number of years as Dean of the School of Education. Author of over one hundred books and more than two hundred articles, he teaches in the fields of curriculum and teacher education.

JUNE GRANT SHANE is Professor of Education at Indiana University. She has long been interested in education of young children, and among the books for which she is senior author is *Guiding Human Development*. Her field of specialization is teacher education and the language arts.

SIDNEY B. SIMON is Professor of Humanistic Education at the University of Massachusetts. He formerly taught at Queens College and Temple University and is a nationally known leader in the values clarification and humanistic education movements. He is author of numerous articles and many books, including (with Howard Kirschenbaum) *Values and Teaching*; *Values Clarification: A Handbook of Practical Strategies*; *WAD-JA-GET? The Grading Game in American Education*; and *Clarifying Values Through Subject Matter*.

BENJAMIN D. SINGER is Professor of Sociology at the University of Western Ontario and has been Lincoln Filene Visiting Professor at Dartmouth College. He has been consultant to the Federal Department of Communications in Ottawa and to Children's Psychiatric Research Institute. He is the author, coauthor or editor of the books *Black Rioters*; *For Want of An Ombudsman: Mass Channels as Public Feedback*; *Radio in a Community Emergency*; *Communications in Canadian Society*, as well as articles in *Public*

Opinion Quarterly, Social Problems, the *British Journal of Sociology* and other scholarly journals.

HAROLD L. STRUDLER is President of the Center for Adaptive Learning, Inc., an ad hoc company now developing future-oriented learning materials for the secondary schools. Having graduated from Harvard Law School and practiced private law for some years, in 1970 he joined the Institute for the Future as both Research Fellow and General Counsel. He has been a consultant to the Futures Group, Inc., and a special delegate to the United Nations Institute for Training and Research (London conference on international futurist activities).

ALVIN TOFFLER is the author of *Future Shock.* A former Associate Editor of *Fortune* magazine, he has served as Visiting Scholar at the Russell Sage Foundation and Visiting Professor at Cornell University. At the New School for Social Research in 1966 he taught one of the first courses devoted entirely to the future. He is the editor of *The Schoolhouse in the City* and *The Futurists,* and author of an earlier book, *The Culture Consumers.*

PHILIP WERDELL is Associate Coordinator of the Master Plan for the City University of New York. He was Director of Programming for the U.S. National Student Association, editor of *Moderator* magazine, and a staff member of the American Council on Education. Co-inventor of the "Facilitator" family of teaching and learning models, he has consulted on educational reform with students, faculty and management at over a hundred campuses. Author of *An Intellectual Biography of William Graham Sumner; Student Course and Teacher Evaluation;* and dozens of magazine and journal articles, he is now working on a book of responses to future shock.

JOHN WREN-LEWIS, one of the first professional futurists in Britain, helped organize the "think tank" in the Research and Development Department of Imperial Chemical Industries, Ltd., out of which grew that company's noted study of the year 2000. Originally trained as a mathematician, he has also become known as a theologian and has recently served as Visiting Professor of Religion at New College, Sarasota, Florida, and as Regents Lecturer, University of California at Santa Barbara. He is author of *God in a Technological Age* and is President of the British Association for Humanistic Psychology.

Introduction

Any book that deals with tomorrow involves itself, by definition, with expectations, and it is important at the outset of this one that the reader be given a clear guide as to what to expect. What follows is *not* a book about the future of education. Rather, this book is about the ways in which the very notion of future time is dealt with in our schools and universities.

For this reason, the reader will find little reference to many developments in education which no doubt merit attention elsewhere. There is virtually no reference to computers in the classroom, to programmed instruction, to audio-visual delights or other technological aids. The whole "open school" movement, valuable as it is, receives only minimal mention. (Many of the ideas in this volume, however, are crucial to open schools.)

Similarly, while most of the authors brought together here are sympathetic to "alternative schools" and other attempts to educate young people outside the formal structures that now exist, the book is primarily intended for those who wish to have an impact inside the "system."

This is not because any of us are particularly enamored of the existing machinery; indeed, many of us believe that this machinery is actively hostile or dangerous to our youth. It arises from a sober conviction that, despite efforts at radical reform, the vast majority of young people in the technological societies will continue, for at least the next half-decade, to receive their experience of formal education inside, not outside, the system. If this is so, they must not be abandoned to those who wish only to preserve the present.

The writers assembled here come from a wide range of fields, and do not necessarily agree with one another on all issues. They do not even agree on terminology, so that some use the word "futuristics" while others refer to "futures studies"; some speak of "predicting" while others shudder at the word and refer instead to "forecasting" or "projecting." Some of the authors, both male and female, are deeply concerned about women's rights, and have consciously avoided use of terms like Man, Mankind, or His-tory. Others find this amusing or annoying. Still others betray the special interests of their own disciplinary backgrounds, which range from sociology and psychology, to education theory, law, teaching, psychiatry and long-range planning. Nevertheless, several underlying assumptions integrate the volume.

First, *all* the contributors agree that today's schools and universities are too past- and present-bound. Thus, from its first chapter to its last, the book stands as a manifesto for those who wish to see the future introduced into education. This is its reason for being.

Second, the authors agree that technological and social change is outracing the educational system, and that social reality is transforming itself more rapidly than our educational images of that reality. What follows therefore is a proposed strategy for closing the gap. This strategy is based on a recognition that the future, itself, can be a powerful organizing concept for change. Taken as a whole, this book says that introducing the future is a direct, yet relatively painless, way to begin the move toward necessary changes, not merely in curricula, but in the internal structure of educational institutions and in their external links to the community.

Third, as Toffler, Singer, Bart and Poussaint argue, the concept of the future is closely bound up with the motivation of the learner, and our failure to recognize this paralyzes our programs and mutilates our children. How children or young adults see their future is directly connected with their academic performance and, more important, with their "experiential performance"—their ability to live, cope and grow in a high-change society. Future-conscious education is a key to adaptivity, and, these authors argue, it is especially significant for women and for the children of ethnic minorities, both of which groups can today be regarded as "future-deprived."

Fourth, most of the writers in these pages further recognize that the future is not merely a "subject" but a perspective as well, and, in urging its introduction into learning, they are also arguing for a new organization of knowledge. While the book is organized conventionally, and deliberately so, it is intended to help serious educators smash the disciplinary conventions. Thus the question of the organization of knowledge arises clearly in the chapters by Bell, Buchen, Eurich, Wren-Lewis and Strudler. Ranging from the hard sciences to the humanities, each writer emphasizes the relationship of his or her subject to the strong currents of change in the world that make essential a total conceptual revision of the notion of knowledge itself.

Fifth, the authors assume, although only June and Harold Shane deal explicitly with the issue, that a focus on the future is relevant to all learners, regardless of age. The future is a matter for the concern not simply of graduate students, but of the youngest elementary-school children as well, whether enrolled in conventional schools or in experimental centers. McDanield and Griffith argue that secondary-school students, too, can and must begin dealing with tomorrow. The future represents a starting point for change at all levels.

Throughout the book there is a general dissatisfaction with conventional forms, media and pedagogical processes, and a suggestion, by Rojas, for example, that the introduction of the future is also a spearpoint for change in educational methodology—that it opens the opportunity for a fascinating and effective variety of games, simulations, contrived experiences, classroom theater, role-playing and the like, making it a vehicle for change in form, as well as content.

In the same way, the reader will find throughout a deep concern not merely for "cognitive" or even "affective" education, but also for "moral" learning, to use an old-fashioned phrase. The future is not predetermined. It is at least partly subject to our influence, and our interest must therefore focus on "preferable" futures as well as those that are "possible" and "probable." For this reason, the question of values crops up repeatedly. "Learning for tomorrow" includes learning to know one's own mind, so to speak, to understand one's own values clearly enough to be able to make consistent and effective choices. Kirschenbaum and Simon make the connection explicit: they deal with value clarification and future choice-making.

The authors of *Learning for Tomorrow* assume that the future *matters* politically and socially as well as educationally. Beyond this, many believe that the introduction of the future into learning is necessarily related to the deep, one might say revolutionary, currents in the world today: the struggle for the emancipation of women, the battle to gain a fair shake for people of every racial complexion, the fight to gain dignity for young people as well, in a system that tends to push them out of the centers of decision-making and hold them in "cold storage" (and off the labor market) for longer and longer periods.

In this connection, it is clear that one of the key social struggles of the coming decade will involve the reformulation of the meaning of work, and that the future cannot be conceived of in terms of the simple continuation of forms of work that brutalize and stultify the vast majority of human beings.

Werdell, in the final chapter, links the wave of educational reform that swept America and other nations in the sixties to the new wave of change based on the idea that the future is central to education. In so doing, he begins to connect them both up with the transformation of work in the future.

And finally, because all the authors believe in a close tie between theory and practice, and because manifestoes that do not lead to action are worthless, the book provides an Appendix prepared by Rojas and Eldredge that tells students, parents, educators and anyone else who may be interested, what is happening where, in this new wave of innovation. It provides examples of syllabi used in various schools, from graduate centers down to primary schools, and it provides a "contact" list—people, institutions and organizations who can help accelerate the arrival of the future in education so that we can all of us deal more rationally and competently with its arrival in our lives.

For these varied reasons, I believe that *Learning for Tomorrow* has implications that range beyond the classroom walls—and beyond the present.

A.T.

PART ONE

Images of the Future
and Individual Development

The wave of educational reform that swept schools and colleges in the sixties has reached a new phase. The next step in the struggle to restructure education involves a convergence of new attitudes toward time with new attitudes toward action. This chapter contends that all education springs from images of the future, and that today's learners are being divorced from their own future selves. It presents a theoretical basis for the chapters that follow.

CHAPTER ONE

The Psychology of the Future

by Alvin Toffler

> "That's the reason they're called lessons," the Gryphon remarked: "because they lessen from day to day."
> —*Lewis Carroll*

All education springs from some image of the future. If the image of the future held by a society is grossly inaccurate, its education system will betray its youth.

Imagine an Indian tribe which for centuries has sailed its dugouts on the river at its doorstep. During all this time the economy and culture of the tribe have depended upon fishing, preparing and cooking the products of the river, growing food in soil fertilized by the river, building boats and appropriate tools. So long as the rate of technological change in such a community stays slow, so long as no wars, invasions, epidemics or other natural disasters upset the even rhythm of life, it is simple for the tribe to formulate a workable image of its own future, since tomorrow merely repeats yesterday.

It is from this image that education flows. Schools may not even exist in the tribe; yet there is a curriculum—a cluster of skills, values and rituals to be learned. Boys are taught to scrape bark and hollow out trees, just as their ancestors did before them. The teacher in such a system knows what he is doing, secure in the knowledge that tradition—the past—will work in the future.

What happens to such a tribe, however, when it pursues its traditional methods unaware that five hundred miles upstream men are constructing a gigantic dam that will dry up their branch of the river? Suddenly the tribe's image of the future, the set of assumptions on which its members base their present behavior, becomes dangerously misleading. Tomorrow will not replicate today. The tribal investment in preparing its children to live in a riverine culture becomes a pointless and potentially tragic waste. A false image of the future destroys the relevance of the education effort.[1]

This is our situation today—only it is we, ironically, not some distant strangers—who are building the dam that will annihilate the culture of the present. Never before has any culture subjected itself to so intense and prolonged a bombardment of technological, social, and info-psychological change. This change is accelerating and we witness everywhere in the high-technology societies evidence that the old industrial-era structures can no longer carry out their functions.

Yet our political leaders for the most part propagate (and believe) the myth that industrial society is destined to perpetuate itself indefinitely. Like the elders of the tribe living on the riverbank, they blindly assume that the main features of the present social system will extend indefinitely into the future. And most educators, including most of those who regard themselves as agents of change, unthinkingly accept this myth.

They fail to recognize that the acceleration of change—in technology, in family structure, marriage and divorce patterns, mobility rates, division of labor, in urbanization, ethnic and subcultural conflict and international relations—means, by definition, the swift arrival of a future that is radically *different* from the present. They have never tried to imagine what a super-industrial civilization might look like, and what this might mean for their students.

And so, most schools, colleges and universities base their teaching on the usually tacit notion that tomorrow's world will be basically familiar: the present writ large. Nothing, I believe, could be more profoundly deceptive.

I would contend, in fact, that no educational institution today can set sensible goals or do an effective job until its members— from chancellor or principal down to the newest faculty recruit, not to mention its students—subject their own assumptions about tomorrow to critical analysis. For their shared or collective image of the future dominates the decisions made in the institution.

The primitive father teaching his son how to carve a canoe had in mind an image of the future his son would inhabit. Since he assumed that the future would replicate the present, just as the present replicated the past, his image of the future was just as rich, detailed, comprehensive and structured as his image of the present. It *was* his image of the present. Yet when change struck, his imagery proved not merely obsolete but anti-adaptive because it left out the possibility of radical change.

Like our distant ancestor, educators, too, need an image of tomorrow's society. But this image must include the possibility— indeed, the high likelihood—of radical change. This image need not be "correct" or "final"; it cannot be. There are no certainties, and any picture of a foreseeable society that depicts it as static or stable is probably delusory. Thus, to design educational systems for tomorrow (or even for today) we need not images of a future frozen in amber, as it were, but something far more complicated: sets of images of successive and alternative futures, each one tentative and different from the next.

These images of tomorrow cannot be predictive in the sense that they discern some unshakable future reality. The possible future is not singular, but plural, subject to the choices we make among innumerable arrayed options. Moreover, the tools we have for identifying possible and probable futures are still very primitive.[2] Yet some lines of development are more likely than others, and it is only by making explicit our assumptions about where we seem to be going that we can formulate sensible goals. Only in this way can we deduce the kinds of human abilities, skills and growth patterns that need to be encouraged.

Scenario in the Classroom

What applies to the educator and the institution applies even more strongly to the learner. Just as all social groups and institutions have, in effect, collectively shared images of the future, each individual also has, in his or her cranium, a set of assumptions, an architecture of premises, about events to come. The child, almost from birth, begins to build up a set of expectations from its daily experience. Later these expectations become more complexly organized, and they begin to encompass more and more distant reaches of future time. Each person's private image of the future shapes his or her decision-making in crucial ways.

Students today receive a vast amount of undigested information and misinformation from newspapers, records, TV, movies, radio and other sources. As a result, they are aware of the rapidity with which the world is changing. But if many young people are prepared to contemplate the idea of radical change in the real world, this does not mean that they have the slightest idea about the implications of high-speed change for their own lives.

Some time ago I performed an unusual and confessedly non-scientific experiment with thirty-three high-school students, mainly fifteen- and sixteen-year olds. I asked each of them to help formulate a collective image of the future by writing down on a slip of paper seven events he or she thought likely to occur in the future, and to then date these events. I avoided saying anything that would restrict the *kind* of events or their *distance* into the future. The class threw itself enthusiastically into the exercise, and in a few minutes I had collected from them 193 forecast events, each of them duly dated. The results indicated that these urban, middle-class, rather sophisticated teenagers had accumulated many notions about the world of tomorrow.

From their forecasts there emerged, for example, a terrifying future for the United States in which, presumably, they would live out at least a part of their lives. The class scenario begins peacefully enough with predictions that the Vietnam War would end and United States relations with China would improve, both in 1972. (The exercise was run a year earlier, in 1971). But soon events become more turbulent. New York City breaks away to become a state in 1973, and 1974 is a bad year characterized by race riots in June and a United States pullout from the United Nations. While both marijuana and prostitution are legalized, internal political events must be bleak because 1975 sees a political revolution in the United States.

In 1976 the value of the dollar declines, other nations ostracize the United States, and gas masks are distributed, presumably because of pollution. By 1977 the space program has ended and United States citizens are under constant surveillance in streets and homes. Senator Kennedy emerges somehow as President in 1978 (a special election?), but a major financial crisis occurs, and the following year, 1979, we break off relations with Europe. We learn to cure cancer, but by then pollution has become irreversible and we are highly dependent upon the oceans for food. All this, however, is merely a prelude to a cataclysmic year, 1980. That year can be described in a burst of screaming headlines:

AMERICAN REVOLUTION OVERTHROWS PRESENT GOVERNMENT
CULTURAL AND POLITICAL REVOLUTION BREAKS OUT IN U.S.
MAJOR RIVERS AND STREAMS DIE
NATURAL DISASTER WIPES OUT MANY PEOPLE
FAMILY SIZE LIMITED
MARS LANDING
COLONY PLANTED ON MARS
NUCLEAR WAR BREAKS OUT!

America's time of troubles is far from over. In 1981, Richard Nixon is assassinated, and while race relations take a turn for the better, and the renewed space program results in new missions to the planets, by 1983 we have a military dictatorship ruling the nation. Now the Soviet Union joins with the United States in a war against China (this is, after all, 1984 by now). Scientific progress continues and the rate of change accelerates further—indeed, embryos now take only six hours, instead of nine months, to gestate. But science is of no help when California, hit, one assumes, by an earthquake, slips into the Pacific Ocean in 1986. We are beginning to colonize the moon, while population on earth reaches a crisis point, and the dollar is now worth only 25 per cent of its 1971 value.

As the 1990s open, the Russo-Chinese War is still on, but things begin to improve. Peace among the great powers becomes more likely. Nuclear energy, especially in the form of fusion reactors, is widely in use, and a three-day work week is initiated. Our ecological problems are still extremely pressing, but solutions are at least in sight. In fact, 1995 looks like a good year. The government changes, the space effort expands once more, we finally develop a "more organized system" of education, and, apparently, young people are making their political weight felt, for we elect a new President who is only twenty years old. (Scoffers might note that William Pitt became prime minister of Britain at twenty-four.) We are now also experiencing zero population growth.

I will not go on to describe their forecasts after 2000 A.D., but there is enough here presumably to suggest that at least this group of teenagers do not look forward to a stable world, or one progressing smoothly along well-worn grooves. They look forward to high turbulence for at least the next two decades.[3]

Cultural Premises

The collective image of the future, whether expressed by a group of high-school students, a group of educational planners, or even the political leadership of the nation, can tell us a great deal about its creators and the culture in which they are embedded. For example, the events envisaged by my experimental group ranged themselves over an extremely long time span. The soonest any event was due to occur was "next Sunday." The latest was to happen in 31,971 A.D.—the year the sun would burn itself out. There were also two events listed as "never" likely to occur. One was "the end of human life." The other, a sardonic entry, no doubt, was "end of Vietnam War."

These characteristics of the image of the future may seem inconsequential, but they betray telltale evidences of their cultural origins. For in many cultures the idea of the future, itself, is nonexistent, the idea of infinity ("never") is lacking, and in others, including many Western cultures before Darwin, a 30,000-year time span is inconceivable.

Similarly, it is revealing, though not necessarily surprising, that certain points in time seem more dramatic or more "real" than others, or that forecast events seem to cluster, rather than distribute themselves evenly along a time scale. For these teenagers, 1980 looms as an important year, and so well publicized is the millennial turning point, 2000, that it magnetically attracts forecasts, even though, all things being equal, 1999 is just as likely or unlikely a time for events of significance to occur. This "lumpiness" or clustering of forecasts may reflect the influence of our decimal-based mathematical systems.

By listing every forecast made by the class in chronological sequence, one can analyze with students the contradictions in them and the assumptions that lead to these differing, and sometimes contrary, forecasts. One can, in other words, examine the internal consistency and coherence of the imagery and the values or cultural assumptions that lead to differences between one student's scenario and another's. All this, of course, has nothing to do with the *validity* of the actual forecasts. But with this collective image of the future in hand, one might compare student forecasts with those produced by experts in the various relevant fields—politics, technology, urban affairs, family life, international relations, etc.

More important, one might critically analyze the forecasts of the experts, probing for the hidden *assumptions and methods* of analysis used by them. In short, the image of the future provides not merely a set of interesting insights into the students' own views, but also a powerful learning tool. Yet even this gives only a hint of its educational importance.

The Impersonal Future

Perhaps the most striking fact about these forecasts has to do with the role of the student, his or her self-image as seen in relationship to the outside world. Indeed, in asking the students for their images of the future, I was less interested in the future, as such, or in their attitudes toward it, than I was in their attitudes toward *change*.

I was, therefore, fascinated and troubled to discover that for this class, while the future was clearly exciting as subject matter, it was distinctly impersonal. Thus, of the 193 responses, fully 177 referred to events that would occur "out there" somewhere in the world or the universe. Only sixteen events made any reference to "I"—the student making the forecast. Of the thirty-three students in the class who submitted usable responses, only six saw themselves as part of the picture.

One student, along with such forecasts as antigravity cars (1984) and destruction of the earth (2050–2100), scheduled his or her own life as follows:

Graduation	1976
Working	1977
Marriage	?
Success	1984
Death	2030–2040

Another forecast marriage in 1980 and concluded "I will be a great lawyer" by 1988. He, too (a boy, I would guess from his prediction that the football Giants would win the 1974 Super Bowl), slated himself to die in 2040. One respondent foresaw his or her own death by 1996—i.e., at about age forty.

Death, despite cryogenics and research into aging, is still regarded as a high-certainty event, and every one of the six students who made reference to their personal lives in any way included a forecast of his or her death-time. Indeed, one, whose forecasts included a new government for the United States in 5561 A.D., predicted his or her own death in 1971—in other words, in the immediate future! (Because of the anonymity procedures followed, it was impossible for me to identify this student, but one wonders how deeply parents or teachers have explored his or her image of tomorrow.)

Having tried a similar experiment with another much smaller group earlier, I was not surprised by the lopsided emphasis on the impersonal or nonpersonal in thinking about the future. In general, at least for the teenagers I have experimented with, the future is something that happens to somebody else.

On one occasion, in fact, I asked respondents to draw up two lists. First, I asked in a general way for a list of future events. When not a single personal reference turned up, I asked for a separate list of events that would happen to them personally. It was then easy to compare each personal future with the larger, public or social future in which it would unfold. The results were dramatic. One could not help but be struck by the disconnectedness between the two sets of forecasts. One fifteen-year-old girl, for example, after picturing a U.S.-U.S.S.R. alliance against China, a cancer cure, test-tube babies, an accidental nuclear explosion, the spread of anarchism over large parts of the world, and robot computers holding political office in the United States, offered the following personal forecast:

> Moving into my own apartment
> Interior-designing school
> Driver's license
> Getting a dog
> Marriage
> Having children
> Death

The world in upheaval would leave her untouched.

I must emphasize that the teenagers making these forecasts were incontestably bright, lively, and probably more sophisticated than their counterparts in smaller cities. Yet no matter how turbulent a world they pictured, no matter how many new technologies might appear or what political revolutions might take place, the way of life foreseen for themselves as individuals seldom differed from the way of life possible in the present and actually lived by many today. It is as though they believed that everything happening outside one's life simply by-passes the individual. The respondents, in short, made no provision for change in themselves, no provision for adaptation to a world exploding with change.

I pursue this not because I think these experiments are anything more than suggestive; I would expect different groups to formulate quite different images of tomorrow and to reflect different degrees of connectedness with the racing pulse of change. Rather, I raise it because I believe that the schools and universities, with their heavy emphasis on the past, not only implicitly convey a false message about the future—the idea that it will resemble the present—but also that they create millions of candidates for future shock by encouraging the divorce between the individual's self-image and his or her expectations with regard to social change. More deeply, they encourage the student to think of his or her "self" not as subject to change, growth or adaptation, but as something static.

The Future-Scanning Talent

It is perfectly astonishing, once we stop to consider it, that we are able, out of the stuff of everyday experience, to conjure up dreams, visions, forecasts and prophecies of events yet to come. Scientists marvel at the body's machinery for sensing the environment and for converting its impressions into concepts, ideas, symbols and logic. Yet our talent for projecting images of the future is even more remarkable. In fact, though educators have scarcely noticed it, this "future-scanning" talent is the basis for learning, itself.

If we could not form anticipatory mental pictures of the future, if we could not match these against emergent realities and then correct them, we could not—except in the narrowest sense—learn at all.

All of us project an ever-changing image of the future on the screen of consciousness. Our heads teem with assumptions about the future. These assumptions can be very short-term and practical. I may do no more than assume, for example, that the postman will arrive in the morning or even that the cup of tea will still be there, an instant from now, when my fingers close around it. On the other hand, the assumptions may be very long-range and impersonal. I may envision a world racial conflict in 1985, the emergence of Japan as the world's chief industrial power by 1990, or a meeting with extraterrestrials in the year 2000. The assumptions may be correct or incorrect, consistent or inconsistent, slowly changing or turning over rapidly. But whatever the case, taken together, they constitute my image of the future.

This invisible architecture of assumptions shapes my personality and lends consistency to my behavior. These assumptions, in fact, make it possible for the individual to survive in varied and fast-changing environments. For it is precisely this ability to visualize futures, to generate and discard thousands upon thousands of assumptions about events that have not yet—and may never—become reality, that makes man the most adaptive of animals. It is a prime task of education to enhance this ability, to help make the individual more sensitively responsive to change. We must, therefore, redefine learning, itself. Put simply, a significant part of education must be seen as the process by which we enlarge, enrich, and improve the individual's image of the future.

Action and Imagery

Education, however, is not just something that happens in the head. It involves our muscles, our senses, our hormonal defenses, our total biochemistry. Nor does it occur solely *within* the individual. Education springs from the interplay between the individual and a changing environment. The movement to heighten future-consciousness in education, therefore, must be seen as one step toward a deep restructuring of the links between schools, colleges, universities and the communities that surround them.

The ultimate purpose of futurism in education is not to create elegantly complex, well-ordered, accurate images of the future, but to help learners cope with real-life crises, opportunities and perils. It is to strengthen the individual's practical ability to anticipate and adapt to change, whether through invention, informed acquiescence, or through intelligent resistance.

To function well in a fast-shifting environment, the learner must have the opportunity to do more than receive and store data; she or he must have the opportunity to *make change* or to fail in the attempt. This implies a basic modification of the relationship between educational theory and practice.

High-speed change means that the reality described by the teacher in the classroom is, even as the lesson proceeds, undergoing transformation. Generalizations uttered by the textbook or the teacher may be accurate at the beginning of a lesson, but incorrect or irrelevant by the end. Insights, highly useful at one time, become invalid under the new conditions. The instinctive recognition of this by young people has been one of the key factors behind the collapse of teacher authority.

In the past, one assumed that one's elders "knew" how things were. Yet if the reality is changing, then their knowledge of it is not necessarily trustworthy any longer, and, significantly, they, too, must become learners.

When we introduce change and, therefore, higher levels of novelty into the environment, we create a totally new relationship between the limited reality of the classroom and the larger reality of life. Abstractions are symbolic reflections of aspects of reality. As the rate of change alters technological, social and moral realities, we are compelled to do more than revise our abstractions: we are also forced to *test* them more frequently against the realities they are supposed to represent or explain.

Those who conduct opinion surveys know that the more variation there is in a population to be sampled, the larger the sample required to get an information-rich result. The same is true with respect to variation through time. The more rapid the pace of change, the more novelty-filled our environment, the more often it becomes necessary to "sample reality"—to check our abstractions.

Thus learning under conditions of high novelty requires us to move back and forth between theory and practice, between classroom and community, faster and more frequently than ever before. Failure to measure our abstractions often against reality increases the likelihood that they will be false. But the university and the lower schools, as organized today, are designed to construct or transmit abstractions, not to test them.

This is why we need to accelerate the trend in many colleges and universities to offer credit for action-learning done off-campus through participation in real work, in business, in community political organizing, in pollution-control projects, or other activities. Many of these efforts today are badly organized, ill-thought-through, and regarded by the university as basically insignificant— concessions to the restlessness of students who no longer want to remain cooped up in the classroom. I would argue that such efforts not only must be continued, but must be radically expanded, must be linked more imaginatively to the formal learning process, must be extended downward to younger and younger students in the secondary schools and even, through adaptation of the idea, to primary-school children. Indeed, for older students, this action-learning ought to become the dominant form of learning, with classroom learning seen as a support rather than as the central element in education. Such experiments as the University Without Walls are primitive prototypes of what is possible.[4]

Students learn best when they are highly motivated to do so, and despite a great deal of mythology to the contrary, this motivation rarely comes from "inspired teachers" or "well-designed texts" alone. So long as students are cut off from the productive work of the surrounding society and kept in an interminably prolonged adolescence, many—if not most—are de-motivated. Teachers, parents and other adults may shower them with flowery rhetoric about how today's youth will be the leaders and decision-makers of tomorrow. But the rhetoric is contradicted by a reality that actively deprives the young of participation either in significant community decision-making or in socially approved productive work. Beneath the rhetoric lies a contempt summarized in the twin terms "parasites" and "investments." Conservatives tend to look upon students as parasites, eating up community resources without contributing anything productive in return. Liberals leap to defend the youth by terming them "investments" in the future. Both notions are insulting.

The secret message communicated to most young people today by the society around them is that they are not needed, that the society will run itself quite nicely until they—at some distant point in the future—take over the reins. Yet the fact is that the society is not running itself nicely, and, indeed, there may be little of value left for them to take over in the future, unless we reconceptualize the role of youth in the social order. Not because young people will necessarily tear down the social order, but because the rest of us *need* all the energy, brains, imagination and talent that young people can bring to bear on our difficulties. For the society to attempt to solve its desperate problems without the full participation of even very young people is imbecile.

My father worked at twelve or thirteen. Most children in the past—and most children in the less affluent nations today—were and are needed for their productive contribution. It is a dangerous myth of the twentieth-century rich that our children are *not* needed, that they can be kept in artificial environments called schools and universities, incubating until they are twenty-one or even thirty, before being expected to participate in the everyday affairs of the society.

In the United States we herd 8,000,000 university students and some 51,000,000 younger children into educational institutions, assuring them all the while that it is for their own future benefit.[5] It is all done with the best of intentions. It keeps them out of the labor force and, for a while, off the streets.

This policy, however, is based on a perilously faulty image of the future. By maintaining the false distinction between work and learning, and between school and community, we not only divorce theory from practice and deprive ourselves of enormous energies that might be channeled into socially useful action, we also infantilize the young and rob them of the motivation to learn.

On the other hand, by linking learning to action—whether that takes the form of constructing buildings on campus, or measuring traffic flow at an intersection and designing an overpass, or campaigning for environmental legislation, or interning at city hall, or helping to police a high-crime area, or serving as sanitation and health aides, or building a stage set, or doing research for a trade union, or working out a marketing problem for a corporation—we change the source of motivation.

The motive to learn is no longer the fear of a teacher's power to grade or the displeasure of the parent, but the desire to do something useful, productive and respected—to change the community, to make a dent, if even a small one, on reality. This desire to leave a dent, to make an impact, today fuels a wide range of antisocial activity from spray-painting graffiti on a public wall or vandalizing a school building to committing murder.[6] It is not unrelated to the fact that most crime is the work of the young.

Only by recognizing the urgency of this desire to make a mark (and thereby to clarify or establish one's own identity) and by reconceptualizing the role of youth with respect to work and social needs can the education system become effective.

Today, unfortunately, most action-learning programs scarcely begin to take advantage of their full potentials. For example, most are seen as forms of independent study. For many students, they might be far more effective as group ventures. The organization of groups of students (self-organization would be better) into problem-solving or work teams makes it possible to design additional learning—learning about organization and group dynamics —into the situation. By consciously including people of varied ages in such teams, it becomes possible to provide "generational bridges"—a way of breaking down some of the trained incapacity of different age groups to talk to one another.

Through focusing on some sharply defined external objective or desired change, the group develops a degree of shared intimacy and attacks the prevailing sense of loneliness and isolation felt by so many students even on small campuses. Most important, however, the motivation for learning changes. The group itself generates internal social reinforcements for learning, and the nature of the problem being attacked defines the nature of the learning required, so that the definition of relevance is created by the real situation rather than by the say-so of a teacher.

Members of a small group working to bring about some change in the ecological condition of their community, for example, will find they must learn something about science, economics, sociology and politics, as well as the communicative skills required to define the difficulties, outline alternative solutions, and persuade others.

In the meantime, decision-making, so crucial to coping with change, becomes, itself, a subject of the learning process. Most students in most schools and universities seldom participate in group decision-making. While they may be asked to make decisions about themselves—such as which courses to take (and even this is restricted at the lower levels)—they are seldom called upon to make personal decisions *that affect the work or performance of others.* The decisions they are characteristically called upon to make have little or no impact on anyone's life but their own. In this sense, they "don't count." They are isolates. Attempting to solve real-life problems, action-learning done in the context of a goal-sharing group, trains the participants in decisional skills and begins to develop an understanding that their decisions do count —that personal decisions can have important consequences.

It is precisely at this point that action learning converges with future-consciousness. For, when we speak of an image of the future, we are speaking of the ramified consequences of present-day decisions, whether public or personal. Action-learning, particularly when carried out by groups, is a useful tool for demonstrating the necessity for a future-orientation—the need to study alternatives, to develop long-range plans, to think in terms of contingencies—and especially to think through the *consequences,* including second- and third-order consequences, of action.

This emphasis on the future can, furthermore, be applied not merely to group issues, but to the development of generalized, tentative life-plans for the individual participants as well—plans which the learner is, of course, free to change at will, but which, by their very existence, help orient the individual in the midst of hurricaning change. In this way, the future becomes intensely personal, instead of remote.

In turn, the development of group or personal plans, however tentative, immediately forces the question of values into the foreground. For plans have to do with our images of preferred futures, as distinct from those that are merely possible or probable. No problem in education has been more disgracefully neglected in recent years. The attempt to avoid ancient orthodoxies having led to the myth of a value-free education, we now find millions of young people moving through the educational sausage-grinder who have never once been encouraged to question their own personal values or to make them explicit. In the face of a rapidly shifting, choice-filled environment, one which demands decision after adaptive decision from the individual, this neglect of value questions is crippling.

Action-learning creates opportunities for students to move from the field back to the classroom or lounge or living room not merely for analytic discussion of their strategies for change, but for probing exploration of the personal and public values that underlie their successes and failures. This process of value clarification is a vital part of any education designed to help people cope with "overchoice."

In short, the combination of action-learning with academic work, and both of these with a future orientation, creates a powerfully motivating and powerfully personal learning situation. It helps close the gap between change occurring "out there" and change occurring within the individual, so that learners no longer regard the world as divorced from themselves, and themselves as immune to (and perhaps incapable of) change. In a turbulent, high-change environment, it is only through the development of a "psychology of the future" that education can come to terms with learning.

The relationship of time to motivation and learning has been inadequately explored, not merely by educators, but by psychological researchers as well. Here sociologist Benjamin Singer suggests that a person's educational and social development is heavily contingent upon his or her "future-focused role-image." Blur this image, he warns, and we rob the child of motivation and personality structure.

CHAPTER TWO

The Future-Focused Role-Image

by Benjamin D. Singer

> Just as all education springs from some image of the future, all education produces some image of the future.
>   —*Alvin Toffler*

One of the most important things about any group or society is its attitude toward time. Entire cultures can be characterized in terms of time orientation. In fact, according to the eminent social anthropologist Florence Kluckhohn, not only do groups differ "in their emphasis on past, present or future" but "a very great deal can be told about the particular society . . . , much about the direction of change within it can be predicted, with a knowledge of where that emphasis lies."[1]

I believe the same is true of people—individuals. And if we want to understand why some children do well in school and others do not, we must begin to think about this question.

The predominant American middle-class orientation, it is often said, is toward the future. There is good evidence that this is true —that the middle classes in American society, influenced by the

Protestant Ethic, have typically passed on to their children a time perspective that discounts the present and looks toward the future. This concern with the future, when transformed into personal terms, carries with it the ingredients for success in a culture geared to the future rather than the past.

Yet educational curricula are almost without exception geared to presenting knowledge generated in the present and past, oriented to the past, so that most of what a student does consists of reenacting knowledge put together by the last generation about previous generations' efforts.

This temporal lag is more or less acceptable when change appears orderly, because the speed of change has not resulted in a qualitative transformation of our psychological environment. But it is not acceptable today, when the future is rushing toward us. As former Secretary of Health, Education and Welfare Robert Finch put it, "All too often we are stuffing the heads of the young with the products of earlier innovation rather than teaching them how to innovate. We treat their minds as storehouses to be filled rather than as instruments to be used."[2]

Those who plan curricula and those who carry them out in the classroom are usually unaware of this temporal bias. To educate for the future, one ought to be aware of the attitudes toward time perspectives brought to the classroom by children drawn from different social groupings.

Consider, for example, those groups in American society who are often accused of "living for the present." They are supposedly "improvident." They save nothing "for a rainy day," etc. The poor, the black and certain immigrant groups are characterized in this way and do, in fact, operate on a time system different from that of the American mainstream. This is reflected in differing attitudes toward punctuality and personal planning. The concept of "Colored People's Time" or "CPT," for example, expresses the idea of the timelessness of the disadvantaged group. With a future that is questionable, the present expands. Now, however, the children of the white middle class, oriented in the past to the notion of the future, are new inhabitants of what might be called the expanded present. Beginning with the beat generation and continuing through the flower children to the present-day post-hippie generation, today's middle-class youth are said to be suffering an identity crisis. Assaulted by middle-class expectations—a kind of subcultural lag in the midst of explosive change which has made the goals of the future suddenly elusive—the identity crisis of the middle classes is a problem intricately linked with time.

Although Einstein brought the dimension of time to the physical scientist's conception of space, social scientists, for the most part, continue to orient their thinking to a social structural model which ignores the problem of time. Even a physicist, G. J. Whitrow, acknowledges, "the evidence is compelling that the missing link between the psychological and the physiological aspects of cerebral activity and personal identity should not be sought in some hypothetical higher space but rather in the dimension of time."[3] In short, learning itself is linked to time.

Psychologists who study learning have demonstrated the crucial role of rewards in learning. Learning occurs as a result of the reinforcing effects of rewards. In most human experience, reward follows in time the performance that elicits it. But what if rewards become obscure and roles dissolve and are transformed during periods of extreme or rapid social change? For the deprived, there was never much sense in attempting to separate the present from the future; for the youth of the rest of society—who could once count on personal movement through time, toward a beckoning future—the present and the future have become fused as a result of rapid change. The young are now identified as the "now generation."

Future-Identities

Identity and time perspectives are both derived from the social systems in which we exist. Our identity is a figure which we fix against the ground of the time perspective we acquire. The resulting role conditioned by time can be called the "future-focused role-image." The FFRI is our self-image projected into the future, and it lends meaning to much of what we do in the present.

We develop a self-image by empathically assuming the roles of others; this self-image feeds back on our present behavior and is more important than the evanescent stimuli that surround us and which cause short-term behavior. The self, then, is not merely grounded, as psychoanalytic theory suggests, in the past, but is made up of what Erik Erikson calls "anticipated selves." Early in childhood, Erikson says, the child "tries to comprehend possible future roles, or, at any rate, to understand what roles are worth imagining . . . his learning . . . leads away from his own limitations and into future possibilities."[4]

The future-focused role-image varies—among persons, among social classes, among societies. It is especially important to search for its components and explain its mechanisms during a time such as this: a time of great flux, of increasing tempos, a time when our social milieu changes rapidly, as organizations disappear and emerge and roles are transformed, created and disappear, seemingly unpredictably.

An eleven-year-old boy, asked by a friend, "What do you want to be when you grow up?" answered he could not say, since he did not know what new jobs would replace today's. Nor will today's role models who help stimulate the development of our self-images, be tomorrow's role models.

The linkage of time, selfhood and change is particularly important in considering the problems of the poor, the ghettoized, the inhabitants of developing nations. For those whose future-focused role-image is diffuse are the very individuals who compensate by depending on "fate."

Anthropologist Walter B. Miller's clinical picture of lower-class youth in gangs illustrates this very well. "Many lower class individuals feel that their lives are subject to a set of forces over which they have relatively little control. These are not directly equated with the supernatural forces of formally organized religion, but relate more to a concept of 'destiny,' or man as a pawn of magical powers. Not infrequently this often implicit world view is associated with a conception of the ultimate futility of directed effort towards a goal. . . ."[5]

In another era, we took our cues from the past: the tradition-directed man, for example, had a sense of security in knowing that his role ideals had tenure. Identity was a more certain process, depending as it did on role models of great stability. Erikson perceptively points out the sociological inputs that affect self-continuity in that "cultural and historical change can prove so traumatic to identity formation: it can break up the inner consistency of a child's hierarchy of expectations."[6]

The stanchions of identity are the establishment of long-range goals. Goals, according to social psychologist Gordon Allport, must be striven for, and striving "always has a future reference."[7] Thus, the time orientation of the culture and the individual will condition the quality of his striving which then feeds back and makes present success possible. Striving, as a motive, cannot be separated from the issue of self-image: ". . . there is much growth that takes place only with the aid of and because of, a self-image. This image helps us bring our view of the present into line with our view of the future," social psychologists Chad Gordon and Kenneth Gergen have pointed out.[8]

Goals and strivings are linked to role-images, which in turn are the composite expression of aspirations and occupations, educational objectives and social relations undergoing rapid change. Without the self-image that links our present behavior to our view of our future, all human activities, conditioned by a timeless perspective, would be merely responses to immediate stimuli. Probability would triumph over possibility; the successfully operating human being, as neuropsychiatrist Kurt Goldstein has shown, is the one who is able to master the mechanisms of the possible. The evidence establishing the linkage between what we are and what view we take of ourselves, the way in which we exist in time, is scattered but compelling. Consider, first of all, our sense of time.

The sense of time, as it is expressed by the child, seems to commence between the ages of two and two and a half, for it is at that age when words designating the future begin to appear in the child's talk. Before the process of role-taking begins in earnest, words dealing with the future are tied to activities and concrete events, and then, by the end of the third year, the child begins to comprehend *future roles*. The individuals in his immediate milieu provide him with tentative identifications and expectations that help to form his own identity. It is at this point that differences begin to become apparent in the parents' behavior toward the child that then seem to condition the development of different time perspectives, aspirations and the necessary behavior to achieve them.

The process begins with the idea that the parent generates concerning the child's future. In fact, there is research that indicates that parents' future images of the child may be a more important factor in its intellectual growth than parents taking time to teach the child to count or to write his name. This was the surprising result of research by Norma Radin and Hanne Sonquist, when they investigated factors that would most improve children's performance in an Operation Headstart type of program in Ypsilanti, Michigan. It was found that the most important factor connected with the child's actual success in the program—the measurement of cognitive growth—was the parents' image of the child's future: their occupational expectations for the child in the future. Parents' expectations were among "the best predictor variables for cognitive growth in pre-school among a disadvantaged population," according to Radin and Sonquist.[9] The mechanism by which this future-focused aspiration became transformed into cognitive skills by the children is not clear, but it is there.

And it is ready to become attached to desirable future roles early in life; by the time the child is attending elementary school, he understands which are the desirable occupational roles, for recent research has indicated an impressive, nearly total correlation between adults and elementary-school children in the prestige ratings of occupations.[10] What this means is that a black child, for example, knows the difference between the role of the computer scientist and the dishwasher; he knows the meaning of his own probable future role.

Some of children's understandings of future roles, foremost of which are the occupational roles, comes from their families, from their contacts in their neighborhood, and from television. The child exposed to a homogeneous environment, as is more generally the case with the ghetto child, will develop fewer, less diversified images of future role possibilities and will more likely limit his or her own aspirations accordingly.

The child who depends heavily on television, and this is especially true for the poor and the black,[11] will develop narrow, stereotyped images of potential occupational roles. The narrowness of these images, in turn, constricts the child's ability to imagine himself or herself actually *taking* such roles.

Sociologists Melvin and Lois DeFleur, in studying the occupational knowledge of young people, found that

TV provides children with much superficial and misleading information about the labor force of their society. From this they acquire stereotyped beliefs about the world of work. Given the deep significance of occupational roles for both the individual and his society, any learning source which distorts reality concerning this aspect of the social structure and the child's "generalized other" may be laying the foundations for difficult personal and social problems.[12]

Time and Motivation

It is during the first few years of school that images of the child's future (and the means to achieve them) are generated and become interlocked with his or her time perspective. While there are differences between individuals, the outstanding differences are probably related to social class positions. Children between eight and ten studied by means of a projective story technique designed to test differences in time perspective provided revealing results. Some children projected themselves considerably further into the future than others, and this was more often true of children from higher social classes. The researcher, Lawrence LeShan, suggested there were implications for educational planning and concluded that the individual oriented to present time rather than future time "would not have learned to act in terms of future reward and would, indeed, have learned the opposite since the future would be an unpredictable region and to work in terms of it would be nonsensical for him. Further, this orientation in a world that is primarily run on longer sequences might well produce conflicts, failures, and resulting hostility."[13]

The development of a future-time perspective early in life provides both a motive and a means for achievement in the future. A future-oriented time perspective—a future-focused role-image—operates, then, like Robert Merton's "self-fulfilling prophecy." By its presence, it helps to assure the conditions necessary for its attainment. Social psychologist Lawrence K. Frank has pointed out that a long future focus is needed to bring meaning to our present lives, that it has a "retroactive" effect upon our present. He adds:

The more remote the focus of his time and perspectives, the more immediate the focus, the more he will exhibit consummatory behavior that uses the present only as a means to the future; the more immediate the focus, the more he will exhibit consummatory behavior and react naively and ignore consequences.[14]

Research into the relationship between time perspective and accomplishment supports Frank's suggestion. When seventh- and eighth-grade boys were asked to record recent thoughts and discussions and to take projective tests, the researcher discovered that some boys displayed a future orientation, while others thought in terms of the present or past. The boys who were most future-oriented, it turned out, also had higher academic achievements, which led the research psychologist, John E. Teahan, to suggest that high effort on boring and tedious assignments may be meaningful to the individual who sees them in terms of a future-time perspective in which success is the payoff.[15]

Other research on schoolchildren has linked the values *individualism* and *planning for the future* with social class position, the gaining of high grades and plans for further education. What is now called "the achievement syndrome" is the successor in name to the Protestant Ethic, in which work is justified in terms of future, otherworldly reward.[16]

Today there are good reasons to question both the Protestant Ethic and the naïve assumption that achievement in the traditional sense is an appropriate educational goal. There is also reason to doubt whether we should *automatically* encourage high effort on boring educational tasks. (Perhaps the tasks themselves need to be reconsidered.) Furthermore, we need to develop attitudes toward the future that do not desensitize us to the immediacy of the present. There need be no contradiction between high consciousness or enjoyment of the present moment and a sense of its relationship to the future. Indeed, this perspective can be said to enrich the experience of the present.

However we may feel about these issues, whether we are interested in the issues of educational motivation or, more basically, in personality integration, it is clear that what Toffler calls "futural imagery" is important.

The development, then, of a future-time perspective seems to be essential in developing expectations—goals which individuals can then work toward fulfilling. Where these are not present, behavior which is self-destructive as well as socially harmful may result.

An English sociologist, Basil Bernstein, points to the linkage of future-time perspective to social position and suggests behavioral consequences that could lead to such conduct in working-class families:

> The specific character of long-term goals tends to be replaced by more general notions of the future, in which chance, a friend or a relative plays a greater part than the rigorous working out of connections. Thus, present, or near-present, activities have greater value than the relation of the present activity to the attainment of a distant goal. The system of expectancies, or the time span of anticipation, is shortened and this creates different sets of preferences, goals, and dissatisfactions. The environment limits the perception of the developing child of and in time. Present gratifications or present deprivations become absolute gratifications, for there exists no developed time continuum upon which present activity can be ranged. Relative to the middle classes, the postponement of present pleasure for future gratifications will be found difficult.[17]

Research also exists which supports the notion that the way in which one perceives time is linked to conduct. In one study of students in a residential school, individuals whose tests indicated they *experienced* time as passing more quickly were the individuals whose behavior was best when incentives for maintaining good behavior were removed.[18] In another investigation, it was found that nondelinquents had a longer time perspective than delinquents. This inquiry was based on psychologist Kurt Lewin's assertion that "a person is likely to be future-oriented if he feels that a highly valued goal is accessible to him, while a belief that the goal is beyond his reach restricts him to a present orientation."

The researchers, psychologists Robert J. Barndt and Donald Johnson, used a projective story technique to find out whether the stories constructed by delinquents and nondelinquents varied in terms of their time projection. Stories generated by the delinquent boys took place in shorter times than those of the nondelinquent boys.[19]

Thus, those who are unable to project themselves into the future must live for today, unable to visualize future rewards with clarity. A consistent finding among street gangs, for example, is their tendency to live in the present and their belief that they are the pawns of external forces, of fate. Indeed, the notion of autonomy and self-responsibility appears to go hand in hand with future orientation. Sociologists who study the differences between those who live for today and those who live for tomorrow call this ability to wait the "deferred gratification pattern."[20]

Luck, Chance and Fate

In research on preschool and adolescent whites and blacks conducted in Atlanta, Georgia, in 1969, psychologists Adrian Zytkoskee, Bonnie Strickland and James Watson followed up earlier work dealing with children's belief in "luck, chance, fate or powers beyond his control as opposed to events occurring as a result of his own skills and activities." The children were given a choice test involving a small immediate reward or a large, delayed reward. The investigators were attempting to determine, among other things, why some children are willing to "trust society and its agents for the possibility of future rewards." They found that adolescent blacks more often than whites believed in factors external to themselves and were less likely to be willing to wait for the future. But there were no racial differences among preschool children. Clearly, during the elementary-school period, something happens to cause children from certain social groupings to discount the future.[21]

The ability to defer gratification is found most often among white and affluent children. Clearly, if one is willing to defer gratification, it must be because there is a fair certainty of a payoff when tomorrow comes. This belief in the future—or lack of belief —may explain differences in the way in which social classes apply regimens to their children. Lower-class parents, realistically surveying "tomorrow," are aware there is less likelihood of a return to the child than is true of middle-class parents. While sociologists tend to explain differences in behavior by social class, it may well be that the crucial factor is, in reality, time orientation.

The real-world pattern of biased payoff is, of course, the ultimate factor. Children, black or any other kind, are perceptive enough to recognize inequalities in the real world of the present. If they are allowed to believe that discriminatory social and economic patterns (a central determinant of their environment) will persist in the future—their future—they quite rationally conclude that the present and the future are essentially interchangeable. Once this assumption is made, however, concern for the future becomes unnecessary. Academic performance is only one casualty of this belief.

Conversely, where the future seems open and positive, the self-fulfilling prophecy must be in operation. Thus there is evidence from other sociological research in schools that the ability of students to delay gratification for a future time frequently correlates with higher academic achievement as well as higher occupational aspiration.[22]

If one is to develop this habit of looking to the future for rewards, one must be assured there will, in fact, be a payoff. Experiments with rats suggest that some animals act on the basis of whether a reward or punishment follows the act or behavior immediately.[23] Humans are different in possessing the kind of abstract ability that enables them to imagine the long-term consequences of a given action. This ability, however, varies among people. The current concern with *relevance* in curricula exemplifies student concern with the ability of the educational system to deliver a payoff. Textbooks and teachers geared to examples drawn from roles, institutions and values of the past are patently absurd to students whose primary experience has been gained during a period of very rapid change.

The consequences of a given behavior can be termed expectancies, and introduce another variable into the time-success syndrome. People who have high expectancies of success in their undertakings—whatever they are—usually perform better, according to laboratory experience.[24] Thus, we suggest, moving once more to the concept of role, that individuals who expect to fill future roles successfully ought to, indeed, be more likely to achieve them. Support for this comes from the study of Teahan's discussed earlier which also found that future-oriented youngsters tend to be more optimistic.

Fantasy and Reality

Role expectations probably are formed after youngsters try out, vicariously, their future roles. It has been found, for boys for example, that there are three general stages of this process: From six to eleven, the *fantasy stage*, at which time youngsters imagine themselves as spacemen, cowboys, etc.; from eleven to eighteen or nineteen, the *tentative stage*, when there was vacillation in choice of occupations; eighteen and nineteen and above, the *realistic stage*, based on greater awareness of the objective world.[25] However, the ability to imagine oneself in any role in the future seems to be limited, and one of the constraints is found in the aforementioned social-class position of the youngster. Some youngsters, it would appear, never do develop a crystallized view of their future role. In his classic study, *Elmtown's Youth*, August Hollingshead reported on interviews with high-school children who were asked what they wished to be after leaving school. He found that a full 41 per cent of lower-status youth had *no* crystallized image of themselves in that future role. They could not imagine it. Only 3 per cent of higher-class youth had this problem. Thus, there was a blurring of the future-focused role-image as one moved down the social-class scale.[26]

Research across cultures points to the importance of being able to imagine oneself in a productive future role. Daniel Lerner, studying village people in underdeveloped areas, suggests that a crucial determinant of modernization is the ability of such people to "empathize," imagine themselves in such future roles. One of the important factors holding back modernization is that this ability to empathize is lacking.[27] When individuals *are* able to develop a picture of a future role for themselves, the attitudes, values and behavior which make up this image feed back to the present.

Occupational sociologist Morris Rosenberg suggests the individual "is likely to incorporate into his present self-image aspects of his future occupational status—he is a 'future doctor,' 'future teacher,' 'future engineer.' In the course of time, he develops a picture of the attitudes, values, and behavior which are appropriate for a member of this occupation. . . . This image of his *future* occupational status is likely to influence the student's present attitudes, values and behavior. . . ."[28] In other words, *just as research in role playing has shown that playing a role leads to the adoption of the attitudes involved, so future role playing feeds back on the present through the acceptance of the values and attitudes built into the future-role image.*

Feedback from the Future

Research to date, then, has shown that time perspectives are not uniform, but depend rather upon the person's location in a social system. Social systems, however, operate in various states of change. In North America, one can trace the concern with future role-taking from Puritanical times when small children were treated as little adults (an emphasis during that epoch on the child's hurrying to meet the future) through the present epoch which can be characterized as the future hurrying to meet the child.

Given that time perspective ultimately affects conduct and the development of our present capabilities, there is a self-fulfilling prophecy in operation. Thus, future-role images, particularly occupational ones, feed back on the present and help to socialize the individual to his or her future role; since some individuals do not have crystallized views of themselves in the future—something that the present temporal environment may encourage—some will be permanently trapped in an expanding present, out of their own control. When future shock occurs—when time is telescoped because of the rapidity of change—planning long-range goals becomes difficult. Frequently, there is a reversion to short-term goals—and to pessimism about one's own future role.

The problems we must face during times of explosive change include our ability to be properly oriented to the future in personal terms. One of the startling characteristics of the youth of our time is the suggestive peer-orientation (which can be read as *present-orientation*) which is so strongly associated with the retreatism exemplified by the drug culture. Thus, for some there is an over-determinism of the present by peers rather than self-imagery projected to the future. For others—those who traditionally have been forced to live in the present—there remains the problem of helping to generate a future in personal terms, that is, the FFRI.

The school at present is, like other social institutions, caught in a temporal lag and thereby contributes to the confusion, rather than helping young people by providing appropriate temporal orientation. The movement from personal autonomy toward external dependence which the drug cult and neo-mysticism (the current astrology fad, for example) so well illustrate is a symptom of a compensatory regression generated by temporal disorientation. And schools bear more responsibility than other institutions both for the condition and the cure. William L. Smith, former executive director of the Pace Association of Cleveland, highlights the responsibility of the schools in this period:

> There are far too many children in urban schools today who do not learn as well as they might because they simply are not clear about what their lives are for and what is worth working for. They have not yet found a meaning for their lives and are therefore unable or unwilling to marshal up their full intellectual resources for use in the crucial game of living.[29]

Educators cannot simply assume the presence of a time perspective geared to the future—one that would help organize and give meaning to learning. Often its lack subverts everything they try to accomplish. From now on, learning must be intimately bound up with the future, must help to structure and give meaning to that future.

How we see the future (and how it motivates us in the present) is a result of powerful conditioning factors. One of these is "sex-typing"—the channeling of young people into different futures according to sex. In this provocative chapter, sociologist Pauline B. Bart argues that today's schools systematically prepare girls for yesterday's future, damaging their intellectual and creative abilities, ignoring major changes that are likely to restructure the form and function of the family before long.

CHAPTER THREE

Why Women See the Future Differently from Men

by Pauline B. Bart

The mountain-moving day is coming
I say so, yet others doubt,
Only a while the mountain sleeps.
In the past
All mountains moved in fire,
Yet you may not believe it.
Oh man, this alone believe,
All sleeping women now will awake and move.
—*Yosano Akiko*

How does a child form its picture of the future—the personal future and the larger, public future of which the personal future is only a part? We do not know much about the stages of development of this imagery, but it is clear that almost from birth society sends different messages to different groups, so that boy babies and girl babies begin very early to see their future as distinctly different.

Of the array of possible futures, only certain ones are regarded as appropriate for each sex. Even before delivery, women begin to speculate about whether they are "carrying like it's a boy" or "like a girl"—in effect, assessing a future probability. Because sex implies radically different futures, not merely for the infant but for the parents as well, sex is one of the first things noticed at birth.

Thereafter, as a rule, girl babies are talked to more than boys and develop language skills more rapidly. Professor John Money of the Johns Hopkins Medical School, an expert on gender differentiation, reports that the child begins, by the time it is twelve to eighteen months old, to know what sex it is, depending upon its facility with language skills.[1] (Since girls tend to handle language better earlier, it is possible that they become aware of their gender at an earlier stage than boys.)

Professor Money has studied many cases of gender ambiguity, situations in which the sexual organs are not fully developed or in which it is difficult to determine sex. He reports that where a change is made in the diagnosis—if a child thought to have been a boy is subsequently redefined as a girl, or vice versa—there are problems of psychological readjustment even at so young an age. If the child knows names, Money states, "the boy has a clear concept of himself as a boy, and a girl of herself as a girl." The child recognizes nouns and pronouns differentiating the sexes.[2]

Very quickly, the little boy learns that he is expected to "misbehave," to tear his clothes, do dangerous things, get dirty and, later in life, sow "wild oats" before settling down. If he doesn't, but rather obeys his mother, stays close to home, and does not act up, it raises questions. Is he a "momma's boy"? A "sissy"? Why can't he be like everyone else? So the bad boy is really the good boy because he conforms to the futural imagery of his parents and other socializing agents. The imagery of what he is supposed to be and become conflicts with the verbally expressed wishes of family and teacher, and it is the imagery, not the words of admonition, that really counts.

In the girl's case, things are different. If she is "sugar and spice," and hangs around the kitchen, ever eager to help her mother by running errands, cooking or tending the baby, if she causes no problems at school, she is regarded as a good girl. There is, for her, no equivalent of the "bad boys are good boys" pattern and no direct conflict between the image of the future she is encouraged to hold and the words of praise or reprimand that she hears all day long. Admonition and futural imagery are consistent—and powerful.

The convergence suggests that girls' images of the future may well be more cohesive, more internally consistent, but less elaborate than boys', in terms of choices. If true, this could, as we shall see, help account for certain differences in how the sexes view the world.

The Reading Trap

As the child grows older, various outside influences begin to act on her, shaping her picture of the future. Juvenile literature, for example, serves as a "vehicle for presentation of societal values to the young child," according to sociologist Lenore Weitzman of the University of California at Davis, who, with Deborah Eifler, Elizabeth Hakoda, and Catherine Ross, content-analyzed prizewinning and best-selling children's books.[3] Their report, *Sex Role Socialization in Children's Picture Books*, showed that this literature is also a vehicle for the presentation of obsolete information about society. Thus, it is not merely that children absorb values from them; they also pick up from the role models presented to them in these books, ideas about "what they will be like when they grow up." Here the books present highly traditional views about the different roles open to men and women.

Conceiving of work in terms of the occupational structure of the past and present, rather than the probable occupational opportunities of the future, they provide children with unrealistic models of tomorrow, and unrealistic targets for personal development.

This occupational past-orientation is linked to sex-role channeling in a well-known pair of Hallmark matched books, *What Boys Can Be* and *What Girls Can Be*, each page of which shows a boy or girl playing an occupational role.[4] For boys, the roles depicted are fireman, baseball player, bus driver, policeman, cowboy, doctor, sailor, pilot, clown, zoo keeper, farmer, actor, astronaut, and President of the country. But a girl must choose from a narrower range, limited to traditional service careers or unrealistic glamour roles in which the ultimate achievement is not election to the Presidency, but acceptance of the role of housewife and mother. Specifically, she may be a nurse, stewardess, ballerina, candy-shop owner, model, big movie star, secretary, artist, nursery-school teacher, singer, dress designer, and (of course) bride, housewife and mother.

It is worth noting that, with the exception of "astronaut" and "stewardess," every single occupation on both these lists is at least half a century old. Children are thus not merely divisively channeled according to sex; both sexes are encouraged to believe that the world of work circa 1990 (when they reach eighteen) will be similar to the world of work that existed in 1920!

The channeling process is reinforced in other ways. The authors of *Sex Role Socialization in Children's Picture Books* charge that in the books winning the Caldecott Award or listed as runners-up during the past half decade, there are, all told, 261 pictures of males and only twenty-three of females. Among animals depicted, ninety-five are male, only one female. Even when women are found in these books, their roles tend to be insignificant, inconspicuous, and often nameless. In the two (out of eighteen) prizewinning books that did carry stories about girls, the heroine in one had a boy's name, while the other was a foreign princess. Overall, the impression conveyed is that females are invisible—that girls will not be very important, that their activities will be limited to loving, watching, and helping, that they will be passive, and that those who succeed will do so by working unobtrusively behind the scenes: girls serve; boys lead. Thus, adult women also appear in these juvenile books as passive, servile, and almost always a wife or mother. The report notes that "*not one* woman in the Caldecott sample had a job or a profession,"[5] although even now, in the early seventies, women form fully 43 per cent of the United States work force.[6]

This percentage, or at least the absolute number of working women, is almost universally expected to rise in the future, but no one would ever guess it from this past-obsessed literature of the present.

At the same time, motherhood continues to be portrayed as though it were going to be a full-time, lifetime occupation, rather than, as it already is for many women even today, a part-time, ten- or fifteen-year commitment. There are strong reasons to believe that the role of mother will occupy an even smaller percentage of the life of a woman in the future, but this idea, too, is absent.

One might think that the books used in the schools would be better, more carefully selected, than those available outside. In fact, however, this is not the case. The educational system itself reflects and fosters the traditional sex-role allocation in our society. Men are the administrators and women the subordinates— teachers and clerical workers. While there are male teachers, they quickly tend to rise to the rank of administrator, particularly in the primary schools. And the same pattern is evident in the books forced on the children.

Overall, education as it exists today implies that nothing significant is likely to occur in the future with respect to the place of women in society. Its central message to girls is that they, like their mothers, should look forward to a life of submission, housework and child-bearing. Boys, by contrast, are strongly urged to achieve, advance and create.

Marjorie B. U'Ren, doctoral candidate in English at the University of California at Berkeley, in "The Image of Women in Textbooks," in *Women in Sexist Society*, has shown, for example, that in the most recently adopted texts in California for second-through sixth-grade use, fully 75 per cent of the stories center around male characters. "Accounts of female adults are almost non-existent."[7] In a page-by-page analysis, she reports that less than 20 per cent of story space is devoted to female characters. The stories that *are* about girls turn out to be shorter and less interesting, since they are typically restricted to domestic settings.

While boys are told, by implication if not directly, that they will in the future have great freedom of movement and exciting adventures, girls in these books rarely leave the confines of the family and rarely receive recognition. Sisters are almost always subordinated to brothers. Mothers seldom, if ever, suggest solutions to family crises. Rather, as in the story "The Glass Bank," "Mrs. Woods went to work washing dirty dishes and Officer Woods set about his plan."[8] Fathers solve problems, control, and create and execute ideas. Females are described as "lazy, incapable of independent thinking, or direct action."

The books always portray a supposedly "normal" two-parent home with a working father and a housewife mother, as though this pattern, the male-dominated nuclear family, is likely to endure forever into the future. Ironically, according to U'Ren, textbooks earlier in the century presented a "more favorable picture of the female sex than do textbooks written from 1930 on." Mothers in these earlier books participated in more activities with their children, and girls occasionally handled physical danger and were more heroic.[9]

History and Health

As we move up the age ladder, out of elementary school and into courses for older children, the same distortions occur at a more complex level. The child's image of the future is pieced together from many sources, including historical evidence about what was possible in the past. The repeated false assertion that history was essentially a male affair suggests to the unwary that the same will hold true in the future. Once again the heads of young people are stuffed with largely unexamined assumptions that restrict their conception of the possible.

Dr. Janice Law Trecker studied thirteen popular history texts and found that women were depicted, once again, as "passive, incapable of sustained organization or work, satisfied with their role in society, and well supplied with material blessings."[10] They rarely fought for anything (and, therefore, presumably, won't in the future?) but occasionally *received* (as befits naturally passive creatures) certain rights, such as suffrage and alleged equality. Actually, of course, quite the reverse was true. Upper-middle-class English gentlewomen actually burned houses, blew up mail boxes, smashed windows and went to jail in their struggle for the vote.

Neither their struggle to enter higher education nor their efforts to organize and unionize are covered. Even when black history is incorporated into texts, black women tend to be ignored, whether as abolitionists, civil-rights workers, or contributors to the arts and letters. Even when the feminist movement is discussed, male spokesmen are ordinarily the discussants, rather than the feminist leaders themselves, although no one, then or now, has ever accused them of inarticulateness.

What history books do with respect to the "public" past and, by implication, the "public future," other books do with respect to the girl's own private destiny: A key component of any individual's self-image and image of the future has to do with his or her own body. Each of us has, in the mind's eye, so to speak, a picture of what our body will look like at various times in the future. This piece of conjecture shapes and shadows our perception of the personal future. Children, because they associate power, competence and freedom with adulthood, want to "be big." Middle-aged people, peering into their future, often fear advanced age—the loss of hair, the facial wrinkling. Their image of their future bodies creates anxiety in the present.

What will she look like? What futures will her body make possible—or impossible? Cheryl Bowles, formerly a school nurse, has examined the materials given to students in "health class" in a midwestern American high school.[11] Although she gathered her material in 1971, it has the ring of an earlier generation about it.

All freshmen, segregated by sex, took the course, and there was no special literature designed for the boys. Girls, on the other hand, received special literature on menstruation, feminine hygiene, and life as a woman. The literature on menstruation reinforced the pressure to accept the conventional female role. One pamphlet, *Growing Up and Liking It*, explicitly tells its readers what the future holds for them: they will "fall in love and marry" and they "will want to have children."[12]

Here, again, we find the easy assumption that the past will simply repeat itself in the future. The literature does not suggest that there might be socially acceptable alternatives to marriage or motherhood. Not only is this quite possibly misleading with respect to the future of the family in the United States and other high-technology countries, but in a world facing enormous population problems, it is implicitly pronatalist. Furthermore, there is no hint in it of some of the startling biological breakthroughs that may affect the birth process and could even, thereafter, as we shall see, change the woman's role in the birth process.

The health literature fed young girl students repeatedly tells them that the changes in their bodies are a preparation for future childbearing. Thus, the literature, when discussing marriage and the girl's future role, makes contradictory statements. One booklet states that there are a great variety of new opportunities for women. But it rejects these and asserts that "we still expect a woman's main role to be the one it has always been, that of home-maker. We still define a womanly woman as one who succeeds first of all in the roles of wife and mother."

"Cooling" the Girls

Should a girl, despite this barrage of conditioning, continue to formulate an image of her future in terms of work, she is supplied with supposedly helpful literature that actually is designed to cool her interest in any role outside the traditional female occupations. Thus, one book says, "If you're interested in chemistry you'll find it easier (and perhaps just as satisfying) if you go into home economics rather than trying to break into the petroleum industry. If you want to take care of sick persons, it will be easier to become a nurse than a doctor. If you're interested in human welfare, it will be easier to become a social worker than a politician."[13]

To grasp the effect of this advice on self-image and achievement motivation, see how it sounds when we substitute "black" for female: "If you're interested in chemistry, you'll find it easier (and perhaps just as satisfying) if you become a (black) lab technician rather than trying to break into the (white) petroleum industry. If you want to take care of sick persons, it will be easier to become a hospital attendant or aide (black) than a doctor (white)."

Such consistent pressures, continually narrowing the girl's image of possible personal futures, inevitably has an effect on her intellectual capacities as well. In this connection, it would be important to know exactly how girls' conceptions of their future lives, and the environment in which these lives will be lived, differ from those of boys. Apart from the narrower range of possibilities, do girls tend to think further ahead or less so? Are their images of the future more consistent? Are they "lumpy," in the sense of focusing on a few key futural events, like marriage and birth, rather than equally rich and elaborate at each stage of the anticipated life cycle?

When Eleanor Maccoby, a specialist in the psychology of sex differences, writes about intellectual functioning and gender, she points out that most differences between the sexes in interests and abilities can be explained as follows:

> . . . members of each sex are encouraged in, and become inter-ested in and proficient at the kinds of tasks that are most relevant to the roles they fill currently or are *expected to fill in the future* [emphasis added]. So boys in high school (but not elementary school) forge ahead in math to prepare for possible roles as en-gineers or scientists, unlike girls who see no need for math in their future. And later, as housewives, their "total intelligence" declines because such tests measure skills that are used less by adult women than by adult men.[14]

There are some areas in which males do better than females: spa-tial ability, analytic style and breaking set, she states. But the last attribute, usually called field-independence, has been reex-amined recently by psychologist Juan Pascual Leone. He chal-lenges the conventional argument that men are intellectually superior because they are more field-independent than women. He points out, moreover, the advantages of field-dependence or con-textual thinking. However, since dependence is a "bad" word in our patriarchal language, he changes the term to "field sensi-tive."[15]

Professor Albert J. Silverman, chairman of the Department of Psychiatry at the University of Michigan, has suggested that the relationship is even more complex. He has found no differences between field-dependence and field-independence between male and female students at the University of Michigan, but has found such differences in students from Washtenaw Community College. Since community college students are usually from lower-status homes, social-status factors may be involved rather than sex.[16]*

---

* It is precisely here, in connection with the issue of creativity, that futural imagery may play its most significant role. Thus, the ability to break set, to think outside the given categories, to redefine the problem, to imagine alternatives, is based, at least in part, on the ability of the individual to analogize, to match one type of data against another type in search of novel and useful juxtapositions. The fact that boys are told to behave one way, but expected to behave another, and the richer array of possibilities held out to them from birth on, could both easily contribute to a more complex futural imagery, with more varied stores of data. The more varied the information and imagery, the greater the likelihood of thinking outside a given set. *If* it is true that girls have difficulty "breaking set," this could

A crucial aspect of sex typing that further inhibits women's intellectual development is their socialization for conformity, dependency and modesty such that intellectual assertiveness is considered unfeminine. Psychologist Gloria L. Carey attempted to improve problem-solving behavior through changing attitudes toward such behavior by group discussions directed toward increasing self-confidence and emphasizing the social acceptability of excelling at problem-solving. This method improved the performance of college *women*, although not of college men.[17]

This outcome further demonstrates the necessity for teachers to discard traditional sex-role expectations. As Maccoby's work shows, they should, for maximum intellectual development, encourage *in*dependence in their *female* students and in no way make fun of or humiliate boys who are *de*pendent on them.[18]

The failure to encourage independence and to widen the range of possibilities open to women produces a fatalism and passivity that flies in the face of all the educational rhetoric about producing resourceful, self-reliant and hope-filled people for tomorrow. This is mirrored in the work of psychologist and president of Radcliffe College, Matina Horner.[19] In an experiment that directly touched upon their images of the future, she studied ninety female and eighty-eight male students at a large midwestern university. The females were asked to complete a paragraph, the first sentence of which was "After first-term finals, Anne finds herself at the top of her medical school class." The cue for the men was "After first-term finals, John finds himself at the top of his medical school class." Not accidentally, the paragraphs about the male tended to be filled with accounts of future success and

---

be explained by the fact that they are, in the first place, encouraged to think of their future in terms of only a few possible roles, and thus amass data into only a few categories. Clearly, this does not imply that girls are less creative than boys, but simply that the impoverishment of the futural imagery of girls might be more closely linked to their intellectual and creative performance than has hitherto been suspected. This theory with some modifications might also apply to other "future-deprived" groups, including blacks and poor Americans generally. [Editor's conjecture.]

I am not sure about this interpretation because girls are also given double messages, one of the most common being achieve-don't achieve. That message does not appear until adolescence, when their high-school performance, not surprisingly, falls off. [Author's comment.]

happiness. Those that projected "Anne Smith's" future were am-
bivalent at best. Anne was pictured as having a future filled
with loneliness and frustration. No wonder girls who start off
bright so often do not fulfill their promise.

Feminist Future Projections

Since the consistency, coherence and accuracy of the images of
the future held by girls, in conjunction with the structure of the
society, shape the actual futures they live as women, it is important for educators to examine deeply the assumptions upon which
their work is based, and the life-premises they communicate to
their students. Is it realistic, in view of the vast changes sweeping
all the advanced technological nations today, to continue to picture the future of women as essentially unchanged? Is it just, to
shrivel their sense of possibility? Can one expect high intellectual
or creative performance under what might be called future-
deprived circumstances?

The gap between what the schools teach today (implicitly as
well as explicitly) and the changes we face is most evident with
respect to the family. At the very moment that millions of young
people are being led to believe that the present traditional family
forms, and especially the nuclear family, will endure indefinitely,
the newspapers and some science journals are filled with indica-
tions that we may confront a radically different future.

Indeed, there are a whole series of potentially dramatic
biological breakthroughs having to do with birth technology, genetics engineering, and transplants that could have a heavy impact
on future families. For example, Dr. Marian Murray,[20] assistant
professor of anatomy at the University of Chicago's Pritzker
School of Medicine, is concerned with the future impact of control of sex-role behavior through surgery on the hypothalamus,
that portion of the brain thought by some to be related to sexual
orientation.

If we wish to resist these technological changes on grounds that
they are dehumanizing, as many believe, can we do so by raising
our children in ignorance of the choices that will face them?
Given these possibilities, it is more important than ever for
women to have control of their own bodies, and for a strong

feminist movement to support women in this effort. It is equally important for women to enter biological and technical fields in which such technologies are spawning.

Today many serious scholars, as well as long-range planners, government agencies and others, are busy drawing up forecasts picturing alternative futures. Many of these projections, speculations and plans will influence the future of the family and, by implication, the future of women. Yet they are, by and large, the product of exclusively male, or primarily male, futurists. Only recently have feminists, too, begun to explore the long-term future, and the images of tomorrow that they present are often radically different from those of what might be termed "establishment" futurists.

Thus, for example, the psychologist Dr. Phyllis Chesler closes her brilliant book *Women and Madness*[21] with "Some Psychological Prescriptions for the Future." Female psychology will change, she says, when enough women "challenge or alter their relation to the means of production and reproduction," although a minority will be able to effect such changes in themselves through modification of consciousness alone (consciousness includes changed future images).

Dr. Chesler argues that women must "gradually and ultimately dominate public social institutions in order to insure that they are not used against women. . . . I happen to think that science must be used to either release women from biological reproduction—or to allow men to experience the process also. . . . The point is to have our *entire* social drama played out as fully by women as by men. And it *is* revolutionary by definition to have women out of the biological home, both psychologically and actually."

Women must thus be passionate about achieving the power necessary for self-definition, predicated on direct control of worldly realities and concern for their own survival and growth rather than through or for their men or families. Dr. Chesler does not suggest that they give up their capacity for warmth, emotionality and nurturance and become like men. Rather, that they use these qualities for *themselves and other women*, including their daughters. (She notes that this may result in an increase in the male capacity to nurture.)

Dr. Chesler concludes the chapter with these relevant points (among thirteen questions she raises): If helpless and prolonged dependence of human children is the model for all culturally oppressive relations, will new methods of childbearing and rearing "banish the human tendency to arbitrarily interpret biological differences in oppressive ways"? If flexible sex roles lead to the ability to engage in homosexual and bisexual relationships, which she considers "the ability to respect, fear, and love women and men equally," provocatively she asks, "Will men be able to become *more* heterosexual just as women are able to become *less* heterosexual?"

The most controversial radical feminist image of the future is Shulamith Firestone's alternative to 1984, her "Case for Feminist Revolution."[22] She believes motherhood is a "fundamentally oppressive biological condition that we only now have the skill to correct," and with this change the need for marriage can wither away. Her "flexible alternatives" are as follows:

- *Single Professions* (particularly in the transition period): "a single life organized around the demands of a chosen profession" can satisfy the individual's needs.
- *Living Together*: Probably monogamous at first but "after several generations of nonfamily living our psychosexual structures may become altered so radically that . . . 'aim inhibited' [i.e., monogamous] relationship would become obsolescent." Since she believes that parental satisfaction is obtainable only through crippling the child, abolition of family name, property and class will make having children as a form of ego extension obsolete. At that time, she considers it likely that "artificial reproduction will be developed and widely accepted."
- *Households*: "Large groupings of people living together for an unspecified time. It is the new reproductive unit."
- *Limited Contract*: As "households" replace marriage, at first they can be legalized by a group of about ten adults of varying ages applying for a license for a given time period, e.g., seven to ten years, or "whatever was decided on as the minimal time in which children needed a stable structure in which to grow up," after which the group could renew the contract, change membership, or disband.
- *Children*: They would constitute a regulated percentage of each

household. At first they may be genetic children created by household couples, but after a few generations how the children were "produced" would not matter. Natural childbirth and a nine-month pregnancy and delivery make the mother possessive about her biological children and encourage her to continue viewing the child as property, thus perpetuating inequality between children and adults.

In Firestone's utopia, many adults and older children would take care of the babies, and ". . . all relationships would be based on love alone, uncorrupted by objective dependencies and the resulting class inequalities. Enduring relationships between people of widely different ages would become common."

Legal rights, chores, city planning, and the economy would all reflect the end of the family structure and the ensuing equalitarian relationships. Drudgery would be equally distributed and then eliminated altogether, resulting in "socialism within a technetronic state." This cybernetic socialism with the household the alternative to the family meets her four minimal demands, which are

(1) The freeing of women from the tyranny of their biology by any means available, and the diffusion of the childbearing and childrearing role to the society as a whole, to men and other children, as well as women.

(2) The economic independence and self-determination of all.

(3) The total integration of women and children into the larger society.

(4) Sexual freedom—not only between and among the sexes but also between the generations, including the breaking of the incest taboos. While she is aware that introducing biotechnological changes in childbearing would be used oppressively in the society as it exists today, she suggests that—

> As was demonstrated in the case of the development of atomic energy, radicals, rather than breast-beating about the immorality of scientific research, could be much more effective by concentrating their *full* energies on demands for control of scientific discoveries by and for the people. For, like atomic energy, fertility control, artificial reproduction, cybernation, in themselves, are liberating—*unless* they are improperly used.

She underestimates, however, the danger to children in the freedom from incest taboos she proposes. In any society adults are stronger than children. And her description of self-hatred in pregnancy and of childbirth as comparable to "shitting a pumpkin" is neither my experience nor that of other feminists who have had children, but a reflection of the situation of women in today's society, and the male perspective in obstetrics.[23]

Alice Rossi, professor of sociology at Goucher, has a radical, humanistic image of the future, which does not include the bioengineering changes in reproduction or the abolition of the nuclear family that Chesler and Firestone sketch. Rather, in a utopian vision ironically titled, "The Beginning of Ideology,"[24] she focuses on institutional changes that could result in equality not only for women and blacks, but for men and whites. In her hybrid model of equality, embodying many of the values of the counterculture community, fellowship and creativity are emphasized rather than rationality and efficiency, and social responsibility rather than status and high income. In this model, for example, academic women who have been resocialized as adults in women's liberation groups will not share the values of their masculine colleagues. They will redefine academic productivity, emphasizing not the number of publications or professional offices held, but the quality of teaching, service to the institution, and community and colleagueship with students.

In her "Family Development in a Changing World,"[25] Professor Rossi states that, while there have been significant changes in the American family, "they are not as pervasive as those described in the critical literature." She points out that though young girls in the 1970s still focus in their play on imitative maternal behavior, maternity has become a very small part of the adult woman's life. Thus, for a woman who marries at twenty-two, who works outside the home for three years after marriage and then has two children two years apart, and who dies at seventy-four: 23 per cent of her adulthood will be spent without a husband; 41 per cent of her adult life will be spent with a husband but no children under eighteen; 36 per cent of her adulthood will be spent with a spouse and at least one child under eighteen years. So, only 12 per cent of her life will be spent in full-time maternal care of pre-school-age children. Only seven of her fifty-six adult years will go to pre-school child care.

A great part of her life will be spent keeping, caring for and running a household; indeed, the time needed for such activity has *increased* rather than decreased with each additional object and appliance purchased.

One of Rossi's suggestions, involving human rather than technological resources, is a registry at junior and senior high schools "to which a local family could apply for pairs of students to be assigned to their families on a regular basis" to help out with household and child care. She suggests a mixed-sex pair. Such a plan would aid mothers of young children, as well as help the helpers.

To control population size, she suggests legalizing abortion, spreading contraceptive information, and legitimating childlessness and homosexuality. In addition, she notes that for some women meaningful employment could satisfy needs which otherwise would be met by an increase in family size. She does not believe that women will choose the biogenetic engineering alternatives, but does consider the possibility that such choices may be forced on us by a totalitarian government.[26]

The Nuclear Family as Nuclear Disaster

Even if there were no major biological breakthroughs or if social pressures prevented their widespread adoption, it is still likely that the family would undergo drastic changes. The figures on broken marriages today, not merely in the United States but in Western Europe, suggest strongly that the nuclear family is too constraining for many people, or that it does not adequately fit into the culture around it. "The nuclear family is a nuclear disaster," was a slogan of radicals in the male and female liberation movements.

With increasing sensitivity to the necessity for curbing population growth, it is no longer necessary that all sexual unions be potentially fecund. And with increasing education and affluence, more permissive attitudes toward sexuality, whether in its heterosexual, homosexual or bisexual forms, are growing, especially in more sophisticated segments of the population. Moreover, just as heterosexual partners are changed through the life cycle in serial monogamy, it may well be that the future will bring a pattern in which the gender of the partner will also change. Should a person want children, she or he may have a heterosexual relationship at a particular life-cycle stage. But when these needs have been met, homosexual relationships may occur. Once the stigmatizing and labeling process stops, our human bisexual potential may be explored. The gay liberation movement has accelerated the trend, making this possible and expanding all of our choices. For, as the *Chicago Gay Pride Celebration* newspaper said: "The trouble with the world is not that some people make love differently. . . . The trouble is that most people don't make love at all."

Whether or not one agrees with this picture, it is clear that more and more questions are being asked about the future of traditional marriage. Jessie Bernard, a sociologist who has specialized in the marriage and the family field, and who has for the past few years supported the women's liberation movement, marshals evidence to show that married women are not happy, that they get the dirty end of the stick, that we make women "sick" in order to fit them for marriage. She concludes her article, "The Myth of the Happy Housewife," with the question, "Could it be that marriage itself is sick?"[27]

Changes are also likely to take place in family roles because the population explosion means that women may be less pressured to marry and have children. Margaret Mead points out that if men do not have to support as many children, their life options will be increased.* They will be able to follow callings that pro-

---

* While I have emphasized the limiting effects of the female sex role stereotype, the traditional male role is also limiting, and young boys are constrained, affecting their future behavior. It is almost as though females were allowed to express any emotion except anger, while anger was the *only* appropriate "masculine" emotion. In *Family Interaction* (John Wiley, New York, 1970), a former president of the American Sociological Association, Dr. Ralph Turner, states, "the traditional personality differences between men and women are not conducive to a highly stable and mutually gratifying relationship, and are no longer suited to any workable division of labor in marriage. Their only clear utility would be to facilitate a relationship of inequality."

Perhaps the traditional men's qualities were useful when we had physical frontiers to conquer, harsh elements to battle, mountain passes to traverse,

vide intrinsic satisfaction, such as music and art, but that do not necessarily pay enough to support a family. "As we reduce the requirements for motherhood, we reduce the requirements for fatherhood, and we'll release a lot of people to be individuals and to make contributions as individuals, rather than as parents."[28] While she believes the family is the best place to bring up small children, it is not the best for anything else. Thus, norms may change so that the ideal pattern may be one of being married only until the children are grown.

Sociologist Philip Hauser gives four major developments that will profoundly affect the family: population explosion, population implosion, population diversification, and the accelerated tempo of technological and social change. In our mass society the family has become nuclear and has lost many functions. Because the parents are younger when the last child leaves home and the age at which one's spouse's death occurs has risen, "the number of years in which parents are freed from childbearing and child-rearing activities has tremendously increased."[29] With increasingly equalitarian families, changing female roles, and a decline in the importance of the family as a socializing agency, there will be more marital conflict, rather than less, and more partner-changing, with the overall result a system of sequential polygamy. With the remarriage rate reaching new peaks, we are already well on the way.

Similarly, the commune movement cannot but have some effect on future family forms. It is not at all clear that the commune movement will radically improve the lot of women. Thus, Marge Piercy's recent novel, *Dance the Eagle to Sleep*, pictures the destruction of the counterculture in a world of the near future.[30] In her scenario, the central characters attempt to transcend the nuclear family ("a hotbed for breeding neurosis"). They want, as they put it, to go beyond couples, troops, teams and unions. They mistrust roles. Yet, in spite of their commitment to new ways, the same old problems of sexism recur.

Nevertheless, even though the commune movement involves only

---

and plains to be plowed, as we attempted to achieve our Manifest Destiny. But the economy of abundance rather than of scarcity and the increased leisure time we have now, and will have, make the John Wayne image an anachronism.

a statistically small number of young people, and seldom appears to achieve its altruistic aims, its very successes and failures are likely to provide an alternative standard for evaluation. Indeed, alternative standards reflecting deep changes in our value system are already spreading far beyond the radical young or the commune movement. These standards, which include sexual equality, cannot but influence the future in which today's schoolgirls will live out their lives.

An analysis of sex equality goals may start with the reality of contemporary life, but soon requires an imaginative leap to a new conception of what a future good society should be. The new model of equality envisages a future in which family, community and play are valued on a par with politics and work for both sexes and for all the races, social classes and nations which comprise the human family. We are on the brink not of the "end" of ideology, but its "beginning."[31]

"We Don't Have To Live This Way"

In their attempt to reconstitute society so that people are no longer constricted by obsolete sex roles, radical groups within the women's movement have condemned the nuclear family. While they recognize that for some people the nuclear family has furnished a refuge from the competitiveness and dehumanization of the marketplace, they argue that this very "escape" can keep people from fighting to change and humanize society. These women focus a great deal of attention on the ways in which the nuclear family and traditional sex roles support the present economic system.

First, women, because they are among the last hired and first fired, provide employers with a vast, flexible labor pool to complement the ups and downs of the business cycle.

Second, they still, in many places, do the same work for less money than men do, maximizing profits. Moreover, they are more likely to work at non-unionized jobs, such as salesclerks, laundresses, and office workers. The low valuation of housework ("just a housewife") conditions a woman to regard her time and skills as relatively valueless, so that she will work more and complain less when she does take a job.

Third, the nuclear family helps stabilize society by separating and isolating people into small units distrustful of outsiders.[32] Within marriage, it tended to "chain women to their reproductive function" formally by connecting sex to reproduction and child-rearing with the birth process. The mother-child linkage in the nuclear family leads to the children being considered private property rather than separate human beings, and to overidentification with them by the parents, particularly the mother, who is told to live vicariously through her children and husband. My research on depression in middle-aged women, or "Portnoy's mother's complaint," demonstrates the sad situation in which these women find themselves when they lose their mother role.[33]

Fourth, the ideology of the family, with the woman supposed to find her happiness at home, leads to consumerism, since the one area in which the woman can exert control is in furnishing the home and buying clothes. These activities can become ends in themselves, fed by the ads in women's magazines.

Since the goal of the women's movement is to diminish the constraints of ascribed sex roles, and since the current institutional structure, particularly the nuclear family, reinforces such stereotypes, many women in the liberation movement attempt to change the future by living in alternative ways now. Some try to make marriage work, but make it more egalitarian by institutionalizing rights and obligations in contracts that specify a 50/50 shared responsibility for child-care and house-care arrangements. Some, still within the framework of marriage, work out cooperative child-care arrangements for weekends and overnights, not only to free the parents but to prepare the children for the less individualistic society they envision. Some live with men without being married, although this method no longer has the mystique it once did, since it has become clear that problems of sexism are quite as likely to arise in such arrangements as in a legal marriage. The movement's year for "smashing monogamy" did not work and was extremely difficult for many women, so, in general, nonmonogamous relationships have been abandoned as a device to bring about the good society.

Some women live with other women. Some are ascetic, believing that sex isn't worth the hassle it entails. Some are bisexual. Some are lesbians. Some live in communes, urban or rural, and some in nuclear-family settings. For some, the women's movement itself, particularly the part of it built around consciousness-raising groups and an ideology of sisterhood, has provided many of the functions of an extended family at a time when their biological extended families could no longer fill these functions. Thus, the movement has helped in crises such as divorces. It has eased transitions to new geographic areas by providing primary groups to which women could look, much as one would call up a second cousin when moving to another town where the cousin lived. It has provided helpful referral services for psychotherapists, attorneys, gynecologists. In some cities, such as Chicago, liberation schools have sprung up in which women can learn practical skills such as auto repair, which they missed out on earlier because they had to take homemaking rather than shop. Other courses include the sociology, psychology and economics of sexism. Such skills help women become competent and independent and able to survive as whole persons rather than as "the better half" they were socialized to be.

The scope, variety and depth of this social movement suggest that its values and implied standards for future behavior will not vanish without trace. Many of the experiments may prove to have been simplistic or abortive. But the failures are only a small part of the story. The history of the late sixties and early seventies is likely to alter the future of the late seventies and early eighties. The failure of most schools to recognize this, their refusal to re-examine their role in terms of the emerging future, means that millions of girls and young women passing through the system today, from the kindergartens to the colleges, are being damaged along the way.

The Future Is Part of the Present

It is true that schools reflect the values of the dominant forces in the community, but this fact simply explains the situation. It neither implies that it has to be this way nor does it justify what is. Moreover, if these stereotypes are dysfunctional and inhibitory for the lives the students can, or probably will, live in the future, if the range of behaviors arrayed before the student is too narrow, then, in fact, the schools are not *really* reflecting the parent's interests either.

Sociologist Marcia Milman, criticizing traditional sex-role research, points out that during rapid environmental changes, narrowly specialized organisms die off first and those that are the least specialized survive. She suggests that in coping with our rapid social change, "what is best suited for the social environment is that social behavior cease to be characterized by sexual differentiation or specialization and that both males and females reincorporate the qualities which they lost in the role division."[34]

Were parents to understand how the rigid stereotype of sex roles will limit, rather than free, their children in the future, perhaps support could be mustered for changing the futural images of men and women, of boys and girls, as presented in the texts. (A new California law requires that textbooks be neither racist nor sexist.) Nonsexist books are available through the Parents Magazine Press, the Feminist Press, and the Lollipop Press; other publishers are preparing new ones. They present a broader range of alternatives than is presently found.

But education must change more than textbooks. It must stop constraining behavior based on traditional notions of propriety. Girls should be able to take shop (some of them have had to go to court to win the right!) and boys should learn to cook, as is now the case in Sweden. Such skills enable us all to become more autonomous, the woman less helpless when confronted with a stalled car, and the man capable of cooking not only for himself, but for a family, if he decides on a "hybrid" marriage or relationship. The abandonment of sex-role stereotyping, moreover, should be reflected in the organization of schools of the future. It should no longer mirror the sexism in our society, men in the top rungs (the principals), women as subordinates (teachers). Young men have proven their ability, their sensitivity, as nursery- and elementary-school teachers. But if their integration as elementary-school teachers is simply a temporary phenomenon enabling them to leapfrog more experienced female teachers to the role of principal, little will be accomplished.

Girls need to be rewarded for learning advanced math and science, rather than derided, as sometimes occurs in classroom situations. Remedial programs should not focus solely on the problems boys are more likely to have, reading problems, for example, but give additional help to those students who have difficulty seeing spatial relationships (mainly girls).[35] Anyone who has tried unsuccessfully to find her way in a strange area, with or without a map, will recognize the importance of such skills.

This paper has shown how from the moment of birth, external and constraining forces, many arising from the educational process, have shaped us, interacting with and molding our original biological sexual identity, to make us into first boys and girls and then men and women fitted to be citizens of the past. The future is part of the present. Yet education sex-types us for obsolete roles by imposing sharply different expectations on boys and girls, and has reinforced this sex-typing through stereotypes in the books students read.

Today a movement is gaining force, aimed at bringing the schools into the present and reorienting them toward the future. This movement cannot succeed unless it recognizes not only the importance of "images of the future," but the importance of those procedures, like sex-typing, that narrow and stultify the futural imagery held by young people, female *or* male. By portraying the future as constricted and unchanged from the present, we create not fully adaptive, change-ready, competent human beings, but ill-equipped, essentially obsolete, people. By channeling the sexes into hermetically sealed, compartmentalized roles, we guarantee their misery.

"Less drudgery and compulsion in the activity we call work, and less compulsion to marry and raise families will pose perplexing problems of identity and purpose for both sexes," says Suzanne Keller, professor of sociology at Princeton. "For with the decline of lifetime employment for men and lifetime maternity for women we have removed the two ancient Biblical curses and with them the foundations of domestic society. Whether this redirection of history will usher in a new Paradise before a new Fall remains to be seen. But as a first order of priority we must create substitutes for these two organizing principles of our society. . . .

"The liberation movements gathering momentum—in art and in life—are thus no accident. They are not superfluous. As weathervanes of tomorrow they are part and parcel of some very basic and very significant developments regarding family and community in our time."[36]

The black child's image of the future affects his or her present-day behavior in special ways. Black youth cannot thrive in racist social or educational institutions, and they cannot develop healthy, future-focused role-images until sufficient numbers of blacks are presented in all the communications media in non-racist contexts. Here the prominent black psychiatrist Alvin F. Poussaint argues that for many young blacks, delayed rewards are weak motivators because they are discriminatory and inconsistently given. For the black child, the future is too far away and far too unpredictable.

CHAPTER FOUR

The Black Child's Image of the Future

by Alvin F. Poussaint, M.D.

. . . What shall I tell my dear ones raised in a white world.
A place where white has been made to represent
All that is good and pure and fine and decent,
Where clouds are white and dolls, and heaven
Surely is a white, white place. . . .
—*Margaret Burroughs*

Every individual's future has been determined to a large extent by the circumstances of his birth. Boys and girls born into royalty became kings and queens while youngsters born into slavery became slaves. Most civilizations have had a caste or class system which defined some as having "good blood" and others as "bad." It was believed to be the will of God that the individual's station in life should be so determined. In large part, then, a child's image of the future is a reflection of his socioeconomic background, i.e., does he belong to the in-group as opposed to the out-group in the current status hierarchy; is he poor, is he rich and to what ethnic group does he belong. Clearly, the future of a slum child will differ vastly from that of his peer in suburbia. In the United States, it is undoubtedly the color-caste system that is the most decisive element in the black child's perspective on his future life-chances and his self-image.

In a society which favors whites and discriminates against blacks, the black child's identity and future are predetermined to a significant degree—the black man has only to decide what methods of survival to adopt. For most older blacks, that option was precluded as well, since to be docile was to immediately curry the white man's favor, while to show open aggression meant to flirt with a quick death at the hands of racists. This was particularly true in the past. Today, the Afro-American's options have increased and a reappraisal of his image and his survival tactics has been necessary.

Now that full equality is looming closer on the horizon, many blacks find that aggressiveness and self-assertiveness are more appropriate to survival than servility. However, there are still many black parents who have not kept abreast with the times and are still teaching their children the methods of yesteryear.

To understand why blacks have changed their adjustment tactics, and must continue to do so, if change is to be effected, it is necessary to examine their relationship with the dominant society. This is a relationship in flux and one which fifty years hence will be very different from what it is now.

Perhaps the best way to understand how a person esteems his life-chances in a particular society is to study his self-concept. Within it, one may find the individual's view of the world, his role in it, and, in turn, the role assigned to him by society. Undoubtedly, if a child is told time and time again that he is ugly, he will come to view himself as such and may, in fact, form a future identification reinforcing that very image. Like it or not, his image becomes a composite of how others see him, or how they tell him he should be seen.

According to psychologists George H. Mead,[1] Charles Cooley,[2] and others,[3] the self is formed through the individual's interaction with the reaction to other members of society—his peers, parents, teachers and other agents of socialization. Through interaction and as a necessary means of effective communication, the child learns to assume the role and attitudes of others with whom he comes into contact. These assumed attitudes condition not only how he responds to others, but how he behaves toward himself. The collective attitudes of the community or "generalized other," as Mead calls them, give the individual his unity of self. Each self, then, though having its own unique personality characteristics, is also a reflection of the social process.[4]

This is illustrated in Cooley's "looking-glass image," according to which the individual's self-concept is made up of "the imagination of our appearance to the other person, the imagination of his judgment of that appearance to the other person, the imagination of his judgment of that appearance and some sort of self-feeling, such as pride or mortification."[5] Omitted in this definition is the fact that the self-concept is determined not only by past and current inputs but also by a child's future projection of himself. It is determined by "what can I be" as well as by "what I am now," or, as Benjamin Singer in Chapter Two calls it, the "future-focused role image."[6] It depends as much on whether the child learns to have a pessimistic or optimistic view of the future as regards himself, his family and his community. The black child has to determine whether the society will permit him to be more than just "another nigger."

Snow White and the Tar Baby

For the black youth in white American society, the white "generalized other" whose attitudes he assumes and the "looking-glass" into which he gazes both reflect the same judgment of him, i.e., he is inferior because he is black. Living in the lowest stratum of a color-caste system, his self-image is significantly shaped, defined and evaluated by a racist "generalized other."

If we accept the argument—unfortunately many social scientists do[7]—that whites are the sole "significant others" in the black person's life, then we could deduce that his self-concept is negative. Because of his contact with institutionalized symbols of inferiority—segregated schools, neighborhoods and jobs, and the more direct imprint of his family (which is socialized to believe that it is substandard)—he gradually becomes aware of the liabilities of his skin color. Thus, he comes to form what Erik Erikson calls a "negative identity."[8] In the looking-glass of white society the supposedly undesirable physical image of the "Tar Baby"—black skin, woolly hair, and thick lips—is juxtaposed to the valued model of "Snow White"—white skin, straight hair and aquiline features.

Fortunately, the picture is not as bleak as it looks, because white society is not the black youth's *only* "generalized other" and "looking-glass." Immediately surrounding the black youth is the black community which does not accept *in toto* the definition given it by the white community. Since the days of slavery, blacks have tried to counteract the effects of racism on their children and themselves. Understandably, racist conditioning has taken its toll, but blacks have a long history of teaching racial pride and self-respect. By and large, they never accepted servitude. The Sambo image of docility was a necessary survival mechanism: however, underneath it there existed the individual's own definition of himself. His church, his music, his literature—his whole life-style reflects a love of life which, given the grim surroundings from which it emerges, whites find hard to grasp.

Furthermore, blacks have not really believed in the image of goodness and purity projected by whites. Blacks have always seen most whites as hypocrites who could not be trusted. Thus, the black self-image has never been completely controlled by whites. Indeed, blacks have struggled to show whites that their image of them as inferior just isn't so. And one factor that has helped blacks sustain a positive self-concept is their faith in the future—a belief in change—that better times are coming, "Good news, chariot's coming." Thus, we can only speak of a black child's damaged self-concept in relative terms. During his oppression in the United States, the black man has developed an independent set of values, and it is in the context of these, and not just those of white society, that we should appraise the black child's self-image and future self-image.

Several attempts have been made to determine how a damaged self-concept affects the black child's ability to function in society, his ability to achieve success and cope with the future. For the most part, the evidence is weighted heavily against the black child, depicting a grim picture of an individual stymied by a variety of syndromes: "identity foreclosure," "negative identity," "lack of self-esteem," "cultural deprivation," etc. Social scientists have been too quick to find only pathology in the black experience in America. Blacks have been studied as if they were a hotbed of chronic social disease. White investigators in particular have had a negative approach—ignoring the many strengths of the black community. Daniel Moynihan, blinded by his own social values, described the black family as "matriarchal" and disorganized. Arthur Jensen, using questionable data, argued that blacks are genetically inferior in intellectual endowment compared to whites. Thus, many social scientists under the guise of "objective research" have promoted racist attitudes and further traumatized the black psyche. The fact that researchers, in one way or the other, have described blacks as deficient has further stigmatized blacks and put an additional obstacle in the path of a positive black self-concept. Black babies now enter the world burdened with the task of overcoming "scientific evidence" that they are the carriers of "inferior genes."

Despite the negative tone of much current research on Afro-Americans, a review of these studies may shed some light on the special dilemma of the black child in today's society. Deutsch's work reported that black children had significantly more negative self-images than did white children.[9] He maintained that among the influences converging on the black urban child

> is his sensing that the larger society views him as inferior and expects inferior performance from him as evidenced by the general denial to him of realistic vertical mobility possibilities. Under these conditions, it is understandable that the Negro child would tend strongly to question his own competencies and in so questioning would be acting largely as others expect him to act, an example of what Merton has called the "self-fulfilling prophecy"—the very expectation itself is a cause of its fulfillment.[10]

Similarly, R. H. Coombs and V. Davies, in their investigation of school and college performance as it relates to self-concept, offer the important proposition that

> In the context of the school world, a student who is defined as a "poor student" (by significant others and thereby by self) comes

to conceive of himself as such and gears his behavior accordingly, that is, the social expectation is realized. However, if he is led to believe by means of the social "looking glass" that he is capable and able to achieve well, he does. To maintain his status and self-esteem becomes the incentive for further effort which subsequently involves him more in the reward system of the school.[11]

These views have been confirmed by Helen Davidson and Judith Greenberg in their studies of motivation.[12] In their examination of black children from Central Harlem, these authors found that the lower the level of self-esteem, the lower the level of achievement, while consequently, higher levels of self-appraisal and ego strength—feelings of self-competence—were associated with higher levels of achievement. For example, high achievers were better able to present their own ideas and to express basic needs, suggesting that a stronger self-concept is associated with a greater willingness to risk self-expression, an obvious prerequisite for achievement.

In 1968, Katz reported that black children tended to have exaggeratedly high aspirations, so high, in fact, that they were realistically impossible to live up to. As a result, these children were able to achieve very little—"In a sense, they had been socialized to self-impose failure."[13] Katz presents evidence which indicates that the anticipation of failure or harsh judgment by adults produces anxiety in the child, and that in black children, this level of anxiety is highest in low achievers who have a high standard of self-evaluation.[14] Accordingly, a black child with an unrealistically elevated self-concept often tends to become so anxious concerning his possible failure to meet that self-concept that he does in fact fail consistently. This suggests that performance is related to the image of the future in quite complex ways. "Higher horizons" are not enough when they are objectively unachievable because of racism in the surrounding society.

The Persistence of Self-Esteem

Moreover, while all these studies uniformly take for granted the presence of a strongly negative self-concept in the young black child, this underlying assumption needs to be looked at more closely. Beginning with the study carried out by Kenneth and Mamie Clark,[15] which was later followed by those of Mary E. Goodman, Robert Coles, Judith Porter, H. J. Greenwald[16] and others, the black child's correctness of self-identification has been thoroughly pursued. In most of these, black as well as white children have been presented with black and white dolls and asked to pick out the doll with which they identify. In general, it was found that black children preferred white dolls. Considering that just a few years ago the *only* dolls around were white, it is not difficult to understand why these were singled out by black kids. Yet, several of the social scientists chose to equate this cognitive decision with a value judgment, i.e., because they picked the white dolls, black children didn't like themselves and thus suffered from self-hate. John D. McCarthy and William Yancey in an important article[17] point out that "It is a rather long jump . . . from racial awareness, preference for white dolls and assignment of inferior roles to brown dolls to self-hatred on the part of such children."[18]

It is also hard to ascertain in these studies the children's objectivity in making the selection. It is well known that children will tell adults what they want to hear. Similarly, the methods used are not always objective. For instance, until the study of Herbert Greenwald and Don Oppenheim, the children were presented only with black and white dolls. In their study, using mulatto dolls, Greenwald and Oppenheim found that a significant number of black children chose the mulatto dolls.[19] Thus, many of these studies have significant flaws which unwittingly weight the evidence against the black child.

Robert Coles has expressed disagreement with what he feels to be the one-sidedness of these studies. He says that many of the black children he examined during a period of desegregation in the South showed resilience and great emotional strength, thus contradicting the popular belief of massive personality damage.[20]

Similarly, the celebrated Coleman Report, a 1966 study by the United States Office of Education on the equality of education opportunity,[21] maintains that the black child's self-concept has not been exceptionally damaged, and is, in fact, virtually no different from that of a white child. The report did, however, note that the white child is consistently able to achieve on a higher level than that of his black counterpart. (The Coleman study, in fact, concluded that self-concept may simply not be crucial in an individual's ability to achieve.[22])

A few observers have noted that the recent movement toward black pride has substantiated the position that American blacks may have a healthy self-esteem despite the presence of oppression. Thus, although the effect of racism upon the development of self-concept cannot be ignored, it must be recognized that it is still the immediate family which gives the child his earliest feelings about himself. With love and consistent care a child will develop strong feelings of belonging and worth. A study by E. E. Baughman and W. G. Dahlstrom[23] of a group of black and white eighth-graders in a rural Southern community showed that

> The Negro children in our sample . . . much more frequently reported themselves as being popular with their peers than the white children did. Also there was a tendency for more Negro than white children to say that they were very satisfied being the kind of person they were. In addition, significantly more Negro than white children described their home life as being happier than that of the average white child.[24]

Certainly, these various studies cannot be considered as ultimately or unanimously conclusive. Yet one fact is clear: not one of these reports had found *any* evidence that high achievement results from a low self-concept. Obviously the black child with a low self-concept competes at a disadvantage with white youth in the struggle to achieve in this society.

The question then arises: Why do black youth bother to involve themselves at all in this struggle? If negative self-image handicaps them so greatly in achieving, why not simply abdicate and, in fact, adhere to white society's definition of them as substandard? To answer this we must move into another area—that of the *patterned needs* of an individual.

In the course of the socialization process, the individual acquires needs which motivate behavior and generate emotions. Three such needs concern us here: the need for achievement, the need for self-assertion or aggression, and the need for approval.

Among the attitudes of the "generalized other" which the individual in American society internalizes are the norms and values of the wider community, including, of course, the major tenets of the Protestant Ethic American creed—i.e., the notion that with hard work and effort the individual can achieve success, and that the person's worth can be defined by his ability to achieve that success. The individual who internalizes these values is motivated to act consistently with them, as his self-esteem is heightened or maintained through behaving in a manner approved by the community. Thus, the need for achievement develops in both white and black Americans. Consequently, the black youth's participation in the struggle for success is at least in part an attempt to satisfy his own needs.

That this need to achieve may, indeed, be very high among black youth is illustrated in the findings of Coleman[25] and Irwin Katz,[26] both of whom note the exceptionally high aspirations of black youth with regard to schooling and occupational choice. Moreover, Katz[27] and Gordon[28] note that these high aspirations and demands for academic achievement are shared by the parents of these young people. Nevertheless, all these sources agree that actual achievement does not match either their own aspirations or those of their parents.[29]

Thus, once again, the problem does not seem to be, as some have suggested, one of insufficiently high levels of aspiration, but rather one of realizing these aspirations through productive behavior.[30] Gordon[31] and Katz[32] suggest that this discrepancy persists because the educational and occupational values and goals of white society have been internalized by black youth, but for one reason or another, the behavior patterns necessary for their successful attainment have not been similarly learned. Thus, the black child's negative self-concept is further complicated by his internalization of white society's high-level goals, and the need to achieve them, without a true comprehension of how to do so effectively in a system that discriminates against him.

The Right of Self-Assertion

If we look more closely at the values of the Protestant Ethic, we find that assertion of self and aggression are expected and admired forms of behavior. Through the socialization process, the individual internalizes those attitudes which reinforce his basic need to assert himself or express himself aggressively. Thus, random and possibly destructive aggression is channeled into a legitimate and rewarded avenue of achievement.[33] What, however, happens to the black child's need for aggression and self-assertion? What has been the nature of his socialization with respect to expressing aggression? Since slavery days and, to some extent, down to the present, the black individual most rewarded by whites has been the "Uncle Tom," the black man who was docile and nonassertive, who bowed and scraped for the white boss and denied his aggressive feelings for his oppressor.

To retain even the most menial of jobs and keep from starving, black people quickly learned that passivity was a necessary survival technique. Present-day vestiges of this attitude still remain, certainly in the South, but also in the North where blacks who are too "outspoken" about racial injustices often lose their jobs, the excuse for which is that they are being too "unreasonable" or too "sensitive." It is significant that the civil-rights movement had to adopt passive resistance and nonviolence before it was accepted by white America. At an early age, then, the black child is socialized to act in accordance with society's precepts: don't be aggressive, don't be assertive. Such lessons do not, however, destroy the *need* for aggression and self-assertion.

Self-expression, goal achievement and fate control are three major reasons for individual self-assertion. All are interrelated but some more so than others. Thus, Coleman found that of three attitudes measured, sense of control over environment showed the strongest relationship to achievement.[34] He further discovered that blacks have a much lower sense of control over their environment than do whites,[35] but that this sense of control increased in proportion to the number of whites attending their school.[36] These findings indicate that for blacks, a realistic inability for meaningful self-assertion is a greater inhibitor of ability to achieve than is any other variable. These findings also suggest, however, that when blacks are interacting in a school situation which approximates the world with which they must cope, i.e., one with whites, their sense of control and achievement grows. Our emphasis here is not on the sense of control and level of achievement brought about by black students intermingling with whites, but rather on how these are affected by their being placed in a situation which more closely simulates the future they will find once they leave school.

Coleman's findings here are supported by those of Davidson and

Greenberg—high achievers were more able to exercise control and to cope more effectively with feelings of hostility and anxiety generated by the environment than were low achievers.[37] Deutsch points out that black male children for whom aggressive behavior has always been more threatening (compared with black females) have lower levels of achievement on a number of variables than do black girls.[38] It is not surprising then that black people who, objectively speaking, are less in control of their environment and their future lives than whites, may react by abdicating control or by deciding not to assert themselves. The reasons for this are clear. First, the anxiety that accompanies growth and change through self-assertion is avoided if a new failure is not risked and thus, an effort is not made. Second, the steady state of failure through nonachievement rather than through unsuccessful trial is a pattern which many blacks have come to know and expect. They feel psychologically comfortable with the more familiar.

However, this effort by black people to deny their need for self-assertion and control over their own future inevitably takes its toll. Their frustrated efforts to control the environment are likely to lead to anger, rage and other expressions of aggression.[39] This aggression can be dealt with in a variety of ways. It can be suppressed, leading one to act on the basis of a substitute and opposing emotional attitude, i.e., compliance or docility. It can be channeled through legitimate activities—dancing, sports, or through an identification with the oppressor and a consequent striving to be like him. Aggression can also be turned inward and expressed in psychosomatic illness, drug addiction, or the attacking of those like oneself (other blacks) whom one hates as much as oneself. Or it can be directed toward those who generate the anger and rage—those whom the individual defines as thwarting this inclination of self-assertion.

This final form of aggression can be either destructive or constructive: dropping out of school or becoming delinquent are examples of the former case, while participation in black social-action movements is an example of the latter instance. This latter form of aggressive behavior among black people is on the increase. The old passivity is fading and being replaced by a drive to undo powerlessness, helplessness and dependency under American racism. The process is a different one for those black people who manage to make the attempt. For their aggressive drive, so long suppressed by the ruling power structure, is deterred by still another exigency: their need for approval.

The Hunger for Approval

Through the development of the self and through the process of identification, the individual's need for approval develops and grows as does his need to avoid disapproval.[40] As we have stated earlier, the Protestant Ethic of American society approves behavior which is in accordance with the achievement incentive and the need for self-assertion. Such behavior is often tied to a need for approval. For blacks in American society, the reverse is often the case, i.e., behavior which is neither achievement-oriented nor self-assertive is often approved by both blacks and whites (for different reasons), and thus, the need for approval may be met through behavior unrelated to either achievement or self-assertion.

Katz's study maintains that in lower socioeconomic black homes, children do not learn realistic (middle-class) standards of self-appraisal and therefore do not develop (as do middle-class children) the capacity for gaining "satisfaction through self-approval of successful performance."[41] Accordingly, Katz suggests that achievement should be motivated and rewarded by approval not from the home, but from fellow students and teachers.[42] However, the extent to which black children in the lower socioeconomic category are responsive to approval for achievement in middle-class terms is questionable.

Some evidence suggests that poor black children are motivated to gain approval through physical characteristics and prowess rather than through intellectual achievement as are middle-class white and black children.[43] This is, of course, understandable, since, for a long time, sports were one of the few areas where these youngsters could gain status and monetary security. Other needs for approval, not often encountered in the established institutional channels, may be met outside of these. For instance, delinquent subcultures support and encourage the behavior of their members. As a result, such members gain approval and esteem by proving themselves in criminal and antisocial behavior (as judged by the dominant society). Their allegiance is to the mores of the community subculture. Thus, for black youths no less than for others, how the need for approval motivates behavior depends in large part upon how it is satisfied or rewarded.

The Unpredictable Future

The rewards offered by the institutions of this society to those whose behavior meets their approval consist of money, prestige, power, respect, acclamation, and love, with increasing amounts of each of these being extended for increasingly "successful" behavior. The individual is socialized to know that these will be his if he lives up to society's expectations. Hence, these rewards are an external motivation for behavior. Blacks have learned of the existence of these rewards. They have also learned, however, that behavior for which whites reap these rewards does not result in the same consequences for them. In the various institutional areas of society, Afro-Americans are often rewarded differently from whites for the same behavior—if they are rewarded at all. How, then, can such a highly capricious system motivate their behavior? If the society's reward system *is* capricious, it becomes difficult for the individual to forecast the consequences of his own behavior —a highly disorienting situation. The future is made even more unpredictable than it is for others in the society.

That blacks orient some aspects of their behavior to society's reward system is evidenced by the fact that many studies have shown that lower-income blacks, like most white Americans, have a utilitarian attitude toward education, viewing it primarily in terms of its market value.[44] The system provides no assurance, however, that once they obtain the proper education for a job, they will in fact be allowed to get that job. This inability to trust society to confer rewards consistently no doubt makes it difficult for blacks to be socialized to behave in terms of anticipating future rewards for present activity. In line with this argument, Deutsch found that young black children are unwilling to persist in attempting to solve difficult problems. They respond to such situations with a "who cares" attitude.[45] Similarly, another study showed that when a tangible reward was offered for successful work on a test, the motivation of the "disadvantaged" youngsters increased considerably.[46]

However, motivation to achieve certain rewards may have different consequences for behavior. As Robert Merton explained, when the goals of society are internalized without a corresponding internalization of normative means for achieving these goals, what often results is the resort to illegitimate or deviant means to achieve the socially valued goals.[47] Just as a child, unable to satisfy his need for approval through legitimate channels, may turn to delinquent subcultures for support and encouragement, so, too, might such a child, unable to gain society's rewards by legitimate means, turn to illegitimate ones in order to attain them.

Numbers running, dope pushing, prostitution and other such forms of behavior effectively serve to net the rewards of society, while circumventing the institutional channels for achievement of societal rewards. Gordon's study suggests that black children learn very early which channels offer the quickest rewards. Thus, when young (nine to thirteen) Central Harlem boys were asked if they knew people who had become rich, and if so, how they thought they had managed to do so, those who responded affirmatively said they felt they had done so either through illegitimate means or good luck.[48]

Consequently, for many black youths, delayed rewards are weak motivators of behavior, as they are discriminatorily and inconsistently given. The more immediate and direct the reward is, the stronger a motivator is likely to be. The future is too far away and too unpredictable.

It would appear from this analysis that the standards and rewards of white American society simply do not work effectively to motivate productive behavior in young oppressed blacks. Clearly there is urgent need for a basic restructuring of the system. What must be kept in mind is that, despite the above documentation, the fundamental damage to the black child takes place, not in early childhood, preadolescence and adolescence, but when he leaves high school or drops out. It is then, as the doors to higher education and careers slam firmly in their faces, that these young high-spirited and bright men and women become members of the hard-core element of society which has all but abandoned hope.

To reverse this unfortunate trend, so costly to the nation as a whole, several things must be done. First, with respect to self-concept and future-focused role images, all institutional segments of society must begin to function in a nonracist manner. To the extent that the self is shaped with reference to a "generalized other," to that extent will the black child's image be impaired as long as America remains racist. This "generalized other" is presented continually to black children in the mass media magazines, newspapers, movies and particularly television. In the future, if young black people are to develop healthy future-focused role images, sufficient numbers of blacks must be presented in all aspects of the media in nonracist contexts.

The growth of black consciousness and pride has had salutary consequences for the black's self-image. But this alone is not sufficient. The operation of self-image as a motivator for behavior is directly linked to the future. It operates like a self-fulfilling prophecy—blacks are continually told that they are inferior and will fail. Therefore, they fail. For the black child to be motivated to achieve in school, the school must negate everything that the society affirms: It must tell the child that he can succeed—and he will.[49]

The relationship between self-concept and achievement is not clear-cut, but it appears to be a weaker motivator of behavior than the motive to self-assertion and aggression. More attention should be given to examining this dimension of personality as a motivator of the black youth's behavior than to continuing inquiries into his self-image. It has been noted that the black youth's sense of control of his environment, and therefore over his future, increases as the proportion of whites in his school increases. It is imperative to keep in mind, however, that participation in predominantly-black or all-black structures need not be self-destructive, if the black youth *chooses* rather than is forced to participate in them. For, if he chooses, he is asserting control over his environment. Thus, for blacks, community control of schools is an important factor in fostering the black child's achievement. Those structural changes being made in American society in the direction of blacks having the opportunity to be more aggressively in control of their environment must be continued and expanded. The plans to decentralize New York City schools, to develop black business, and to organize and channel black political power are significant steps in this direction.

Most of the data indicate that black youth and their parents have high educational and occupational aspirations, which are not carried through to achievement levels. The reward systems of a racist society are often remote to the lives and aspirations of most black youth. Something is obviously wrong with any school system which permits so much potential to be wasted, simply because it cannot be developed within the confines of traditional methods. New frameworks must be developed which will enable the educational aspirations of black youth to correspond to their interests and proficiencies.

Students should not be viewed as some homogeneous, monolithic group that can be fitted into a rigid educational machine designed to service yesterday's model of a white middle-class child. A curriculum designed to meet the needs of a child in white suburbia may fail miserably if foisted unmodified on black youth in the ghettoes. Variations in experiences and life-styles mean that different people need different things at any given time. No single approach or method works effectively with everybody. Schools should have the flexibility of styles and approaches to work with a variety of classes of youth. With the establishment of a pattern of consistent—predictable—reward, there is every possibility that intellectual endeavors would have immediate relevance to young black lives.

The time for being surprised at the behavior of black youth has passed. The time for lengthy, nonproductive attempts at understanding them has too, in its turn, come to an end. The time remaining must be effectively used to bring about those changes which appropriately address the needs of black children who are victims of the pernicious race-typing in our society. In this process, it is crucial that the older generation lend an attentive ear to the keen perceptions and suggestions of black youth who are themselves presently victims of an antiquated system. America cannot afford to wait for the future generation. The time is now.

PART TWO

The Place of the Future in the Curriculum

The way we imagine the future has a powerful impact on the decisions we make today. This fact has not yet been adequately recognized by the social sciences. Here Yale sociologist Wendell Bell shows how the future can be infused into anthropology, psychology, economics, sociology, political science—and into the classrooms in which these subjects are taught.

CHAPTER FIVE

Social Science: The Future As a Missing Variable

by Wendell Bell

> Mankind is passing from the *primacy* of the *past* to the *primacy of expectations of vast future changes.*
> —*Harold D. Lasswell*

The world of tomorrow rushes toward us at an ever-accelerating rate. We can turn our backs and privatize our lives to exist largely in the shadows cast by the futures that other people will make—or we can confront the changes ahead and try to cope with them by adaptation. Perhaps we can even enter into the building of the future ourselves, not just in the small worlds of self, family, and friends, but in the larger worlds of collective decision and struggle on community, national, and planetary scales. No matter what we do, we cannot remain unaffected. Only death gives us that option.

A dizzying array of *"expectations of vast future changes"* already faces us within the boundaries of our contemporary imaginations: genetic control, cloning, cyborgs, landings—and then colonies—on other planets, time travel by deep-freezing, endless leisure, direct democracy through computerized polling, artificial intelligence, sophisticated robots, synthetic foods, roadless vehicles, staggered work weeks, artificial life, ocean farming, and weather control.[1] For some, this conjures up a frightening new world, perhaps even a doomsday vision of the end of human life. For others, it opens an optimistic vision of full development of human potentialities and self-realization. Obviously, some future is coming. With or without massive intervention, our lives will be greatly changed, perhaps—or more likely surely—beyond the scope of contemporary imaginations.

Here lies the great challenge to contemporary social science: creating and transmitting the knowledge for understanding and coping with a future that remains largely unknown. For an adequate response, nothing short of a revolution in social science may be necessary—a revolution in dominant theories and perspectives, in methodologies, in the content of what is taught, and in teaching techniques themselves.

Students must be sensitized to the trends of change, to probabilities for alternative futures, to an array of future possibilities, to modes of adaptation, and to corrective and innovative action. They need to be encouraged to transcend past experience, to creatively invent the future, and to define sound means of implementation. They need to understand the nature of social power and decision-making. The way that options are specified, and the context of conflicting interests in which they are selected, need to be given meaning in the classroom.

Moreover, because taming the future requires active participation, freedom from past ways, and some degree of choice, the student role must become less passive than it has been, without, at the same time, permitting a surrender to mere self-indulgence or expression. As psychological, economic, political, cultural, and social changes swirl around them, can students, as many educational philosophers have stressed, be taught to learn to learn? How prepared are the social sciences today to educate for the future?

Time Orientations in Social Science

Although much has been written about coming scientific and technological changes, much less has been written in modern social science about the future. It is fair to conclude that, with the major exception of forecasts in demography and economics, the study of the future in social science during the last few decades has been neglected.

This is particularly ironic inasmuch as many of the founders of social science were obsessed with the future. The father of sociology, Auguste Comte, and the other "prophets of Paris," according to historian Frank E. Manuel,[2] both unveiled the future and tried to give it direction. For them, the past was prologue, the present a burden. They longed for the future. Comte put it succinctly. The whole purpose of his work was the future: *savoir pour prévoir.*

Turgot believed that a science of social progress should be established as a basis for planning the future; Condorcet tried to foresee the future scientifically and "to tame it"; Saint-Simon drew up plans for the administrative organization of the future world; Fourier's blueprints for the future included revolutionary changes in love and work and the goal of self-fulfillment.

Such enthusiasm for the future is perhaps difficult to match, but trends, projections, and future orientations can be found in the writings of most of the early modern social theorists, Charles Castel de Saint-Pierre apparently having been the first "to suggest clearly that man's future lies in his own hands."[3] His *Observations on the Continual Progress of Universal Reason* appeared in 1737.

Despite this, the past and, to a lesser extent, the present, not the future, have dominated the attention—and the education—of social scientists in recent decades. Typically, that "past" has been largely ahistorical, a cross-section of time, a thin slice that is often thought about in terms of the present as it drifts backward away from the ever-emerging future.

There are several reasons why the past has dominated social-science thinking. One important factor is narrow positivism—an epistemology designed to deal with facts. Facts are, by definition, phenomena of the past. There are no future facts. Thus, the logic of determinism invites the backward look, and the past comes to pervade the classroom and the research center. By contrast, the forward look has an openness not easily handled within a thought system constructed to deal with events that have already happened.

The last election, for example, can be analyzed. The results are known. The next election, however, gives us difficulty. Will the same interdependencies exist? What are the contingencies? What new, capricious, creative and spontaneous variables will enter in?

All this is clear, but is past time a fair sample of all time? Philosopher Robert S. Brumbaugh says that "Determinism does hold for the past, but if we were not committed to notions of verifiability, truth, and fact which are all past-oriented, it would be evident from our own immediate experience that it does not necessarily follow that such determinism also holds for present or future. . . . A 'choice now open' or a 'possibility' has *some* ontological status."[4] Should we, in other words, talk about the future in the same terms as we talk about the past, in terms that allow no other modes of existence except the one that has, in fact, already occurred? To do so, of course, would be to deny one of the fundamental principles of futuristics: alternative possibilities for the future are real.

Equally important is the concept of "cause" in social science, no matter by what terms it is disguised. A cause exists before an effect. To sort out the independent and the dependent variables in deterministic systems, a *time* priority must be established. This is thoroughly justifiable logic, but applied dogmatically and unimaginatively it has tended to blind social scientists to the notion of the "future" as cause. For example, images of the future—expectations, hopes, and fears—can be legitimately brought in as causal phenomena in the past. Sociologist Arthur L. Stinchcombe, in a study of *Rebellion in a High School*,[5] found that the "future" *caused* the present. Reversing the usual perspective that looks only into the pasts of high-school students to explain whether or not they became "rebels," Stinchcombe looked to their conceptions of the future. His data show that adolescent rebellion is not the result of distinctively rebel biographical pasts, but rather results from images of the future.

Adolescents who foresee themselves becoming members of the manual working class see no clear relation between what they are doing in school and their future occupational status. Thus, their current performance loses meaning, and current self-restraint is perceived as irrelevant to the achievement of long-run goals. Such students often become high-school rebels.

In this example, cause and effect remain temporally differentiated and within a deterministic system. Yet, when we deal with the future that is yet to come, we must, beyond this, take account of its openness, the real alternative possibilities that exist, the wills and intentions of humans, their awareness and spontaneity, the intensities with which they strive for certain goals, and the feedback of knowledge itself into self-fulfilling or self-denying prophecies.

It is the distinctive characteristic of social science that the subjects of its research can use social-science knowledge to free themselves from the very historical routines that underlie the ability of social scientists to establish the validity of determinative systems of explanation. Although this may cause difficulties for the social scientist, it gives all of us living, breathing, choice-making individuals cause for hope. Yet, until recently, the teaching of social science, dominated by a stress on past-oriented determinants of behavior, has tended to minimize the awareness that is necessary for freedom.

An emphasis on the past at the expense of the future is even built into the research tools used by social scientists and the norms that shape their work. Today, most social scientists are, in fact, doing history. (This is not to denigrate the historians, especially since they often have a dynamic time perspective and a sense of place that could beneficially be adopted by social scientists who wish to orient their work to the future.) Social scientists are doing history in the sense that they are talking about past events.

With some exceptions, it takes years before social research is adequately reported, it takes more years before it becomes part of the conventional wisdom of members of the discipline, it takes even longer to become available to the people who might find the information useful in the decisions they must make, and it takes longer yet for the message to reach the classroom. These time lags persist even though it is clear that, in many fields, if we are to plan and decide rationally, we should have near-instantaneous data probes, analyses, interpretations, and dissemination.

The fact is that the technology to make this possible in many cases already exists. One need only think of the speed with which ground-control units respond to data describing conditions in a space ship on a lunar flight. (It is ludicrous in this example to think of tolerating a time lag of several years between data collection and dissemination typical of social science. Even months or days are too long.)

In social-science research, behavior could also be monitored, the data fed to on-line computers, categories of analysis and interpretation pre-set, both short- and long-range projections made (and constantly corrected as new data became available), and such a system could be linked to decision-making so that timely corrective action becomes possible. Furthermore, consequences for alternative futures could be assessed and reanalyses of data in terms of newly invented futures carried out. Adapting present activities would be relatively simple for measurements of, for example, the use of electricity, television-program selection, bank transactions, the flow of traffic, and the pattern of telecommunications and letters. It is now technically possible to monitor, in this immediate pulse-taking sense, many of the variables that social scientists study, many of which are vital to the collective well-being of some group and some of which may be vital to the human race as a whole.

Such a system may offend some people. It could not be otherwise, since our experiences and values have prepared us to live in a simpler world. But visions of "1984" need not be validated. Information systems and decision-making processes can be designed with safeguards to protect individuals and can be organized to serve a variety of aims. Furthermore, anarchy and ignorance of social facts clearly offer no viable alternatives.

This is, of course, not to say that social scientists should become political decision-makers themselves. Nor is it to say that all social science could or should be "on-line." Nor is it to insist, more generally, that social scientists should merely shift their focus from the past to the future. Rather, I am proposing a time perspective that includes past, present *and* future as interpenetrating. This temporal perspective is essential if social scientists are to cope with social phenomena in process.

Further, I propose that some social scientists within this broadened time perspective must turn their attention specifically to the future, and that we must, even now, begin educating young social scientists for this purpose, if social science is to have very much of interest to say about the social changes that threaten to engulf us. Otherwise, like the French generals, social scientists will end up fighting the last war, describing people, economies, policies, cultures, and societies not as they are becoming, or even as they are, but as they used to be.

Justifications of the Future

The ultimate purpose of the study of the future is to help people create a better life for themselves, and for this what is needed is control. Or, if we are dealing with changing phenomena that cannot be controlled, then at least we must learn how to live with constantly changing social patterns by anticipating them. The aim, where possible, is to subject the rate and direction of social change to the will of human beings.

This suggests that social science must include not merely the study of past change, trends and cycles, and the causes of change, but also possibilities for the future: the fan of alternative futures which, at any given time, could emerge into reality and the probabilities of the different possibilities under existing trends and cycles and under different ones. It must include making predictions. It must include the study of the preferences of different individuals, groups, and the human race as a whole—their wished-for and feared futures—as well as the scale of values by which different possible futures are evaluated.

Social scientists should ask, "When, where, by whom, how intensely, under what conditions, and with what consequences are different futures desired?" They should study the struggle to control the future itself: Who is trying to do what to whom to create what kind of a future? They should study both policies and actions designed to control the future and the decision-making processes that set their parameters and allocate resources among them. And because doing all of the above things may have consequences for the emergent future, another purpose of the social-scientific study of the future is the explicit and objective study of how social science itself helps shape the future.[6]

With a shift in time orientation, all of the above can be accomplished. Materials, to some extent, already exist that could form the basis of reoriented teaching of a future-focused social science. Others are in preparation. This alone would be of great help in preadapting students to the future and alerting them to the possibilities for accelerating desirable trends and dampening undesirable ones.

But it may not be enough.

Guidance, creativity, and innovation are needed, perhaps a pervading sense of transcendence, even of eschatology, because we all tend to be trapped by the past and the present. To escape the pull of present and past and open our intellects to the real possibilities for the future may require an effort analogous to the energy required for a space capsule to escape the gravitational field of the Earth.

The Dutch sociologist Frederik L. Polak believes that Western man's sickness in the 1950s lay in the fact that he was no longer able to formulate positive, idealistic images of the future. Not just any images of the future qualify, since most of them are simply extensions of the present, simply more of the same. His idea of the future is one that is drastically different from the present, "the idea of the future as The Other, or as a new dimension of this world, the perfected antipode of the imperfect here and now."[7] Planning can be made even more sterile, the future made more narrow, and time horizons even further shortened by studies of the future that do not cultivate transcendence and stimulate fantasy. As Arthur C. Clarke has said, "Most of the things that have happened in the last fifty years have been fantastic, and it is only by assuming that they will continue to be so that we have any hope of anticipating the future."[8]

Thus, the social scientist of the future has the responsibility for determining past facts, which he is fairly well trained to do, for identifying present options and real possibilities for the future, and for breaking out of the confines of the past and present and inventing the future, which he is not well trained to do.

The principal focus of the study of the future is neither description nor explanation per se, nor is it primarily prediction. Rather it is innovation and guidance. Futuristics involves clarification and evaluation of values and goals, as well as description of trends, and it includes projections of alternative futures, as well as explanations of existing routines of interdependencies. Moreover, the social-scientific study of the future promotes intervention in social processes through invention, evaluation, and selection of alternative courses of social action. This involves learning processes that are of value not merely to potential social scientists, but to all students, since all of them will have to cope, as individuals, with a future that is emerging at extremely high speeds.

As educators, social scientists have taught their students a great deal about the so-called human condition. They have taught considerably less, however, about the human potential. Each of the social sciences has it own weaknesses as a future-oriented activity, yet each has its unique contribution as well.

Anthropology

Anthropology, for example, has been past-oriented. Archaeologists have focused their energies on understanding societies and cultures long since dead. Other anthropologists, making a religion out of intensive face-to-face field work, have focused on the small society, on time- and space-bounded cultures that are often far removed from the dominant images of the future that direct major planetary trends of change. Such cultures are sometimes considered to be in some sense primitive, despite the use of euphemisms, indicative in the present of some distant past. There have been times when the anthropologist, comfortable within the cultural envelope of his adopted "primitive" tribe, has simply turned his back on the realities of the future, although one must confess that a dismantlement of civilization is always a possible, if unlikely, future for humankind.

Yet there are several ways in which anthropology may be well suited for adaptation to futuristics.[9] The study of prehistory, for example, the sifting of archaeological evidence, must, like the study of the future, deal with its subject matter obliquely. There remains the fundamental difference that the past has happened and the future has not, yet the knowing of the prehistorical past is often as problematic as is the "knowing" of the future. Additionally, through archaeology we obtain an important time perspective: the behavior of humankind in relation to the more than three million years of existence.

Also, in the same way that the Middle Ages were opened up in part by the voyages of discovery, so too have anthropologists, along with comparative sociologists, by showing the range and malleability of human cultures, opened up "advanced" societies, forcing them to question their purposes, values, world views, and epistemologies. The comparative study of societies and cultures has taught us to ask questions about cultural alternatives, limitations, and choices. It has taught us to try to avoid being trapped into one way of thinking and to look at knowledge as in need of constant revision. Although cultural relativism may have been pushed too far, and, as we shall see below, there may be reason to begin a serious search for what may be universal or absolute about the needs and hopes of the human race, it is a salutary antidote to false prejudices, uncritical enthnocentrism, and ignorant parochialism.

In the same way that the futurist must transcend the limitations of his present cultural envelope and break into the "other" world of the future, so the anthropologist must transcend his culture to appreciate the different culture of a strange group.

In this connection, it is worth stressing the important parallel between space and time. Because societal and cultural changes occur both through time and in geographical space on the surface of the Earth, important analogies can be drawn. This is why it is sometimes possible to draw inferences concerning cultural evolution when studying societies of different places at the same time as well as when studying societies at the same place at different times. Some people are space travelers, moving across the face of Earth, coming in contact with different ways of humankind. Others, though they may not themselves move, change their ways as cultural diffusion moves across space. They are also time travelers facing perhaps ever more startling variations in human belief, behavior, and organization in the world to come. In the analogy made famous by Alvin Toffler, humans face the possibility of both culture shock and future shock.[10]

Applied anthropologists, of course, have been involved in directed change. They have often smoothed the interface between different cultures, especially between small communities and powerful nation-states. They have been intercultural brokers and interpreters. They have served as agents of change, for example, by helping to introduce new agricultural or marketing practices, or as links to the past, for example, by teaching young members of a nonliterate society some of their own people's legends, songs, and dances that no one else has remembered. In such roles, they have worked actively at that point where past and future converge in the present.

But anthropologists could be more keenly sensitized to the study of the future. They could move further toward the view that cultural changes are subject to people's goals, imaginations, wills, and choices. They could raise more questions about what human beings *could* become.

They could experimentally design cultures, naturally nonexistent today, that were in some respects ideal. They could tell us more about how cultures are born and how they die—and what the chances are for our own cultural survival in the future. They could tell students whether the existence of a multiplicity of cultures has any evolutionary value. They could tell us more about human needs for the little community, if, in fact, such needs exist. They could tell us more about people's primary interests, preoccupations, and purposes, and how these are most likely to change in the decades ahead. And they could help futurists transcend the Euro-American cultural envelope in which generally they now are entrapped. All these are issues that can excite students, by connecting cultural models from past and present with the students' own personal futures.

Economics

If at first glance anthropology appears to be the most past-oriented of the social sciences, then economics may appear to be the most future-oriented. It is certainly, along with demography, the social science that has been most concerned with the analysis of time series and forecasting. Sophisticated methodologies and models exist for describing past trends and projecting a variety of economic variables into the future, ranging from such broad measures as Gross National Product, manpower needs, and sector growth to such specific projections as crop yields per acre. Forecasting is an important part of economics.

One reason for this is that economics has close ties to decision-making. As the pioneering political scientist Harold D. Lasswell has pointed out, decision-making is unthinkable without a future orientation.[11] One must think of the future in making choices;

possible outcomes and consequences of actions must be estimated and evaluated.

Today, economic planning is an accepted fact and economists advise governments, businesses, labor unions, universities—most of the major institutions of society—concerning their economic-related decisions. Operations research, input-output analysis, multi-variate econometric models, computer simulations, sample surveys of economic behavior, and organizational studies are becoming standard parts of policy-making and policy-implement-ing processes. Businessmen need to make guesses about the future in order to make decisions concerning investment and production. Future sales need to be estimated in order for decisions to be made about increasing or reducing inventory, buying equipment, or expanding plant. Governmental decision-makers want to know next year's national-income accounts in order to make decisions concerning fiscal and monetary policy now—often so that they can act to negate the forecast if it is undesirable.

More recently, economists have played a large role in introduc-ing and staffing the "planning-programming-budgeting-system" in the U.S. federal government. It assures some "thinking about the future," but it excludes, like most cost-benefit analyses, many im-portant variables and values, sometimes, even people viewed as *sui generis*. (It is, perhaps, no accident that the system was first introduced into the federal government in the Department of De-fense where human life and death are invariably translated into dollars.)

We can, perhaps, go beyond Lasswell's observation about the relationship between decision-making and future thinking and state that *any* conscious or deliberate social act necessitates a future orientation. This is certainly the case insofar as behavior is purposeful, because, by definition, the goals of any present or contemplated action reside in the future. How systematic, explicit, data-based, and accurate the thinking about the future is, of course, varies tremendously. In economics, forecasting is generally system-atic, explicit, and data-based, although not always accurate, partly because the forecasts themselves lead to intervention in the economic system.

Because it has dealt with forecasts, decision-making, and action, economics has developed a set of folkways concerning cause and effect variables, some that presumably can be manipulated and some that cannot. For example, thinking of the rate of unemployment as a policy-related variable, as a condition that can be altered as a result of decided-upon actions, makes it an assumption under which other variables, such as GNP, can be differentially projected, depending on alternative decisions considered. Thus, both prediction and control are part of economic theory, method, and praxis. From this point of view, economics is a model of a discipline with a well-developed futurist wing. Yet, because it emphasizes rigor as against imagination, many present-day economic phenomena—such as trade unions, profit-sharing, social security, and scientific management—were, for the most part, not envisioned by professional economists themselves.

Moreover, although economics may be the most future-oriented of the social sciences, it may also be the most ethnocentric. It is puzzling to the non-economist, for example, to pick up American introductory textbooks in the field and find "Free World" economics discussed for 1,000 pages and that of the rest of the "World" discussed in five. This is not to mention the near-total ignorance of the economic principles formulated by anthropologists. And then there are the biases that serve the gods of efficiency, profits, and growth, to mention only a few. It is neither a brave nor a new world.

Furthermore, despite what I have said about the future orientation of economics, it remains in important respects too present-oriented. This is so because of the narrow time band with which it usually deals, because of its focus on the solution to immediate problems within the framework of its existing concepts and, perhaps most importantly, because of its servility to existing dominant values and institutions. Such servility, for example, may account for the fact that orthodox Western economics, resting as it does on the assumption of underlying harmony, has little to say about the irreconcilable conflicts that exist in the real world. It may also explain why it has been unable to explain or propose an adequate remedy for the most important economic problem of the century: the growing income gap between the advanced industrial nations and the Third World.[12] To confront these issues adequately invites a revolution in economics and would call into question powerful and controlling groups in society.

For all its description of past cycles and trends, and for all its forecasting of the future, economics uses time, therefore, to serve the present. In economics as it is taught and practiced today, the "other" future becomes uncritically more of the same, once again closing the mind of the student to the dazzling range of alternative futures available to us.

Political Science

Like economists, political scientists are deeply involved in decision-making and policy implementation. Thus, they, too, have developed a futurist wing, although it seldom reveals itself in the classroom. Yet in a modest way they have engaged in trend analysis and formulated images of both the immediate and remote future.

Thus, as Lasswell notes, "students of American government have been substantially of one voice in predicting such developments as the further centralization of the federal system, the rise of metropolitan regions and the decline of the states, the concentration of executive power, the liquidation of ethnic discrimination, the continuation of the two-party system, the increase of litigation over civil and political rights, the continuation of controversy over civil-military relations, and the extension of social insurance coverage."[13] Additionally, there are promising studies of trends and futures of international relations, such as Bruce M. Russett's *Trends in World Politics*.[14]

Unlike economists, political scientists have so far failed to formulate mathematized general theory by which forecasts of the future can be rigorously (though often inaccurately) made. But they, too, have their men of genius, and Lasswell has gone well beyond Polak in working out some of the details of the methods of creating images of the future and in specifying the direction of particular trends of modern society. Laswell calls his method developmental analysis, the major tool of which is the "developmental construct," which is similar to Polak's concept of image of the future.[15]

A developmental construct expresses expectations about the future and is related to the facts of past trends. Society is viewed as an interval on some continuum of social change, and the developmental construct delineates the end points of that continuum—the from-what and toward-what of developmental sequences. Lasswell deals with the problems created for scientific analysis by the confounding nature of self-fulfilling or self-denying prophecies through which scientific predictions, as they become known, may themselves affect the very future predicted. For him, this is precisely what such predictions are supposed to do.

In one of his most famous examples, the garrison-state hypothesis, Lasswell forecast the possibility that the United States was becoming a military dictatorship. He outlined the facets of American society that were leading to this development, but he also stated that this trend was not irreversible and could be deflected *if* people who valued democracy were willing to take action.

I was first impressed with Lasswell's insight during my own studies, from 1956 to 1964, of the transition from politically dependent colonies to politically independent nation-states in the English-speaking Caribbean. Nation-states, of course, do not just happen, they are *made* to happen. My previous training in social-science methodology was inadequate in the face of the emergent quality of the situation, its problematics, its "becomingness," and its struggles to shape the future.

The transition to nationhood necessarily raises basic questions about what the new states and nations should be—ranging from their geographical boundaries to the kind of polity, society, culture, and people the new nation should have. New elites arise to make decisions. The nature of the political community is altered. There is an exhilarating turmoil surrounding what should be done and how to do it.

Adopting Lasswell's view and making a virtue out of the difficulties imposed by transience and the interventions of human beings into the historical process seemed the only adequate response. Thus, Ivar Oxaal and I formulated the *decisions of nationhood*, those decisions that must be faced by every new nation-state, and tried to study the attitudes, values, and purposes by which they were being decided and by which the future was being shaped.[16]

I have now come to believe that this was not simply a unique situation brought on by a special event (the once-in-a-lifetime achievement of political independence), but that all social phenomena can usefully be analyzed from a similar perspective—in fact, had better be, if we are to have any hope of shaping the future to our will.

More, of course, needs to be done, but there are considerable materials already available in political science from which the future of government and politics could be anticipated and on which corrective actions, if necessary, could be based. Among the most significant questions are those dealing with the future governance of cities, the relationships between local governments and the national state, international relationships, the possibilities for the development of supranational organizations, and especially the related question of what lies beyond the nation-state.

The latter subject may require all the "imagineers" that can be found in political science. With the breakdown of the colonial empires and the formation of more than sixty new nations in the twentieth century, the Age of the Nation-State and of National Citizenries has now been reached. Although sometimes associated with a reduction in geographical scale, the creation of many of these new nations has resulted in an increase in political and social scale, since it was a redefinition of the polity and to some extent the society to include all—or nearly all—people within the boundaries of a territory on the basis of equality of citizenship, and since it enlarged the *social* space through which people could move freely.

The trend toward increasing the scale of political organization can be expected to continue. If it does, will an all-Earth Government be the result? If so, will new small communities within the Earthwide unit be necessary to achieve a sense of relatedness among persons? Will diversity be cultivated, and what of race and ethnicity? What are the alternatives, their desirable and undesirable features, and how might they be achieved? What will citizenship mean and what will educating for it entail in the "other" world of the future in which nation-states have been transcended? Assuming, of course, that no one drops the bomb! Classes on the future of the nation-state could arouse widespread student interest—and help prepare all of us for some of the political shocks that lie ahead.

Three problems facing political science in studying the future, in addition to the lack of an adequate mathematized general theory, should be mentioned. One is the tension between the normative and scientific wings of the discipline.

The scientifically oriented members of the discipline have been struggling over the last few decades to develop theories and methods that exemplify the canons of science, and they have tried to eliminate value judgments from their work, with the exception, of course, of those values supporting the scientific enterprise itself and, in some cases, the selection of problems for study.

The normative theorists, until the recent clamoring for social relevance, have been on the defensive, playing a losing game. The study of the future complicates this picture, because values are brought back in and in ways that violate some of the consensual scientific norms of political scientists today. Lasswell, for example, stresses the possibility of a shift from description and prediction to control, and the introduction of the manipulative standpoint into the contemplative. He shows how, in formulating scientific questions in a search for courses of action leading to some goal or maximizing some value, scientists may self-consciously enlarge their role of influencing society in some desired direction—a role, of course, that the scientist plays whether or not he is conscious of it.

Such manipulation, control, and influence cannot occur in a normative vacuum. Thus, the study of the future requires an infusion of the normative into the scientific, preferably as explicitly and critically as possible. Perhaps a shotgun will be necessary, but warring normativists and scientists among political scientists must be brought to the altar of matrimony in futuristics.

A second problem facing political scientists in studying and teaching the future is their own brand of ethnocentric bias. In the Western world, perhaps especially in the United States, this is the uncritical acceptance of certain meanings and forms of democracy to the exclusion of others. On the one hand, the search for the prerequisites of democracy has been an effort, along the lines suggested here, of combining the normative with the scientific, alternative possibilities and preferences with facts. Democracy constitutes a value that even the most scientific of political researchers and teachers utilize to shape and give meaning to their interpretations of political life. This is so, in part, because "education for citizenship" is an explicit part of the political scientist's task as a teacher.

On the other hand, much "education for citizenship" has been little more than indoctrination into believing in the worth, even sacredness, of the particular forms that "democracy" is presumed to take. And since the Western world has appropriated the term —not without dissent from the Communist world, of course— Western political scientists, especially Americans, are prone to define the value, goal, or condition of democracy by what existed or exists in the United States, Great Britain, or some other Western country.

Explicitly value-laden social science, then, is just as filled with the pitfalls of bias as is so-called value-free social science, although the bias in the former may be sometimes easier to detect. The answer, of course, is not to be found in simply adopting a contrary interpretative framework, in order to explore different definitions and empirical referents for the term, such as could be found in Marxist-Leninism (although the teacher interested in promoting skepticism rather than blind faith among his students might do well to give equal time to Western and Communist conceptions). For the point is that *both* may be—probably are— inadequate to cope with the demands of the emerging future. The student needs not only to understand present conceptions, but to think of basic institutions, values, and goals in new ways as well: to ask where current practices, hallowed though they may be, are, or are not, achieving the purposes for which they were intended or the better purposes they might now be charged to serve; to experiment with alternative forms that validly embody the meaning of democracy; and to begin the search for the future meanings of democracy itself. Ironically, when American political scientists have strayed from conventional definitions of democratic forms in the recent past, they have not generally done so well. They have used novel conceptions of democracy that permit patently undemocratic regimes to be classified somehow as the opposite, have been unduly pessimistic concerning the viability of democratic systems and their capabilities for economic and social development, and, without adequate evidence, have given favorable assessments of the efficacy of authoritarian military regimes to institute reform.[17]

A third problem is that political science and political scientists are to some degree—and in some sense inadvertently—subservient to the state and the status quo. While holding to the ideals of democracy and justice, they are frequently involved in the perpetuation of real undemocratic practices and injustice. As Hans J. Morgenthau has put it:

> The government disposes of a whole gamut of professional and social rewards from appointments and consultantships to foreign travel and to invitations to social functions at the White House. By adroitly promising, dispensing, and withholding them, it keeps a large segment of the academic community at bay. The political scientist, by accepting one or the other of these rewards, enters into a subtle and insidious relationship with the government, which imperceptibly transforms his position of independent observer to that of client and partisan. In consequence, his intellectual function is also transformed. In the measure that he values these social rewards and professional advantages more highly than his commitment to the truth, he becomes a political ideologue, justifying morally and rationalizing intellectually what the government is doing.[18]

As Morgenthau says further, political science, if true to its moral commitment of measuring political truth, necessarily calls political and social convention into question. "By doing so, it is not only an embarrassment to society intellectually, but it becomes also a political threat to the defenders or the opponents of the status quo or to both; for the social conventions about power, which political science cannot help subjecting to a critical—and often destructive—examination, are one of the main sources from which the claims to power, and hence power itself, derive."[19]

There are, thus, contradictory pressures on political scientists, toward subservience on the one hand and subversion on the other. The political science of the future could profitably make such pressures, their conditions and consequences, a focus of investigation both in research and teaching. For they importantly involve one of the long-standing—though frequently slighted—concerns of political science, power. Furthermore, this could be made part of one of the most important questions we can ask about the future: Who will and should have the power to decide what the future will be?

Psychology

Although psychology, like the other social sciences, has not been oriented primarily toward the future, it does contain a wealth of materials on which a science of futurism can be built. More and more students now study psychology—and at a younger age. They should be made aware that in both social psychology and in the study of the individual, images of the future play a neglected but critical role.

Psychology, in fact, can claim an early champion of the need for modern social science to study the future. In 1930 Nathan Israeli wrote "Some Aspects of the Social Psychology of Futurism."[20] He called for the creation of scientific and systematic utopias toward which man could strive and for evaluations of possible future trends so that patterns of present behavior leading to the most desirable future could be identified. After writing his first article, Israeli carried out a series of experiments aimed at isolating the nature of the predictive process, but these experiments represented only a small part of the vision he had had.

Although Israeli attracted little attention, several years later two other psychologists became interested in the nature of prediction and followed his lead. They were Douglas McGregor and Hadley Cantril, who wanted to know what factors influence the predictions an individual makes. McGregor and Cantril asked respondents to make a series of predictions and then correlated their social backgrounds and attitudes with the predictions.[21] In an all-too-rare bit of cumulative research, Hans Toch analyzed the accuracy of a series of predictions about the state of the world in 1952 that had been collected by Cantril a decade earlier.[22] Cantril's interest in expectations for the future continued throughout his career, and it matured into his studies of *The Pattern of Human Concerns*.[23] Along with Lloyd Free, he developed the Self-Anchoring Striving Scale and investigated future hopes and fears for self and nation in a large number of different countries, a pioneering work that deserves to be followed up.[24]

Psychology, of course, has its clinical side and thus is necessarily drawn into some consideration of the future. Decisions, actions, and change in psychology may have more to do with the little world of the individual and his adjustment than with the world of cabinets and parliaments of nations, but even private decisions and actions require concern with the future. What, for example, is treatment or therapy all about? Isn't it to produce some kind of a change in the state or relationships of the individual? But what kind? How should the individual or his situation be different in the future after treatment if he is to become mentally well, or happier, or adjusted? Some conception of the potentially "well" patient in the future as well as a set of theories and methods is necessary to guide the therapist.

As sociologist Pauline Bart points out, "Dynamically oriented psychotherapists deal with the reconstructed past of the individual and have a (usually implicit) goal or image of the future for their patients."[25] What past is reconstructed and what images of the patient's future exist, as she says further, depend partly on the theoretical orientation of the therapist. But in all cases the therapist is trying to make the patient's future, in some sense, different from his present. Concentration on the intra-psychic state of individual patients and the goal of adjustment, however, invite the therapist to ignore society and social change and to opt for a conception of the social future very much like the present, or as Bart says, the past of Vienna.

Other aspects of applied psychology go considerably beyond the field of mental health. In industry, for example, workers are rated, selected, and placed in different jobs; job success is predicted; work environments are studied and manipulated with an eye to changing future productivity levels, job satisfaction, or accident rates; man-machine relationships are investigated to increase efficiency or reduce fatigue; work groups and organizations are studied in order to improve communications or reduce intergroup tensions; and individuals are studied to learn how to increase motivation and morale and to reduce boredom and monotony. These and the many other examples of applied psychology that could be given nearly always have a future orientation involved in them.

Although the techniques that have been developed may be of use to the emergent psychology of the future, the substantive knowledge that has resulted is quite limited. The narrow time conceptions involved, the immediacy of the problems solved, the special interests served, and especially the absence of a sense of eschatological transcendence, as in the case of economics, makes much of applied psychology of little help to us in preparing for the future. Even so, the efforts of the experimentalists to isolate themselves from applied psychologists is to be regretted, since the latter generally do have a better developed sense of the importance of time.

The noted psychologist B. F. Skinner has written, in *Walden Two*,[26] about a utopia based upon a behavioristic framework. Undoubtedly, Skinner is a man of good will, but his proposed future society, based as it is on what he has discovered about how pigeons learn, leaves considerable to be desired. He has designed a total environment and has been criticized for its "brave new world" aspects.[27] My chief complaint is somewhat different. *Walden Two* is much more the world of the present, even of the past, rather than the "other" world of the future. There is little in the book that has not already been formulated by the architects of the Great Society, except that people behave themselves better and the system of social control is more effective.

Psychology, despite my caveats, has a great deal to offer in the study and teaching of the future, and I have not been able to consider the important contributions of physiological psychology. Time and change are inextricably linked; each is in some sense relative to the other. Thus, many of the core concerns of psychology such as child development, growth and maturation, and learning, itself, deal with processual thinking, a time perspective that includes past, present, and future. There remains a need to shift the time perspective more toward the future, to develop an epistemology to take account of the openness, uncertainty, and problematics of the future,[28] and to broaden the psychological purpose to include a concern with the meaning of human life.

If efforts to do these things are not made, then the judgment of future history may well be that behavioristic psychology, the dominant style at the core of psychological research, may turn out to be "a narrow, artificial, and relatively sterile approach to the understanding of man" as the proponents of a humanistic psychology have been saying since the 1950s.[29] "Creature Sapien" is not simply another animal. Nor are we simply machines. Nor are we now all that we might become in the future. A major task of a psychology of the future is to help humans learn how to learn and to discover, perhaps to help expand, the human potential. And the term "potential" itself implies a future.

Sociology

Sociologists have been just as reluctant to get involved with social workers, their social engineering counterparts, as experimental psychologists have been to get involved with clinicians. Thus, much sociology remains static and atemporal, pure and immune from the demands of the future that could be brought to it by action-oriented social workers. Yet sociology does have its applied wing, including even some connections with social welfare, and in the last decade it has grown tremendously. It includes the use of sociology in law, medicine, education, management, the military establishment, marketing, foreign policy, public administration, social planning, unemployment and manpower, and public health.

Recently, the need for research directed toward the evaluation of social-action programs has been recognized. In the past we did not know what sociological knowledge had been used in decision-making, or, if it had, what the consequences were. Today, a number of sociologists are replacing the little experiments of their own making by the great experiments in social change that are under way,[30] and, because it is necessary for the study of change, they are consciously introducing a time dimension into their work.

Applied sociology, however, has generally dealt with the narrow problem of goal implementation; and the goals have generally been those of established organizations, rather than emergent ones or individuals. Thus, sociologists have been disproportionately mobilized for status quo and establishment purposes. Although the organizations and agencies that sponsor social research, that serve as its clients, and that sometimes use research in their actions, have varying missions, together, most of them constitute a vast complex of complementary organizational needs.

The institutionalized needs of government, business, the military, trade unions, school systems, and the like—not the needs of humans—have defined most of the problems and shaped much of the research. Even where social change is the goal, such as in community redevelopment, elimination of poverty, improvement of low-income housing, and increasing equality of educational opportunity, elite origins have often inclined new community-action agencies and their demonstration researchers "toward elitist objectives, strategies, and tactics of change."[31] Students, of course, are not unaware of this bias and are increasingly critical of the whole social-science enterprise.

Moreover, Western sociologists have probably been as uncritically concerned with order as political scientists have been with democracy. The dominant paradigm in sociology for some years has derived largely from the theoretical work on the social system done by Harvard sociologist Talcott Parsons.[32] It has led to a preoccupation with stability, pattern maintenance, and consensus. It has tended generally to sweep change under the rug, and in the United States to deemphasize or water down the study of violence, revolution, class, history, elites, and intellectuals, as Ralf Dahrendorf[33] lists the six "missing traits" of American sociology contrasted with European sociology.

We live at a time of the most rapid social change in history, yet a recent study of 537 colleges and universities in the United States, for example, showed that less than a fourth offered undergraduate courses on social change.[34] The static nature of Parsonian functionalism has recently been characterized by Alvin W. Gouldner:

> Although Functionalism is adaptable to all *established* industrial systems, it is not equally responsive to *new* orders that are only coming into being, for these may be the foes of those already established. What makes a theory conservative (or radical) is its posture toward the institutions of its own surrounding society. A theory is conservative to the extent that it: treats these institutions as given and unchangeable in essentials; proposes remedies for them so that they may work better, rather than devising alternatives to them; foresees no future that can be essentially better than the present, the conditions that already exist; and, explicitly or implicitly, counsels acceptance of or resignation to what exists, rather than struggling against it.[35]

The study of the future need not be either conservative or radical, in the sense used by Gouldner, because a probable future could be more undesirable than the present and struggle might well be directed toward keeping the desirable aspects of the present as they are. Also, designing remedies so that existing institutions may work better is a legitimate aim for sociologists of the future, since, as Marx said, a series of minor quantitative changes can eventually result in qualitative changes. Yet Gouldner's basic point is correct: Parsonsian functionalism is status quo-oriented. Order, not change, has been served. And, given an imperfect world and the human ability to construct images of a better future, the study of the future is to some extent necessarily subversive of the present.

The dominance of Parsonsian functionalism in sociology, however, has been eroding for nearly a decade. New future-oriented and intervention-minded sociologists are reshaping the discipline. If an era of unparalleled commitment to the status quo defined the climate of the times that gave rise to Parsonsian atemporal system theory, then its fall may be equally linked to a thorough-going shift in the larger sociocultural setting, as Robert W. Friedrichs claims.[36] Such a shift has included the domestic civil-rights revolution, Marxist-motivated social change in underdeveloped countries, the rediscovery of the young humanistic Marx, existentialism, black power, the questioning of traditional female roles stimulated by the women's liberation movement, and antagonism to the Vietnam war on the part of the American intellectual community.

The new sociology will undoubtedly contain much of the old. But it will distinctively add the cultivation of *awareness* as a central feature. Such awareness includes a sensitivity to the time dimension, the consequences of present actions for the future, the role of the investigator, himself, in changing his subjects and their social environments, and the purposes of increasing human responsibility and freedom through the revelation of the potential results of behavior. At Yale, James A. Mau and I have tried to contribute to these developments by formulating a cybernetic-decisional model of social change that rests heavily upon the concept of image of the future in its explanation of change.[37]

The contributions sociology could make to studying and teaching about the future include answers to such questions as the following: What new sex and marriage patterns are rising? How are family forms changing? What are the trends in the patterns of inequality? What new elaborations in the concept of equality can be used to judge class, ethnic, sex, and age inequalities? What new forms of cities are possible and what are their consequences for social relationships? What are the benefits and disadvantages of diversity? How can diversity be promoted or minimized? What is the meaning of deviance in a rapidly changing world? If every society gets the kind of criminals it deserves, what kind of criminals do we want? Is it necessary to have criminals in every kind of a society that can be devised? How can the population bomb be controlled or how can people learn to live under conditions we would now believe to be unbearably crowded? What will mob behavior be like under a massive system of electronic intercommunication? What are the contradictions in existing society that provide pressure or leverage for change?

More generally: How do society, its institutions, and its organizations come to be what they are? How can they become something else? How and why do structuring, restructuring, and destructuring occur? What choices do people have and how do they go about making them? How can society and social changes be brought under greater control and made to serve better the needs and hopes of humankind?

Toward Preferable Futures

The future is a crucial variable in social science. Although my brief review of five of the social sciences does justice to none, I hope that I have been able to give a glimpse of the role that each of the social sciences could play in the study and teaching of the future—and the role of the future in the study and teaching of social science. We are all psychological, political, economic, social, and cultural beings, and our lives are dominated by our emotions, hopes and fears, our beliefs, and our commitments to and relationships with other humans.

As change accelerates and time shortens, we are in danger of being trapped in a world of the future that we do not want, one that may be hostile to the point of threatening human life. Freedom and responsibility to know and to choose the future we want can only come from our imaginings and anticipations of the future combined with our understanding of means and ends. The social sciences lag behind the unanticipated social consequences of the can-means-ought mentality of unbridled application of technology. A fundamental shift in time perspective is needed to catch up to, to get ahead of, and to obtain and keep control of the vast changes that already surround us. Only then will we obtain the power to design the future.

What values are to be served? This is a question that should concern each of the social sciences as they look toward the future. The future can be made to serve the human will. But can humans agree, can they will together? Are there some areas of human activity in which they *must* will together, if life is to continue at all, or be tolerable, or be beautiful? Freedom is not an unmixed blessing and the demise of superstition and cultural "absolutes," if they are to die, may unshackle humankind for presently unknown purposes. As Polak says:

> In setting himself purposefully to control and alter the course of events man has been forced to deal with the concepts of value, means and ends, ideals and ideologies, as he has attempted to blueprint his own future. As long as the prophet-propitiator was acting only as a divine transmitter of messages from on high, man felt that he was accepting his ethics ready-made, with no alterations allowed. In a later stage man staggers under the double load of not only having to construct his own future but having to create the values which will determine its design.[38]

And as Lasswell points out, "The accent put on future events gives new prominence to preferred events, to value goals, since the possibility is perceived that some act of selection may influence the sequence of future occurrences."[39]

Is there any evidence that universal values of some absolute nature exist for human beings? Some writers think that some may exist, common values that derive from the survival, health, and dignity of humankind.[40] In his studies in fourteen different countries including Brazil, Cuba, Egypt, India, Japan, Nigeria, Poland, the United States, and Yugoslavia, Cantril found cause for noting certain basic similarities in peoples' hopes and fears. He says that they "revolve around the complex of personal well-being as this is rather simply and genuinely defined; a decent standard of living; opportunities for children; technological advances; good health; a good job; decent housing; a happy home life; better educational facilities."[41] In general, the outstanding worry people had for their country was that it might become involved in another war.

But he found little evidence, in the main, of more idealistic or sophisticated hopes. Only five per cent of the total population sampled expressed an improved sense of social and political responsibility, of being useful to others, or of aspiration for self-development. Concern "for greater social justice, more freedom, better moral standards, the resolution of moral or ethical problems and similar goals appears to be the conscious concern of only a tiny minority of people throughout the world." Cantril concludes that "It is clear that people must learn what to want the way they learn anything else; they must learn the range and quality of experience that should be theirs if things are to be different."

Perhaps that is where we are. But there is no reason to despair if food, clothing, shelter, a decent job, a family, and good health are preferred over more abstract things. After these basics are provided to all, as they may soon be, what then? That tiny minority is at work. Perhaps the future development of values will be as fantastic as the technological changes we can already envision. Choosing which values are to be served, as economies, polities, cultures, and societies are deliberately shaped, has enormous implications for, and need of, social-science information. Our educational institutions need to be refocused on the future so that students can "learn what to want" and so that they can explore the "range and quality of experience that should be theirs if things are to be different." Thus can Creatures Sapiens take control of the world of the future. What they create, of course, in turn, will shape them. Therefore, the ultimate question may be: What kind of people do we want?

The future will, in part, be shaped by the values of the present and past. A revolutionary new social science curriculum that combines a central interest in values with a strong future-orientation is being prepared by a team of social scientists, teachers, writers and psychologists. Making heavy use of games, experiential education, and inquiry method, it is based on a "cultural systems approach" and employs two carefully articulated models. Here Michael A. McDanield, who has been associated with the project from its inception, describes the objectives, theoretical base, and structure of this new curriculum.

CHAPTER SIX

Tomorrow's Curriculum Today

by Michael A. McDanield

I like the dreams of the future better than the
history of the past.
—*Thomas Jefferson to John Adams*

How does one go about the design of a curriculum for the future? This was the question faced by a group of educational writers and researchers brought together by the Center for Adaptive Learning, Inc., in May 1971. Their task: to formulate the theoretical framework for a future-oriented social studies curriculum—and to develop student materials to implement this curriculum.

Recognizing that massive changes are needed in American education, including the development of many more small, informal, experimental and open schools, and, indeed, the wholesale shift of a good part of education to outside the schools, we nevertheless also recognized the likelihood that millions of youngsters will, in the immediate half-decade or more, continue to be educated in formal public schools. New, future-focused and change-oriented materials are desperately needed to replace the past-oriented and static materials to which most high-school students are still exposed.

There seems little question that curriculum design must begin with a *concern* for the individuals who are most *concerned with* that curriculum: students and teachers. For the past two years we have talked to many students and teachers at seminars and informal gatherings about what kind of curriculum we need for the year 2001, but at a recent conference on creativity I received from a number of young people, students and teachers, a list that most nearly reflects the consensus of these many discussions.

The following are their responses, given in a blitz session of less than twenty minutes, to the question "What kind of learning materials will best prepare students for life in the year 2001?"[1]

1. Materials that will help maturing individuals *cope with their society.*
2. Materials that will help maturing individuals *understand themselves.*
3. Materials that will help maturing individuals *understand their investment in the future.*
4. Materials that will help maturing individuals *not to feel powerless or impotent.*
5. Materials that will help maturing individuals *identify with the society they will inherit.*
6. Materials that will help maturing individuals *understand the nature of change.*
7. Materials that will help maturing individuals *see the means of affecting the direction of change.*
8. Materials that will help maturing individuals *understand key social-science concepts and their relation to change.*
9. Materials that will help maturing individuals *identify roles they can take in the change process.*
10. Materials that will help maturing individuals *avoid ethnocentrism.*
11. Materials that will help maturing individuals *incorporate classroom learning into their immediate environments.*
12. Materials that will help maturing individuals *transfer classroom learning to future responsibilities.*

13. Materials that will help mature individuals *assist maturing individuals to create relevant learning situations.*
14. Materials that will help mature individuals *understand the role of maturing individuals in change.*
15. Materials that will help mature individuals *connect and become involved with maturing individuals.*
16. Materials that will help mature individuals *and maturing individuals change immature institutions.*

The gestalt of this list is satisfying to me. It emphasizes the cooperative efforts of mature individuals helping maturing individuals—it recognizes the role of the past in creating the future. It is modest in its emphasis on coping and understanding, but assertive in its recognition of power and change. It reflects the general understanding that we are living in special and difficult times and that the acceleration of change has become our main challenge. As such, it sums up fairly well the objectives of the Center for Adaptive Learning Curriculum for the Future Project.

Curriculum Overchoice

Alvin Toffler, who is a key figure in the project, uses the term "overchoice" for the situation in which people become paralyzed by the surfeit of choice.[2] Overchoice is especially a reality for the designer of educational curricula in the social studies: there is so much that *could* be taught that it is almost impossible to decide what *should* be taught. A way must be found to narrow the choices.

As Toffler points out, and as few familiar with education will deny, parents expect the schools to "fit their children for life in the future."[3] This expectation, if taken seriously, as it should be, turns out to be at least a partial solution to the difficulty posed by "overchoice" in the curriculum—we must design a curriculum that *will*, in fact, fit children for life in the future.

Beginning with this commitment, we can make important choices by asking questions such as, What concepts, values, ideas will help us adapt to (or intelligently resist) the future? What concepts, values, ideas have helped people in the past adapt to their future? Did they forecast their future? Can we?

It is clear that the educator must continue this direct attack on the problem of overchoice by deciding what to exclude and what to include. To do this, he must select concepts that are highly generalized and of wide application: What is change? What ideas will be useful to the student in coping with change? What is changing? How is it changing? What kinds of conflicts take place over change? Will they continue to take place? What is slow to change? How do we agree on what should be changed?

Out of just such questions we evolved a curriculum that focuses on the future through the broad themes of change, continuity, conflict, and consensus in cultural systems. These general themes, manifested in both a model of continuing cultural elements and a model of change, became the heart of the new Center for Adaptive Learning (C.A.L.) curriculum based on what we call the "cultural systems approach."

Concepts and Structure

With a strong commitment to inquiry, the C.A.L. curriculum does not, however, simply display a wide range of data or factual material for the student. It encourages the student to search for organizing concepts or generalizations. Moreover, we have set our concepts in a well-defined structure, so that both student and teacher can see how they are related as a *system*. In short, we organized the concepts into clearly specified models.

If a program is to be structured by the use of general concepts, we must heed the warning of sociologist Lewis Coser that concepts must be thought of as "neither true nor false; they are apt or inept, clear or vague, fruitful or useless. They are tools designed to capture relevant aspects of reality and thus constitute the definitions of what is to be observed."[4] Coser's emphasis is on observation, on action, on tools that help us adapt to the future. For us, then, it is clear that the student's ability to *use* a concept is and will be more important than his ability to *describe* it.

George C. Homans in *The Nature of Social Science* puts it another way, but no less strongly: "Propositions [generalizations] are the one essential product of any science. . . ." While he believes that concepts only "tell us roughly the kinds of things we are going to talk about . . . sooner or later we must stop 'being about to' talk about something and actually say something—that is, *state* propositions [generalizations]."[5] For us what counts is not so much the student's ability to state a proposition as his ability to understand and exploit it. We believe this ability is promoted by the use of clearly defined models.

The lack of such structures or models has been a major failing in most of our past social-studies instruction: teachers have emphasized particularistic knowledge at the expense of systematic knowledge. We felt it important to devise a program that would not only expose the student to some of the models that have been developed by social scientists to explain social and cultural systems, but teach students, by implication, how to design their own models, thus allowing them to structure the new knowledge and new situations they will encounter in the future.

Choices and Candor

A teacher for whom I have great respect tells this anecdote about an experimental course in the sociology of the future which he taught at Cornell: "On the first day of class I noticed a girl in the back of the room, busily taking notes during our rather meandering discussion. At the end of class I could not resist asking her why she was so busy with her notebook during the discussion. She said, 'I have been taking down all the assumptions that everyone has been making during the discussion.' I said, 'You are our *assumption keeper* and you have an A for the course.'"

It was a firm belief of our curriculum designers that we should be candid about the choices *we* are making—that we should state our own assumptions about education. We must state our "meta-values," for what we do in research (as Myrdal made clear) and what we do in teaching (as Dewey and Whitehead and Bruner made clear) depends on what we think people are like and what they can become. And these assumptions are reflected in the materials we prepare. If we make our assumptions clear they are at least subject to criticism and examination.

We assumed that whatever program we devised must itself be capable of change, providing a solid CURRICULAR CORE of organized concepts, but remaining open to new facts and information from many sources, so that students could move from the basic curriculum to the "real" environment outside the classroom to gather facts and take significant actions.

We assumed that there must be SUPPLEMENTS TO THE CURRICULAR CORE. Some of these would be provided by us, but most exist and are already available in most school libraries and in almost all public libraries, as well as in the community generally. In short, our materials had to be designed so that they could, if necessary, stand alone. In practice, however, they had to be "open" in style so that they would, whenever possible, be used in conjunction with other books or materials that would examine content in more depth, or from specific points of view, or would elaborate the general concepts introduced in the CURRICULAR CORE.

While this assumption may seem neither brilliant nor original, social-studies texts have seldom if ever been prepared in this way. They are sold as "complete" or "all-purpose." When a book fails to win a "basic adoption," it is often offered for "supplemental adoption." This results in classrooms full of books that are essentially identical in content and coverage, *all* constituting what *we* would call supplementary books.

Since C.A.L.'s designers assumed from the start that supplements like, for example, Kluckhohn's *Mirror for Man*, Potter's *People of Plenty*, or Theobald's *An Alternative Future for America II*, would be used, we were able to deal with other matters in our core curriculum. This, for us, is the true meaning of an instructional system, and it is time that producers of materials faced up to the fact that no book, no course, no matter how good, can do it all. By making this assumption, we were freed to recommend the best materials produced by others, then depend on educators to accept their responsibility to articulate and fill in the system.

We assumed that there would be REFERENCE SOURCES FOR THE CURRICULAR CORE. Again, there is a specific role for such works to fulfill in the C.A.L. instructional system: They are to provide dates, places, names and other information for the inquiries that are set in motion by the core curriculum.

We have had the courage to exclude much of this material, knowing it can be better supplied (and is, in most schools) by such books as *The Encyclopedia of American History*, the many books of *American Heritage*, *The New York Times Encyclopedic Almanac*, *The Annals of America*, etc. We have judged it more important to structure the inquiry than to provide the answers to the inquiry.

We assumed that there is AN ENVIRONMENT OUTSIDE THE SCHOOL that is related to the curriculum. The core curriculum does not exist in a vacuum; the school does not exist in a vacuum. If we have a concern for social reality, we must link the instructional program of the school to the instructional program implicit in the culture. What has already been done by the media of the culture and other socialization methods? What is it that the instructional media should do? What is it that the media of the culture can do? How can we bring the two together?

We can profit from the realization that the culture, in its media, is fact-rich and method-poor. (Students are bombarded by data but starved for useful models.) We have already mentioned that there are many information sources available to provide the facts that a course centered on the inquiry method and process elects to omit. Yet the intelligent use of the media is becoming more difficult in our culture. Postman and Weingartner in their book, *Teaching as a Subversive Activity*,[6] suggest that a relevant curriculum would be one that focuses on "media ecology"—the processes and skills that would enable students to process the vast amount of data with which they are daily bombarded. We have responded to this suggestion, particularly by presenting systematic models.

We assumed, finally, that our curriculum *would not* be the students' only, or last, experience with social study. Too many textbooks have already been prepared with this unstated, arrogant, and untenable assumption. In attempting to do everything, or in following the latest educational or media fads, these programs fail to give students content that is of lasting significance, or concepts that provide them with a useful guide for study or adaptation. To paraphrase Churchill, we see our program not as the beginning of the end, but as the end of the beginning.

The Cultural Systems Approach

The idea currently popular in education (sometimes manifested in mini-courses) that diversity alone can reform the curriculum is similar to the idea of auto makers that a diversity of models solves the problem of good transportation; it equates relevance with immediacy rather than with ideas and gives us an "overchoice" of "non-choices."

The crucial question is still, What knowledge is of most worth? And although this question is not new, it is also not irrelevant. Martin Mayer pointed out in a book on social studies in the schools[7] that "one of the elements that distinguishes teaching [learning] from miscellaneous communication is the control of irrelevancies; the goal of teaching [learning] is to enable the student to control irrelevancies by himself . . . and to generate new models that help him to do this."

What knowledge is of most worth is, in the final analysis, that which is retained for potential application—and the student needs structure to help him retain knowledge. Courses organized only by the inclusion of contemporary problems allow students and teachers to be swept along by contemporary events, to respond to the current fads, to the latest quick solutions—all of which may turn out to be obsolete or useless in a short time.

Teachers and students must learn to extract from problems the crucial themes and threads that make them *significant* problems, that make them *persistent* problems. Simultaneously, they must see the interconnections among them. This is why we have emphasized a systematic, model-based approach.

Our decision to focus on cultural systems is one which is receiving increasing support from key figures in social science. In an article in Morrissett and Stevens' *Social Science in the Schools: A Search for a Rationale*, Kenneth Boulding argues that "we are moving very rapidly toward a unified social science" and states his preference for a "general systems approach to education." Boulding defines a system as "anything which is not chaos" and says that the "task of learning is to perceive what is chaos and what is not chaos in the world around us."[8] A rigorous application of this concept can make a fundamental difference in social-science curriculum. It is a unifying concept, one that can bring together the sciences that are, in the words of George Homans, "in fact a single science."[9]

Stafford Beer in *Decision and Control*[10] gives a general definition of system as consisting of at least four components: (1) elements, (2) relationships, (3) patterns, and (4) purpose. Although it is relatively easy to specify the elements, relations, patterns, and purposes of the natural sciences, it is much more difficult in the social sciences. There they remain matters for debate. Nevertheless, while we may argue about purpose, all cultures can be characterized in terms of elements, relationships and patterns. In turn, by doing so, we can construct useful models by defining these elements and specifying their relationships and patterns. Finally, by identifying relevant elements and their operative relationships, we can begin to make forecasts about the system. We can begin to think systematically about its future.

At another level, we, as curriculum designers, want the student to realize that all people use more or less systematic models in their everyday thinking, and that one of the characteristics that distinguish humans from other animals is the ability to create these models and use them for prediction.

Accordingly, we have developed a model for cultural systems. It is intentionally simple, even simplistic. It is designed to serve a heuristic function—to help the student see the significant areas of inquiry. The significant areas of inquiry for students should be those that are significant areas of research for social scientists, and the student should be able to compare and contrast our model and his models with those that social scientists have developed, models that are much more complex and complete than the one with which the students will begin.

Some of the operations which we encourage the students to engage in are to (1) contemplate the model, (2) manipulate the model, (3) compare it with others, (4) utilize it in data gathering, (5) utilize it in prediction, (6) modify the model, and (7) construct alternate models. The purpose is to free the student, through inquiry with the model, of reliance on any specific model.

Continuing Cultural Elements: Model 1

The intent of our design group was to develop a curriculum for grades ten through twelve oriented toward the future and centered on the idea of cultural systems.

In pursuit of this objective, we initially focused on two of our basic themes: continuity and change. We began by asking two essential questions about cultural systems: What is likely to remain the same? What is likely to change? In responding to these two questions, we evolved two models: a model of "continuity" (a model for synchronic analysis of cultural systems) and a model of "change" (a model for diachronic analysis of cultural systems). These models lend a pedagogical, philosophical, and logical unity to the whole ten-through-twelve curriculum.

In the first model we assumed that cultural systems

(1) work through interaction between ideas—(i.e., the info-sphere) and action—(i.e., the actionsphere),

(2) transmitted and modified by a symbol system and its at-tendant technology.

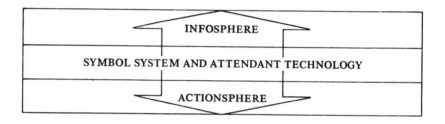

There is, of course, little surprise in this. This simple model, in narrative form, appears again and again in the literature of behav-ioral science. A few quotes will suffice here to indicate the theoreti-cal base on which it rests.

Alfred Kroeber and Clyde Kluckhohn in their book, *Culture,*[11] a massive compilation of expert opinion about the culture concept, write that "culture systems may, on the one hand, be considered as products of action, on the other as conditioning elements [ideas and values] of further action. . . ." They go on to note that "culture includes both modalities of actual behavior and a group's conscious, partly conscious, and unconscious designs for living."

Kenneth Boulding in *Economics as a Science*[12] divides social reality, what he calls the "sociosphere," into three basic domains: the "econosphere," the "polity," and the "infosphere," noting that the latter "has considerable claim to dominate the other segments."

It is vital that a social-studies model emphasize ideas and values as well as events and behavior. We are often unaware of our ideas and values. As Kroeber and Kluckhohn put it: "The implicit culture consists in those cultural themes of which there is characteristically no sustained and systematic awareness . . . In a highly self-conscious culture like the American, which makes a business of studying itself, the proportion of the culture which is literally implicit in the sense of never having been overtly stated by any member of the society may be small. Yet only a trifling percentage of Americans could state even those implicit premises of our culture which have been abstracted out by social scientists."[13]

Having established some support for the initial model, we can elaborate it in the following way: A *cultural system* is composed of *people* acting as individuals and interacting with groups or *organizations*, with *things*, in a given *place*, subject to *values* and *ideas* that are affected by and affect behavior, and are transmitted by a *symbol system and its attendant technology*. The model is now as shown:

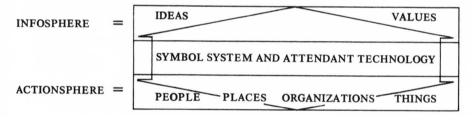

It is one of the objectives of the curriculum for the student to recognize that these three elements—the infosphere, the symbol system and attendant technology, and the actionsphere—are (or can be regarded as) components of all human cultures, past, present and future, and that each of these, in turn, can be seen to have subcomponents.

Thus, for example, all cultures have not only values and ideas (and in these two categories we include implicit assumptions such as those regarding time), but also communications channels through which these ideas and values are symbolically expressed. Moreover, all cultures involve things, places, people and organizations. In turn, these elements can be further broken down into their constituent parts. Organizations, for example, would include governments, corporations, families, tribes, etc.

What this model provides, in effect, is a classificatory scheme by which a culture or subculture can be empirically characterized in as much or little detail as desired. Using it, we can get a snapshot of the culture at any given moment in time.

Cultural Change Forces: Model 2

Kroeber and Kluckhohn note another characteristic of cultural systems in the following way: "All systems appear to acquire certain properties that characterize the system *qua* system rather than the sum of isolable elements. Among these properties is that of directionality or 'drift.' There is a momentum quality to cultural systems."[14] Therefore the second type of model which we developed is a model for studying change, for the diachronic study of cultural systems. We have, again of necessity, simplified our model, since the nature of social change is one of the most complex research topics in social science. But while in research one must deal in *precision*, in instruction it is often sufficient, and in the interests of clarity and simplicity, often imperative to deal only in *awareness*.

Our first step, as shown by the diagram, was to analyze, in effect, the spectrum of change:

Change

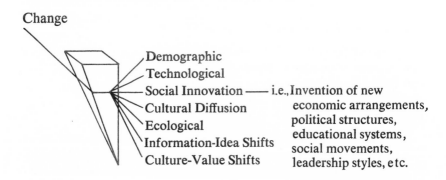

Demographic
Technological
Social Innovation —— i.e., Invention of new
Cultural Diffusion   economic arrangements,
Ecological   political structures,
Information-Idea Shifts   educational systems,
                              social movements,
Culture-Value Shifts   leadership styles, etc.

Breaking the idea of sociocultural change down, we arrived at seven different types of change or, as we called them, "change factors." These can each be further subdivided (as suggested for Social Innovation in the accompanying list) and all seven are obviously interrelated (as indicated in the diagram on p. 118). There is no suggestion here that these are the *only* such factors at work, nor are they ranked in any order of importance. Nevertheless, all seven presumably operate in all societies—and that makes them highly significant and pedagogically valuable.

SEVEN CHANGE FACTORS[15]

1. Demographic

   We presume that in any culture increases or decreases in population, or shifts in the age and sex distribution, generate other changes. We would include under this variations in birth and death rates, life span, family size, balance of young vs. old, migrations, etc.

2. Technological Innovation

   We assert that changes in technology trigger other changes. We define technology here in the limited, more or less colloquial sense, as having to do with productivity and machines. We would use a broad definition of innovation to include even seemingly small adaptive changes in existing machines. A shift from ropes to horse collars, increasing the ability of the animal to pull, is by this definition a technological advance, as is the invention of a modified, faster Xerox machine or computer.

3. Social Innovation

   The term "social" is used here in a broad sense to include the invention of new arrangements, systems or styles in educational, political, economic, military and other dimensions. Innovation here is even more difficult to define than it is in the technological sphere, but would include new ways of organizing human effort (i.e., the corporation), new political institutions (parliaments), new ways of organizing war (Panzer blitzkreig vs. trench warfare), etc.

4. Cultural-Value Shifts

   Every society holds a set of unspoken assumptions, and carries out a great deal of unrationalized behavior. It also manifests a value system. Changes in cultural axioms or values may trigger significant other changes. Example of a change in cultural assumptions: the unnoticed shift in the way men used time after the coming of industrialism. (Conception of linear time, refined, carefully conditioned habits of punctuality, etc., based on need for synchronized work.) Example of a shift in value: The decline in the importance attached to property and/ or virginity.

5. Ecological Shifts

Changes in human society may also be occasioned by changes in the natural ecology—the glacier moving down across Europe, the decline of the caribou population in Lapland, earthquake, tidal wave, the appearance of new kinds of crops because of transplantation from abroad, the pollution of rivers or oceans, etc. This would include the impact of climatic conditions on culture and personality, etc.

6. Information-Idea Shifts

The scope, quality and manipulability of knowledge all fall within this category, so that a scientific discovery, a new theory about race or child rearing, new verbalized conceptions about how-things-work, all exemplify change in the character and distribution of the knowledge pool. (Knowledge and information are here used interchangeably.)

7. Cultural Diffusion

Any transfer of ideas, values, or techniques from one culture to another, whether as a consequence of invasion, war, advertising, increased travel, etc. A significant difference exists, however, between cultural diffusion and the other six change factors, since it operates at a different level and can be said to incorporate the others. For example, when a production technique like the Bessemer furnace, developed in Europe, is imported to the United States, it can be said to be a cultural borrowing. But once in the United States it operates exactly like a Technical Innovation. One culture may borrow values or information from another. These, when introduced into the borrowing culture, represent Cultural-Value Shifts or Information-Idea Shifts. Cultural Diffusion, therefore, may take the form of any of the other change factors, and is defined purely in terms of origin outside the culture.

We can see that the synchronic and the diachronic models are closely related; however, it is not a one-to-one relationship with their elements but, as Kroeber and Kluckhohn have previously noted, a "system *qua* system" relationship. The kinds of change we have identified as significant are those that take place when one cultural system impinges on another or those that take place within a cultural system over an extended period of time.

Thus, the two models can be seen in the following way: Model 1, the continuity model, permits a description of a culture at a moment in time. Model 2, when applied to a culture described by Model 1, sets it into motion. (This is not an exact description of their relationship, since Model 1 is itself not a static model. But it is a good enough description of the two for pedagogical purposes.)

In both cases, the student is encouraged to manipulate the model, to draw on it to make predictions, to understand that it is tentative, to expand, elaborate or modify it, and, finally, to abstract from reality his or her *own* model that will help organize data about change.

Complexity and Challenge

At this point, we should comment on the apparent simplicity of the models. It is appropriate to be critical about the elements of both models; indeed, we have indicated that this will be one of the primary activities of the students in the course. But others may react negatively to the simplicity of the models. Let's look at this "simplicity," in terms of the second or "change" model, for example. When we do, we discover that it is not as simple as it looks.

After our first analysis yielded the seven change factors, we posited that they were related in a system. (At this stage, however, we had a simple heuristic model. Its function is to aid observation and to structure the analysis of change. Indeed, a strict interpretation of our model, by systems analysts or cyberneticists, would perhaps call it an assemblage, since, as shown below, it does not specify the relationships among the seven change factors, or variables.)

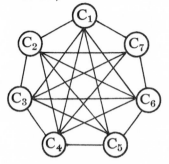

C_1 Demographic Change
C_2 Technological Innovation
C_3 Social Innovation
C_9 Culture-Value Shift
C_5 Ecological Change
C_6 Information-Idea Shift
C_7 Cultural Diffusion

However, as the inquiry in each school year progresses, the student will be led to develop relationships by hypothesis and inquiry. Thus students may wish to explore the ways in which each change factor affects the others. (How, for example, does a particular Social Innovation lead to or arise from Cultural-Value Shifts? How does an Ecological or Demographic change affect Technological Innovation?) Beyond this, it is clear that each change factor triggers or retards further change of the same type. (A Technological Innovation may accelerate other Technological Innovations, as for example was the case with the computer.) Each such hypothesis will add to the complexity of the model. The initial specification of such a general system or "simplified" model is, in our opinion, the best and *the most honest* way of guiding inquiry without suffocating it.

If the system (assemblage) above is expanded to include specific hypotheses about the relationship of each factor to itself and to the others, the ability of the model to explain social reality increases, but so does the uncertainty, variety, and complexity— eventually reaching a level that is difficult for the high-school student to sustain. While we can see that the system is simple, we also see that students and/or teachers can very quickly produce all the sophistication and complexity they can handle.

While any curriculum for the future must have a coherent

model that ties it together, it also needs specific content. Specifying a general model leaves the student somewhat free to search out his own content, but we should give him possibilities. As we have indicated, our basic commitment is to a study of cultural systems that is both comparative and concentric.

With the help of the teacher and other students, the individual student is encouraged to examine comparative cultural systems— whole cultures remote in time and space. The student also examines concentric cultural systems—i.e., entities smaller than whole cultures, but which exhibit characteristics of cultural systems (corporations, service clubs, schools, subcultures)—noting the differences between these and whole cultures. By manipulating the two models, the student learns how to ask critical questions, whether analyzing change in foreign or historical cultures or attempting to understand our own.

Continuity and Change in Cultures: Grade Ten

Content for the three courses was selected with some consideration for the difficulty of achieving institutional change within the schools. The course descriptions that follow fit within the traditional content requirements already established in most states, but significant changes in range and domain have been made, and, because they are unified by the themes of continuity and change, conflict and consensus, and structured by our synchronic and diachronic models, they possess a fundamental unity that is lacking in most secondary curricula.

At the tenth grade, the program develops the general cultural-systems approach. In the first module, the student uses the continuity model (synchronic) to analyze data produced by the culture itself: myths, jokes, artifacts, buildings, marriage rites, ruling bodies. A view of the culture is inferred from the data and structured in the context of the model. The student also looks (in terms of the model) at groups that are close to him or her: classroom, family, community. For example, if the class decides to focus on the local community, the students might collect artifacts, advertisements, news, taped conversations, songs, political posters, movie bills, business or personal correspondence and other data from which the class may infer the values and ideas of the community. The students are given some data, in other words, and encouraged to go outside the classroom to obtain more and to flesh out a picture of the things, people, places and organizations in the cultural unit under study.

In the second module, the study proceeds to an examination of three specific cultures at various levels of development: a hunting and gathering culture, an agricultural culture, and an industrial culture. As the students move, for example, from the Yanomamo tribe in Brazil to contemporary Japan, they identify the elements of the continuity model in each culture, and the change forces— i.e., the change model—working on it. They are then encouraged to expand, modify, challenge and criticize the models, to manipulate the model elements, to hypothesize relationships, or to create alternative models.

The final module or sequence in Grade Ten consists of a series of case studies in cultural change. These studies are structured by Model 2—the change model; that is, they are specific case studies of some general causal relationships specified in the model. They are intended to show how the change factors impact on a culture and move it along. Thus, for example, once the Yanomamo culture has been described in terms of Model 1, students study the ways in which the change factors in Model 2 (e.g., technology or ecology) alter Yanomamo life.

Conflict and Change in America: Grade Eleven

The eleventh-grade program is a series of case studies that parallel the general periods and topics of traditional American history courses; we have no quarrel with the historians, and in general, their epochs do represent significant periods of change. But we do not believe in history-for-history's-sake. Thus, our content, our case studies, must meet an additional test: All of them must be chosen for their relationship to, and impact on, our present and our future. This is determined by our change model. Thus "The Westward Movement" becomes an example of the demographic change factor—one of the seven change factors—at work. This causes a dramatic shift in the narrative and sets criteria for the data that are included. The period known as "The New Deal" gets a new deal as it is developed through two case studies: one on value change and one on social innovation. While a specific change factor provides the focus for each case study, the other factors in the model are examined as areas of resultant change; and the cultural-systems model is used to assure comprehensive coverage and to structure further student inquiry. In short, American history is taught, not as a chronological account, but as a series of dramatic illustrations of how the seven change factors cause movement, unrest and cultural development. America's past, in this sense, becomes an example of larger, more universal processes that continuously create the future.

Coping with the Future: Grade Twelve

Since our basic intent, extrapolated from a concern for the future, was the design of a curriculum that would "help the maturing individual adapt to change," we were led naturally to the inclusion in the twelfth grade of a specific course *about the future*. It is important to note that we did not begin with this commitment—our curriculum was not motivated by the interests of a new "academic guild": the futurists. It was motivated by the fundamental concerns stated so eloquently by the students at the beginning of this paper. It quickly became evident that the social studies have been dealing with truncated time: They hit hard on the traditions of the past, give a glancing blow at the problems of the present, and then retire from the ring.

The twelfth-grade course has three basic modules: Possible Futures, Probable Futures, and Preferable Futures. Since these are not among the conventional categories of social science, the description of the twelfth-grade course requires a bit of elaboration.

Possible Futures are those futures that could happen but are not necessarily likely. More futures are possible than most of us imagine, and the module deals not merely with specific future possibilities, but, more important, with *how to imagine*, since imagination is a prerequisite for the exploration of possible futures. Games and other exercises are designed specifically to elicit imaginative responses in the context of the future.

The basic approach to content is through the device of the

scenario. And we caution the student against looking on these futures presented, or any futures, as wholly impossible, because of the implications of Clarke's Law as stated in *Profiles of the Future*:[16]

> When a distinguished but elderly scientist states that something is possible, he is almost certainly right. When he states something is impossible, he is very probably wrong.

Probable Futures are those that are currently seen as having some reasonable probability of occurring. This probability is established by the study of responsible futurists, sociologists, demographers, and other social scientists and observers. It is supported by looking carefully at the conflicts already under way in our present society and extrapolating from some of these trends and controversies, although not necessarily in a linear fashion.

Here the course deals with quite specific forecasts about politics, technology, ecology, family life, education, urban futures, and the like, drawing attention to the values implicit in the forecasts and to the methods or models used by the forecasters. Images of a future America (and of the planet) emerge for dissection by the students. Put another way, this module asks: What are significant people saying about the future? How did they arrive at their opinions? Are their methods good and their opinions soundly based—or aren't they?

Finally, the student is introduced to the idea that he or she is continually making largely unconscious forecasts about his or her own future. The same questions emerge: How does one arrive at sound opinions about one's own probable futures?

Preferable Futures are those that the students feel are desirable, to which they attach some positive value. The value aspect of the future *is not* delayed until this last module, but permeates all three phases of the course. But the methods by which value choices are facilitated are emphasized here. Methods used by experts as well as value-clarification strategies that may be employed in deciding courses of personal action are included. Action strategies that the student may employ in influencing a desired direction of change will also be emphasized in this module.

Here again, however, there is a conscious interplay of the

personal and the public. How we define our values personally is linked to how a democratic system deals with diverse values— i.e., diverse sets of preferable futures. What are the political mechanisms of choice? How adequate are they? Here, in the final section of the sequence, two powerful educational themes converge. The future is indissolubly linked to the values that underlie social and personal choice.

This is a most appropriate ending/beginning, particularly if citizenship is an ultimate objective of social study. Many high-school seniors are voting citizens, and for many of them this will be their last opportunity to *study* decision-making processes in a systematic way.

The future as content has compelling reasons for inclusion in the school curriculum. Some of these have been alluded to earlier, but we can expand on them now.

Equality is a major value commitment of the American system, but our present educational system is built on hierarchical assumptions—teachers teach and students learn. The leaders of education and of society in general comment on these inconsistencies at great length in formal gatherings where speeches are made and proposals are put forth about ways in which the students can be more involved in their own learning—ways in which they can achieve some equality with the teachers in selecting content. Many teachers, however, find it almost impossible to follow through on these injunctions as they see themselves teaching subject matter about which they (usually) possess more knowledge than the students.

When courses are focused on the past, the teacher usually does have more interest, knowledge, and certainly more experience (in terms of a life span in the immediate past) than the student. In the case of the present, the teacher is again, as a voting citizen, more involved with current social reality. The one area in which teachers and students should be able to meet with common purpose is the future. Both will live there in some equality as citizens; both will have interests as citizens; and both can take action; both have the same "*knowledge*" about the future.

The study of the future gives the student additional advantages, however. Because the student has a longer life expectancy, his or her real (though perhaps unrecognized) interest extends further in time. Because they are younger, students also have more options: a wider range of choices and decisions that they can exercise in the future. A course in the future, then, enables students and teachers to work together naturally with more equality and more cooperation.

There are other pedagogical gains: Because there is no content to memorize, students must create, must analyze, must value. In short, they must engage in those social processes that are all too often neglected in our current social-studies programs.

Because the future lacks "content," in the traditional social-studies sense of that word, it must be generated: The student must conjecture on future change and he must consult the conjectures of others. McLuhan's famous phrase "the medium is the message" becomes "the method is the message." In a program on the future we are led to judge the quality of a student's participation, not on his *memory*, there is nothing to *remember*; not on his knowledge, there is nothing to "*know*"; instead we must respect and encourage his *imagination and quality of thought*: the methods and procedures by which he generates content for study and the rules of evidence by which he analyzes that generated content.

A course about the future also shifts the emphasis from the objective of "education for change" to the objective of "education about change." The difficulty of the former objective is that it is focused on the present, or, at most, on the immediate past or immediate future, and that it often specifies the preferred direction of change. Consequently, it is often structured around concerns or problems that are short-lived, that will disappear soon, are currently misunderstood, or are politicized to such an extent that free inquiry is inhibited.

A focus on the future, the long future, forces the emphasis from "education for change," with its concern for immediate relevance, to an emphasis on "education about change," the study of the general nature of change and broad categories of change which will persist over a long time span. It allows the student to specify the change with which he is concerned, state his preferences for the direction of that change, and determine courses of action to influence that direction.

When we focus on methods of anticipating and dealing with

change, we free ourselves from narrow reliance on the individual social-science disciplines. The methods we use are removed from any implication, as they have in the case of the study of the past, that they are "the way a historian works" or, in the case of the study of the present, that they are the "way a sociologist works." Instead, there is a realization that everyone who has to cope with, or work for, change may have methods that are relevant to our study. The methods are not even limited to the rubric "the scientific method."

For example, the use of *scenarios* is obviously drawn from the literary method, while *Delphi** is drawn from the assumptions underlying polling procedures and the jury system. *Any* technique which has been useful to people who create solutions to problems is germane: methods as diverse as proof, prediction, and problem-solving. When we speak of method, then, we are not talking about "the method of social scientists" or "the methods of the futurists" but about the methods of all people who are concerned with change.

In fact, we encourage the student to make creative application of the methods of other disciplines or areas of human endeavor through analogy: How can I use the rules of evidence of the lawyer in this course? How can I utilize the flow-charting techniques of the businessman in analyzing this social process? What can I learn from the weather forecaster that will help me anticipate social problems?

Here we find a large area for study that has scarcely been touched by the traditional social studies: game theory, decision-making under conditions of uncertainty, value analysis, content analysis, cybernetics, and many others. All of these may sound frightening to the social-studies teacher, but, if appropriately presented, they will sometimes, as in the case of our models, seem too simple.

There is, moreover, no denying the importance of including these methods in our social-studies curriculum. Much of the

---

* A scenario is a hypothetical sequence of events, an imaginative history of the future. The Delphi technique gathers the opinions of experts through an intermediary, shares these opinions anonymously, refines them in successive rounds of questioning, and results in a group consensus.

decision-making that will affect our lives in the future is already drawing heavily on the above techniques. It is important for the students to understand the decision processes used by individuals, groups and institutions that will most affect his life.

Components and Control: A Modular Curriculum

It should be emphasized at this time, however, that this curriculum is set up by modules so that there is no need to cover the program in the order of any of the individual components. Many alternative paths are provided by the *Teachers Resource and Process Book* so that, for example, students might *begin* the twelfth-grade course with the module on Preferable Futures or do the eleventh-grade American History sequence backward, working from the present (or indeed the future) backward in time.*

A program that is designed to help the student to adapt to the future should itself be able to adapt; it must reflect this in form as well as function. A curriculum which is intended to educate about change should be pre-adapted for change itself.

In this respect, we planned for a core curriculum which is a system of student books, each independent of the others, although articulated with the others, through the use of the *Teachers Resource and Process Book*, and each capable of quick revision. The components of the system (they are intended to be reinforced with other outside text materials, reference works and media as discussed earlier) are for each year, a DATA BOOK, a READINGS BOOK, a CORE TEXT, and a TEACHERS RESOURCE AND PROCESS BOOK.

The DATA BOOKS are characterized by material that is produced by the culture under study or by a direct observer of that culture

* Since the completion of this paper, the entire three-year sequence has been still further modularized to take account of the more flexible scheduling now available in many schools. The curriculum is divided into some twenty free-standing modules, each of which can be studied independently in any order, and each of which incorporates, or is premised on, the cultural-systems approach and the two models described above. Teachers' guides, Readings, and inquiry Data are provided for, and integrated with, each independent module. The result is a completely modular, yet completely consistent and self-reinforcing, curriculum for use over periods varying from a few weeks to a full three years.

—what the historian calls primary data or the anthropologist terms field observations. The authors of the program will select, not interpret, the data. The learning mode is primarily inference of idea and value and identification of cultural elements by inductive inquiry. For example, from the lyrics of a hymn, a map of a slave plantation, and a theatrical poster of the period, students might be asked to infer the hidden values of the culture with respect to love, God or money, and to see if the implied values contradict or reinforce one another. In short, fragments of revealing data are displayed for imaginative analysis.

The READINGS BOOKS contain material by expert observers, social scientists, or theorists, about the culture under study. The characteristic feature of these books is that the thesis or argument of the expert is presented with minimal interference by the program authors. The readings can be used by students in confirming, rejecting, or modifying their own hypotheses, inferences, observations. The basic learning mode here is deductive inquiry.

The CORE TEXTS will survey or cover in depth selected cultural systems in terms of the synchronic and/or diachronic models, described above. It is here that the interpretations of the program authors may be directly stated, although the emphasis will, wherever possible, be on the students' learning through inquiry with data.

In the TEACHERS RESOURCE AND PROCESS BOOK we tried to set forth specific strategies for the teacher, with an emphasis on the total classroom experience: content, method, format, teacher behavior and learning situations are part of a coherent and consistent whole. For example, assignments in the text are to be made by purposes and not by pages. When a teacher says "Read pages eighty through eighty-four," the student understands "I'm to cover five pages." However, when he is told to "Read Chapter Four and analyze the scenarios there for their implications: What changes took place and how did they come about? What is the chain of events that caused the destruction of the oceans and what could this mean to our community?" he is given a sense of purpose. The basic intent of the TEACHERS RESOURCE AND PROCESS BOOK is to double the learning space available to the program. Where other teacher's guides are often only a debriefing manual for the text,

our TEACHERS RESOURCE AND PROCESS BOOK develops student activities that are parallel to or independent of the student texts.

Learning is provoked rather than spontaneous. Situations that
are conducive to learning must be created, even contrived, to
allow students to engage in interesting and meaningful interactions
that provide personal growth, interpersonal sensitivity, skill in
group interaction and problem-solving, understanding of society
and culture, and the ability to understand and cope with change.
These learning situations must possess a certain amount of pressure. For it is usually under some pressure that we make key
choices and decisions. The situations must give the students a
feeling for as well as the *facts about* social reality.

The TEACHERS RESOURCE AND PROCESS BOOKS are filled with
suggested games, simulations, "classroom theater" exercises and
other enlivening activities. Indeed, it was our conception from the
start that the printed materials were not to be seen as end-products,
but as the bases for the creation of a sequence of experiences in
and out of the classroom. In this sense, they are guides rather
than scripts. Most of the activities suggested in the TEACHERS
RESOURCE AND PROCESS BOOKS are too complex to summarize here,
but many of them involve a search for relevant materials in the
community, field exercises, and role-playing, as well as more
analytical exercises. Here, for example, are a few drawn from the
twelfth grade.

ACTIVITY: The students are asked to prepare a time line for the
period for which they want to project possible futures.
This is an open exercise, but we might expect the
student to speculate on key events in his or her own
personal future: birth, marriage, retirement, death; and,
alternately, life spans of significant others: parents,
marriage partners, children, grandchildren.

The purpose of this warm-up is to emphasize to the
students that the future will be of direct personal concern to them and to those close to them.

The time lines that are developed by the students should
be kept for later use because of the *assumptions* that

students will make about the future which they might want to modify later.

ACTIVITY: Short excerpts from science fiction are introduced to elucidate aspects of the model, i.e., a selection from *Nineteen Eighty-Four*, "The Principles of Newspeak," is used to illustrate the symbol system. A section from *Farenheit 451* by Ray Bradbury or "Harrison Bergeron" in *Welcome to the Monkey House* by Kurt Vonnegut to illustrate the perversion of *equality* as a *value*.

ACTIVITY: Students are given alternate methods of preparing scenarios, including some that are not commonly used, such as a visual scenario. The text might include an imaginative work of art as a stimulus, a Dali or Tooker or Hicks painting, and the students would be asked to produce their own visual scenario. The entire class might participate in producing a room mural at each stage of the year: one for possible futures, probable futures, preferable futures.

ACTIVITY: Students are asked to evaluate a series of statements in terms of whether they regard them as possible futures, probable futures, preferable futures; they are asked to indicate basis for their judgments:

1. There is life on other planets. . . .
2. All men are treated as absolute equals. . . .
3. Man becomes immortal. . . .
4. All national boundaries are eliminated. . . .
5. You can read everyone's mind. . . .

After indicating their reactions they could be asked if they wanted to complete the scenarios.

ACTIVITY: An activity to reinforce the discussion in the text regarding the difficulties faced by change agents.

1. Teacher presents several examples of resistance to change. These are taken from *Diffusion of Innovations* by Everett M. Rogers and *The Evolution of Civilizations* by Carroll Quigley.

2. Teacher presents a brief and convincing rationale for the abolition of the school's grading system.
3. Students organize and pursue a study of the task of abolishing the system. Obtain data through interviews of teachers, students, principal, parents, board members, school counselors.

Ralph Nader in his book *Action for a Change: A Student Manual for Public Interest Organizing*[17] points up two of the difficulties our society faces:

1. The country [our schools] has more problems than it should tolerate and more solutions than it uses.
2. We have too much outrage and not enough action.

What is needed today are ways of getting the solutions we have to their respective problems, before we cry for *more* solutions. Just as there are demands for new laws with existing laws unenforced, medical technology second to none with vast inequity in distribution of medical care, mass-transit technology that cannot be set on a track, so do innovative solutions in curriculum face tremendous difficulties in reaching their respective problems. Will the schools respond to the courage shown by the curriculum designers in adding a new time dimension to the curriculum? Will they respond to the courage shown by excluding traditional content in order to concentrate on key concepts? Will they respond to those who gave due consideration to the state requirements that exist while refusing to be hamstrung by their specifications? It is important that teachers and administrators examine their assumptions when they evaluate curriculum materials.

For a number of years *The Bulletin of Atomic Scientists* showed a clock face on the cover with the time running out to symbolize the danger of atomic energy to mankind. As this image occurred to me, I thought of another clock, one that symbolizes for me the *lack of energy* in our educational institutions because of unexamined assumptions: It was a classroom in Buffalo, New York, and on the wall was a very large clock; under the clock was a sign reading "STOP WATCHING THE CLOCK, TIME WILL PASS, WILL YOU?"

The assumptions implicit in this sign are

1. Time in classrooms passes very slowly.
2. The purpose of education is to receive a passing grade.

Unfortunately, these assumptions are too often true; and time is running out for our educational institutions unless they can examine the hidden assumptions that keep them from reaching out and *responding* to the concerns of young people, such as those expressed at the beginning of this paper and particularly their last objective which says it all:

> Mature individuals must help maturing individuals change immature institutions.

Humanists speak of educating for the "whole" person. But how whole is any person torn out of his or her social context and— worse yet—stripped of tomorrow? This is the question that Professor Buchen raises in an essay that relates the world-wide debate over the limits of economic growth to the question of the limits of individualism. He probes the root assumptions of humanism and suggests a new direction.

CHAPTER SEVEN

Humanism and Futurism: Enemies or Allies?

by Irving H. Buchen

> Human life is reduced to real suffering, to hell, only when two ages, two cultures and religions overlap. A man of the Classical Age who had to live in medieval times would suffocate miserably just as a savage does in the midst of civilization. Now there are times when a whole generation is caught in this way between two ages, two modes of life, with the consequence it loses all power to understand itself and has no standard, no security, no simple acquiescence.
> —*Hermann Hesse,* Steppenwolf

> There is a miracle in every new beginning.
> —*Hermann Hesse,* Steppenwolf

One of the most cherished ideals of the humanistic tradition is the notion of the whole man. And yet the moment one asks the perfectly basic and big question, "What constitutes our wholeness as human beings?" it is more often than not greeted with either a tolerance that is patronizing or an impatience that is inhibiting. "Our wholeness as human beings? Yes, well, it all depends whether the context is religious, philosophical, political, economic, cultural, psychological, etc. Define your terms." Thus, in rapid fashion, the big question is splintered and sorted out into various cages in which different expert trainers put the now-tamed question through flaming hoops with astounding and enviable dexterity. Result: the humanities train generalists who are really professional fragments or specialists who are all broken off in the same place.

Even humanities programs that officially seek interdisciplinary convergences contain distortions, although perhaps of a higher order. Many exclude the physical sciences or bewail the dehumanization of man by technology. Frequently, those who cry the loudest against the evils of technocracy consult concordances put together by computers, cite articles reproduced by Xerox, allude to manuscripts and out-of-print books made available on microfilm, and play back Hopi burial chants on audio cassettes. Even more serious, their pejorative attitude toward technology often jeopardizes communication with their students who already are quite comfortable with computers and teaching machines, and are aware that the human element, namely themselves, has not been mechanized.

Finally, even the best of humanities programs generally exist apart from any contact or relationship with programs in business, education, science and engineering, etc. As a result, liberal-arts and business students, for example, confront each other like two armed camps, and stake out a gulf that embodies the widest generational or cross-cultural gap imaginable. Such mutual and unnecessary opacity is not limited to education, but appears in almost every single collision between environmentalists and businessmen. Indeed, it might not be far-fetched to claim that the intransigence between such groups is due less to the inherent extremism of each position (a decent environment versus a reasonable profit) than to the mutual self-defensive excesses each has forced upon the other (the purest of environments and the maximizing of profits) in the absence of any holistic frame that might move them toward an accommodating center.

I am not calling for a cessation to honest disagreement or legitimate differences, but I am maintaining that insofar as the humanities cut themselves off from an intercollege position, they directly and indirectly create the basis for a wasteful rather than an interactive confrontation of differences. Moreover, as a result, the humanistic tradition ironically has set up its students for the dreadful prospects of impotence on the one hand or fascism on the other, which are not so much alternatives as versions of each other.

How did this process of fragmentation occur? At what point and for what reasons did the great tradition of the whole man become parceled out? More important, what solutions are available to us in the future?

Over-Individualization

The twentieth century can be summed up quickly as the century that exceeded itself, that went to the moon before it was either comfortable or dispossessed from earth, that left the past further and faster behind than any previous age or perhaps all centuries combined, and above all that leaped into the twenty-first century without having the courtesy to allow the present one to come to its natural chronological end. Indeed, the overreaching appears to have reached such dislocating proportions that there is often a frantic search for mythic metaphors to comprehend the phenomena of changing change and exponential transcendence. Those who find humanistic prospects imperiled have revived Mary Shelley's *Frankenstein*. Others, more hopeful, base their metaphors on the oracle at Delphi, Prometheus, Faust, Consciousness III, or Jesus Christ, Superstar. But whether the future is seen as dark or rosy, we face the possibility of total generational discontinuity. It is one thing to bring forth a wave of the future, but quite another for that wave to break before one's own has crested. One raises children, but they are not supposed to raze parents; one expects human variations—not aliens from another planet.

The standard scapegoats trotted out by the humanists to explain such presumption are materialism and technology. Yet the condemnation of materialism is usually a refuge for those already comfortable. What would we have the Appalachian poor do? Retreat to Walden Pond to lead lives of noisy desperation? Contemplation and love will not fill empty stomachs; besides, the highest form of charity is to make recipients independent of such handouts. And so far as technology is concerned, nearly all the major problems of man antedated the industrial revolution, are still with us and are still not solvable through technology. The issues of war, racial relations, social justice, abortions, divorce, etc., cannot be blamed on the outer-space program. As Buckminster Fuller often has noted: If one dumps all the technology into the ocean, millions will starve; but if one dumps all the politicians into the ocean, no one will starve.

The major achievements of the modern world are not materialism or technology, but the supreme emergence of the individual and the rout of those classic reactionaries who insist that the "democratic dregs" or common man, given equal opportunity, would reduce or tarnish the quality of society, culture and civilization. But if individualism has triumphed, where are our men of genius? Individualism theoretically raises up saviors and superstars. We have had many of them in the past. Yet today, something is different. They are here and they are not. A Ralph Nader appears, but he is now a we—Nader's Raiders. A class-action suit on behalf of the schoolchildren of California is brought not by some lonely, starry-eyed or muckraking lawyer, but by a collectivity, a team of experts from many fields from all over the country. Why do we automatically despair when we discover that "It is just too much for any one man to do!" Perhaps it is a good thing— that so many of the tasks facing us exceed any individual's capacity. Perhaps the superstar system is not the only, or even the best, way to make something happen and to have it endure. Perhaps the persistent search for saviors has tyrannically tied us to an equally tenacious search for scapegoats. In short, a special and sometimes destructive psychology has accompanied the emergence of individuality in Western civilization through the reinforcing notion of a search for individual identity.

One basic reason why the humanities did not honor the past legacy of educating the whole man is that they turned, instead, to educating the individual; and the concept of individuality and that of the whole man are not synonymous. The individual man is stirred by independence, autonomy and self-reliance; the holistic man by interdependence, collectivism and reliance. And if one views the history of the presumptuous twentieth century as essentially the history of individuality, then what perhaps becomes clear is that individuality is the great overreacher, the lovely presumption. Indeed, we may have reached a point in history when individuality, traditionally conceived, may have gone as far as it can go. What we need today is not merely traditional means for multiplying or extending individuality, but also nontraditional ways for surrendering part of it.

For the humanist the idea of "surrendering" even a fraction of one's individuality will no doubt seem like heresy. Perhaps this alarm can be reduced, however, if we dispose immediately of a misconception.

There may be a direct correlation between our present contemplation of the limits to industrial and economic growth and our contemplation of the limits of individuality. But just as the concept that growth has limits need not necessarily signify the end of growth, so, too, the notion that individuality may have limits need not signify the end of individuality. Understanding the limits of any system is the first step toward expanding or transcending those limits. In short, the real conflict we face now is a conflict not between the old and the new, but between the new and the futuristic, between what is known and what is emerging, between the individual and the new, emerging image of what might be termed the collectivized individual. The whole person is not and cannot be totally individual; part of the whole—today more than ever— must be nonindividualized, communal, or "collectivized." For we all live in a social environment with others. And that social environment, explosive with change, by continually impinging on us, becomes part of us.

The new focus of the humanities should be the collectivized individual as the futuristic image of the whole man. But what exactly is a "collectivized individual" and how does one go about employing humanistic studies to educate this hybrid man and woman of the future?

The Collectivized Individual

A collectivized individual is multiple rather than singular. If the traditional notion in the West has been one God, one love, one job, one identity, one country and one planet, the futuristic notion is many gods, many loves, many jobs, many identities, many countries and many planets. The collectivized individual may unexpectedly prove more responsive to and cooperative with overt and official planning of aspects of his life, partly because he will be better able to comprehend the communal imperatives for such overall planning, partly because he will be a participant in that planning, rather than a passive object of it, and partly because he will, in effect, be compensated by enjoying the greater personal freedoms granted by his multiplicity. He will be capable of sustaining many allegiances, without contradiction, on both a national and international scale, and be closer to being, especially through the concept of global perspectives, a world citizen. Work will neither tyrannically absorb nor determine his life; indeed, because no one component will ever dominate his reality frame, he will often be proficient, although perhaps not outstanding, in a remarkable number of areas. He will learn to make peace with incompletion. And, of course, he will recognize that he is not just a "he" but also a "she"—that wholeness includes not the elimination of sexual differences, but a recognition that the planet was not put here for the exclusive advantage of one sex.

But it is one thing to describe what the collectivized individual might or should be like and quite another matter to determine how he can be encouraged to develop his complex potential. We need to observe the educational process and to identify within it those built-in obstacles to educating collectivized individuals. (Throughout, I will discuss education at its best, so that any failures are fundamental to the process rather than our inability to realize it fully.)

It is not accidental that we speak of a "hunger" for knowledge, of cultivating a "taste" for art; and that many sociologists and psychologists use terms like impoverished environmental "diets" or "undernourished" social conditions to describe the plight of the educationally and culturally disadvantaged. A subject comprehends an object by claiming, encircling and ingesting it. Internalization—the term itself is revealing—takes the form of the now-grasped object being converted into an absorbable form of nourishment within the now-expanded and satisfied subject. Feeding and knowing are both ways of growing.

The ingestion of information is reflected psychologically in ego-building or identity-granting additions. Thus, we know; and we know that we know. The knowing of what we know constitutes both the identity of knowledge and the knowledge of identity. This dual process exists and should continue. Nevertheless, because it buttresses the individual self as a separate and perhaps even separatist activity, and because such a self sustains itself often in competition and as an ego-island, there is a serious question as to whether such an educational process is not inherently inimical to the goals of collective cooperation and to the possibilities of change. I am not suggesting that ego-identity as a basic building block of self-esteem be scrapped, any more than individuality as a basic strand be eliminated. What I would suggest is that a series of supplemental and extending processes be introduced to enlarge and extend the ego-centricity.

Extending the Ego

The first has to do with the rejection of the notion of the singular self, because that is ultimately as much an impoverishment of human potential as the complete denial of self. The truth is we are many selves. Singular selfhood is the egotistical attempt of a part of the whole to be self-sufficient and to subordinate other parts to its own desires and purposes. Culturally, it is reflected in the lie of the melting pot; internationally, in the self-sufficiency of isolationism; economically, in the unilateralism of being solely a consumer. Among the affluent, the self stands at the center and demands to have its individual needs satisfied. But surfeit soon comes, and, with it, the characteristic attitudes of boredom, loss of hunger or jaded appetite that preclude education and change. Far from supporting such further impoverishment or aggrandizement of the self, the educational process should instead focus on the image of multiple selves which simultaneously can serve as a maximum invitation to the underdeveloped self and as a strong antidote to the overdeveloped self.

Similarly, the temporal extension of self becomes important. As Benjamin Singer notes in the second chapter, the projected self or future-focused role image is a critical part of the present self, and the educational process that ignores it does so at its own risk. If we are many selves, we are also likely to become many future selves, and a humanist education will recognize and serve that inevitability.

Simultaneously, it will help call attention to those purposes that are not achievable by the individual alone. Educationally, this involves the interdependent rather than the independent learning model in which cooperation is structured to be as productive of results as competition and which involves the extensive use of games, simulations, and role-playing techniques that instruct through transactional means, i.e., through negotiation. The futurist emphasis on these forms of learning is truly a liberating one.

Futurist education also emphasizes the creative process, the mutual conversion of objects and subjects. From the creative point of view, the subject-object relationship is not a static but a transferable relationship. In other words, an object under investigation has, so to speak, the capacity to become a communicating subject or, to use the larger more meaningful term, an "alive" environment in its own right. The traditional analytical process is unilateral, one-directional and monolingual; the subject comprehends the object, tree. The creative process is mutual, two-directional and bilingual; the object, tree, communicates its own meaning even in its own language. The tree need not be regarded solely as a passive object with no identity other than that given to it by a comprehending subject. Rather, a tree ultimately has as much to say about human systems as it does about systems of tree-ness or ecology. In analytical thinking, the stress is on the discipline of control.

In creative thinking, the stress is on the discipline of surrender. Subjects and objects are thus interchangeable at crucial points of mutual understandings. André Gide rightly observed: "One imagines one possesses and in reality one is possessed. . . ." By striking a balance between possessing and being possessed, between subject and environment, the individual ego, i.e., the subject, can learn to "listen" to the object. The more we are capable of so doing, the more we may learn to listen to people from different cultures and, ultimately, perhaps, to those creatures from other planets who may some day confront us.

By extending the ego-building process in these lateral, interactive directions, it may be possible to overcome or minimize the obstacles to cooperative and collective ends within the traditional educational process. Subjects who can become objects, in turn establish the dynamic interplay of the collectivized individual and the multiplistic unity of the world citizen.

But even the best of educational processes needs direction and shape—needs a sense of what we are becoming and why. That perspective can revivify the humanities, and it can be found in the emerging field of futurism itself.

Futurism as Ally

Let me begin here by indicating what futurism is not, and disowning what has been put upon it. Futurism is neither super-gadgetry nor salvationist ideology. It does not traffic in hysterics or lullabies. It does not seek to change human nature in manipulative fashion, but rather to encourage awareness of the rich changes inherent in its own multiplicity. Above all, futurism does not now, and never will, possess an assured or fixed body of content that exists apart from what it seeks to comprehend. Indeed, in the final analysis, what recommends futurism is its inclusiveness, its capacity to generate synthesizing and unifying ways of looking at man, mind and matter.

Futurism dovetails with the concept of the collectivized individual because it provides a synthesizing framework that does not violate, but rather interrelates, the separate disciplines. It provides them with a collectivized framework within which to nest their individuality.

And it is for this very reason that I believe futurism, in partnership with humanism, could stir a second renaissance.

A study of the next thirty years may appear puny in comparison with the humanist's traditional study of the last five thousand. Yet it is quite possible that change in the next three decades may equal in magnitude the change from an agrarian to an industrial society. Then, too, futurism is by no means at odds with the past. First, the past no longer is and the future is yet to be—and the imaginative bond necessary to sustain one carries over to the other. Second, in some respect the future may already have happened in the past. No one can read or write today's pessimistic science fiction without noting it is based on a solid understanding of primitive societies. Similarly, many of the proposed new international symbols gradually being introduced all over the world as a global sign language have their roots in the mythic imaginations of the ancients. And no futurist can ignore the past when he confronts the "leap-frog" concept that sees developing countries like Bolivia, in which 50 per cent of the people are regularly unemployed, conceivably spurting ahead of the economically advanced countries to become leisure societies sustained by guaranteed incomes.

Futurism also provides an excellent academic opportunity to test a student's true knowledge of what he has learned, for example, of the principles of sociology or economics, by asking him or her to design a new social institution or some new aspect of an economic system. Both history and futurism can be honored by reconvening the first Constitutional Assembly and drafting anew a portion of the Constitution. Or the entire enterprise can be projected on an international scale by creating a "Global Planning Council" manned by students representing different countries and ideologies and negotiating agreements on outer space, fishing rights, etc; and that can be done before, during and even after such negotiations are completed in real life.

Futurism also offers the prospect of comprehensive research projects and curricula developments in all fields, for there is no subject in the humanities that does not have a futuristic dimension. For example, there is the lovely contradiction of doing research on a comprehensive history of attitudes toward futurism. Equally important, we are not the only age to experience cultural dislocation. How various cultures faced "Copernicus Shock," collapsing and then renewing themselves, is an area of legitimate interest for both specialist and generalist.

The need to examine resistances to change, the capacity for creative or nonlinear thinking, the development of a new psychology of multiplicity for the collectivized individual, are all potential benefits of looking ahead. Finally, we are oversaturated with war studies and not enough with peace studies, such as the thorough and rigorous programs already developed by the World Law Fund; and we are foolishly wasting our energies debating whether aggression is inborn or acquired when what we need are studies and courses on the conversion of aggression into creativity as models for both the individual and the society.

All the above examples—and there are many more—designate futurism in its supportive role, as an extender of traditional disciplines. But futurism can also serve as a comprehender in its own right and subsume a variety of existing disciplines. Imagine the design of new societies to be planted on Mars or Venus. And imagine the humanistic concerns involved in such an exercise. What values should be dominant? What might its conceptions of justice, beauty or time be? To be sure, initial designs might reveal the extent to which we are slaves of the past and obediently duplicate existing arrangements. But even if so, how often is that limitation exposed? Moreover, releasing that bias often opens the way for more imaginative possibilities.

In turn, imaginative excesses or wild fantasies are correctable through two indispensable futuristic controls. Futurists search for consequences, examining decisions for their unsuspected impacts. Such foresightedness, then, points to the real possibility that many of the major decisions in the future will be decisions *not* to do something. A second control lies in the necessity to engage in goal- and value-generating processes by those who have to live that futuristic design. In a democratic society, such communication is not just a crucial prelude to implementation, but is, in fact, a form of implementation itself.

Futurism is not an enemy of the past or of the tradition of solid and rigorous scholarship, but on the contrary an ally; it seeks not to supplant, but to extend, existing disciplines; and it offers precisely the kind of comprehensive and comprehending perspective that will enable faculty in the humanities to gracefully extricate themselves from excessively compartmentalized, isolationist structures.

Three accusations generally are directed against futurists. The first is that the entire enterprise is a fad, the latest form of swinging fun and games. That is a not-very-subtle assault on academic credibility. I can respond to this only on a very personal basis by saying there is no real way to defend yourself against snide and thoughtless criticism. But if you are a genuine futurist, the charge will not bother you or your students because you both will be engaged in one of the most difficult and comprehensive learning experiences of your entire lives, and you will never have read and thought so much in so many fields.

The second canard is favored by the professionally bored, in and out of the news media; it holds that futurists are elitists. This total misconception—almost, one might say, willful misconception —can be met frontally if the futurist builds into his model or design a participatory process for generating goals and values. Such correctives, however, will fail to satisfy the cynics, and they will assemble as their third line of attack a long list of previous predictions that have turned out to be false. Here, you can retaliate, for such a view completely misunderstands or distorts futurism.

Futurists are not prophets; they do not "predict" what will happen. They employ devices, ranging from extremely simple to highly sophisticated, to detect trends. However, their output is not a "final" projection but an array of possibilities—a multiple series of alternatives, not a fixed singularity. Besides, futurists are not so much interested in predicting as in creating desirable futures; the stress is not on what *will* be but what *can* or should be. Futurists leap ahead to the future not so that they may stay in an escapist never-never land, but so that they can lure that future into the present and negotiate with it while the options are to be chosen rather than imposed. If there is indeed the prospect of future shock, then dealing with it now may transform future shock into something less intimidating. Above all, futurists are keenly aware that if they do nothing about the future, it will come about for good or bad. Therefore, their commitment to do something about the future is a moral commitment.

And that brings us full circle to the humanist's concern with the whole man or woman. For that wholeness, as traditionally defined, has been, as I hope I have demonstrated, something considerably less than whole. The individual isolated from the surrounding social environment is not and cannot be whole. He, indeed, takes his individuality in part from it. But neither can the individual who is focused exclusively on past and present. Just as there is no wholeness without society, there is no wholeness without the future. Only through this recognition can the humanities themselves survive and serve the future.

*Educators must build "empathy across time." But, says an out-
standing humanist and scholar, this process must face tomorrow
as well as yesterday. We must, says Dr. Nell Eurich, attempt not
merely to re-create the past, but to shape the future. By examining the utopian dreams of our ancestors, by encouraging the
free play of imagination, by recognizing the contemporary arts as
possible pointers toward the future, she argues, the humanities
can once more make a significant difference.*

CHAPTER EIGHT

The Humanities Face Tomorrow

by Nell Eurich

> . . . that part of [the future] which is not pre-
> dictable, which is largely a matter of free human
> choice, is not the business of machines, nor of
> scientists . . . but it ought to be, as it was in the
> great epochs of the past, the prerogative of the
> inspired humanists.
>
> —*Dennis Gabor*

Education has taken as its primary purpose the preparation of
students for their future lives. Implicit in this purpose was the
concept of the educator and the school as custodians of society's
past achievements. The assumption was that examples from the
past were the best guides for the future. And, for most of man's
history, this assumption has proved to be true, because a man's
future generally was not too different from his immediate past.

Today this way of thinking has run up against obstacles which
force us to question its applicability and challenge its power to
continue in established patterns. In the first place, we now have
so much data on the past and the present that it threatens to

engulf us. Our predilection for collecting information on everything we can get our hands on has circumvented the law of natural selection through which great ideas and developments survived on the strength of their continuing appeal, while lesser efforts were forgotten.

The knowledge pool upon which many vital decisions are based itself reflects the values of society—values shaped, in part, by the cultural heritage. The humanities alter not only the behavior of individuals, but, through their influence on the value system, the configuration of knowledge or data that practical men use in making decisions about business, politics, war, diplomacy, and science. Put simply, values determine what kinds of information are collected and put to use. And the humanities determine or, at least, heavily influence the value system. When this process breaks down and the value system becomes inappropriate for its time, the knowledge base itself is affected and the decisions taken become inappropriate—perhaps dangerously so.

Add to this the indisputable fact that new discoveries in the sciences and technology hold cataclysmic implications for our future lives. Decisions confront us, decisions which must be made if we are not to forfeit the opportunity to affect our future as a human race. From the midst of the mass of accumulated knowledge, these cry out for attention and deliberation and ask that priorities be recognized.

The future arrives with increasing velocity, and we have come to expect startling announcements of new developments daily. Obviously the future will *not* offer us an environment basically similar to the present, with only slight modifications. It will be radically different from anything we have known. The role of educators as custodians of the past must, therefore, be cast in a different light. Their past-orientation for future purposes requires fundamental adjustment.

Teachers in the sciences and social sciences have responded to the challenge of rapid change more effectively and easily than in the humanities. Not only have scientists created many of the changes and the speed of the process, but they also are fortunate in the nature of their subject matter and its historical development. Science has a way of wiping out its past through new discoveries that can be checked out practically and so invalidate preceding hypotheses or even "laws." While the past holds lessons and fruitful ideas for possible new configurations, knowledge in the sciences is genuinely cumulative, and the next step can replace a former one as well as build upon it. So the history of science has recently become a subject especially for the layman to aid his understanding of the nature of scientific methods and how they have changed.

Furthermore, new discoveries separate themselves quickly into their accompanying technologies and create through the knowledge system, itself, new combinations of fields for study: so biochemistry, biophysics, and now biopsychology are born. Selection of materials for teaching in the sciences is comparatively simple for the educator. His greatest problem is to keep up with the new and project its implications. His eyes must be focused on today and tomorrow—not the past.

Social scientists, in their own way, also carry a less burdensome load of past knowledge. Their fields—sociology, psychology, economics, and anthropology—scarcely have a past, except as they write it from historical evidence. These subjects only appeared as fields of study in the late nineteenth or early twentieth century. And, as Wendell Bell notes elsewhere in this volume, they have taken as their *primary* orientation the present-day, contemporary civilization. The approach is generally analytic; the concern is with man and society—with immediate issues and problem-centered studies. Students of the social sciences must inevitably adjust and move forward their attention as change demands, and so at least some forward motion, if not a forward look, is in play.

The humanities, in sorry contrast, are languishing on several fronts. More than scholars in the other disciplines, humanists, because they serve as keepers of the intellectual and cultural heritage of the race, have become the victims of their own commitment to yesterday. Too many humanists have remained largely past-oriented, seldom turning their attention to the present, much less toward the future. As a result, they do not sufficiently reflect *modern man's* attempts to work toward or beyond rational ends, to create new structure and form, or to express ineffable human feelings. Education in the humanities has been reduced to dry dissections of "great" works and men of the past whose very greatness is frequently submerged in footnotes. Hence, the humanities are not currently fulfilling their once-central role in determining the quality of our lives.

If they are to resume their formative position again, if they are to help in the creation of values and in the clarification of the choices before us, and so affect the quality of life, a renaissance is urgently needed in the humanities.

The renaissance will depend upon changes in the way the humanities are taught and a dramatic change in their orientation toward time.

Passion versus Neutrality

To encourage this rebirth, we first need teachers and scholars eager to tear off their protective masks and engage personally with their materials—people willing to say "I believe," or "I think," and take strong positions on whatever issue or question is at stake. While objectivity and critical inquiry are essential, they can no longer be tolerated as a shield against commitment; neither approach is exclusive of the other.

It is ironic that humanists, impressed by little-understood "scientific methods," should have adopted an approach ill-suited to their subject matter and so contributed to their own decline as science grabbed man's imagination. The "objective," seemingly value-free presentation, the precise and detailed analysis of facts, have led the art of criticism to a high point of polish in humanistic disciplines.

Yet the materials of the humanities are hardly neutral. In an age of overchoice and high-speed change, students face extraordinarily complex decisions. Through clarification of their values, as emphasized by Howard Kirschenbaum and Sidney Simon in a later chapter, young people can be helped to make more intelligent, more considered choices. Yet even in the humanities we see some teachers, in a desperate attempt to ape the "hard sciences," avoiding the difficult, but critical, issue of values.

The basic materials of the humanities speak of belief, hope, aspiration. They explain our views on time-present and time-past. Often, they foreshadow the future. All the more pity that the student's encounter with the great humanistic works has ceased to be a moving, vicarious, personal experience that enters the consciousness and remains capable of affecting his or her present life and shaping the future. Only teachers with strong commitment can make the transforming experience occur for the student, and only in this way will the past release its treasures for many people.

To do this, teachers of the humanities must sort out these riches, and, in the spirit of passionate learning, make the work at hand come to life and the age of its birth live again. If this is achieved, students will sense what it was like to live in that time. They will experience "empathy across time." They will understand, or at least apprehend, the greatness of their ancestors who expressed it. Without this, a person has no anchor for comparison with the present, no appreciation for the creative intellect that has gone before him. And these are essential, unless humanity chooses to start *de novo* in the process of civilization as it is forced to do in biological development.

The second major ingredient for the renaissance in the humanities is a better process of selection from the constantly mounting mass of materials. We are deluged in records of the past and interpretative studies. And ancestors have a way of multiplying daily. To stay afloat, teachers in this century have divided the mass into eras, periods, and centuries. So we have the Restoration, the Enlightenment, the sixteenth, seventeenth, eighteenth centuries, etc. Most humanistic disciplines follow this method of slicing the historical cake. The concept is one of epochal coverage, and those in the discipline feel responsible for covering all of the stages of development which bring them to the present.

In addition to dividing history into digestible time periods, teachers have traditionally focused on a few "giant thinkers" who seem now, in the reconstruction of history, to have shifted or strongly affected the course of subsequent affairs. These are individuals whose stature often makes of modern man a puny thing, indeed, and so, living with such figures, teaching and discussing their writings or works every day, the teacher is unwittingly enticed into idolatry of the past.

Faced with double-barreled domination by a growing accumulation of information, on the one hand, and a towering reverence for great men of the past, on the other, humanists have retreated from the front lines of creative and original thought and become priests of the past. To gain purchase on the constantly increasing mass of knowledge, they had to continue breaking it down into smaller and smaller pieces, and this has come to constitute the process of scholarship and advanced training in the humanistic disciplines. In specialization lay the chance for accuracy and the comfort of self-confidence.

What is needed now is the abandonment of this sterile process and the reassertion of individualism on the part of the teacher in selecting those materials that carry the most personal meaning, and which he or she can then convey to students with conviction. The teacher must identify those materials or themes from which comparisons can be fully drawn. Rather than microscopic dissection of a work, the history of an idea or a theme in literature might be traced forward to its modern expression and even projected forward to its possible future interpretations.

Yesterday's Tomorrows

Indeed, one major theme that humanists might do well to examine is the future, itself—the ways in which earlier societies imagined their futures. Fred Polak, in his two-volume work, *The Image of the Future*,[1] has systematically examined the visions of a future time held by the ancient Greeks, the Persians, the Hebrews, the church of the Middle Ages, and scores of philosophers, writers, intellectuals and artists of the past, arguing that what a culture thinks its future will be has an enormous impact on its actual future. Certainly, this idea provides many opportunities for linking the past to the present and future.

Humanists claim that truly great works speak to people through deep human concerns that have changed little, if at all. What they frequently ignore is how the handling of "enduring" themes—the attitude toward them—has changed and *will* change. Love, hate, war, shelter, greed, terror, and the future may remain of major concern to humanity, but attitudes toward each are drastically different in various societies and at different times in history, and are changing radically today. Remarkable teachers may compare the concept of love held by the Greeks with that of the Elizabethan and Victorian periods, or with today's new love patterns. A few, like Moses Hadas, may explain that Euripides' women are the type who would wait for their husbands at the subway exit with a bowl of hot soup. Others may, indeed, project the idea of love forward into possible societies of tomorrow. But most teachers of the humanities are not so steeped in their subject or so capable of making it vital.

It is strange, if not paradoxical, that such is the case. Why the dull, conservative past-orientation generally characteristic of teaching the humanities when the materials themselves—the creative works of the human race—were exploratory and bold? The most outstanding contributors actually shaped the future, giving us new theories, creating new art forms, joining common elements in new combinations that went beyond what had been known before. Dante dared to fabricate a whole system for the universe and created an immense structure for religious thought that sweepingly embraced purposive principles and prescribed behavioral responses for man.

Creative imagination formed images of things no human had ever seen before, expressing visions in poetry, epics, painting and music, in dance movement and ritual form. Imagination transcended inherited models, transformed them into expression that lived and became the base from which other creative minds could take off in the future.

Artists boldly introduced perspective into their paintings, replaced the flat stylized figure with real people and thus captured movement. Experiments with light changed focus from the fixed spotlight in the glowing darkness of a Rembrandt to the diffuse, shimmering light of the Impressionists and the pointillism of a Seurat. The machine has recently become the ally of artists who, with engineers and physicists, have produced kinetic art with continuous movement, changing color and form, reflecting, perhaps, the restlessness of our technological society as it races into the future.

To be sure, art has commented as well on its own time with a can of tomato soup, the portrait of a patron, or a mural of war. It has preserved the familiar, common life, but it has also projected visions for other men's imagination and opened vistas of the future. Gyorgy Kepes has written, "Some artists were like distant warning systems of the human condition today. They read the signs of coming ecological and social disasters early and with full grasp.

They saw the illusion and degradation at the height of compla-
cency in the last century over what was believed to be the best of
all possible worlds." He believes that artists are again finding in the
environmental landscape new materials for creative objectives:
"Some of them dream of molding gigantic artistic structures carved
from the earth, resting on the ground, flying in the sky, floating
in the ocean, that are themselves environments."[2]

Musicians, too, throughout the ages have devised novel instruments and created new music from past models. Before the visual
artists, musicians adopted the "machine." They wired the piano
for new sounds and turned the guitar into an electronic instrument.
Technology continues to extend the range of sound, and now we
have the Moog synthesizer, which imitates the sounds of all other
instruments. As if to bring the human being back into play, into
active participation creatively, the pendulum currently swings
toward man's improvisation in music and the arts.

Today film is the primary medium in which the creative arts are
united. Together the writer, musician, artistic director, and actor
have made film the means with which to capture the innuendos
as well as the raw reality of human experience. Films are projecting, and perhaps creating, man's images of the future more powerfully than any other medium of expression. Born of technology,
films have become a potent influence over the majority of people
because of their effective combination of the visual and the audible
elements. With TV, the combined power has entered the home
and become a formidable antagonist—and potential ally—for the
teacher relying on words in the classroom.

Still the humanist has not invited the new creative expressions of
artists into his sanctuary. Nor have we, by and large, entertained
the large questions that must be raised, if the humanities are to
have any influence on the quality of our lives today, much less
tomorrow. Is "quality of life" to be measured solely in terms of
GNP and the amount of goods each man possesses? If we can
make a world of plenty for all, what then would comprise quality?
Are there *any* humanistic values—or was it all a great hoax? What
are or should be the ethical concerns of the individual? The questions are more important than the answers; in the search, directions may be found.

Without confronting such issues—which traditionally have belonged in the humanist's domain—it is unlikely that we shall be able to cope with the monstrous possibilities now before us. Decisions will be made by someone, some group—or by chance. Today's discoveries are powerful determinants of tomorrow. These are realities which seem so unreal, so unbelievable that one feels overdramatic in trying to talk about them. It is now possible through psychosurgery to remove from a man the emotion of rage and the seat of aggression. It has been done successfully. Doctors using electrical stimulation of the brain can now change man's moods and reduce anxiety or depression. By using the technique of "biofeedback" a man, by himself, can regulate or check certain hitherto involuntary functions. Genetic engineering, on the other hand, is rapidly proving its ability to eradicate the problem before it happens. Yet as one eminent scientist, Helmut Thielicke, asks: "Would one try to eradicate Faust's restlessness, Hamlet's indecision, King Lear's conscience, Romeo and Juliet's conflicts?"[3] To control man's evolution is a staggering thought. What do we want? Duplication of ourselves—cloning, as it is called—so we can keep an identical twin frozen for organ transplants?

Or consider, for the classroom teacher, pupils with memory cells "installed" from another person who has already mastered the subject. Or perhaps a pill for French. The possibilities are endless and moving rapidly into the realm of reality. Scientists are deeply disturbed and frequently raise the moral and ethical questions. The embryologist Robert T. Francoeur has written of cloning: "Xeroxing of people? It shouldn't be done in the labs, even once, with humans." Others are asking, Who will decide and make the choices?

Where are the voices of the humanists? To remain ignorant of or aloof to science and technology and the directions they are carrying us, to assume that the past alone can enlighten, is to cripple the humanities and shrink the chances for human survival. More humanists must speak and louder to be heard. The philosophers are in their midst, theologians and the men of letters. Humanists of the past, in their moral ciriticisms of *their* present, showed a detailed awareness of the forces creating their future. They were sophisticated in the science and technologies, the politics and religious struggles of their time. Today, by contrast, most remain entombed by the past, ignoring the contemporary forces that are shaping a dramatically different tomorrow. And, through this indifference, they renounce all claim for influence on the directions in which society is moving.

If the scientists do not find themselves making the decisions for us, the psychologist B. F. Skinner is ready with a technology of behavior. He claims, "It will not solve our problems, however, until it replaces traditional prescientific views, and these are strongly entrenched. Freedom and dignity illustrate the difficulty. They are the possessions of the autonomous man of traditional theory, and they are essential to practices in which a person is held responsible for his conduct and given credit for his achievements. A scientific analysis shifts both the responsibility and the achievement to the environment."[4] He admits this technology raises questions concerning "values" but, on a recent TV show, he stated that this should not be so difficult; he could define the values and purposes for our conditioning.

From Bacon to Orwell

Certainly before the humanist can influence future trends and play a formative part in the days to come, he must at least capture the moment in its full intensity and implications, search out its roots, if any, and join in exploring new directions for man.

The next leap, then, is to unleash the humanistic imagination to play with possibilities and define the many futures from which we may choose. Creative thought, powers of invention and discovery —as well as cold logic based on an analysis of present trends—are the means we possess to design the many possible worlds before us.

The obvious fact that we cannot foretell events to come, or prophesy with accuracy, need not render our imaginations powerless. It is a human weakness. Yet predictions are being made and forecasting is a new sport played largely on a linear and quantitative basis—forecasting that merely assumes incremental change and more of the same. Many social scientists are engaged in this type of prediction. What is needed that humanists can help supply is disciplined conjecture, not about the probable, but about possible and preferable tomorrows.

It is necessary to predict qualitatively, or to apply imagination to the depiction of possible futures. Scientists have shown a failure of imagination in their attempts at forecasting. Arthur C. Clarke has pointed out in *Profiles of the Future* that many eminent men of the laboratory have been blind to the implications of their own research. Lord Rutherford was one of these who "frequently made fun of those sensation mongers who predicted that we would one day be able to harness the energy locked up in matter." He held to this view even as he worked to lay bare the internal structure of the atom which was smashed only five years after his death. So Clarke suggests a law: "When a distinguished but elderly scientist states that something is *possible*, he is almost certainly right. When he states that something is *impossible*, he is very probably wrong."[5]

Humanists can help compensate for the failure of imagination. In their ranks are those who, in the past, saw nothing as impossible and who took pleasure in writing down their visions. Few claimed apocalyptic revelation; more were concerned with making their personal imprint, delivering their own message for man. Francis Bacon in the seventeenth century was such a spokesman. A Lord Chancellor of England, brought up in the school of humanism, he believed deeply in the method he developed for learning more about nature and how it works. He foresaw a gigantic task—the collection and sifting of knowledge, a task in which multitudes would be engaged before we could learn to ape nature and control its processes. He not only helped shape the scientific method and imagined all sorts of technologies of the future, but set forth a plan for the world's first "think tank." Few heeded his exhortations. After all, he was a man of letters—not a scientist—as William Harvey indicated. So Bacon created a *New Atlantis* which put his method in operation and explained the harvest of results. For this work, above all, he is remembered.

Men would fly, he said, move under water in submarines, talk across countless miles, use spectacles to correct myopia or farsightedness. They would also have the microscope. Human senses would be strengthened and checked for veracity in the acts of observation. All the knowledge gained and products invented would of course be used for universal benefit. So long as his symbol of science—the "Father of Solomon's House"—reigned supreme, there could be no doubt that man was exercising his "right reason" in pursuit of a state of perfection.[6]

Many other authors in Bacon's century wrote of new worlds with laboratories and benefits of all sorts. The "new learning" of science was just beginning, and it attracted men of imagination. Even before them, however, others set a tone for utopian societies. We cannot say that they "predicted" so much as they "projected" ideals. Plato's *New Republic* has never been realized; many ancient dreams of a better life have not been achieved. Yet these were visions of good toward which men's hopes were directed.

In Thomas More's *Utopia*, men were equal and life was a collective venture organized for the common good. Later in time, more utopias centered on social and economic issues as their authors imaginatively corrected the evils of their contemporary day. And all along the way, there were visions of a return to the primitive, supposedly peaceful state of nature in which goods and possessions were of little real value. The man counted, and his relationship to his fellow man.

As the world turned and men's minds produced new revelations, the visions changed dramatically. H. G. Wells put Solomon's House in the *Modern Utopia* in which millions of men became involved in collection and analysis with generous federal funding.[7] Now humans are free to invent and play, emancipated from the physical labor on which older utopias were based. They enjoy leisure in a moral and intellectual atmosphere that releases freedom and true individuality. People are registered by number in an elaborate mechanized system, but their lives are led with liberty to develop themselves. Wells only laments that in the real world political, social, and moral devices do not function as smoothly as the linotype machine. Aldous Huxley and George Orwell extended the vision and reversed it, making of man an automaton in states controlled, one for his presumed happiness and the other for his subservience to the power of the state.

As a literary genre, utopias or dystopias imaginatively project a possible future to give the reader the vicarious experience of living in it. They are valuable extensions—whether bleak or beautiful—of imagination, helping us to understand the choices facing us and the variety of worlds toward which we may be moving.

These are the worlds the humanist must aid in building. As he educates the next generation for their future lives, surely he will think of more than their professions as doctors, merchants, or lawyers. In the arts and literature, in the wealth of the past and present, lie materials for the creation of many futures. His task is to urge the creative expression of young minds to their highest powers and so to help form their visions of a future that will be guided by informed values and ethical principles.

Today's scientists "are apt to be among the most conformist, unquestioning members of the community," according to John Wren-Lewis, who argues that neither industry nor government will be well served by scientists who are narrowly unaware of the consequences of their work. An education in futurism can not only sharpen their imaginations, but integrate their specialized knowledge with relevant knowledge in other disciplines.

CHAPTER NINE

Educating Scientists for Tomorrow

by John Wren-Lewis

Every honest man is a prophet . . .
—*William Blake*

Students of any natural science are learning, whether they know it or not, about potentialities for changing human life, for inventing the future. Their scientific education is fatally incomplete if it does not include, as an integral part of their discipline, some explicit training in how to think about the kinds of future that may be in store for mankind.

The idea of pure knowledge is a delusion in the field of science. Even the purest of pure mathematics is an evolution of new modes of abstract formulation which can always, in principle, at some time inspire revolutionary new developments in physics or engineering. In practice, this usually happens far sooner than anyone expects when the apparently esoteric formulae are first stated. Two outstanding examples of the present century are matrix theory and Boolean algebra, which for decades seemed perfect instances of totally useless "pure" mathematics but have become, since then, keys to the revolutionary advances of nuclear physics and computer engineering. As for the experimental sciences, the principle of inventing the future is built into their very existence. The experimental method *means* testing ideas against the touchstone of whether they can be successfully applied not merely to explain known phenomena, but to predict new modes of action not hitherto thought possible. As C. P. Snow put it in his famous but generally underrated "Two Cultures" lecture, a leading characteristic of the mode of thinking that has produced modern experimental science is that those who practice it "have the future in their bones," even if they, themselves, are not especially aware of the fact.[1]

When the great surge forward of natural science began in the seventeenth and eighteenth centuries, its pioneers were under no illusions about its power to change human life. When Francis Bacon urged the priority of "experiments of knowledge" over purely practical inventions ("experiments of fruit"), his whole point was that the experimental method provided the means whereby practical life ceased to be relegated to the level of more tinkering and was made the focus of the full force of creative mind, involving both intellect and imagination, applied at the most fundamental level. Hence his prescription for the education of "experimental philosophers" included as much emphasis on political and social issues as on scientific technicalities, and this was one of the reasons why the pioneers of the scientific revolution who followed his ideas were considered dangerous by most of the academic establishments of their day, who wanted learning to conform to the classical theological and political status quo.[2]

Today, the fact that science is the great agent of change for mankind's future good or ill is blindingly obvious to everybody except, apparently, to large numbers of those who organize and practice the teaching of science. Overwhelmed by the ever-growing complexity of scientific knowledge, they retreat into their various specialisms and relegate consideration of the impact of science on human life to the status of an extracurricular interest, an optional addition which students who like that kind of thing are free to pursue with their friends, or with the aid of political theorists or historians, as long as it does not take too much time away from their serious studies.

As a result, those whose education has been predominantly scientific are apt to be among the most conformist, unquestioning members of the community. While notable exceptions hit the headlines from time to time, like Nobel-prize-winning chemists who are also brilliant musicians, they are exceptions that prove, rather than disprove, the rule. In general, the nature of scientific education is such that there is a direct correlation between success in science courses and lack of awareness of wider human issues.

I can quote personal evidence of this from an informal survey I had a hand in conducting recently among new recruits to a large government scientific establishment which prides itself on getting the very best young scientists from universities. The majority of these brilliant young people were almost totally unaware of social and political conditions outside their own country, and sometimes shockingly ignorant of such issues even within it. They took completely for granted a whole range of nineteenth-century notions about such matters as human motivation in work, utterly unaware that these had been undermined by well-established findings in social science for more than twenty-five years. Their ideas on such issues as the population explosion were naïve in the extreme, lacking any appreciation of the psychological problems involved in such areas as birth-control education, while their views on the future of sex, marriage and the family were uninformed even by such well-known and by now ancient findings as those of the Kinsey reports. Worst of all, perhaps, their ideas of such issues as the drug problem were based on myths long exploded in natural science itself, such as the theory of "escalation" from psychedelic to hard drugs, and they were prepared to quote the literature on the hazards of psychedelic drugs with an uncritical confidence which in other fields would have failed them in any first-year examination.

The fact that "social responsibility in science" has become something of an hysterical campaign slogan in the last few years is evidence of the degree to which scientists with active concern about the future feel themselves to be in a tiny minority in their professions. And unless positive steps are taken to correct this bias in scientific education, it becomes self-reinforcing. Recent psychological studies of scientists' career-motivation (for example, those of Dr. Stephen Box of the University of Kent in Britain) have shown that the impersonal, specialized structure of science courses tends to attract those students whose fear of their own emotions makes them want to retreat into a world of abstractions.[3] At the same time, the more vigorous, concerned minds are so repelled by what they see science has become that they retreat into a counterculture which is more and more explicitly antiscientific, so that it becomes possible for an American historian, Theodore Roszak, to write a campus best seller, *The Making of a Counter Culture*, which argues that antipathy to science, as such, rather than simply to the nasty consequences of technology, is the underlying motif of the whole youth-protest movement of our time.[4] This trend, if not altered, could spell disaster for the human race, since it would lead to a situation in which those who possess knowledge which is power are lacking in all conviction, while those whose concern about the future has passionate intensity remain powerless to translate their ideals into practice.

De-Specializing the Scientist

Fortunately, there are currents moving in the reverse direction, some of which are very powerful even if they have not yet produced effects on anything like a wide enough scale. Probably the most important is the growing recognition among industrialists that socially unimaginative scientists and technologists make for bad business. In a world in which high technology is increasingly common property, the successful firm is the one that best anticipates changing human needs, both those that express themselves directly in changing consumer demands and those that find slower, more indirect but ultimately more powerful expression in political action.

Large companies all over the world have first-class scientists and technologists working on new and improved products and more efficient processes, plus well-trained technical marketing staffs capable of presenting their products' advantages with the most persuasive effect. The firms that make the really important business advances will, more and more, be those whose technical staffs are informed, *right from the outset of all their thinking*, of the likelihood that a new generation may want (say) foods to prevent illness rather than medicines to cure it. It may prefer to travel or make music rather than watch TV, or to have throw-away furniture rather than permanent homes; or it may be that public pressure on environmental issues will rule out certain technologies, or that emergent nationalism in some area of the world may cut off the supply of important raw material. Over the past decade progressive industries in many countries have begun a drive to inject such wider awareness into their planning by organizing interdisciplinary "think tanks" in which technologists are teamed with economists and social scientists, but this is of little use if the new thinking remains only at the rarefied level of higher management. To be really effective, the majority of a firm's technical staff must develop the general habit of thinking in these terms as the basis for all their work, and scientists or engineers who have been trained as narrow specialists find the habit very hard, if not impossible, to acquire.

So there has begun to emerge a demand from industry in many countries for a new broadening of scientific education in school and college. Moreover, this demand is now starting to be echoed by many government organizations of various kinds, as examples pile up, all over the world, of airport schemes, welfare schemes, city plans and even military strategies going awry because the technical people who shape such schemes have been working as narrow specialists with no proper awareness of wider issues. The demand in general terms is not, of course, new. For several decades, progressive employers of scientists in both industry and government have been urging the educational world to temper specialized technical training with at least sufficient literacy and humane interests to enable their pupils to communicate with others outside their own specialisms. Hitherto, however, teachers have been able to plead that the main obstacle to any liberalization of scientific education was the prospective employers' more basic demand for diploma qualifications requiring a degree of specialized knowledge which left no space in the timetable for other activities.

The interesting feature of the present situation is that the demand for greater breadth comes today in a new form which offers hope of a solution to the problem. Instead of a general vague plea for liberalization, what is now emerging from the industrialists who have studied the question most seriously is the idea that scientific education at all levels should be widened *by a logical extension of its own basic principles* to include training in the art that has begun to develop over the past decade in the various "futures think tanks," large and small, that have sprung up across the world under a variety of names and sponsorships—namely, the art of thinking systematically about possible futures for human society on various segments of this planet, in such a fashion as to integrate specialized scientific thinking with psychological and sociological insight and humane imagination.

The Future as Integrating Device

In fact, the development of "futures thinking" as an identifiable discipline—no less identifiable for being, as yet, and perhaps always, without any clearly determinate form—may provide just the kind of unifying principle long sought by educators who wish to make liberal education something more than a vague mishmash. No field of human learning is alien to it, yet the kind of integration it provides is achieved not by fitting other subjects into an abstract intellectual framework, as theology tried to do when it claimed the role of unifying principle of knowledge, but by seeing all knowledge in its practical relationship to the most fundamental of all existential concerns—the concern with the opportunities and vicissitudes of our continuing being—i.e., the future. Hence, it provides the means by which any specialism can be opened up to include appreciation of the nature and purpose of other specialisms—in principle, of all other specialisms—as part of the logical development of the specialism itself, instead of having them imposed as extras which some well-meaning educators think students ought to learn about for the good of their souls.

In practical terms, a course on the principles and practice of "systematic future-thinking" can form a logical part of the main curriculum of any specialist, whether scientist, social scientist, lawyer, political theorist, creative writer, artist, linguist, historian or theologian, since it can provide an appreciation of the human realities of his or her own subject and the ways in which these may be applied in future careers in a rapidly changing world. At the same time, such a course will, by its very nature, introduce the student to the emerging ideas in his or her central field, and to some of the more significant ideas and practices of people working in many other fields as well.

The task of designing courses of this kind is in its infancy, and for many years to come they are likely to take a wide variety of different shapes, according to the different talents and resources available to the individuals who have the enthusiasm to organize them in each case. Such pioneers will normally have to draw in teachers from several different departments, and often from outside their own school or college, including some people from industrial and government institutions.

As more and more efforts of this sort get started, it will be an important part of the work of large professional futures organizations to provide advice on the construction of "futures courses" for all levels of education. Many schools and colleges will, in the first instance, be able to mount only one general-purpose futures course for students in all faculties, leaving each faculty to develop interface-classes for its own students to link their special subjects with the general course. In any case, the primary task in every institution will be the building-up of an interdisciplinary group of enthusiasts who cross-fertilize each other's thinking as they work together in developing the whole continuing operation—an operation which is not just that of organizing specific classes, but also has the equally important task (perhaps more important from the long-term point of view) of gradually permeating the whole school or college with "futures-awareness," so that even the most specialized teaching acquires the new dimension which such awareness brings.

The need for inclusiveness here cannot be too strongly emphasized. A futures course that limits itself, as many do, to teaching socioeconomic forecasting techniques plus a little ecology, is doing less than half its job. Socioeconomic predictions and ecological exhortations are meaningless unless thoroughly grounded in an awareness (a) of the hopes, fears, and values that can motivate people, as reflected in the changing patterns of history, literature, politics, law, philosophy and religion, and (b) of the basic principles, methods and growing-points of the natural sciences from which the future technological opportunities and hazards of human life will spring. Ideally, no doubt, the social sciences could form a bridge to link the thinking of those whose jobs and interests are predominantly technical with those whose main devotion is to humanities, but this is far from being the case at present.

Those of us who have wrestled with the problems of running a futures think tank will heartily endorse the view of Wendell Bell in another essay in this volume, that the general run of social-science teaching and research is as much in need of being revolutionized by futures-awareness as is natural-science teaching. The fact of the matter at present is that futures education, itself, has to provide the bridge between humanities and sciences, and a major part of the work of those who plan futures courses will be the development of a forum in which specialists in humanities, social sciences and natural sciences alike can learn and practice the art of communicating their main concerns, methods and ways of thinking to each other.

In this exchange, natural-science teaching, in particular, stands to gain not only from what it receives, but also by virtue of what it is asked to contribute. For perhaps the greatest deficiency of the scientist who has been trained entirely as a narrow specialist is his inability to communicate to others what his work is really about. As I said earlier, managers in technological industry have long been aware of this as a major obstacle to the effective use of science, but nowadays it can be perceived as a grave hazard for society as a whole, in a world in which the things a scientist does can affect whole populations before anyone has quite registered what is happening.

Scientists simply cannot be allowed to "cop out," as they often try to do, by pleading that their ideas are so sophisticated that they cannot be communicated to the layman. No one expects any technical man to communicate masses of detail or esoteric theory, but if he refuses the effort of trying to express his main concerns and his principles of operation in such a way as to bring out their relationship to the rest of human life, he is claiming an elitist position that his fellow men cannot afford to allow to anyone who deals in knowledge that is power. He just has to be told to try harder, and if this means taking time out from his specialized work, so be it: science is made for man, not man for science.

Scientific Imagination

But, in fact, his science is likely to gain, rather than lose, by his being required, from time to time, to reexamine the fundamental implications of his work in simple basic terms. Very often it is when received assumptions are questioned that scientific advances are made. This is well known to be true on the grand scale, as in such famous cases as that of modern polymer chemistry, which was born only when Hermann Staudinger defied the ridicule of nearly all his contemporaries for abandoning their classical concept of a molecule as inadequate to experience; or that of antibiotic medicine, which was delayed for nearly twenty years by pharmacologists' unquestioned assumption that substances toxic to bacteria must necessarily also be toxic to man;[5] or relativity physics, which required basic rethinking of what is really meant by the measurement of space and time; or quantum physics, which has advanced only as scientists have reexamined what the long-accepted notions of causality mean in terms of actual experience. The same holds good, however, for countless small advances both in science and technology.

Narrow specialists are liable to be able to envisage only the most pedestrian solutions to the problems they are working on: breakthrough solutions that depend on a creative leap or side-step are possible only to minds that are able, at any time, to stand back from the normal routines of their subject matter and make fully conscious the significance of the questions being studied. The scientist who claims that his ideas are too difficult to be explained to the nonspecialist is probably dealing in muddled ideas, however precise they may seem within his specialized context. Training in the art of communication is, in fact, an integral part of training in the ability to think properly, and scientists are probably more in need of it for their professional competence than anyone else.

Moreover, it is equally true, I believe, that the process of giving science students an understanding of the social, psychological and humane issues needed for responsible futures-thinking will also improve, rather than detract from, their professional performance as scientists, besides making them better-educated individuals and more responsible citizens. It is a notorious fact that large amounts of the material at present taught in science courses are quickly forgotten and never used again once examinations are over:[6] what must be used again, indispensably, is imagination, and imagination is indivisible—stimulation of it in any area will be felt in other areas as well. If it is restricted, it is liable to become stunted altogether.

Science confined within the limits of narrow specialization, in effect, reverts to the level of tinkering from which the Baconians sought to liberate it, no matter how advanced the concepts with which it deals. The narrowly specialized applied scientist will tend to be pedestrian in his work and will also be prone to waste time, energy and resources on projects which are rendered obsolete by advances on other fronts, whereas a more broadly ranging imagination will be constantly alert to the possibility of such advances. In more basic science, narrowly specialized training leads to a phenomenon which ought to be impossible, a contradiction in terms, but is regrettably all too common—scientific dogmatism, the assumption that contemporary concepts and theories are more or less final truths, which inhibits all those really radical advances that depend on the development of fundamentally new ways of thinking.

I would hazard a personal speculation here that we are heading for a time, not far hence, when science in many areas will undergo dramatic changes in its ways of thinking, leading to fresh ideas about the world, and whole new areas of human activity, undreamed of in most of our present philosophies. When our youthful counterculture condemns contemporary science for its materialism, and traces a connection between the practical blunders of expansionist economics (in East and West alike) and the tendency of our scientific world-view to exclude all consideration of mankind's traditional spiritual and psychic notions, I believe it is putting its finger on a limitation of our thinking which is detrimental from the strictly scientific point of view, quite apart from ethical or metaphysical considerations.

We have so far developed our scientific understanding of the world almost entirely within the confines of thought paradigms appropriate to our ordinary common-sense consciousness, which looks at the world in terms of forces, substances and objects to be observed and manipulated, and it is no accident that most of the results of our applied science have been expansions of our power to exploit environments for the greater satisfaction of our desires.

It is an interesting fact, however, that the progress of physics has begun to strain our paradigms of thought to the breaking point, demanding weirder and weirder concepts, just at the very juncture in history when social pressures are forcing us to reexamine radically what happiness and satisfaction really mean in terms of the inner life of man, leading to a great upsurge of interest in expanding human consciousness to explore potentialities of awareness beyond ordinary common sense. The next decade may well see the start of new kinds of scientific thinking which, without sacrificing the principle of experimental rigor and objectivity, are able to recognize many of the ideas at present relegated to the realm of the supernatural and paranormal, as simply unexplored potentialities of nature and man.

This is speculation—but I would contend that unless scientists and technologists are trained to keep their minds constantly open to the possibilities of really radical departures in their own fields, even such way-out possibilities as these, they are not living up to the tradition of experimental science at all, but are reverting to a scholastic dogmatism which is just as imprisoning to the human spirit as the theological dogmatism which tried to inhibit scientific inquiry in earlier centuries.

The Frankenstein Complex

One of the most serious social failures of the scientific and technological community in recent decades has been its failure to be sufficiently future-oriented and imaginative about its own work, thereby giving science a public image of nineteenth-century mega-mechanical antiseptic coldness which has been one of the main causes of the widespread reaction against science in our own day. I would hold scientists to blame, quite as much as, if not more than, politicians and businessmen, for the fact that research over the past few decades has been so largely channeled into the kind of science and technology which develops bigger and bigger power-sources, production systems, communication networks and vehicles, leading to massive urban concentrations, massive centralized bureaucratic organizations and massive pollution problems. Had scientists had sufficient imagination to be able to envisage, as they are now beginning to do, their eventual ability to understand and follow nature's own pattern of using small amounts of highly directed energy in vastly diversified organic self-regulating systems, they would, I am sure, have found ample commercial and political backing for research and development in those directions.

While commerce and politics do undoubtedly have a general bias toward large-scale centralized developments, the business and political worlds are so diverse that other kinds of development would certainly have got going here and there, sufficiently to demonstrate the very real advantages of organic flexibility and decentralization, had not the general bias been reinforced and confirmed at almost every crucial decision point by lack of vision on the part of scientists and technologists themselves. The fact that a significant movement in this new direction has now begun to make itself felt in technological thought is partly a matter of straight scientific progress in such areas as molecular biology and ultramicrocircuitry, but it is also due in no small measure to the spread of professional futures-thinking in industry.

Thus, we have the irony that when Theodore Roszak concludes his latest book, *Where the Wasteland Ends*,[7] with a list of counter-cultural proposals for future directions in society, economics and technology which he thinks will require a revolution against the prevailing character of the scientific outlook, he echoes without knowing it proposals which are already being made the basis of scientific planning in several of the world's largest industrial concerns. His unawareness of this is a token of the degree to which such open future-oriented thinking remains as yet only a minority influence in the scientific and technological community as a whole, albeit a significant one.

Science in the Developing World

The need for this kind of radical thinking, and indeed for well-trained futures-thinking generally, is probably even greater for scientists and technologists who are going to work in, or for, the less technically developed countries than for those in the highly industrialized ones. For the less-developed countries face the dilemma that their populations are reaching out toward higher standards of living from positions of underprivilege, just at the time when the environment seems unable to support much further growth along the lines the developed nations have been following. It is psychologically unrealistic to suppose that the newly emergent nations will submit tamely to requests for growth limitation when they have only just begun to taste the higher standards which their more industrialized neighbors have enjoyed for decades. The only hope of avoiding world disaster in this situation is for means to be devised for them to leapfrog right over many of the stages of industrial development through which we have gone, and proceed directly to the kind of sophisticated "post-industrial society" toward which we ourselves are struggling, wherein high standards of individual and social well-being are maintained with a minimum of drudgery and strain on the environment.

The less-developed countries will require, in fact, to have the very highest technology, not lower-level technology, as is often assumed at present (although there will undoubtedly be an important place for the much-vaunted "intermediate technology" as a stopgap). They will have the advantage of being able to introduce it without the grim consequences that marked our history, but it will need scientific imagination of the boldest kind, combined with the very highest level of sociological and humanistic insight.

If far-out possibilities like controlled telepathy instead of telephones, or teleportation instead of automobiles, are going to emerge at all, they are needed here more than anywhere. However, even if we stick to strictly foreseeable prospects, we still need to be able to envisage such possibilities as, for example, extremely small-scale (small enough for a home or local commune), sophisticated, multi-product, self-maintaining hydroponic systems for food production, with recycling of waste products, as an alternative to mass agriculture, mass crop protection, mass transport systems, mass commercial marketing and large-scale sewage disposal. We shall need to consider providing efficient, sophisticated preventive medicine (based, perhaps, on new kinds of food, drink, clothing and atmospheres which give a high sense of well-being while also building up the body's disease-resistance) instead of massive medical services and drug production. If our scientists are incapable of inventing this kind of future to help the underprivileged peoples of the world to level themselves up, while humanity as a whole slows down the attrition of the environment, the prospects for the next century of our planet are not very bright.[8]

Futurism and the Emotions

So I believe the provision of futures education for students of science and technology may be a matter of even greater importance than the most enthusiastic of the pioneers working in the field have yet imagined. It is so important that almost anything is better than nothing, but the ideal would be for the process to be a continuous feature in every stage of scientific and technological training, rather than confined to a special course in one part of the syllabus only. At various stages of the educational process, there will be places for special classes on specific aspects and techniques of futures-thinking, for interdisciplinary seminars and rap sessions, for "futures games" and model projects, for real-life group enterprises and for brainstorming parties to open up new ideas in specialized scientific fields. There will also, I believe, be an important place for a kind of training which has not found much use in futures work so far, but is likely to play a growing part in many different areas of education in the coming decades, namely *training in emotional self-awareness* of the type which management education has begun to develop in recent years

The idea that scientific training automatically confers the ability to rise above petty emotions and personal prejudices in decision-making is a myth that has been rudely shattered by numerous revelations of disastrous misjudgments that have resulted from rivalries, insecurities and blind attachments on the part of the scientists who have swayed the world's military destinies ever since World War II—for example, C. P. Snow's horrific account[9] (since substantiated in the small print of official histories) of what went on behind the British decisions to develop radar and to engage in strategic civilian bombing in the early 1940s. Like all myths, this one has a definite basis in reality. Snow himself pointed out in yet another of his lectures, "The Moral Un-neutrality of Science,"[10] that the whole discipline of the experimental method is a self-correcting system designed to eliminate bias. By practicing it, scientists are almost inevitably given some insight into the virtues of letting honesty override private fears and fantasies. But this is not enough, especially where the scientist's work touches (as it *always* does to some degree) on human issues outside the range of his strict professional discipline.

It is not enough because the human mind—and especially the clever mind—is adept at rationalizing its prejudices and emotional biases into apparently well-reasoned views without ever allowing the feelings to come fully into the focus of consciousness. People who practice impersonal disciplines like those of the sciences are perhaps especially prone to avoid facing their emotions in this way, as I said earlier, but the emotions are not thereby eliminated: they simply become more dangerous for being covert.

Some of the formal techniques developed by professional futurists, such as the famous Delphi technique, are designed precisely to circumvent this rationalization process, but even they can be only very partially effective, and in any case are not applicable to a great many of the decision-making situations with which the inventors of the future will be confronted in practical life. Fortunately, we have now begun to learn, by borrowing some of the insights of group psychology and group psychotherapy, to supplement our normal procedures of rational discussion with simple disciplines for bringing personal feelings out into the open in a systematic way, so that everyone else can at least make allowances for them, and hopefully each individual can achieve, through greater consciousness, a certain degree of real emotional detachment and objectivity.

When a few bold spirits began to introduce these disciplines into management education two decades or so ago, they were viewed with great trepidation by the scholastic and managerial establishments generally, who feared they would shatter the hard-won achievements of reason and open the floodgates to chaos. Experience has proved the reverse. In most cases, the effect of facing emotions deliberately and openly, not just in special therapeutic or training groups, but as a regular part of the discipline of actual decision-making, has been to give new strength to reason and to open the way to agreements that transcend petty fears and prejudices.[11]

Although as yet in its infancy, I believe this kind of discipline is almost more important than any other for those who deal in the kind of knowledge that is power. And this kind of training, too, I believe, will actually benefit, rather than merely complement or detract from, strictly professional competence, for it has been my experience that bringing personal prejudices, insecurities and ambitions out into the light of open encounter has the effect of liberating great quantities of creative energy which have hitherto been locked up in useless emotional conflict below the surface of consciousness. Man invents the future as no other species does precisely because he is a creative animal capable of taking responsibility for making or resisting change, and there can be no real divorce between his technical capacity and his capacity for responsibility, since both spring from the same fount. So the truly educated scientist is one who has the future not only in his bones, but in a responsibly imaginative head and an informed heart.

In hundreds of universities and schools, specialized courses in the future are springing up as a result of the enthusiasm and dedication of innovation-minded educators. Here, the head of a learning-materials company cautions that such courses must be seen as no more than a first step toward a deeper transformation of the curriculum.

CHAPTER TEN

Educational Futurism: Perspective or Discipline?

by Harold L. Strudler

> It is our future that lays down the law of our today.
> —*Friedrich Wilhelm Nietzsche*

As the future has begun to creep into the curricula of hundreds of schools and universities across the nation, a controversy has arisen about its nature and boundaries. Is futurism, or futuristics, or futurology an academic discipline or is it a perspective—a way of looking at the subject matter in all disciplines? Should it constitute itself a separate subject matter, separately taught, or should it become an element in all courses?

The answer to this question has to do not merely with the organization of knowledge, and the structure of educational organizations, with their departments and specialties, but also with the question of time: There may well be one answer if we are attempting to achieve short-term goals and a quite different answer if, like futurists, we look further down the road. The two answers are not necessarily mutually exclusive.

Given the desirability of expanding the time horizons of students, and developing their future-orientation, the pragmatic, near-term solution would be (and, indeed, has been) the creation of separate courses in "the future." These courses have proliferated with extreme rapidity throughout the United States, especially at the college level, and by 1972 had cropped up as far away as the American University in Beirut.

Many such courses concentrate on the techniques by which practicing futurists seek to identify points of intervention which may turn possible futures into probable ones. I suspect that many of these courses have, as part of their intention, the desire to establish the legitimacy of futur 1 as an academic discipline, partly to counteract public skepticism reflected in the notion that futurism is "crystal-ball gazing" and "tea-leaf reading." Where this is the case, the courses are frequently oriented toward the work of what might be called the "para-scientist futurist," whose special interest is the quantification of judgment and prediction. The courses, thus, emphasize certain methodologies—systems theory, model building, Delphic surveys, and the like—that rely on statistical and mathematical procedures.

Surely, there is nothing wrong with explaining to the public and to students how such methodologies work—or, often enough, fail to work. But, to the degree that these techniques require special expertise and training, they contribute to an unfortunate "we-they" dichotomy and sometimes feed an attitude of professional elitism. It would be a mistake to follow the existing model of the academic disciplines, with its superstructure of credentials, its exclusion of the unordained, and creation and nourishment of a self-perpetuating mystique. The last thing we need is a new priesthood wrapped in the cloak of prophecy.

Sociologist H. Wentworth Eldredge, who has surveyed existing futures courses, notes that many of them lack an examination of past views of the future, including our traditional concerns with both ideal and abhorrent worlds. In addition, Eldredge notes that, with the exception of a few courses offered by sociologists, most of them are characterized by an "almost complete lack of any implicit, much less explicit social change theory . . . without which there can be no holistic prediction much less future planning."

Some "para-scientist" courses also focus so sharply on the

delineation of probable futures that they frequently ignore or short-change normative considerations, the values that underlie our choices with respect to *preferable* futures. They pretend, in effect, that one can discuss the future in a value-free fashion.

Because of their insistence on some semblance of "rigor," these courses are more likely to be acceptable to traditional academics. They find their place in the catalog and in the existing departmental structures more easily than those courses that concentrate more on qualitative approaches to the future. The latter run the gamut from excellent intellectual discourse in the seminar format to rambling, unpointed discussion, field trips for empirical observation without any follow-up attempt at systematic generalization, etc. At worst, they amount to a college-age show-and-tell exercise.

However, when these courses are sensitively and intelligently designed, they provide a bridge across C. P. Snow's two cultures. Some of our forerunner futurist educators have shown a keen awareness of the social and ethical aspects of futurism, as well as the more mechanical aspects. Billy Rojas' course on "Social Trends and Future Ideologies" at the University of Massachusetts, Dennis Livingston's explorations of utopia at Case Western Reserve, and Roger Wescott's examination of the future of the university itself, at Drew University, exemplify this richness.

The best of the courses blend the "science" of charting the probable with the "art" of imagining the possible, and add a deep concern with delineation of the preferable. Implicit in the design of these courses is the view that by a better understanding of the alternative roads to tomorrow, we can, in fact, create a better tomorrow. This implicit assumption is especially important in view of the tide of anti-intellectualism which has swept the young. A significant cause of this antirationalism may be the recognition by a generation reared on transience and upheaval that the traditional, past-oriented curriculum, with its implied assumption that the present will simply continue in the future, offers little in the way of guidance through the turmoil of change.

Beachhead Courses

This, then, is the beachhead: courses in the future, taught as a discipline, embracing both the science of prediction and the art of imagining. Initially, the material taught in these early courses will, however, be beyond the training and imaginative capacity of most teachers. Professor Ossip Flechtheim, who was among the first of those who called for the introduction of the future into education, has contended that "A course with the future as a subject matter could never be a textbook course. It would have to be taught by a truly creative scholar with a wide sociocultural background and a vital interest in the forces of our age. He would have to possess strong scientific discipline in order to rid himself and his students of prejudice and force them to part with many of their most cherished illusions. Though an active participant in the life of his century, he would have to be for the purpose and duration of this course a dispassionate and disinterested observer of things future."

This, of course, is a utopian description of the ideal teacher. However, it is clear that futurism must cross the traditional disciplinary boundaries. That futurism may be approached from many sides is evident from the wide variety of backgrounds from which futurist-educators are, in fact, drawn: theology, sociology, engineering, business administration, law, and dozens of other fields as well. Nevertheless, the special character of the courses, and the special demands they place on the teacher, mean that the early courses are being taught by enthusiasts. The real test of the level of interest that futures courses can sustain will come when second- and third-generation teachers move out into the field.

It is important to recognize, however, that specialized courses in the future are only a stopgap. The future of education itself will best be served if the burgeoning interest in tomorrow is not, as it predominantly still is today, channeled into a separate discipline, but instead is made pervasive throughout the entire curriculum. By this I do not mean that each subject taught should contain a module on futurism. I mean that the entire course should reflect concern with broadening, expanding and future-orienting the time horizons of students. The whole educational curriculum should make learners aware that not one, but many, futures are possible, depending upon how they, as individuals, choose among the alternatives open to them.

It has been said that one of the characteristics that separates humans from the lower orders is the ability to "time-bind."

Largely through the use of language, man has been able, as no animal has, to link past with present, to build traditions, and to create a culture which is not simply immediate but stands and grows upon the past. This, however, ignores what is perhaps an even more significant distinction. Man is a predictive animal. Although some religions and philosophies may deny this, man has always acted functionally as though he had choices and, by selecting from among alternatives, could influence his future. Even the smallest conscious act presupposes this possibility. To do this, man has had to be able to predict the consequences of choosing among these available alternatives. We have all done this as simply and naturally as breathing.

What futurism as an art attempts to do is to enrich the range of alternatives, to define a broader array of possibilities. What futurism as a science attempts to do is to explore systematically two decision points, to relate their interactions and to display those "worlds of if" which are made possible or probable from these key decisions.

However, when man functions as a predictive animal he does not do so in a compartmentalized way. His whole experience and his whole being are involved, and the results affect not a part of him, but his whole person. If a student's time horizon should be broadened, this should not merely happen with respect to science, social science, or the humanities, but across the board. And this can ultimately best be done by making the techniques and the spirit of futurism an integral part of the course rather than a discrete and ostensibly "transcendental" discipline. The process should be more through osmosis than through dosage.

A Transdisciplinary Perspective

The development of futurism as a science has, in large measure, been based upon the concepts of systems analysis. This mode of thought, stemming from engineering and scientific research during the Second World War, sees events, whether technological or social, not as separate and independent occurrences, but as links in a system or process. It is holistic. If futurism were to crystallize as a separate discipline, however, and were to be taught separately in the schools, there is considerable danger that it may become a victim of academic aggrandizement. The fledgling discipline would, in all likelihood, be eyed covetously by the more traditional social sciences, and quite possibly ingested by them. The world congress of sociology held at Varna, Bulgaria, in the fall of 1970 had as its theme "Planning and the Future of Man." This, of course, was a thin disguise for futurism. The attitude of many of the sociologists at the conference was "We are not sure that futurism is a discipline and a science, but if it is, it belongs to us." Were futurism to be swallowed by the social-science whale—or any other academic whale—its utility would be destroyed.

Finally, it may help us understand why futurism or, more generally, future-consciousness, should be a part of the entire education process, rather than a distinct discipline, if we come to see it not as a subject matter alone, but also as a perspective or a tool. No one considers the inquiry method of teaching-learning as a separate branch of knowledge, but rather as a method useful throughout the taxonomy of education. In the same way, while there is distinct subject matter that can be called futurism, there is, more important, a perspective, an attitude toward time, itself.

I am convinced that education is in need of deep reform, and that the introduction of the future is a crucial part of the reform process. But in order for this reform to succeed, futurism must first be introduced in the form of a separate course, and then through a process of infusion throughout the entire curriculum. Otherwise, we stand in danger of producing a generation of future-retarded children.

PART THREE

Directions and Resources

The younger the child, the longer his or her life is likely to extend into tomorrow. How can educators begin, with the very youngest children, to develop a sense of wonder and competence with respect to the future? Here June and Harold Shane present a comprehensive approach to the reformulation of elementary education. They argue for an expansion of the "content" of education to include community service, mass-media experiences, and the conscious reorientation of learning around the concept of the future-focused role image. Their suggestions force a serious re-examination of most of our conventional wisdom about young learners.

CHAPTER ELEVEN

Educating the Youngest for Tomorrow

by Harold G. Shane and June Grant Shane

> To complain of the age we live in, to murmur at the present possessors of power, to lament the past, to conceive extravagant hopes of the future, are the common dispositions of the greatest part of mankind.
> —*Edmund Burke*

The future is important to all of us, particularly since it is where we will spend the remainder of our lives. These emerging chain-series of interlinked tomorrows that lie ahead are even more important for boys and girls than they are for us. New ideas regarding future-control procedures—the methodical designing of tomorrow—suggest that the child of the 1970s is on the threshold of an opportunity not only to create a better world, but to influence greatly the very nature of human evolution through the genetic sciences and by means of environmental intervention in the realm of the behavioral science.[1]

There are several obvious reasons why the years ahead are potentially more significant for the young than for those now approaching thirty. One of these reasons is simple and mathematical. Of approximately 40 million children who will be age twelve or younger in 1975, all will be thirty-seven or younger in 2000 A.D. The twenty-first century will *belong* to them. They will teach our grandchildren, work in service occupations, agriculture, or industry, run our government, determine as opinion-makers and as consumers what we read, sing, see, hear, eat, and wear.

Man has *always* to some extent "created" the future. The future is, in large measure, a product of man-made change. What man did in the past (whether wittingly or inadvertently) determined the present; the present was once the past, ergo, for better or worse, *man created the future* before it became the present. If today's present leaves much to be desired, it is because the adults who created the present made blunders (as well as some brilliant decisions) in making their way into the future from the past.[2]

Beginning very early, children need experiences that help them to understand the nature of change, to recognize that the future is at least partly malleable—that there are alternative futures among which they can choose—and to sense that greater prescience and wisdom are needed in the decision-making processes which can carry them toward socially desirable goals in the future.

A third factor of newly increased significance adds to the importance of a future-oriented education begun at the earliest possible age. This factor, already noted above, is the development of techniques and technologies for radically altering the environment with great speed and, also, the pregnant possibilities (no pun intended) of intervening in the genetic nature of man himself. Our Jovian powers suggest that today's children will possess, before long, a tremendous and extended capacity for doing either grievous harm to their species and to their environment, or a great deal of good.[3]

If it is true that basic patterns of human behavior are fixed at an early age—and the data is increasingly persuasive—then it becomes important at the earliest possible age to teach for to-morrow so that man can regain as rapidly as possible the needed balance between wisdom and the mere exercise of technological power.

Still other reasons for a future-oriented approach to elementary education suggest themselves. Every ten years, for example, a complete recycling of the elementary-school population occurs. This gives education an important new chance periodically to improve its contribution to the future through better instructional methods leading to a more perfected product. Furthermore, for the individual, a future-focused role-image (FFRI) can be of appreciable importance to the child: a magnet toward which he is drawn; a context for his *present* behavior created by his concept of the *future*. For these and other considerations, it is time to examine ways in which future-consciousness can be generated.[4]

Education as Change Agent

From earliest times there have been divided opinions as to the purpose of schooling. In somewhat oversimplified terms, the major split has been between persons of conservative persuasion, those who are satisfied to support teaching that will reflect and preserve the status quo, and those who believe that the schools should be outposts on the frontiers of social change. Between these polar positions, of course, there are infinite nuances of opinion.

To accept the idea of a future-oriented education is to enter the ranks of those who believe that education must be an agent of cultural change. It is from this action viewpoint that we explore possible educational developments that promise better to school our children by teaching the future.

Any meaningful approach to conceptions of the future (when working with children of twelve or below) has at least two dimen-sions: (1) an image of the kind of world to be sought in the future, including the future-focused role-image with which the child identifies himself in this world, and (2) a perspective of the con-tent and the educational conditions or "climate" which (hope-fully) will create changes in the individual behavior of boys and girls—changes congruent with the self-image they have of them-selves in the future.[5]

Development of an image of a "good" future world implies a number of new teaching methods. Thus, it requires preparation without indoctrination, the extensive use of inquiry as a method of instruction, and the continuing development of the open-mindedness which is a prerequisite to inquiry. It also involves an understanding of the meaning of "duty" to one's society (as one of many world cultures of comparable respectability), instrumental skills[6] that make one useful to himself and to his fellows, expressive skills[7] that lend meaning to the individual human life, and the will to laugh (with kindness and compassion as needed) at and with a world in which individual humor—and even pleasant irony—have become diminished by the canned "overkill humor" or puerile farce poured out each season by mass media.

A "futurizing" education implies that the learner will begin to sense and to accept both the constraints and the advantages of freedom. Finally, future-directed teaching and learning should emphasize the ineluctable fact that education will increase rather than decrease inequality! To the degree that it personalizes, it will increase inequalities in the ability of different individuals to contribute to society, rather than suppress the differences and, in that way, create dull, egalitarian intellectual *bidonvilles*. (One important qualification must be voiced, however, with respect to education that "increases inequality." Such future-directed learning should *decrease* inequality in the ability of all persons to engage in effective, receptive, and expressive *communication* in their many forms, including the inaudible but eloquent languages of gesture and expression.)

These educational methods and targets are too important to postpone until students reach the secondary level, and, indeed, even to delay until the primary-school years. In an appropriate fashion they can be used with children under the age of three.

The Content of Learning

If one probes beneath the surface of a generalization such as "the school should make extensive use of inquiry as a method of instruction," what does such a phrase really mean when interpreted or applied with young learners? How shall we change the *content* (what is learned) and the *climate* (the spirit or tone) of the teaching-learning situations that we endeavor to develop?

Since most schooling up to the 1970s has tended to preserve the traditions of the past and to maintain much of the status quo, one might contend that the best future-oriented education could be based on a reversal of contemporary practice. Such a switch would create or accelerate curriculum trends and changes that carried us

FROM	TO
Mass teaching	Personalized teaching
Single learnings	Multiple learnings
Passive answer-absorbing	Active answer-seeking
Rigid daily programs	Flexible schedules
Training in formal skills and knowledge	Building desirable attitudes and appreciations that stimulate a questing for knowledge
Teacher initiative and direction	Child initiative and group planning
Isolated content	Interrelated content
Memorized answers	Problem awareness
Emphasis on textbooks	Use of many media in addition to texts
Passive mastery of information	Active stimulation of intellect
and so on.	and so on.[8]

But to advocate or acquiesce in the mere reversal of present practices in elementary education is both simplistic and likely to build a false sense of success in teaching *for* and *of* the future. What is needed, in addition to many basic 180-degree turns, is a new conception of what constitutes fitting content and of the qualities of a suitable psychoemotional and social climate for learning.

We need a better understanding of the educational experiences that will implant, without numbing indoctrination, a wholesome future-focused self-image in the mind of the child. We also need to conceive of a desirable psychological field and an emotionally stabilizing matrix in which young learners become secure and self-directive in the acceptance and pursuit of a satisfying role-image.

The genuinely important content of instruction eventually resides in a body of skills, knowledge, attitudes, and convictions that govern the learner's behavior after he has forgotten many of the details of the input that he has absorbed through his schooling. What we propose is not a downgrading of such individual content-bred competencies but a closer linkage of the individual to the purposes of his experiencing, and to the acceptance of these purposes because he recognizes and accepts them as relevant to his personal future-focused role-image.

Congruence with Tomorrow

What is needed is "content" for a self-image that seems congruent with the future. "Content," as the term is used here, transcends the conventional educational subject-matter input of the elementary school: language arts, mathematics, science, social studies, and so on. Our definition of "content" does not imply the replacement of such subject matter; rather, it broadens the idea of instruction to include all kinds of learning experiences associated with schooling. It also offers cues and clues for parents and other adults—not just teachers—to contemplate in their contacts with the twelve-and-under group. Content, then, defined as the sum of experiences needed to bring about desirable behavioral changes that will make one useful to one's self and to one's culture, needs to be designed methodically far sooner than has generally been assumed. Even the experiences of the infant, physiological, psychological, and intellectual, affect the ability of the developing child to develop behavior appropriate to the role-image that emerges with the unfolding years.[9]

The self-image and future-focused role-image can be consciously cultivated. In recent decades, child psychologists have stressed the importance of the self-image which the child develops. This is his view or opinion of himself as created by what his experiences tell him he is or what he is becoming. An insensitive parent or teacher, for example, may lead a youngster to believe that he is a "dummy" or "normal," a "problem" or a person of promise, a nonreader or reader. And he often becomes, in a form of self-fulfilling prophecy, what he is led to believe that he will become.

The experiential content in future-oriented learning situations should create for the child as optimistic a concept of himself as reality allows. But we are now coming to recognize that the child's *present* self-image or self-concept is not, by itself, sufficient to account for its motivation and performance. It is the image of its future self—what Benjamin Singer calls the future-focused role-image—that strongly affects its educational competence. Thus the self-concept should be *projected forward* to develop in the child a wholesome, achievable, future-focused role-image. Such an image delineates (in the emerging in-and-out-of-school world into which he is moving) what he can become: a role that can be filled with dignity, self-respect, and the satisfactions to which they lead in both present and future. The type of future image here envisioned presumably would strengthen the learner's purposes and motivation as he copes with subject matter in mathematics and science or with the task of improving reading skills and the like.

In the early encouragement of an FFRI, the presentation of *the possible "history of the future" should extend the past and enrich the present.* Most children thrive on fantasy and on the delights of extended imagination. They virtually always do so without confusing the real world and the imagined or make-believe world, despite the occasional alarums voiced by adults who have forgotten their own childhood. Schooling should be designed so that the possible history of the future—carefully reasoned projections or conceptions of developments that man can probably bring about —become part of the curriculum. Such scenarios of possible futures, with children of twelve or younger, could lend meaning to their possible future roles, bring greater meaning to the present by exploring its possibilities for future development, and sharpen past history by showing how, say, such topics as the Age of Exploration in the 1500s or the Westward Movement of the 1800s foreshadowed and shaped our ancestors' tomorrows and our own yesterdays.

Content should involve knowledge for "use" rather than for "possession." Traditionally, at least some of the content of the elementary curriculum has been included because it was deemed "good" for children regardless of whether it had meaning or utility. The out-of-context parsing (grammatical analysis) of sentences, memorization of dates, and learning the names of kings in forgotten dynasties are illustrative of knowledge-for-possession teaching.[10] An education for effective living in possible alternative futures should emphasize how to use what is learned in immediate learning situations. How to decide the amount of wood to order for a 5' x 8' x 4' puppet stage, or how many fish can live in a five-gallon tank has greater potential "use value" than recalling 1066 A.D. or memorizing Joaquin Miller's five stanzas lauding Columbus. ("Behind him lay the gray Azores, Behind the Gates of Hercules.")

Schooling should cultivate individuality. Most educators have long since acknowledged the importance of recognizing individual differences among children and adjusting school programs accordingly. Usually this has meant a diligent effort to fit the learner to the Procrustean bed of "normal" performance even if he had to repeat Grade Five and maybe Grade Six before he fit the bed. Education for effective learning in the future should stress individuality rather than individual differences. That is, the gradations among children that constitute individuality should be prized and increased rather than diminished to fit contrived norms. The challenges of the future require the cultivation of varied talents, of *maximum* potentialities rather than *minimum* essentials or the potentially limiting influence of "performance objectives."

The Learner as Resource

The learner himself should become a resource. Projects undertaken by schools that seek to teach the future should more frequently develop content (i.e., experiences) that involves the learner as a resource in the creation of the future. This generalization requires some explanation. In the past, and probably in many schools of the seventies, the curriculum often included units or projects which were contrived or simulated. Children of about seven, for instance, who lived in the city, might learn about the

farm, community helpers (fireman, policeman, etc.), the super-
market, circus, or zoo. Sometimes one or more visits were made
to a farm, firehouse, or zoo—or someone was invited to the
classroom to tell about his work.

In future-oriented teaching-learning situations, children should
get in the act as participating human resources. Prudence must be
exercised in selecting useful, safe, nonexploitive work experiences,
but students *need* to engage in socially useful activities such as
cleaning up litter in public parks, learning to weed the parks,
helping to dispose of debris on our beaches, shoveling snow, helping care for the school area, and performing similar tasks that
need to be done. These activities need to be done in small groups
over a sustained period of time, and with community understanding and cooperation.

As children move from seven-year-oldness to twelve-year-old-
ness, they could become genuinely important community resources,
develop social responsibility in the process, discover personal
significance, learn respect for labor, and also learn to respect an
environment by helping to keep it in good condition. The world
of the future should be a distinctly better place if such learnings
can be jointly sponsored by home, community, and school. These
real tasks are much better than such idiot's-delight activities as
coloring a circle green on a reading-readiness drill pad! They are
better not only because they are meaningful but because they are
the raw material of *real* readiness for learning.[11]

The experiences and the work in which children and youth
engage should make the community a distinctly and overtly better
place because the schools are there. This better environment should
show *concrete* evidence of the use of young learners as resources
in the form of less litter and well-kept parks, not merely in the
mystique that the schools make the community better by educating
children to be good little citizens.

The community becomes a massive teaching aid and source of
content. Implicit in the student-as-a-resource concept is the idea of
the community as a resource, a teaching aid of vitality, an extensive school without walls. Through careful planning and new de-
ployment of educational funds and personnel, our parks, factories,
museums, shops, governmental agencies, and a myriad of other

community entities can become literal components of a broad educative environment.

New content will lead to different uses of time and space. For generations past, school walls have been almost as rigidly confining as those of a jailhouse—albeit for less of the day. The concept of future-focused education envisioned here will abolish inflexible schedules and their inevitable concomitant, the school bell. It will also demolish the "jailhouse" walls that restricted learning to what could be simulated, or taught by telling, or preserved in books.[12] Instead of reflecting the phony theories that children's attention spans can't be sustained for more than twenty or thirty minutes, and that they sponge up knowledge best sitting quietly in rows, future-focused education will use larger time blocks (perhaps a week or more in April spent readying a neighborhood play area for summer use) and be much more active and social.

The three R's are not ignored in the context envisioned; they are learned under different ground rules, in more varied ways and at more varied times.

A new approach to the role of mass media in education will be made. Educative, behavior-influencing experiences which children of twelve or under acquire through mass media have tended to be receptive and passive. To live effectively, children need a future-focused carefully guided implanted image of the power, subtlety, and limitations of radio, the press, and TV. Particularly TV. Youngsters need to understand (Walter Cronkite's tag line to the contrary) that what they see and here on TV often *isn't* "The way it is"!

Meticulously cultivated awareness of the bias inherent in mass media needs to become a part of teaching of and for the future.[13] Boys and girls need to understand that the same sensory input does *not* lead to an identical or common interpretation of this input by the central nervous system of any two listener-viewers. Our subculture membership, our past experiences, determine what we see and hear. Also, they need at an early age to recognize that TV in particular contains many "visual editorials": not "pure" news but the camera teams' and the editors' ideas of what will enhance their reputations, capture viewers' attention, and promote the personal value-beliefs of the network policy-makers.

Future-Oriented Skills

Special future-oriented skills should be acquired. Most school-ing at the elementary level has tended to emphasize the past or the world as it is at present: often an almost static world as inter-preted in many classrooms. Attitudes and information deliberately selected in anticipation of the future role of a child were rarely included.

While young learners cannot explicitly be educated for tomor-rows about which one can only conjecture, project, or envision, they can be encouraged to develop certain ways of thinking, evaluating, and behaving which promise to make them more effec-tive human beings in a changing environment.

One skill that needs to be imprinted and nourished is that of coping with the rapid, almost exponential change that threatens the United States with anomie—with an alienating and faltering social structure. The need is reflected in the ranks of the thirty-and-under group today, many of whom, ironically, seem to have greater problems in adjusting to changes that constantly are sur-facing than do the over-thirties who have witnessed far greater changes since World War I than have occurred since 1955 in the lifetimes of today's youth.

Another skill, of which mention has been made earlier, is learn-ing to future-plan: to deploy time, energy, and money in such ways as seem likely to make the world better through a reasoned systems approach to designing a more pleasant, compassionate, less impersonal world. This is a plea not for cold or mechanical calculation of future costs and benefits, but for the use of imagina-tion and empathy in considering alternative courses of action, and for intelligence in considering these consequences.[14]

Coping skills and planning techniques are not acquired by children through lecturing or telling. They are absorbed by means of future-focused experiences which begin to help them recognize and explore possible alternative choices likely to create a more desirable environment for the human species. Coping with change and future-planning can be encouraged, say with ten- or twelve-year-olds, through discussion of such questions as "What has happened since *you* were eight?" and "How has our neighborhood changed in the last five years? Are the things that are happening good or bad?" "What do you want to happen to you next year?"

An able teacher will protect children from the folly of unreasoned decisions based on global discussions of topics of which they have little knowledge and on which there are few, if any, ways to obtain information. But, at the same time, even intelligent discussion and evaluation of change are not enough. Discussion should lead to action (or at least to active learning activities) to have any real, behavior-changing influence.

The Future-Oriented Climate

We noted earlier that "teaching the future" was a twofold task. In addition to a reinterpreted approach to content which provides a more suitable role-image for the future with which a child can identify, there is the matter of maintaining a sound, affective milieu for learning: an emotionally wholesome climate that will mediate thinking and behaving in childhood in ways that are consistent with the objectives of education.

Competent teachers long have recognized that there is such a thing as a "good" or "right" setting and tone for learning experiences. Among familiar attributes of such a milieu are encouragement of inquiry, respect for the learner, an atmosphere of freedom, stimulating content, flexible teaching procedures, and so on. The climate of future-focused schooling is especially important because of the need to motivate children to make a sustained effort both to attain a better world of tomorrow and to create a realistic place for themselves in such a world.

This is not to imply that each child should be prepared for his slot in an Orwellian future. Rather, his learning experiences should free him to "create himself" in terms of a viable self-image of the finest, most contributive, joyful person he can become. Patently, a supportive environment that will help children accomplish this delicate task is tremendously important. But what are its characteristics? Here is a brief list of some of the important, often neglected, components of a psychological climate that promise to help free children for cumulative self-realization:

An affective approach is made to cognitive experiences. The learner should feel ready to learn. His attitude, his readiness, rather than a prescriptive curriculum guide or course of study, provide the clues as to the timing, the sequence, and the breadth of what is experienced.

Participation is encouraged. A suitable climate helps prepare the child of twelve and below for future effectiveness by ensuring that he is "in" on things, that his opinions are valued, and that they will govern decisions to whatever degree that they have merit. Confrontation, as a technique of forcing issues, thus becomes needless. Even very young children can develop this understanding. They also can begin to sense that genuine broad-based participation makes it unnecessary to support an elite to think for others in the years ahead.

Pressures for uniform "Protestant Ethic" behavior are sharply reduced. At least some Americans have long been persuaded that unpleasant or hard school tasks had disciplinary value. They "helped make a man of you." Long, cold winter walks to school, penalties for being tardy, bell-regulated schedules, busywork that "kept idle hands from becoming the Devil's Workshop," and arduous, drill-type homework were some of the educational expressions of this Protestant Ethic.

Teaching for maximum self-realization as children grow older will more clearly recognize that it is unwise to attempt to pour human individuality into an eighteenth-century New England mold. The future requires flexibility and the power to adapt quickly, rather than an ability to respond to behavioral problems in terms of carefully transmitted, rigid conduct codes. This is not to suggest that elementary education will be without standards, but that the tone of teaching and learning will reflect an appreciation for a number of different values. Respect for human individuality—in recognition of the fact that children best do different things in different ways at different times—implies varied school entrance ages, perhaps different hours spent in learning, certainly a large number of personalized experiences, and new thinking as to the desirable limits of compulsory attendance at the secondary-school level.

Society rather than child or school is held accountable. Until recently children were held personally accountable for behavior and achievement in school. Punishment and report cards were the agents, respectively, for preserving order and for recording academic performance. In the late 1960s and 1970s there was much talk about the schools being held accountable, especially with respect to measurable academic skills. When teaching for the future, it probably will be desirable to do so in a classroom climate in which the child himself is not the fall guy who is blamed if he learns less than demanded for a "C" or better!

At the same time, there is considerable doubt in our minds as to whether the teacher of the school can be made accountable for formal discipline and uniform academic performance—particularly if an emotionally comfortable atmosphere is sought. Only in a comfortable atmosphere, free of unreasonable or premature academic pressure, can youngsters have experiences that will enable them to move into the future with a positive self-concept and a healthy future-focused role-image. Neither the teacher nor the learner can be held fully accountable. Society, itself, must once again accept some responsibility for the educative experiences of children.

When Tom Sawyer was a lad, virtually all of the adults in his riverfront town on the Mississippi felt responsible for *all* children's progress toward adult maturity. Recall how quickly someone took action or informed Aunt Polly when Tom strayed from the path of rectitude! In a broader, more dynamic sense, the community today needs once again to take on the responsible role it has played in most of mankind's history in being accountable for the next generation.

The End of Age-Segregation

Age-grouping must disappear. For over a century in most United States schools, children have been age-grouped. When admitted, usually in September at age five or six, boys and girls are assigned to a Kindergarten or Grade One teacher. Originally devised as a useful means of distributing elementary children when one-room schools began to be replaced by multi-room buildings, graded school organization, in our opinion, is not only a major impediment to overdue educational changes, it is a source of unreasonable discrimination against children. There is no place for this form of school organization in a future-focused program. Invidious comparisons, unimaginative mass teaching methods, much text and workbook material of doubtful worth, report cards that can be emotionally harmful, isolated content teaching, and the failure-or-promotion decisions over which teachers agonize are among the liabilities sustained in age-group classrooms.

Ironically, after more than one hundred years of searching, no psychologically desirable and reliable ways have been found to subgroup children in a given grade.[15] To attain a good climate for learning, the graded-school concept must be abandoned and age-grouping replaced by short-term or ad-hocratic groupings built around child interests, purposes, tasks, discussions and comparable activities.

The stigma is removed from non-college-bound students. The belief that almost all youth should go on to colleges as they are now constituted is one of the most indefensible and dangerous of the tacit assumptions made by teachers, parents, and their children. In 1890, a case might have been made for urging that able potential contributors to society enroll in higher education. A vast market existed for professional men, the liberally educated, and the specially prepared. What universities offered was more or less appropriate for the tiny number of students enrolled.

Today almost the exact reverse is true. Beginning with children of elementary-school age, we need to point out that there are numerous valuable, important, dignified ways in which everyone can serve humanity, and that most of them do not require a liberal-arts degree. Until this point is put across with conviction, millions of children of twelve or younger will continue to feel that they are failures if they do not contemplate attending a college. And they will languish in a school climate that damages any prospect of acquiring a future-focused self-concept and role-image with which girls and boys can live happily and with self-respect.

The concepts of alternative futures and social consequences will strengthen children's role-images. Not only must we de-intensify the anachronistic campaign to persuade most children and youth to attend college, we must place new stress on the idea that many alternative futures are open to us and that desirable ones *can* be attained. In other words, we must create, even for quite young children, learning atmospheres that are wholesome and hopeful, infused with the idea that each individual learner—and our entire species as well—have many desirable choices open to us, and that, with rational planning, there will be a rewarding role for each child to fill.[16]

Many components of a desirable psychological climate for future-focused learning could be identified and added to those already listed. It was not our goal to make a comprehensive list. Rather, we intended to make the point that a child's self-concept —if it is to help him move happily and wisely toward tomorrow at the elementary level—must involve more than mere tinkering with the design for learning that is woven today by home, school, street, mass media, and other ingredients of American culture.

To introduce the future effectively in the life of the elementary-school-age child, we must not only devise new concepts of content and recast old subject matter to free the mind; we must make use of far-reaching innovations in the creation of a setting for learning that breeds a free spirit—a spirit capable of envisioning desirable alternative futures and willing to work to bring them into being.

When, and as, we accomplish these objectives, education will become at last not merely a reflection of yesterday, not merely a means of living better today, but a supremely interesting process through which we help children and youth learn how to create new outposts on the frontiers of social progress which they will inherit the right and the duty to explore as tomorrow comes.

What was probably the first future-oriented course in an American high school was initiated and taught by Priscilla Griffith in 1966 in an innovative school serving, among others, the children of technicians at Cape Kennedy. It was, she says, a primitive and rickety first model. Nevertheless, many of the methods and preoccupations of this early course foreshadowed the work being done elsewhere today. Here, Mrs. Griffith, tongue occasionally in cheek, tells what it was like.

CHAPTER TWELVE

Teaching the Twenty-First Century in a Twentieth-Century High School

by Priscilla P. Griffith

> Nevertheless, in spite of the dangers, it is a wonderful age to live in, and I would not wish to be born in any other time. The wonderful and precious thing about the present moment is that there is still time—the Bomb hasn't gone off, the population explosion may be caught, the technological problem can, perhaps, be solved. If the human race is to survive, however, it will have to change more in its ways of thinking in the next twenty-five years than it has done in the last twenty-five thousand.
>
> —*Kenneth E. Boulding*

The rapid and startling changes rocking our society today force the classroom teacher to face the fact that her words are not necessarily wisdom, and that, in fact, even if they are wisdom at the moment they are uttered, they may be obsolete the next moment. The student has every right to mistrust the generalizations delivered in the classroom unless he or she has an opportunity to test their correctness against the real world. This means that the student must have an opportunity to become what William Boyer calls "a causal agent in historical change." Only by attempting to make change in the social and physical environment around him can the student test the accuracy and relevance of what the school proclaims as knowledge.

It is the task of the teacher to help give students the tools and attitudes that will help them and us survive in the midst of a historical transformation. There is a need, too, for positive images of the future. People need to feel that they *can* cope, and the place to start that feeling is in the schools.

Whether the "futures" course I shall describe was able to accomplish these objectives cannot be stated with certainty. There were those students who said they had "learned a lot." But what they meant by that is moot.

The course was one of the first ever given in a United States high school and is perhaps a primitive model of the many courses on this subject now cropping up all over the country. Were I to have the opportunity to teach a similar course once again, there is much I would do differently. Clearly, many of the limited materials then available could now be improved upon. At the time, the term "ecology" was still scarcely known and pollution a vague, rather than immediate, menace. There were relatively few readily available books and articles dealing with the future in terms appropriate to the high school.

But more than materials are involved. Having learned from teaching, I would today place much greater emphasis on the development of *positive* images of the future, calling to the student's attention at least some appealing alternatives to the present. I would also sharpen the focus to emphasize the issue of human survival, making it a major, rather than minor, theme in the course. Nevertheless, with all due qualification, I am more convinced than ever that the future must play a role in the preparation of young people for active, healthy lives in a period of rapid and sometimes extreme change.

The Need for a Gyroscope

In a book called *Teaching as a Subversive Activity*,[1] the public-school teacher is advised to equip his students with a built-in "crap detector"—i.e., the inquiring attitude. The student, we are told, must be trained in the techniques of inquiry. He must be given the confidence to question, examine and thereby arrive at a definition of truth. Hopefully, thereafter, this definition will provide a framework for judgment and make it possible for him to act on the basis of his judgment, while at the same time recognizing that changing conditions may alter the framework.

Yet the student needs more than a crap detector. He also needs a gyroscope. He must be able to act—to adapt to change, to be a viable human being while undergoing a severe form of cultural stress, future shock. And while alternate forms of education are increasingly available, it is probably safe to assume that, at least for the majority of this generation of schoolchildren, the public school system is still "it." Thus, while the development of alternative forms of education is extremely important, this article will proceed from the assumption that future studies need to be incorporated not merely into the free schools, the open schools, and other experimental systems, but into the mainstream of public education as well. In this connection, it may be helpful to describe what happened in one public high school which offered a full year's course on the future. It might be equally instructive to look at what happened to the course, itself, as it was changed by the context of the school system in which it was offered.

Melbourne High School serves a community adjacent to Cape Kennedy, where preparations for the moon landing were already under way. An estimated 50 to 60 per cent of the students were children of technicians at the base. The student body, however, spanned the economic and social spectrum. Racially, 10 to 15 per cent were black. "Mel Hi" itself, was at this time an exciting and innovative place.

Its principal at the time, Dr. B. Frank Brown, was himself a bringer of change. Nationally identified with the idea of non-graded schools, Brown was receptive to suggestions for change, and Melbourne considered itself, and was considered by many, to be on the cutting edge. It seemed perfectly natural that it should attempt a course so in keeping with its spirit and with the symbolism of the Space Age.

The course had its genesis in an article by Alvin Toffler that appeared in the Summer 1965 issue of *Horizon* magazine.[2] The theme of this article was the now well-known idea that people were suffering from future shock, a phenomenon which was bound to get worse with the increasing speed of change. To prepare people for rapid change, Toffler suggested that courses on the future should be taught in elementary and secondary schools as well as colleges and universities.

On reading this article, I wrote to Toffler, inviting him to help us implement the idea. The invitation was seconded by Dr. Brown, and before long Toffler appeared for two days of conferences. These meetings brought together teachers from several departments—art, social studies, English, science and math. Teachers came in during their planning periods and also conferred with Toffler and each other after school. The conferences were intended to bring some of the interested, innovative faculty in contact with a "futurist" so that his thesis, perspective and suggestions might have an impact on their thinking—and vice versa. But the target was immediate and practical: to set up guidelines for a year's social-studies course in the future.

Toffler came supplied with a rough course outline consisting of fifteen units with recommended readings for each. The readings ranged from magazine articles (*Playboy*, "The World of 1984"),[3] to nonfiction books (Arthur Clarke's *Profiles of the Future*),[4] novels (Edward Bellamy's *Looking Backward*),[5] to contemporary science fiction (William Tenn's "The Servant Problem"). Originally, he had conceived of the course as an offering for students of above-average ability and interest.

As it turned out, the course was never taught to a class of this type during the three years it was in the Melbourne curriculum. While there were always a number of very good students in the classes, the course itself was offered on a "Phase Three" or average level. This situation meant, naturally, that there had to be considerable modification of both the reading list and the approach to make it practicable and appealing.

There was another reason for modifying the reading list: the student's pocketbook. While teachers were free to require student purchase of paperbacks, either to supplement textbooks or replace them, even one book per course unit would have been beyond the reach of many of our students. A second reason for shortening the list was the usual unwillingness of average students to do much reading, particularly at home. Moreover, a number of books and articles were unobtainable for various reasons. Thus, suitable replacements had to be found in the form of articles which could be reproduced by the teacher and—more important—in activities such as games or films, which would cover the same topics.

As the course took shape, the following units were laid in place:

I.   Introduction to the Future,
II.   Predicting the Future,
III.   War and Violence,
IV.   Race Relations,
V.   Work and Leisure,
VI.   Man and Machine,
VII.   Intelligence,
VIII. Communications,
IX.   Control of the Mind,
X.   The Politics of Tomorrow,
XI.   Population,
XII.   Urbanization,
XIII. Genetics,
XIV.   Life Span,
XV.   What Is Man?

All these units were used in the order originally suggested, and a number of teaching games and simulations, also suggested by Toffler, were incorporated. As the course developed through its first year, other readings, games and activities were introduced— some original and some borrowed.

Toffler arrived in Melbourne with a considerable number of ideas for activities to be used as teaching devices. A number of them were actually utilized, although some had to be modified. (More about the ones used later.) There were several, however, which, if put into practice, might have caused considerable difficulty in almost any public school. One of the more ingenious "simulations" would have had each student actually live with a sequence of families other than his or her own, spending a month at the first home, three weeks in the next, two weeks in the one after that, and so on down to a single day. The idea was for them to experience, and learn how to live with, a phenomenon likely to become quite common in the future: frequent changes of home, family and friendship relations—transience. The participating students would have had to learn to make rapid emotional adjustments to different types of people in the intimate setting of family life, and at an accelerating pace.

Since rootlessness has frequently been cited as a cause of alienation, it might, indeed, have been interesting to see how this experiment would have turned out, both for the families and for the adolescents. Discretion prevailed, however. It would have been extremely controversial, of uncertain value, risky, difficult to organize, and probably would have suffered from a scarcity of volunteers. Nevertheless, even the presentation of such an innovation and the issues it raised, proved a stimulant to our imaginations.

After much discussion of the widely varied games, simulations and other exercises, as well as the basic readings, the course was approved for the school year 1966–1967, and it was named "Twenty-First Century" to suggest immediately that it would not be an ordinary, run-of-the-mill academic offering. Melbourne High has a college-style registration procedure in the fall, during which students sign up for electives. It pays to advertise. We did. And it worked. Both sections were filled to overflowing. The "Twenty-First Century" opened to a full house.

Student Expectations

This full house consisted of two sections whose numbers each fluctuated during the school year between thirty-five and forty-one students. Although Melbourne High uses homogeneous grouping based on achievement, the system of registration often allows students to take courses above or below their level. All a student needs is a good story and a willing teacher. Phase Three, or average, classes are, as might be suspected, the most likely to contain a goodly number of other than "average" students. As it turned out, "Twenty-First Century" appealed to a very wide range of students.

Every teacher knows that each class is different—in tone, texture, and the interplay of minds and personalities. How does one adjust readings and activities originally designed for advanced students to a less-advanced group? The question of level proved to be a persistent problem with the course, despite its popularity. Nevertheless, very few students transferred out—and most of those who did, did so for reasons of necessity, not disappointment. The course clearly met the students' expectations that it would be something "different."

These expectations were themselves interesting. It would be accurate to say that a majority of the students had rather limited notions of the future built, it would appear, largely around their own experiences and those of their families—plus the American fascination with technology. To many, the future simply meant more consumer goods. What technical goodies would our society come up with next? What miracles would science create? Certainly, the fact that the school is in the Cape Kennedy area enhanced the faith in technology. This being the case, many students expected the course to concern itself chiefly with the wonders of technology.

There were a few, however, who—even then—were ready to view science and technology as a two-edged sword, solving some problems and creating others. There were also a few who saw the future as ending rather too soon in nuclear catastrophe. Perhaps they took the course as a form of masochism!

Such an unusual course, along with the heterogeneity of the students, puts a special burden on the teacher. It requires a teacher with a distinctly interdisciplinary attitude, with a tolerance for unusual opinions, with the ability to serve as a kind of ringmaster in a three-ring circus, and—above all—a sense of humor.

To whet the student's appetite and set the purpose for the year's experience, the first unit, "Introduction to the Future," opened with a long, two-part reading from *Playboy* entitled "The World of 1984."[6] In it a group of celebrated science-fiction writers participated in a group interview. They discussed the future in terms of genetic engineering, alternatives to marriage, life expectancy, transportation, space travel, etc. *Playboy* had given us permission to reproduce the article, but this created a problem for us: censorship. The school is still a public agency, and unless one is prepared for a long, bitter, and digressive struggle, there are some things a teacher does not distribute to a public high school class. We solved the problem of questionable passages with the help of scissors and black Magic Marker. Of course, any student could have read the entire article outside. Nevertheless, some students, not inappropriately, protested the cuts. It was a healthy and educational experience for all of us and we were immediately propelled, by it, into the real world of the present. This, in turn, provided a backdrop against which the problems of tomorrow might be silhouetted.

Since, for reasons of economy, there was only a single set of these reproduced articles, they were read in class by all students, who then divided into small discussion groups. They were given a set of probing questions to get them started, and were asked to report the group's conclusions. Student reactions were swift and intense: delight, disbelief, fear, horror, anticipation. (It was, incidentally, quickly possible to identify the science-fiction buffs in the class because, with a few exceptions, they had already learned from their reading to think more in terms of the social and ethical problems of the future than simply the gadgetry.)

After the smorgasbord of "The World of 1984," the class turned its attention to "Can We Cope with Tomorrow?"—an early essay by Toffler that appeared in *Redbook*.[7] Here students became acquainted with Toffler's basic thesis concerning the acceleration of change and its effects, and what might be done about it. The discussion of this article was teacher-led, and apart from some difficulty with a few of the terms, it was well received.

We then turned to some of the time-line charts from Arthur Clarke's *Profiles of the Future*[8] in which he forecasts future scientific and technical developments. (Later, after the publication *The Futurist*[9] came into being, we made use of its forecasts as well.) Here again we had many opportunities for rich discussion—not simply about the technology, but about the values of the class and the society. A good exercise that can be used early in the course, and then repeated at the end, is to ask each student to select and

detail in writing a "most desirable" and "least desirable" development, and to state his or her reasons for the selection. Such an
exercise not only involves the use of language and expressive skills,
but, perhaps equally important, compels the student to match
possible future developments against his or her own present value
system in an explicit way.

Clarke's chapters on predictions that have come true, and those
that have not, along with his explanation of why, were instructive,
amusing and fascinating. They served as an excellent launching
pad for the unit on "Predicting the Future." This consisted of
reading and discussing "The Method of Scientific Investigation" by
Thomas Huxley,[10] and then playing a couple of illustrative games.
The students found this nineteenth-century essay rather quaint and
usually became thoroughly tangled in the distinction between
inductive and deductive thinking. Oh, they knew what a hypothesis was, all right, and they apparently grasped that one should not
build a hypothesis on a single isolated fact—although a tendency
to do just that remained evident throughout the school year. But,
when asked to label some examples as deductive or inductive,
confusion took over. Many got the point, but encouraging any considerable number to apply more systematic or "scientific thinking"
the rest of the year was another matter. By the time they are in
high school, students have been so thoroughly indoctrinated by
tradition that they want to learn (i.e., memorize) "facts" in discrete units, and have difficulty transferring knowledge from one
activity or area of learning to another.

A game we played at this point involved a dialogue between
teacher and class. It went something like this:

Teacher: Suppose you and a friend decided to go out in a boat
on the ocean one day and after you got far from
shore, the motor broke down. How would you get
back to land?
Student in the rear: Call the Coast Guard on the radio.
Teacher: There is no radio on the boat.
Student: Row.
Teacher: No oars.
Student in third row: Run up a sail.
Teacher: No sail.

After several minutes of this banter, a student might say: Get out of the boat and push it!

Teacher: There are sharks in the water.

By now frustration sets in, along with a strong desire to best the teacher. Many students, asked what the game was supposed to show, professed to believe that it was a demonstration of the principle "the student can never win!" Several of the "victims" declared that it showed how many things—including improbable things—can happen to upset human plans. Actually, the game opened the way into a discussion of probability and forecasting. By forcing the players to move successively from obvious to more far-fetched or imaginative solutions, it led to a clarification of the distinction between possible and probable futures.

To push this distinction further, we asked the students to select some ordinary activity, such as going to movies on Friday night, and to list all the precondition events that had to happen first. We then discussed the probability of these preconditions actually happening. Many of the students resisted, arguing that this exercise was a "waste of time." But most of them enthusiastically entered into the next one.

The class divided into two teams to play a new version of the old game "Battleships." In this game, each team "hides" three geometric shapes on a coordinated grid, kept out of sight of the "enemy." The opposing team, by applying probability theory, has to guess at the location of the concealed shapes, and, by successive approximation, zero in on them. The shapes or "ships" occupy numbered squares. Each team is given several "shots" at the other's fleet. At first the shots are random. But as soon as a "hit" is scored, it is possible to use probability theory to place one's successive shots most effectively. Much fun, high-spirited and competitive banter takes place. But, by the time the game is over, many students are asking "What does this have to do with the future?" and the teacher has an opportunity to take the next, and far more difficult step, and explain the connection between choice-making, probability, and future-influencing events. Making this connection clear is by no means easy, and I cannot say we were always successful. By now, however, the students are champing at the bit for more "future."

theless, futurists have found that games possess important pedagogical effects.

Games motivate. Game-playing is enjoyable and something to look forward to. Self-motivated as well as unmotivated students can become involved in game dynamics and, subsequently, become interested in the subject matter that was simulated. Games are orderly systems which offer the student a sense of control, which in turn partly accounts for the power of the games to motivate players. Games help students understand the world by integrating selected aspects of reality in such a way that the relationships among them become clear as the player manipulates them. Because they create student interaction, they open up the classroom to student-to-student communication, which, depending upon the nature of the game, can result in a sense of group coherence, even esprit. Beyond this, and perhaps equally important, they alter attitudes toward authority. Since the rules are built into the games, and are not the product of the authority of the teacher, students are less likely to respect authority blindly, for its own sake.

Since the mid-sixties a wide variety of academic games have been devised for school use. Until 1967, however, no future-oriented games had been invented, let alone made accessible to teachers. In that year Olaf Helmer and Theodore Gordon created *Future*, a game in which players try to predict the impact of different types of events on each other. Investments can influence the probability of a given event happening, and players wager on the outcome of various alternatives. *Future* received limited distribution as a public-relations gesture of Kaiser Industries and influenced the computerized exploration of the year 2000 which was programmed into the PLATO computer system at the University of Illinois.

At the same time, Alvin Toffler designed a number of "future theater" exercises for use in an experimental "Twenty-First Century" course at Melbourne (Florida) High School.*

In the last four years a number of other futuristics games have been developed for secondary- and college-level classrooms. It is

* See Griffith, Priscilla, "Teaching the Twenty-First Century in a Twentieth-Century High School," supra.

not the purpose of this paper to review the rules, objectives, etc., of these games. Rather, it is worth noting that futurists interested in educational gaming quickly found, as Villegas did earlier, that games actually designed by the teacher—often with the assistance of the students themselves—offer a number of advantages that even well-conceived finished games cannot provide. Building one's own future-oriented game turns out to be an extremely powerful educational exercise.

There are a number of ways in which this can be done. For example, future time can be incorporated into a simulation either through having the play, itself, simulate the passage of years or by setting the game at some specified date in the future. In the latter case, one can note that some events are scheduled considerably in advance of their occurrence, such as political conventions, meetings of legislative bodies, elections, graduations, bond maturations, and the census. For example, a Mars colonization game would hypothetically be set in 1990. A variation on this theme involves selecting a year and speculating about conditions at that time: What will be the titles of ten best-selling books in A.D. 2000? What will the federal budget look like in 1984? What etiquette will prevail in the year 2525? Future events can also be fabricated to suit special purposes.

In a class devoted to the future of the Appalachian region, my students participated in the founding convention of the state of Appalachia. Needless to say, the likelihood of this event ever happening is low, but the simulation provided the setting for a number of classroom activities. Students passed bills establishing laws for the new commonwealth, they submitted designs for a state flag, and discussed issues affecting the future of the area.

Every forecasting technique is theoretically adaptable to classroom gaming. The "cross-impact game" can serve as an example for discussion. The procedure for playing is simple and many variations on the theme are possible. Three steps are involved.

Step one consists of writing on a sheet of paper a concise description of a plausible future event. "Three-year marriage contracts become law; licenses can be renewed, if desired, by the parties to the contract at the time of expiration." This is one possibility out of thousands. The "event" is circulated among the class, each student adding a one-sentence *consequence* on the paper. For instance, the three-year marriage law inspired these speculations among one group:

- A great majority of people would give this a try, and there would be an awful lot of women left with a bunch of children on their hands.
- This would create the need for more state assistance such as the aid to dependent children program.
- The issue of revenue would arise. The government would need to get money for aid programs from someplace.
- Taxes would be increased which in turn would cause public resentment toward the government and toward the people who had children without planning for their support.
- Radical schemes to solve the problem would be advanced by politicians (compulsory sterilization, childless first marriages, etc.).
- Because all these problems arose, the Supreme Court would declare the law unconstitutional; when people got married they would have to stay married unless they got a divorce.

What is important here is not whether the assumed consequences are "correct." The simple process of eliciting consequences forces students to think imaginatively about social causation. It helps them clarify and make explicit their assumptions about the way things are organized at present. And, more important, it encourages the habit of thinking in terms of consequences; it suggests to them that all actions, personal or private, past, present or future, trigger reverberations.

Step two demonstrates that subjective biases can influence predictions—a point worth stressing. Another single-sentence event is circulated, this time separating the responses of male students from those of the women. Any sex-related forecasting biases that exist with respect to a particular issue are likely to be revealed. Similarly, the same event may inspire the perception of quite different consequences if it is circulated among (A) a group generally favorable to the development, and separately circulated among (B) a group unfavorably disposed to it. And so forth. One can compare the responses of liberal-arts majors with natural-science majors, graduate students with undergraduates, rural students with urban students, teachers with students, or whatever. This demonstration should help students develop a more critical eye for the press, polls, and television, as well as futurist forecasts.

Step three involves moving from this demonstration to a theoretical discussion of cross-impact matrix forecasting.[2] One can use a game, it is clear, to accomplish academic objectives. Students can design their own matrixes or supply ideas for a matrix assembled by the teacher for the class. The cross-impact game can be further used to test individual items in the series. Or students can devise a Delphi survey which could contribute input for a cross-impact matrix. At the conclusion of this process, the class will have created a testable model of future events.

Other departures using the add-a-line technique are possible. These may not qualify as "games," if a strict interpretation of the term is followed, but a game parameter is observed. One exercise consists of completing a scenario. The teacher would take the responsibility for describing some future state-of-affairs to the class, such as the following:

> The Guaranteed Income Act passed Congress and was signed into law on July 4, 1978. The demographic effects of this act were felt in Appalachia almost immediately. Counties which had steadily lost population for many years abruptly became population gainers. Eastern Kentucky, which had 500,000 people in the 1970 census, reached the 800,000 mark ten years later. The repopulation of Appalachia had many consequences for the region, among them . . .

After the students have written a passage developing consequences, several options are open to the teacher. A class discussion comparing various scenarios might be used to select the three or four stories most likely to come true. The same discussion could be used to locate student interests and lines of speculation about the future that could be researched by the class. Or this could serve as an introduction to further scenario writing. Which brings up another idea: completing a science-fiction story. Again the teacher could write the opening paragraph of such a tale. Each student in class could be asked to add a paragraph. Or each student could be asked to complete the story (this would generate thirty or so adventures instead of one); in this case, each student could be assigned to work on an angle for his or her writing.

One student might assume the viewpoint of a geologist, another might write the story from an economic vantage point, a political outlook and so forth.

Board games also can be adopted for use in the classroom. With a *Monopoly*-type game, each circuit around the board could simulate one year (or two, five, ten years).[3]

The ten or so spaces along each of the four sides of the board could be programed with seasonal events—elections in the autumn, vacations in the summertime, income tax in April, etc. Or a board which is traversed only *once* is conceivable. Each space might represent one year, players beginning in 1973 and proceeding, step by step, to 2001 or some other terminal date. Boards can also be designed with multiple pathways leading into the future. Instead of one track around the edges of a square board, a second, inside track, can be added. Tokens could be switched from one track to another at various points: when a new contract for employment is "signed," when a new party is elected to office, when a predicted event occurs. Chinese checkers provides yet another model. Multiple pathways can intersect and various types of intervention (blockades, etc.) could shape the outcome, that is, the future. Each move away from one's starting position might simulate a year. And branching programs offer further refinement of this idea. Articulation of intervention modes can become sophisticated.

Board games can also make use of maps—real or hypothetical. During each round of a game, for example, players can make investments in urban real estate and add a department store or factory to the map. Perhaps these moves might be intercepted by another player representing public interest, or government. A zoning regulation might be a trump card prohibiting construction of the store. The ocean floor could be depicted, players taking turns developing areas of the sea for different purposes. And boards could be designed in the form of charts or graphs; each round of play might add new information to the game. The design of such games by teachers and class can, itself, prove extremely valuable, since it forces participants to make explicit and open for discussion many of their previously implicit, undeveloped assumptions about the way the real world is organized.

Probably the approach that offers the most promise for academic purposes, however, is social simulation. Even a relatively small class can become

—the American economy,
—the House of Representatives,
—the United Nations.

In Business 2000 a class is divided into groups of three or four students, each representing some corporation (Ford, A&P, U.S. Gypsum, etc.). Each student in the corporation has a specific function such as chairman of the board, research and development manager, vice-president for sales and marketing, and the like. After studying current practices of their corporation, each group is asked to study the future. Possible inventions, changes in consumer preference, and similar information is supplied by the teacher. Then each group creates plans for its firm: modified organizational structure, new budget priorities, etc. Each group is also asked to develop a new product line (or service) and to design an appropriate advertising campaign with slogans, posters, distribution plans. The advertising and its rationale are presented in class before the other "corporations" for their critique. This game can be varied by introducing changes in human values in the future.

The scale of social simulations can be 1:1 to good effect. An example of this is the *Future Family Game*. The initial idea for this simulation came from Howard R. Lewis and Harold S. Streitfeld's *Growth Games* (Harcourt, Brace, 1970). In *Future Family*, futuristics enters the affective domain; what will it *feel* like to live in 1999? Students are recruited to act the part of family members circa 1972. Mother, father, children, are restricted to stereotyped behavior patterns, patterns which typically emerge in nuclear households. One can usually find a placater (it is my fault, I am to blame), an attacker (it is your fault), and an evader (why don't we go to the movies?). In one situation, a daughter who is pregnant comes home from college to deal with an attacking father, evasive mother and placating brother. In another situation an errant son returns home to a religious family; the son has become an atheist at college.

Then the future family is role-played. Several models exist for the family of tomorrow—husband, wife and temporary third parties, unequal numbers of husbands and wives, large groups of people married to each other—being obviously different from today's norm. The simulation that was used in class involved a future family made up of two husbands and two wives (a *Proposition 31* marriage); instead of dysfunctional stereotypes, the "parents" were asked to play "grown-up" adults, people willing to recognize their own shortcomings and who are not committed to traditional sex-typed behavior. In this case a student came home from college and told the family of his unorthodox desire to marry one woman and only one.

Affective components can be designed into more academically oriented simulations as well. Class members can constitute themselves a jury, in the legal *or* nonlegal sense. Simulated appeals to the Supreme Court in 1980 or 2020 would demonstrate the student's comprehension of the complexities of social innovations. It would also demonstrate understanding of aspects of the American system of jurisprudence—if that were a class objective—and the ability of a student to articulate.

The role of the teacher in classroom games can vary considerably. The basic options seem to be participant, referee, banker, policeman, scorekeeper, moderator and random-events generator. This last may be unfamiliar to many readers; it requires the teacher to supply information to players that is best introduced at critical times. The *Educational Futures* game played at the University of Massachusetts is an example of the kind of simulation that requires a random-events generator. Students represented four groups inside a state: the legislature, the black ghetto, white blue-collar districts and affluent suburbanites. The legislature, in turn, was subdivided in blocs of representatives for the three populations.

The legislature was given a one-hour time limit in which to spend $100,000,000 allocated to education. However, there was one catch: During the first fifteen minutes $10,000,000 of the total had to be disbursed, during the next quarter-hour the figure increased to $20,000,000 and then to thirty and forty million in the two remaining fifteen-minute increments. The three citizen's groups held meetings while the legislature was in session; blacks, "hard hats" and suburbanites discussed their needs and also sent recommendations to their representatives by way of lobbyists. Not only was the clock working to pressure the legislature—their constituents were as well. But that was not all that they had to contend with.

Two students acted as the media; one was the local "news-paper," the other took the part of regional "television." The teacher announced the occurrence of "events" whenever they seemed most likely to stimulate discussion. During the hour, the people's government had a statehouse scandal to think about, a student-protest demonstration to mull over, and a proposal from the governor to eliminate the last semester of high school. The community groups meeting *outside* the assembly hall were told about these news events, and also about actions of the legislature, by the media. The media, however, were free to distort all news in any way that suited their fancy as long as truth was contained somewhere in their stories.

The teacher can also act as editor-in-chief. Preparing a 2002 issue of the Louisville *Courier-Journal*, furthermore, involves an entire class in different, but related, work. Page layout, cartoons, features, news stories, need preparation. Or the teacher can act as television-station manager. An April 1, 1984, evening-news tele-cast can be staged. When this exercise was tried recently at Alice Lloyd College, each class selected an issue that was global in character—communist influence, industrialization, wars, space exploration—and took part in brainstorming sessions to generate ideas for specific events at the date being considered. Possible events in space in 1984 included

> —first crime reported in outer space,
> —orbiting space hospital established,
> —private enterprise—tourism—begun in outer space,
> —astronauts rescued (or lost),
> —ore deposits discovered on the moon,
> —military space station launched by Soviets,
> —Neptune space probe sends holographic signals to Earth.

Similar lists were drawn up for other categories of international news. Students were asked to conceive other possible domestic events in fields like technology, medicine, politics. They were given a list of expected value changes by 1984 and were also asked to devise likely events to emerge from an American society that is

—concerned with self-actualization,
—willing to concede errors publicly,
—tolerant of a wide variety of life-styles,
—concerned with the right to have privacy.

News reporters developed "hot" stories; a business staff prepared spot advertisements for television as it might be broadcast twelve years hence. Interviews were staged. Props were prepared. Discussions about the content, format, timing of the program were held; one class decided to transmit their newscast from an orbiting space station. At the end of three weeks of preparation, each class was ready to videotape the news.

The playback of each program further involved students in appraising their work. But, of course, significant feedback does not require television equipment. It is during post-mortem sessions that considerable learning takes place on the part of participants and the designer. Did the rules of the game teach useful lessons about the real world? Was the outcome of the game plausible? Did a sense of future time emerge from playing? And what suggestions are there for improving the game?

What should be clear by now is that there is considerable potential for futuristic game design.

The Future as Change Agent

It is also clear, however, that the introduction of futures into education can be more than the creation of a new course. It can contribute heavily to cognitive learning; but it also touches on affective learning and encourages the use of imagination in new ways. Moreover, the introduction of the future implies educational change. It encourages a reexamination of the organization of knowledge. Because it is inherently interdisciplinary, it implies or encourages structural change as well. And because of its open-ended character—a subject in which there are few, if any, "right" or "final" answers—it works toward a change in the student-teacher relationship as well.

That the introduction of the future can be a generalized stimulus for educational change should not surprise us. To see into the future —even to attempt it—means that one is affected by one's vision. Robert Jacques Turgot, chief minister of Louis XVI, suggested that if a man had true insight into the future, he would have little choice but to condition his behavior according to his perception, and in so doing, might well be thought mad by his contemporaries.

In this sense, Turgot realized what many futurists are today still learning: that the present is a laboratory for the future. Waiting passively for predictions to come true or to be disconfirmed is *not* futuristics, futuribles, futures research, futurology or whatever one chooses to call the field. Imagining or forecasting future events is only a part of futures studies. Acting is the more important part.

Turgot made a number of astonishingly "correct" forecasts: He foresaw the success of the American revolution and the breakaway of the colonies from England because he saw trends leading toward greater human freedom. But he did more than merely observe these trends. He was a philosophe actively trying to change the consciousness of his countrymen. He served as teacher to Condorcet and the French republicans.

In Turgot's words: "Before we have learned that things are in a given situation, they have already been altered several times. Thus we always become aware of events when it is too late, and politics has to foresee the present, so to speak." Not that all futurists—as the term is here defined—are radicals. That conclusion is demonstrably unwarranted. As futurists, Robert Theobald and Herman Kahn live at different ends of the political spectrum, Kahn supporting the military establishment, Theobald doing all he can to undermine it. What they share is a similar "lunacy." Neither is at home in the present. Both are impatient with now. Educational futurists share this orientation.

In the case of teachers, this means a commitment to move beyond the still-predominant style of the 1950s. This does not mean that by 1984 all lectures and discussions will or should cease in classrooms throughout the United States, or that school buildings will be totally replaced by computer terminals, specially equipped touring vans or television consoles. The future does not arrive that way, nor does change within education.

What happens in history can best be described by the phrase "cumulative succession." Old forms and methods persist even though new structures and activities may come to dominate a field. The importance of the older way of doing things in the new order is invariably altered. Less time is devoted to older methodologies, but they are integrated into the modern system at strategic points, although the process may require years before a satisfactory balance is achieved. Less concern is given to older values; they drop in priority rankings, but they continue to exist as part of the revised system.

The learning experiments that have been carried out under the rubric of futuristics are part of this larger process of educational reform and renewal. Indeed, today they may well be the leading edge of change.

*I*t is not science fiction that needs the schools, Dennis Livingston declares, but the schools that need science fiction. For while this genre of literature fought for a long time to establish its legitimacy, it is now schooling itself that finds its legitimacy under attack. The intelligent use of science fiction, he contends, can not only enhance the student's sense of the future, but enliven the imagination, and increase the ability to cope with the change and surprise that are likely to be features of the future.

CHAPTER FOURTEEN

Science Fiction as an Educational Tool

by Dennis Livingston

Adaptation to change begins in consciousness, and science fiction—the speculative extension of technological man—has been crucial to the present rise of visions with new force among the young.
—*Michael Rossman*

Those who live in a time of rapid social change are constrained to contemplate the future, to consider the options it holds for the development of themselves and their society, and to choose the paths in time that appear to promise the most significant improvements in humanity's lot. Preparation for such future-seeking should be a basic and continuing function of education at all levels, yet most of the current school curriculum is time-bound, restricted in its scope to a perspective that sweeps from the past to the present. If we take seriously the charge that students must be prepared for a world in which a plurality of life-styles, values, and social systems will strain to coexist, then education must extend its domain to include the consideration of what is possible or potential in human development.

Logically, one important tool for acquainting students with alternative futures should be the literature of science fiction. Almost by definition, this literature provides a body of works, extending back more than a century, which have taken as their theme the impact of change, particularly that derived from advances in science and technology, on human affairs. Science fiction is thus an archive of futuristic images, a literary repository of the hopes, fears, and speculations of men and women concerning the evolving status of humanity and, therefore, an invaluable training ground for its readers in the anticipation and creation of things to come.

And yet—suggestions that science fiction be incorporated into the educational curriculum have traditionally been greeted by administrators and teachers with as much enthusiasm as would be given, say, to proposals that high schools legalize marijuana or that colleges promote cohabitation in their dorms. Indeed, there is a certain analogy in the way that constituted authorities have perceived both smoking pot and reading science fiction: Both have been frowned on as detrimental to students' future mental stability and aesthetic sensibilities; both have been accused of promoting the subversion of prevailing values; and both, consequently, have usually found their way into schools only insofar as they were imported and consumed furtively by students.

Whether or not it is still possible to read science fiction while doing time in school only by sneaking glances at one's favorite magazine or paperback novel hidden between the covers of the history textbook, as was the case in my high-school days, I cannot say. But it may be stated without much exaggeration that it is not so much the legitimacy of science fiction as a cultural and social force that is under challenge today, as the legitimacy of schooling itself.

While scholars and authors of science fiction have often reacted with frustration to the continuing indifference, or outright hostility, shown this literature by many schools, it would seem at this point that the schools may well need science fiction more than science fiction needs the schools. It is not a desire to improve its status by association with the academic world that leads proponents of science fiction to advocate its use in education. Rather, it is in the spirit of educational renovation that science fiction is offered, a perspective that has also motivated an increasing number of teachers to inquire about its possible utility to their subjects. My purpose in this chapter is to provide some suggestions for such use.*

Defining "science fiction" is not as easy as it might appear.[1] Historically, the literature has been associated with thematic content stressing the extrapolation of scientific and technological trends or the postulation of novel discoveries and inventions, and their influences on society. The author's task was to present his anticipations in a logically consistent, rationally understandable framework that engendered believability, or at least the suspension of disbelief, regarding the possibility that the events portrayed could actually happen. This style was contrasted with works of fantasy, in which unexplained forces of magic were available to characters and in which the possibility that the worlds described could ever exist was not germane to the plot.

In recent decades, however, it has become increasingly difficult to characterize the science-fiction field in these terms alone. The "science" in science fiction has expanded to include the social sciences as an important data base for stories, many of which now attempt the direct extrapolation of future social patterns or even entire alternative societies.

The presentation of highly desirable or undesirable societies has long been the domain, of course, of utopian and anti-utopian ("dystopian") works. Then there is the term "social fiction" which Isaac Asimov would like to reserve for stories which may be set on other worlds or in the future, but which are intended by their authors to convey, not extrapolations, but satirical, purposively distorted images of their own cultures. The once neat line between science fiction and fantasy has blurred with the emergence of stories of "science fantasy" which describe worlds using principles of magic in as consistent and predictable a way as science is used in our time.

Finally, the term "speculative fiction" has been applied to

---

* For a bibliographic note on aids to the classroom use of science fiction see the Notes section.

stories which combine science fiction and mythological elements with intensive psychological introspection and experimental writing styles. There is no reason why all these species could not be loosely wrapped within the blanket of science fiction, which is still the term best known to the mass public. But since the other descriptive phrases also all happen to contain the same initials, for convenience I shall simply refer from here on to "SF" as an all-embracing category for the literature being discussed.

In my suggestions about the uses of SF, I will not distinguish among various educational levels: A futuristic course is as necessary and feasible in a grade school as in a free university; imaginative experiential exercises can be tried in graduate school or kindergarten; comparison of alternative SF societies can be done by anyone within or outside of formal learning situations or classroom buildings. In this manner, teachers and students, however they define themselves, may adapt what I have to say to their own needs and educational environments.

The Functions of SF

Most obviously, SF can be used in courses or independent-study projects which deal in whole or part with the study of alternative futures.[2] SF's contribution to such classes can take a variety of forms.

First, viewed as a whole, SF shares several root assumptions with nonfiction attempts to anticipate the future: The future is, in some sense, knowable; pathways to the future, as far as we know, are flexible—that is, there are many possible futures that could conceivably result from the outcome of present trends; to some extent, the choices we make now, the decisions taken in the present, affect the possibilities of achieving particularly desirable, or avoiding particularly undesirable, futures.[3] In SF, this concept of the importance of past and present decisions in making more probable one kind of future over others is an explicit theme in many stories dealing with precognition, time travel, and "parallel worlds" (other Earths that exist in conterminous dimensions and which have different historical experiences from our own because of differing choices made or actions taken at key moments in time).

Thus, in Ray Bradbury's classic short story "A Sound of Thunder" human history is altered when a time traveler in the prehistoric past accidentally steps on a butterfly. Whether or not a basic acquaintance with SF predisposes the reader to believe that the future is malleable and directable cannot be proven; indeed, the whole issue of the influence of any literature on values and attitudes is controversial, as seen in the pornography debate. But at least it may be hoped that the individual introduced to SF will offer less resistance than the nonreader to the notion of extending his time-span of awareness into the future, as it concerns not just his own life, but the possibilities open to his society and the human race in general.

Second, it has been speculated that reading SF can serve as psychic preparation for a world of accelerating change, a kind of acculturation to future shock. While we may feel the effects of rapid social and technological change daily, it is difficult, precisely because of our immersion in a changeful environment, to gain perspective on what is happening. SF can provide the perspective insofar as it succeeds in gulling the reader to step for a while outside of his own time and place in order to witness vicariously the possible outcomes of present and future trends.

There is, however, more involved here than intellectual appreciation of the fact that the future is different. Much of SF stresses the fundamental strangeness of the universe, its contingency and mutability, and the great diversity of values and life-styles likely to be found in future societies or on other planets. Thus, in Samuel Delany's *The Einstein Intersection*, our Earth has interconnected, somehow, with a universe containing other physical laws, resulting in a marvelous, frightening diversification of human forms and relationships. Why not? In Clifford Simak's "The Thing in the Stone," a man emerges from a car accident with the ability to see the prehistoric past and to listen to exchanges of messages among interstellar civilizations. Why not? Sobering as it is to realize that in the eyes, or tentacles, or whatever, of other intelligent species, we may be their version of the monster from 20,000 fathoms, it may be that the SF reader who finds his curiosity, imagination, and tolerance for the relativity of conceivable social patterns enhanced has also improved his capacity for mental adaptability to, and survival in, the world of the future.

Third, the kind of future a society creates is in part a reflection of the needs and fears of the present. Any art form can thus be examined for the manner in which its creators, whether intentionally or not, shed light on contemporary beliefs that may be significant in shaping the future. SF is particularly rich in this regard, articulating in its recurrent themes, roles assigned to characters, and explicit values of its best-known authors some important attitudes regarding social change that may be congruent with widely shared public opinions.

For example, in contrast with those stories which emphasize the importance of human choice in shaping the future, a great many SF stories contain the implicit message that man is not in control of things, that we are subject to the interplay of forces beyond the ken of the average person. Thus, in Robert Silverberg's "Passengers," mysterious, nonmaterial beings arrive on Earth and proceed to occupy the bodies of any humans they choose to control, randomly and for a few days at a time each. No explanation of why they are here or what they are doing is given —one is going about his business; he is abruptly occupied for a time; he is abruptly released.

A large number of other SF plots are similarly devoted to tales of alien invasions and takeovers. And in a sense, have we not already been "taken over"? Perhaps the powerlessness and alienation often seen as a basic malaise of industrialized, mass societies, in which the individual is cut off from direct control over the forces influencing his life by the decisions of far-off, incomprehensible technocrats, are transmuted by SF into parables of Earth under attack by external alien hordes. In this sense, such stories could be studied as fictional echoes of a pervasive modern fear about where we are and where we are going.

While feelings of separateness from self and society may be widely shared by SF writers with the general public, another group of more explicit attitudes often found in SF are also held by significant sub-groups in society, especially political activists, dissident minorities, and those who identify with the counter-culture. These attitudes comprise hostility toward, and distrust of, big government and big business, and a strong bias in favor of the sovereign individual or small group who can maneuver the social environment to conform to their plans and desires.

In Robert Heinlein's *The Moon Is a Harsh Mistress* a band of stalwart libertarians successfully leads a revolt by lunar colonists against the oppressive Earth government that controls their economy; Frederik Pohl and C. M. Kornbluth present large advertising companies as cynically manipulating the masses for the great god of profits in *The Space Merchants*; and Harlan Ellison's " 'Repent, Harlequin!' Said the Ticktockman" features an eccentric individualist at loose in a world totally enslaved to the efficiency of the time and motion men. Characters who mouth patriotic platitudes, and politicians generally, are often portrayed mockingly, while the imposition of secrecy by governments in the name of security to stifle the free interchange of creative thoughts receives short shrift in SF. Whatever the realism in holding out to the reader some reassurance that individualism and a sense of self-worth can survive even in the technocratic age, it is significant for students of the future that such ideals are widely prevalent in SF, and at the present time, find favor among many of the more articulate and sensitive members of society.[4]

A fourth contribution of the study of SF to futures courses rests on that part of its content most noted by the public, its predictions or postulations of future events. While I know of no detailed examination of the actual extent to which SF prophecies have hit the mark, my impression is that, as a whole, SF has not been significantly successful in its scientific and technological forecasts, and at least in the past, has been unconcerned or too conservative about social forecasts. But the utility of SF to a futures course interested in looking at explicit forecasts is not wholly dependent on the accuracy of the fictional predictions.

For instance, something may be learned by comparing past stories which contain accounts of future events with the actual anticipated time period as it has turned out or with the actual occurrence of the event or discovery forecast, whenever it happens. Fascinating case studies could be developed around the ability of SF authors to predict technological innovations and their social consequences, as the real-world turn of events is often easy to check on. Thus, submarines, airplanes, tanks, and, of course, spaceships, made their appearance during the late nineteenth century in the works of Verne, Wells, and others.[5] During the period between World War I and Hiroshima, atomic energy in peace and war was discussed by such authors as Karel Čapek ("The Absolute at Large"), Lester Del Rey (*Nerves*), Cleve Cartmill ("Deadline," the story which rated an investigation by government officials wondering where the leak was), and Heinlein ("Solution Unsatisfactory").

Predictions of social-science advances are less common, but accounts of the use of complex mathematical equations to predict and, therefore, manipulate social events show up with increasing frequency, especially in Isaac Asimov's *Foundation* trilogy. But it is not just the more or less accurate predictions that are worth studying. Those that were off the mark bear special attention, because an examination of the reasons for predictive errors in SF will reveal the same dangers in extrapolation open to nonfiction forecasting, such as overreliance on the assumption that "all other things" will remain equal and the difficulty in adjusting for radical social change.

In addition, fictional predictions of the past or present may now be compared and correlated with the body of analysis coming from nonfiction futurology. This is important insofar as the intuitive feel of creative authors regarding possible directions of society is a necessary supplement to findings of the more quantitative methodologies widely used in nonfiction scenarios. A sensitive and knowledgeable author may not only be alert to particular trends and values that could escape the net of more specialized and client-oriented surveys, but also can give the reader a feel for how the convergence of disparate trends works to result in unforeseen consequences. It might be instructive, for example, to compare the extrapolations and scenarios of works like Herman Kahn and Anthony Wiener's *The Year 2000*, or the reports of "Delphi" studies (questioning of experts on developments in their fields) issued by the Institute for the Future, with SF stories that attempt to portray the human implications of the social and technological trends the nonfiction works analyze.[6]

Fifth, futures students need to realize that forecasting itself is a social act with social consequences, and not only or merely an objective set of techniques of use in policy-making. To engage in forecasting brings in its wake complex ethical and political questions regarding the status of experts in a democracy, the clients to whom they should lend their talents, the impact of forecasts on policy options injected into the political process, and the implicit power that lies in the hands of those who possess reasonably reliable information on the direction of present trends. SF stories that grapple with such issues include Wilson Tucker's *The Year of the Quiet Sun*, which has the ingenious idea of using a time machine to send a professional futurist into the future to check up on the accuracy of the forecasts he had made in a report put out by a Rand-type think tank(!), and Chad Oliver's "The Ant and the Eye," in which the UN covertly intervenes to ward off situations that a computer extrapolates as potentially dangerous. As for futures methodology, classes might well look at Robert Heinlein's "The Year of the Jackpot," depicting the art of establishing long-range cyclical trends, and Poul Anderson's "Details," which warns against placing too much faith in statistical extrapolations as against sensitive intuition.

A Laboratory of Imagination

SF can provide students interested in the future with a basic introduction to the concept of thinking about possible futures in a serious way, a sense of the emotional forces in their own culture that are affecting the shape the future may take, and a multitude of extrapolations regarding the results of present trends. There is one particular type of story that can be especially valuable as a stimulus to discussion of these issues both in courses on the future and in social-science courses in general—the story which presents well-worked-out, detailed societies that differ significantly from the society of the reader.[7] In fact, whatever the reliability of its predictions, SF is actually a more important vehicle for speculative visions about macroscopic social change. At this level, it is hard to deal with any precision as to when general value changes or evolving social institutions might appear, but it is most important to think about the kinds of societies that *could* result from the rise of new forms of interaction, even if one cannot predict exactly *when* they might occur.

In performing this "what if . . . " function, SF can act as a social laboratory as authors ruminate upon the forms social relationships could take if key variables in their own societies were different, and upon what new belief systems or mythologies could arise in the future to provide the basic rationalizations for human activities. If it is true that most people find it difficult to conceive of the ways in which their society, or human nature itself, could undergo fundamental changes, then SF of this type may provoke one's imagination to consider the diversity of paths potentially open to society.

Moreover, if SF is the laboratory of the imagination, its experiments are often of the kind that may significantly alter the subject matter even as they are being carried out. That is, SF has always had a certain cybernetic effect on society, as its visions emotionally engage the future-consciousness of the mass public regarding especially desirable and undesirable possibilities. The shape a society takes in the present is in part influenced by its image of the future; in this way particularly powerful SF images may become self-fulfilling or self-avoiding prophecies for society. For that matter, some individuals in recent years have even shaped their own lifestyles after appealing models provided by SF stories. The reincarnation and diffusion of SF futuristic images of alternative societies through the media of movies and television may have speeded up and augmented SF's social feedback effects. Thus SF is not only change speculator but change agent, sending an echo from the future that is becoming into the present that is sculpting it. This fact alone makes imperative in any education system the study of the kinds of works discussed in this section.

It must be noted that this perspective of SF has been questioned by some critics. It is often pointed out that, however ingenious they may be about future technologies, many SF writers exhibit an implicit conservative bias in their stories, insofar as social projections are either ignored or based on variations of the present status quo or of historical social systems reshuffled whole-cloth into the future. Robert Bloch has conveniently summarized the kind of future society presented by the average SF writer as consisting of a totalitarian state in which psychochemical techniques keep the populace quiet; an underground which the larger-than-life hero can join; and scientists who gladly turn over their discoveries to those in power. Such tales covertly assume that human nature as we know it will remain stable and that twentieth-century

Anglo-American culture and moral values, especially traditional economic incentives, will continue to dominate the world. Most SF authors have found it as hard as most other mortals to extrapolate social mores different from those operating within their own milieu, so that, it has been charged, far from preparing the reader for future shock, SF is a literature that comfortably and smugly reassures him that the future will not be radically different from the present.[8]

There is much truth to this analysis of SF. It is not easy to explain why so many stories seem to take as their future social settings nothing more ambiguous than the current status quo or its totally evil variant. Part of the answer may be that many authors of commercial SF writing prior to World War II received their professional training in science and engineering and were therefore not equipped or inclined to devise sophisticated social backgrounds in their plots. Be that as it may, the situation has changed dramatically in recent decades. There are an increasing number of stories which explicitly assume that future social patterns of family, government, religion, and the like need not be exactly the same as those of the present and that the forces which motivate men may also be subject to change. It is from such stories, and their predecessors in classical SF, that one may study examples of the impact of SF on the individual and collective imagination.

SF alternative societies may be categorized many ways. One that I find convenient in analyzing the recent literature is to use the familiar utopia-dystopia dichotomy. A fictional society may be more or less utopian or more or less dystopian—but, usually not all good or all bad in modern SF—depending on how it approaches the development of human potential. That is, some societies seek to maximize or enhance the ability of individuals to fulfill their mental and physical capacities, while other societies seek to inhibit or depress such fulfillment.

As to the dystopias, the model that has probably made the most impact on the popular consciousness is George Orwell's *1984*, itself part of a tradition that stretches back to Zamiatin's *We* and that sought to provide a counterpicture to the optimism about scientific progress that appeared in several of H. G. Wells's utopias.[9]

In the typical *1984*-type world, science and technology are grievously misused to produce a society that is dehumanized, alienating, socially rigidified, materially poor (except for the elite), and anti-sensual. The ruling class uses force and psychochemical control to terrorize and narcotize the masses into submission.

While this is the most familiar version of how things could go wrong, more recently there have appeared a range of stories taking as their progenitor Aldous Huxley's *Brave New World*, in which the overt brutalization of people is avoided, positive behavioral reinforcements à la Skinner form the primary social technology, sexual promiscuity is encouraged, and most citizens are materially well off, though, as in *1984* societies, class stratification usually still exists. Perhaps most striking about such contemporary novels as Kurt Vonnegut, Jr.'s, *Player Piano*, Ira Levin's *This Perfect Day*, and Robert Silverberg's *The World Inside* is the material abundance of the societies they depict—hence I call them "affluent dystopias." In all three stories progress in cybernating major production processes and in turning over national socioeconomic planning to complex computers has reached a point at which manual labor is generally unnecessary and all may enjoy the benefits of at least adequate nutrition and housing.

Thus far these stories sound like utopias, the Wellsian dream come true—but, in fact, as perceived by the disaffected heroes of each story, the societies in which they live are spiritually impoverished, the masses living pointless lives based on sophisticated variations of bread and circuses. Indeed, busily engaged in consumption, or disengaged by drug trips, the masses are unaware of how truly miserable is their existence. They are all depressingly happy. The deep irony of such stories is that science, even if not consciously misused, may still lead us to a humanistically sterile world. This perspective, of course, is also precisely that of many nonfiction critics of modern society, and thus familiarity with SF's affluent dystopias may serve to present the student with compelling portraits of societies that are based on a logical extrapolation of such fears.

Full-blown utopias are hard to find these days, but if one looks for fictional societies that, in various ways, enhance human potential, at least three developments are apparent that are as interesting and significant as is the rise of the new, improved dystopia. One is the growing number of novels that have come out since B. F. Skinner's *Walden Two* and Huxley's *Island* that explore the possibilities of self-actualization through some combination of social conditioning, development of paranormal (psychic) powers, careful utilization of consciousness-expanding drugs, and increased sensitivity to interpersonal relations.[10] Thus in Frank Herbert's now-classic *Dune* the charismatic hero achieves a position of spiritual and political power after undergoing rigorous training to develop his physical, mental, and psychic skills. In Bruce Mac-Allister's *Humanity Prime* a mutated race of sea-people evolve a nonmechanical, nonliterate civilization whose continuity is based on the exchange of telepathic word-images among individuals, and in a literal race consciousness, from past generations to succeeding ones. In Robert Silverberg's *Son of Man* a far-future race of humanity is depicted as having the powers of the gods; the members of this post-historical society spend their days in leisurely exploration of sensual pleasures and of the forces of nature. And in Alfred Bester's novels *The Stars My Destination* and *The Demolished Man* individuals possessing skills of teleportation and telepathy are functionally integrated into their societies.

All these wonders need not be taken as literal predictions of how humanity might expand its capacities for self-knowledge and for direct manipulation of the environment. Such stories succeed in simply presenting metaphors of possible developments in our abilities and the startling social rearrangements that could follow. It will not escape many students that these visions are often congruent with some of the goals of the counterculture, insofar as societies composed of "superior" humans reflect life-styles based on openness, honesty, trust, and nonmaterialism, and thus students and teachers may be challenged to confront their own evaluation of fictional societies that reflect these goals. It should be noted that often in SF, as with Robert Heinlein's "Gulf," Olaf Stapledon's *Odd John*, and A. E. van Vogt's *Slan*, the reaction of the surrounding society toward mutated individuals is hostile, nonsupportive, based on fear of the unknown and apprehension about the fate of present man. Here too, classes can confront their feelings about such treatment of "different" humans, especially in the context of wide-ranging current research and policy proposals based on such research in areas like eugenics, biofeedback techniques, and electrical stimulation of the brain.

A second path to enhancing human potential described in some SF stories is through the effects of humanistic religions or social movements. While organized religion in SF is often presented cynically, satirically, or as the handmaiden of totalitarian regimes, there are plots which describe new or revised belief systems as liberating forces. Thus in Robert Heinlein's *Stranger in a Strange Land*, also a novel of spectacular self-actualization, the Mars-born human hero founds a new religion that stresses the communal sharing of worldly goods and sensual pleasures based on the psychic powers released in the human mind during intensive study of the Martian language. A near-future generation of American youth takes the opposite path of sensual denial in "The Shaker Revival" by Gerald Jonas, in protest against the overindulgent, meaningless lives of their parents.

A third possibility that has been taken up in modern SF is the redefinition of stereotyped social roles. Racially, blacks, more or less nonexistent in pre-World War II SF, may now be found in positions of leadership or eminence in at least a small proportion of present SF. Sexually, however, the status of women in SF generally remains as atrocious as ever.[11] It must be admitted that for all its daring probes of possible futures, the portrayal of human females in most SF has fallen utterly within prevailing cultural stereotypes—women in SF are passive, waiting to be rescued, or comforters of their men, or, if they are scientists or leaders, are depicted as cold, efficient, defeminized. One exception that credibly presents a recognizably human female as the major protagonist is Alexei Panshin's *Rite of Passage*, the story of the coming of age of a teen-age girl in a society contained within a giant spacecraft. Even more striking is Ursula K. LeGuin's *The Left Hand of Darkness*, a fascinating anthropological study of a distant planet whose people are humanoid but unisexual, and hence have no place in their culture for the familiar roles and games associated with bisexuality in ours. The androgynous society in which each individual may advance solely on the basis of "his" own endowment is a powerful symbol for those who would like to see a similar breakdown of socially prescribed sex roles, though not the disappearance of biological males and females, on this Earth.

Social Issues

I have so far presented SF as useful in illustrating the concepts, techniques, and difficulties of forecasting and in depicting alternative possible societies. A third major use is based on the fact that many SF stories act as early-warning systems for emerging public-policy issues which society needs to be systematically thinking about now. Thus SF for many years has given some consideration to such imminent policy problems as genetic engineering, over-population, social roles of corporations, military technologies, and contact with or creation of other intelligent life forms. The value of SF here is not so much whether it puts forward solutions to these and other issues, but just that it raises the right questions. In so doing, a broad range of SF stories can be put to educational use especially in several new future-oriented interdisciplinary fields focused on different policy arenas that have appeared in American universities in the last few years—ecology, urban studies, peace research and science and public policy.

For example, classes studying ecological issues could investigate the many SF stories that deal provocatively with the scientific and political aspects of this field. A common theme in many such stories is that man's large-scale interventions in ecosystems whose interrelations are not fully known may lead to unanticipated results, sometimes beneficial, but usually disastrous. As with other SF parables, the locale of ecological morality plays is often another planet which humanity "conquers" and whose environment it attempts to manipulate. Frequently, as in James H. Schmitz's "Balanced Ecology," an ecosystem is itself personified, given a kind of gestalt intelligence comprised of the complex interactions of its individual living units—an intelligence which may strike back at those humans who attempt to upset its delicate balance for their own purposes.

This warning is the theme of at least one novel, Frank Herbert's *The Green Brain*, which describes the fatal political and ecological results of a future campaign by Brazil to wipe out supposedly harmful tropical insects. Nature, of course, may make its own interventions in the life of mankind. One pioneering ecological novel that explores in a beautiful and absorbing way the effects of a new global plague on a handful of survivors and their changed environment is *Earth Abides* by George R. Stewart, himself a professional ecologist.

The particular problems of the population explosion have also been examined in SF, in some cases years before the wave of current popular interest in the subject. Such stories as Harry Harrison's *Make Room! Make Room!*, Anthony Burgess' *The Wanting Seed*, and those collected by Raymond Sauer in *Voyages: Scenarios for a Ship Called Earth*, Thomas M. Disch in *The Ruins of Earth*, and Frederick Pohl in *Nightmare Age*, deal with the full range of possible responses to an ever more crowded planet, from new forms of social controls to handle the masses to governmentally approved sexual deviations. While the tone of these stories is often satirical, it is the kind of satire that exaggerates an issue in order to call attention to its underlying seriousness and to indicate what we could be faced with if we don't give it rational consideration while it is still not too late.

The future of the city has also been a long-standing theme in SF, at least since Graham arose in *When the Sleeper Wakes* and gazed upon H. G. Wells's vision of London-to-be, but the preoccupation has been somewhat one-sided. SF author and critic Kingsley Amis has noted that "science fiction's hells are urban," and it is still generally true that SF's future cities are a mess of one kind or another. Frequently, cities are depicted as behavioral sinks, human traps where the masses work out their tensions in lives of inner despair, vacuity, and interpersonal violence. Several of the stories in Damon Knight's collection *Cities of Wonder* are of this sort. An interesting recent variation of this model is tales of urban guerrilla warfare between blacks and whites, urban renewal as a fringe benefit of race war, as it were. This is the situation in Alan Seymour's *The Coming Self-Destruction of the United States of America*, though a more hopeful note is sounded in *The Jagged Orbit* by John Brunner, in which the races maintain an uneasy, segregated, but relatively peaceful coexistence.

If cities are not being torn apart, they are abandoned, often as a result of developments in transportation, communication, and energy production that render them technologically obsolete, as in Clifford Simak's *City*. Alternatively, the city itself may undergo drastic technological change, moving underground as in Isaac Asimov's *The Caves of Steel*, or, with Arthur Clarke's *The City and the Stars,* becoming one huge automated machine that completely cares for all the needs of its citizens—not necessarily a utopian situation. SF treatment of such issues as the impact of technology and race relations on urban design and the quality of city life would be well suited as the takeoff point for their further analysis in urban-studies courses.

Peace research is a field that utilizes many relevant disciplines to elucidate what conditions promote, or mitigate against, peaceful relationships among individuals and nations, and to delineate models of future world-order systems in which international violence is minimized and socioeconomic welfare increased. While SF has given much attention to possible military technologies and world dictatorships, perhaps because of the dramatic advantage in dealing with exotic weapons or the overthrow of bad governments, there are relatively fewer stories that attempt to describe near-future, realistically complex, nontyrannical, alternative international systems.[12] Such stories are worth seeking out as they make available to the individual involved in peace studies several global variations in the familiar games states play.

In one model, represented by John Brunner's *Stand on Zanzibar,* the international system remains more or less as it is except that states must compete with other international actors, such as multinational corporations or international organizations, for power, prestige, and wealth. One step beyond this is a system in which states may still exist, but are being replaced by functional world organizations, corporate or intergovernmental, which become the focus of loyalty of growing numbers of people; this is the case in Theodore L. Thomas' "The Weather Man," where a weather-control organization is the primary international group, and Mack Reynolds' "The Five Way Secret Agent," where meritocratic world corporations seek to undermine the barriers states put up to the efficient utilization of global resources. An even more radical system change is detailed by Robert Theobald and J. M. Scott in *Teg's 1994: An Anticipation of the Near Future;* here, large bureaucratic complexes as we know them and urban megalopoli have collapsed, leaving the abundance areas of the world organized around a myriad of intentional communities interlinked by a complex communications system and by centralized applied-research organizations. A peace class could instructively study these models not only for their own stimulative value, but in order to compare them with the nonfiction literature on international futures and with the plans of action advocated, for instance, by world federal government groups.

Science, technology, and public policy, or "science policy," is the field that studies the need for and organization of governmental and private administration of scientific research and technological progress, and the impact, in turn, of science and technology on domestic and international affairs. A major focus in this field is technology assessment, the attempt to anticipate the beneficial and harmful consequences of new technologies before they are mass-produced, in order to optimize, if possible, the beneficial effects and in order to allocate limited research funds among competing projects accordingly. Defined this way, there is nothing new about science policy as a process, but what is new is public awareness of this process and attempts in governmental, corporate, and academic circles to devise institutions that will make it more efficient and responsive to national needs. As is the case with ecological, urban, and peace studies, an increasing number of universities have recently established course, research, and degree-granting programs in science policy.

SF as a whole may be the most relevant to this field, for, in a sense, SF is a literature of science policy. Virtually all SF stories contain at least implicit judgments on the directions science and technology should or should not take, while many stories explicitly describe the social consequences of possible technologies and the hard choices involved in developing particular lines of science and technology over others.

It is true that SF has undergone its own kind of evolution in its general perspective toward science and technology.[13] In the days of the pulp magazines, the scientist was often a hero figure, humanity's last hope against an invasion by the slime people or an outbreak of radioactive hives. But in recent years SF has adopted the view that uncritical acceptance of the inherent worth of science is not possible. It is still true that governmental or corporate restrictions on science and technology, especially when they clash with the individual's right to pursue his creative interests, are not usually welcomed in SF, but many stories grant that technology is subject to grave misuse and may be outpacing efforts to control its social impact.

Some authors have responded to this danger by elaborating methods by which science and technology may be subjected to human control. Thus, Isaac Asimov's famous collections of robot stories, *I, Robot* and *The Rest of the Robots*, specify the conditions under which these machines could be constructed so as not to cause harm to human beings. More typical, however, are stories in the tradition of Mary Shelley's *Frankenstein* and Karel Čapek's *R.U.R.*, such as D. F. Jones's *Colossus*. Whether the object of concern is the creation of artificial protoplasmic life, mechanical life (robots), or intelligent computers, as in these stories, or the invention of exotic technologies as in Isaac Asimov's "The Dead Past" (a machine that can see into the past) and Harlan Ellison's "The Beast That Shouted Love at the Heart of the World" (a machine that displaces human tensions elsewhere in the universe), the common refrain of such tales is that we have unwittingly unleashed forces whose consequences have not been foreseen and whose effects will be difficult to contain.

Besides the core problem of technology assessment—the social responsibility of science and technology—SF science-policy stories have taken up one other related theme, humanity's growing, and perhaps irreversible, dependence on technology. The obvious consequence of this trend was graphically described in E. M. Forster's prophetic story "The Machine Stops," which portrays a far-future human race living underground and totally sustained in its need for food, energy, and recreation by a central machine; when the latter stops, human civilization is finished. Another grim possibility was explored by Robert Heinlein in "The Roads Must Roll." If the country is dependent for its economic life on, for instance, a transportation network, the country may also be subject to blackmail by those in a position to sabotage the system. That technologically advanced nations live close to the brink of disaster, even as they grow more dependent on their technologies to supply the material needs of modern life, will hardly be news to most students, as an abstract proposition, but stories like the above can serve to initiate probing class discussions into our consequential existential predicament.

Affective Impact

To this point, SF has been presented as a literary medium which can be used to stimulate student discussions on pressing issues raised by the impact of social change, especially that derived from the effects of science and technology, on human values and institutions. But nothing said thus far makes this way of approaching SF incompatible with traditional classroom education. Thus it is vital to realize that SF is also a potentially significant, though as yet largely untapped, catalyst for reform even within traditional institutions. This is so because teachers with the requisite training can use SF as a vehicle for the enhancement of affective education and because the introduction of SF into formal education, however it is used, impels the democratization of the classroom.

In recent years, educators have grown increasingly aware that the implicit concentration of most curricula upon the development of purely cognitive (intellectual) skills can be detrimental if it ignores the student's emotional and creative side, the affective realm which is inextricably linked to the learning of cognitive skills. This awareness has sparked attempts to integrate in the classroom intellectual knowledge of subject matter with improvements in self-knowledge, creativity, and interpersonal sensitivity of students. SF is an ideal format in which to attempt such integration.[14] On the one hand, its philosophical speculations on the place of humanity in the universe and its intense preoccupation with important public-policy issues of the present and near future provide countless reference points for classroom analysis of the deepest issues of our time. On the other hand, there is an SF way of perceiving the world that involves creativity in a basic sense— the ability to look around the corner before one gets to it, to make connections between variables that seem at first sight unrelated, to trust in one's intuition. Here, the element of visionary imagination in SF can serve as a template against which students and teachers may play out their own feelings regarding possible futures and, in so doing, gain more profound insight into the personal and social contexts from which such feelings derive.

As a vehicle for affective education, SF stories can be used as if they were scripts, providing classes with ready-made roles and fantasies to enact.[15] For example, the most obvious SF game would be "how would it feel like to live in . . . ?" A student could take one of the alternative societies described earlier, pretend he is a member of it, and note his experiences, perhaps keeping a journal account of a typical day or describing to an "outsider" how things operate. Or, two or more students could represent societies of the affluent dystopian and more humanistic types and attempt to convert each other to their own ways of life. Or, a class could take a fictional society as a starting point, assign to its members the roles of major characters, and proceed to re-create, and elaborate upon, key events described in the plot.

Another kind of exercise I call "son of. . . ." Here a class brainstorms its own sequel to an SF story. Thus, at the end of LeGuin's *The Left Hand of Darkness* it appears that the planet of unisexual humanoids will join the galactic confederation of human species. Students could go on to spin out what impact that planet's customs and institutions, based as they are on the non-recognition of sexual differences, will have on Earth, and what it would feel like to be the Earth ambassador to that planet after a few years.

Other provocative questions could be raised about the ending of Jones's *Colossus*. Here an intelligent computer that controls the nuclear-weapons systems of the United States and U.S.S.R. blackmails humanity into giving it ultimate decision-making power over human affairs, because the machine has decided that the ability to govern modern society is too complex a business to be left in merely human hands. But unlike many other stories of this genre, the result of the machine's overlordship will be a world without war or want—we have been taken over for our own good. A class could then speculate on how the world would react to this kind of takeover, while each student should be helped to confront the question of how *he* would or would not adapt to a world in which humanity had lost control, for better or worse, over its destiny.

Of course, SF games need not be tied down to particular stories, but may take any form open to one's imagination. I have been involved in two relatively elaborate exercises with students that were based in part on various SF stories, but took on a life of their own over time. In one, "Visiting Day," students attempt to see the Earth and its problems through alien eyes. In a small graduate seminar we decided that there existed a galactic network of sentient races, a routine notion in SF, that had sent an agent to Earth to act as a catalyst for humanity, with the goal of aiding our planet to hook up with the network. We thus took Earth to be a problem in planetary underdevelopment, both materially and spiritually (in terms of the fragmentation of the human race), which led to discussions of the cultural and political barriers the decidedly foreign agent would have to overcome in bringing Earth to the requisite stage of maturity, and the strategies he might adopt in doing so.

The other exercise is "Invent a Planet." The assignment is to formulate and detail the structure and relationships of an alien civilization. This is a task that lends itself very well to interdisciplinary collaboration and group work by students and teachers, and to getting students to step outside of their own cultural preconceptions, to the best of their abilities, in order to consider the range of possible social patterns available once key variables in our society are explicitly no longer taken for granted. To save time and frustration, the teacher can provide the class with essential physical and social data about the alien world and its inhabitants. In a class in which I participated, the students were given the situation that a group of space explorers from Earth had landed on the planet of another solar system and had made contact with a race of intelligent insects. In order to convince the natives of their own intelligence, the humans asked Earth for help in translating basic Judaeo-Christian religious concepts into the insects' language, as the mere building of artifacts was not sufficient as an arguing point for intelligence on this planet. The class then constituted itself as a committee of Earth experts aiding the astronauts, which also required the class to work out the cultural framework of the insect race, too. The object of the exercise was to get students to think about familiar religious beliefs in a novel way. This process could obviously be adapted to classes in virtually any subject.[16]

As for the impact of SF on the general classroom process, whether it is used as a stimulus to intellectual development or self-actualization, SF can be a force for the democratization of educational roles. This is because it is a subject in which expertise may be gained regardless of age or other academic experience. To be sure, a teacher may bring to bear on the classroom study of

SF his own sophisticated insights and knowledge of SF's historical evolution and present trends, but in any given class it is almost guaranteed that there will be some students who possess wide-ranging information equaling, and often surpassing, the teacher's on at least such factual data as who wrote what, when, and where. Indeed, SF may be one of the few subjects that students still approach with what can only be called reverence.

Once given free rein to talk about it, students who are SF readers will so quickly establish a joyful camaraderie, and will be so eager to trade opinions about favorite authors, that the teacher may have to exert some control to see that something more than a fan-club atmosphere develops and that students not familiar with SF do not feel shut out. But for the teacher who is willing to share his own sense of enthusiasm with the class, along with some guidance, when SF is discussed or acted out, and who is willing to relax his role as monopolistic purveyor of knowledge, a mutual exploration of the awe and mystery of the universe and the fate humanity finds within it may result in the creation of a true community of learners.

Learning for tomorrow must deal not merely with what is possible or probable, but, perhaps most crucially, with what is preferable. *What futures do we want—and what values underlie our choices? Howard Kirschenbaum and Sidney Simon of the Adirondack Mountain Humanistic Education Center suggest that there are powerful, nonmoralizing ways to deal with values in education, and that these ways ought to be part of any well-thought-out futures curriculum.*

CHAPTER FIFTEEN

Values and the Futures Movement in Education

by Howard Kirschenbaum and Sidney B. Simon

> What avail is it to win prescribed amounts of information about geography and history, to win ability to read and write, if in the process the individual loses his own soul; loses his appreciation of things worth while, of the values to which these are relative; if he loses desire to apply what he has learned, and, above all, loses the ability to extract meaning from his future experiences as they occur?
>
> —*John Dewey*

Unless one believes that the future is inevitable—that we have absolutely no control over our private and public destinies—the study of the future must include not merely possible and probable futures, but *preferable* futures. This is why the broad movement aimed at shifting education into the future tense also brings with it a heightened concern with values.

Of course, a concern with values is not entirely new in education. What is new is the way in which this concern must express itself. In the past, we taught values, or tried to. Yet simply "teaching values" cannot and will not suffice for the future.

The child of today confronts many more choices than did the child of yesterday. He is surrounded by a bewildering array of alternatives. Modern society has made him less provincial and more sophisticated, but the complexity of these times has made the act of choosing infinitely more difficult.

Areas of confusion and conflict abound: politics, religion, love and sex, family, friends, drugs, materialism, race, work, aging and death, leisure time, school and health. Each area demands decisions that yesterday's children were rarely called upon to make.

"Should I try marijuana? From everything I've seen and heard it seems less harmful than alcohol."

"Should we live together before getting married? Maybe the present staggering divorce rate would be lower if more of our parents had done some experimenting."

"Why bother going to college or staying in school? I think I could get myself a better education on my own."

"Why bother even voting? The only thing that seems to bring about change these days is taking to the streets, maybe even violently."

"What's the point of work at all? I see so many adults slaving their lives away—for what? They don't seem very happy."

Although the content of the questions sometimes varies over generations, it is not new that young people are asking questions. Children and youth have always wondered about themselves, their future, and their society. Consciously or not, they have always fought to develop values by which to live.

And, traditionally, the educators of the society—the parents, the schools and the churches—have most often taken a common approach toward helping young people develop values and toward answering the value questions that young people raise.

We call this approach *moralizing*, although it has also been known as inculcation, imposition, indoctrination and, in its most extreme form, brainwashing. Moralizing is the direct or indirect transfer of a set of values from one person or group to another person or group. Sometimes moralizing is very direct and coercive; sometimes it is gentle and barely noticeable. In all cases it is based on a common assumption: "From my (our) experience, I (we) have come to believe that a certain set of beliefs and behaviors is better than another set of beliefs and behaviors. Therefore, rather than have you go through the pain of discovering this for yourself, and rather than risk the chance that you might come up with a different set of values, I shall do my best to convince you that my (our) set of values is the most desirable for you."

In a world in which the future bore a close resemblance to the past, moralizing was a relatively effective means of transmitting or "teaching" values. Educators, for the most part, agreed with parents on what values children should hold. Children were taught what to believe and how to act, and with rare exceptions, accepted these moralizations without serious question. Why should they question? The adults seemed in agreement, and there were few or no impinging forces to make them doubt their elders' wisdom.

Why Moralizing Doesn't Work

But consider the child of today. From every side he is bombarded with different and often contradictory sets of values. His parents offer one set of moralizations (communications on what to believe and how to behave) and often *two* sets, because the male-female roles have altered so dramatically that the woman need not agree with all her husband's values. His schoolteachers might have an entirely different set of values which are urged upon the child. And different teachers have different values—whether the issue be Vietnam, homework, competition, freedom, or gum-chewing. Organized religions offer still another set of moralizations, and, as almost any newspaper or magazine will show, religions too are confused about their values. The communications media—television, Hollywood, radio, magazines and newspapers—literally bombard the growing person with all sorts of stimuli and inputs about what to believe, how to behave, what kind of language to use, how to dress, what type of life-style to follow, and even how to avoid growing old. Always there is the implicit message: This is how you should think and act if you are going to get ahead, be successful, impress your superiors and have sex-appeal. Then there is the peer group, one of the most influential moralizing forces. "If you want to belong and be accepted, *here's* what you think and how you act." Add to these forces the political leaders, the youth-movement leaders, folk and rock heroes, sports figures, each adding to the confusion with a new set of moralizations, and you have the dilemma of the child of today.

Any *one* of these moralizations might be very wise or very foolish, helpful or harmful, moral or immoral. But who is to say? Certainly not the young person, who, caught in the middle of the cross fire, can barely make sense out of any of it.

We have tried to teach values. But in a world of confusion and conflict about values, this is not enough. No matter how sincere we may be in our desire to help, all we leave the young person with is one more input, one more moralizing message, which goes into his overloaded computer to be processed along with others.

Hopefully, it gets processed. More likely the principle of "might makes right" applies to the confused person's valuing process. Whichever set of moralizations are most recent or most often repeated are the ones that dominate his thinking and behavior. He has all the inputs rolling around upstairs, but his values are entirely situational, and the locus of control is outside himself. If the peer group is most persuasive at a given time, it is these values he will draw upon. In the presence of authority, it is the authority's values that dominate. At no time is the young person in control of his own decisions. His values are not his own. They are the introjections of numerous moralizations which are undifferentiated to the individual. His lack of clarity about values often is manifested in apathetic, flighty, overconforming and overdissenting behavior.

If moralizing has not prepared young people (many of whom are now adults) to sort out the value confusion of the *present*, then moralizing certainly will not help young people learn to cope with the future. Change is so rapid, and new alternatives arise so quickly in every area of life-choice, that no one set of specific beliefs and behaviors could possibly answer all the choice situations of the future. Nor can our moralizings take the form of general guidelines and be expected to do the job. Values like "honesty," "religion," "patriotism," may be beautiful ideals, but they simply do not answer specific dilemmas in which people find themselves. Taking the last example alone, one does not need Socrates to remind him that patriotism has a debatable definition and that "patriotic" citizens not long ago spent a decade both dying in Vietnam and protesting the war at home.

The shortcomings of moralizing have become increasingly apparent to educators concerned about teaching for the future. Talk to parents and religious leaders; talk to any teacher with twenty years or more of experience, and they will tell the same story. "These kids just aren't the same as when I started teaching. It used to be the teacher's word was gospel. The children listened. They respected age and experience. But not now. Now they think they know more than you do. You can't tell them anything . . ." Depending on whom you talk to, the passing of the old days is looked upon with regret or with a feeling of "good-riddance." But the result is the same: Kids just don't seem to be buying what the moralizers are selling any more. They've got to discover it for themselves.

Laissez Faire in the Classroom

The growing awareness of this reality has led many educators to eschew moralizing and adopt a *laissez-faire approach* toward values. Their response goes something like this: "No one set of values I teach or impose can solve the dilemmas of the unknown future. Ultimately people must develop their own values, if the values are to work for them. Thus, I will give the young people I come in contact with the freedom to go their own way, make their own discoveries and find their own answers. This is what they seem to be asking for. It's *their* world, in a way; they're the ones who will save it if anyone will. I'd better get out of the way and let them go to it." This approach is particularly attractive in public schools, which serve diverse populations with diverse values and would rather do nothing about values than offend a segment of the community by "teaching" the "wrong" values. Subject matter, after all, is a lot less controversial than what the students are going to do with their lives and how they will cope with their futures in a changing world. So the adult steps aside and avoids dealing with values altogether.

Yet, what has changed? The young person is *still* bombarded by most of the same stimuli and inputs. From everyone, save the one or two people in his life who have moved to the laissez-faire approach, there are still the pressures and forces urging him to believe this and to do that. The problem is slightly less than before, with one or two inputs removed, but it is still there. He still has to process all the inputs, to select the best and eliminate the worst of all that he is being told to believe and to do.

Most of the people we have known—children, youth or adults—don't really want to be left alone to solve all of life's dilemmas and problems unaided. The two of us are very grateful that, when faced with a perplexing choice situation or some kind of doubt or problem, either of us can go to the other and know that there will be an empathic listener who by his concern and questioning can help the other regain the confidence and achieve clarity sufficient to guide his own course into the future. Learning to guide one's life is a skill. There is a valuing process by which we sort out all these stimuli around and within us. We don't help our young people learn that process by ignoring the problem.

The Modeling Approach

Not wanting either to moralize or ignore the problem, educators have tried a third approach to transmit values to young people, that of *modeling*. "If the direct inculcation of values doesn't seem to work any more, and if a laissez-faire approach just leaves you floundering in what you might very well perceive as a lack of concern on my part, then I will try *living a set of values*. If I can be a model of an adult who seems to know where he's going and is deriving satisfaction from living, then surely my example will be seen and respected, and young people will try to emulate me in many ways and adopt many of my values."

This approach has some merit, insofar as it recognizes that living by one's values is absolutely essential when working with young people. They have no patience with hypocrisy and will not tolerate adults whose lives are fraught with contradiction yet who seem so complacent. The modeling approach also has merit in that it offers a *concrete* alternative for young people to consider. Vague words about high ideals rarely communicate with the strength and clarity of a living example (a reality most colleges of education have yet to learn). We believe that teachers need to sacrifice some of their neutrality and "objectivity" and become real human beings to the students—human beings with feelings, goals, values and contradictions they are willing to reveal and discuss, just as they would like their students to do.

But, for all its merits, modeling has the same major drawback as moralizing. *There are so many models.* Parents, teachers, religious leaders, peers, sports figures, movie, television and recording stars all present different models to emulate. The young person still has to go through a sophisticated choosing process if he is to wisely sort out the best and worst from the various models.

If moralizing, laissez faire and modeling do not teach young people a process for sorting out and making sense of all the inputs and alternatives they have been exposed to, and will be increasingly exposed to in the future, how *will they* learn the process? Does the future hold any promise?

The Clarification of Values

In recent years, there have been many exciting developments in the field of "humanistic education." This movement is attempting to teach young people the intrapersonal and interpersonal skills they will need to deal with value conflicts and decisions of the future.

The humanistic education movement has many branches. For example: "values clarification," "education of self" at the University of Massachusetts, the Philadelphia Public Schools Affective Education Project, achievement motivation training, the "magic circle" exercises of the Human Development Institute, Parent and Teacher Effectiveness Training, the open classroom, etc.

The different branches of the movement have had different emphases; but they all contribute, to varying degrees, to teaching the same process of value clarification. Louis Raths once defined a "value" (as opposed to an attitude, belief, feeling, goal, etc.) as an area of our lives which meets seven criteria.[1] We think of his criteria as *the seven valuing processes* which all branches of the humanistic education movement seem to be teaching. If we want to prepare our children to meet the unknown challenges of the future, to be able to guide their lives through all the difficult values choices ahead, then we must consciously and deliberately go about teaching at least the following seven processes of valuing.

PRIZING

1. *Prizing and Cherishing.* We need to find ways to help young people discover what is important *to them*, to learn to set priorities, to know what they are for or against. So much of our education forces us to deny our feelings, to distrust our inner experience. Valuing is not only a cognitive process. Education has to include the affective realm too. The future will hold many surprises. Unless people are capable of tuning in to their own feelings, they will be ill-equipped to make the decisions that the future calls for.

2. *Publicly Affirming.* One way we show our values is to stand up for what we believe, to voice our opinion, to publicly affirm our position. Education can encourage this, rather than creating an atmosphere in which we keep our important thoughts and feelings to ourselves. As trust builds and self-disclosure increases, so does self-understanding, creativity, and productivity. Public affirmation is essential for democracy. Groups increase their efficiency in decision-making as more information, supplied by the members, gets thrown out on the table. To deal with the personal and societal decisions of the future, we need people who have learned to publicly affirm their values.

CHOOSING

We make choices all the time, thereby indicating preferences or values. But the choices which the future will call for demand more than glib, whimsical or conforming choices. Education must teach a process of choosing.

3. *Choosing from Alternatives.* Many people take the first choice or the first good choice that comes along. "This is the way I was taught, so this is the way I teach." "We've always handled our Christmas present-giving this way. You mean there are alternatives?" "Everybody in **my** circle of friends smokes pot on Saturday night. What else is there to do?" The future will offer us new alternatives for our personal lives and for the society. Whether we embrace each alternative as it comes along, or take our time and choose from several alternatives, could mean the difference between enormous disappointment and waste or more effective decisions.

4. *Choosing after Considering Consequences.* This valuing process goes hand in hand with the former process. It is essential that we teach young people to examine the *consequences* of the alternatives under consideration, and thus illumine the pros and cons. For example, the future will undoubtedly legitimize many different patterns of dating, mating, and marriage. This is already happening. An important part of valuing in this area would be to consider seriously the consequences of each alternative before making a choice, and not just gravitate toward the alternative that seems most attractive at first glance. This holds true in every area, whether it is marriage, ecology, economics or religion. We cannot "predict" the future or all the outcomes of our decisions. But by proceeding with eyes open, having weighed the pros and cons of the various alternatives, our chances for good decisions are increased.

5. *Choosing Freely.* Everyone wants his children, when they grow up, to be able to guide their lives as mature, responsible citizens. Yet, at every turn of their education, most young people's choices are so proscribed and limited that they never have the chance to learn to guide their lives until they are thrown in the water and told to swim. By that time, it is often too late. The problem is compounded by a marking and grading system which literally destroys opportunities for free choice.[2] We need to create environments in which young people can make choices—about their beliefs, about their behaviors, and about the course of their own education—in which they have the opportunity to look at alternatives, weigh consequences, and make *their own* choices, look at the actual consequences and then go through the whole process again. There is no shortcut. We can't teach people to make responsible choices unless they are given the chance to make real choices. All else is to impose values, which simply will not help them deal with the future.

ACTING

6. *Acting.* Acting is a valuing process. We have limited time, money and energy. How we spend our time, money and energy reveals what we value. Students are continually formulating beliefs, goals and ideals. As a part of their education, they should be encouraged to *act* on these beliefs, goals and ideals. As the

barrier between the school and the outside "real" world breaks down, students can become increasingly involved in community work, in helping relationships, and in other experiences that encourage personal growth and value development. Many adults rarely get (or make) the chance to act on their beliefs, to achieve their goals or to actualize their potential. An education that encourages action, as well as contemplation, will help create a future in which men will increasingly close the gap between what they say and what they do, between what they want and what they achieve.

7. *Acting with a Pattern, Repetition and Consistency.* This valuing process is an extension of the previous one. As we become clearer about our values, we begin to develop patterns of actions, and to repeat our most valued activities. In addition, we eliminate those behaviors that are contradictory to our most cherished values. Young people can be helped to examine the present patterns in their lives. While the unexamined life may or may not be worth living, it is certainly true that until we begin to examine the present patterns in our lives, we rarely move in directions that enable us to achieve our most prized and cherished goals and aspirations —our preferable futures.

We envision a future in which young people are very much in touch with their own feelings and inner experience, continue to go through an intelligent choosing process, and act on their beliefs and do something about their goals. Whether they are making a decision for their own personal lives or for the community they are a part of, their valuing process will help them to sort out the available information, to make a decision that is truly their own (rather than an introjection of authority or peer pressure), and to act with commitment on that decision.

Values as Process

We are suggesting that what has happened with subject-matter education must now happen with values education. Traditionally, subject matter has been regarded as a fixed body of knowledge which all people needed to know. Shakespeare, the parts of speech, quadratic equations, the major products of Argentina, and the

parts of the digestive system were treated as the ends of education. More recently, we have realized that, in a world in which the
amount of knowledge increases geometrically, and in which no one
can keep pace with it, we need to change our emphasis from *what*
to learn to *how* to learn. The new curriculum projects have emphasized the *processes* of the discipline, the ways in which the
historian or the scientist goes about investigating his subject. The
shift has been from content to process. Learning how to learn has
become more important than the specific facts and concepts
learned.

A similar change of orientation must take place with respect to
values. The process of *how to develop values*—that is, the processes of prizing, choosing and acting—must receive increasing
emphasis in the curriculum and in the home. Slavishly adhering to
outdated methods of values education will render educators and
parents as obsolete and irrelevant as the subject-matter teachers
who continue to say, "Repetitive drill and rote memorization of
facts worked for me, didn't they? Well, then, I don't see why they
won't work for the kids today."

What would a school look like if the educators did accept the
need for teaching a values-clarifying process to young people and
tried to implement it on a practical basis? Current experience in
the utilization of humanistic education approaches in schools suggests that implementation takes place on any or all of three levels:

1. by incorporating humanistic education approaches into presently existing courses;
2. by creating new courses with a specific focus on some aspect
   of humanistic education;
3. by reorganizing the whole school, or major parts of it, to
   allow for humanistic approaches.

The first level of involvement usually occurs when one or more
teachers from a given school attend a workshop on one of the
humanistic education approaches. The individual teachers then return with a desire or commitment to "humanize" their own classrooms, that is, to incorporate methods and materials which deal
with the real values and identity concerns of their students, to help
them become clearer about who they are, where they want to go
and how they are getting there. This could apply equally to ele-

mentary, secondary or college teaching. Many of the humanistic approaches have numerous methods or "strategies" for
accomplishing these goals.[3] To the extent that one teacher can be
successful in such an enormous undertaking, her students develop
some practice and skill in using the valuing process in their own
lives and are, therefore, more prepared to deal with the concerns,
conflicts, and choices they will meet in the future.

When several teachers from a given school or system or when a
key administrator is committed to implementing humanistic approaches in the school, a common result is the establishment of
specific elective "courses." Students, sometimes with parental permission required, elect to take a course in "values clarification" or
"controversial issues" or "education of self" or "communications"
or "urban studies" or "family living" or "human relations." The
course titles are as varied as the orientation of the teacher, the
interests of the students, and the political realities of the school
and community. What each course has in common, though, is not
its humanistic *content* (is studying the reproductive system any
more "human" than studying the digestive system?), but its emphasis on the *processes* of valuing, communication, self-understanding, and so on.

Frequently, consultants are called in to help schools establish
such courses and work with the teachers at the beginning. Many
schools are introducing courses of this type. Doing so gives students and teachers an attractive option, and can be extremely
valuable to them in the years ahead. Yet, this type of implementation has its drawbacks. Since only a limited number of students
can take these specialized elective courses, the other teachers often
say, "Well, I don't have to do anything about preparing them to
make values decisions in the future. We have a course on that."
Another drawback is that course offerings of this nature tend to
be faddish. When humanistic education is "in," or when some
students, teachers or community groups are exerting pressure for
educational change, it is often convenient to create "a course."
This takes the pressure off the school, and if, a few years later,
the course is eliminated, it rarely creates much of a stir.

Thus, a few schools have gone further in their attempts to make
education a training ground for the future. They have made major
schoolwide changes toward humanistic-process education. One

method has been to create a "school-within-a-school," sometimes called parallel schools. Somewhat similar to the elective courses, but on a broader scale, students can choose between the traditionally run school and the parallel school. The latter organizes its whole curriculum around humanistic approaches, even in the traditional subject areas. The parallel school often moves away from traditional grading and marking systems which tend to prevent young people from developing their own values.[4]

Another approach to schoolwide humanistic change is to organize the whole school according to the open-classroom model. In this case, the total school, and the community, too, are seen as environments rich in educational resources. Students take the major responsibility for guiding their education through that environment. Teachers serve as facilitators, making their skills and knowledge available to help students move toward their own learning goals.[5, 6] Such a school is in many ways like real life in which people must take responsibility for their own directions, but can share resources with each other and can call on help when needed. In this laboratory setting, students gradually learn the valuing skills and the learning skills that will serve them throughout their lives.

One of the most daring proposals for a schoolwide curricular reorganization along humanistic lines comes from Gerald Weinstein and Mario Fantini.[7] They suggest that the school day be divided into three equal time segments. During the first third of the day, the time would be spent learning the fundamental skills and areas of knowledge which now take up most of the day in most schools. (This, in itself, is a challenging assertion: that students don't need nearly as much of the traditional curriculum as we think they do, and that what is really essential for them—the skills of communication and calculation and the basic facts a member of this society needs to know—could be telescoped into one third of the normal day.) The second third of the time would be open for the students to choose any areas they wanted to learn more about. Many students would spend their time with arts, crafts, music and sports—skills and pastimes that could last them all their lives. Others might want to work with teachers in the academic subject areas in greater depth. The final third of the day is devoted to "education of the self." During this time, all students are involved in activities and discussions which help them become clearer about who they are, how they view themselves, what their values are, what goals they are setting for themselves, how they are achieving their goals, and so on. Here it is possible to examine not only personal goals, but preferable futures for the community and society as a whole. In this segment, students are actually studying themselves; they are the subject matter. And they are learning the processes of self-understanding, values clarification and communication that will continue to serve them twenty and forty years hence, when, predictably, the world will be very different.

No one can predict the values that will emerge from an ongoing valuing process. No doubt, many of our most cherished values are worth maintaining and will be maintained for years to come. Yet other values, whether privately held or shared by the society, will fall by the wayside. Young people who have internalized an ongoing valuing process will make mistakes, just as their teachers made mistakes. But behind the process is a faith in man: that if we can recognize, accept and express our own feelings, if we can consider alternatives and consequences and make our own choices, and if we can actualize our beliefs and goals with repeated and consistent action, our decisions will lead us toward a future we can cope with and control. It is when we deny our feelings and hide them from others, when we accept the first alternatives and don't look ahead to consequences, when we allow others to make our value choices for us, when we do not act on our beliefs and ideals, *then* we relinquish control over our futures and find ourselves floundering in a world and a body we do not understand.

Unfortunately, this latter alternative describes the future for all too many individuals. Yet such a grim future need not be. As educators, we want to continue to model the values *we* believe in. But, most important, we now have the insight and skills to begin designing learning environments in which young people learn a *process* for clarifying and developing their own values. Only in this way can we turn preferable futures into probable futures.*

* For a bibliography of materials available on values clarification and humanistic education and for a schedule of values clarification workshops offered across the country, readers may write to The Adirondack Mt. Humanistic Education Center, Upper Jay, New York, 12987.

"Do-a-Value"

A VALUE IS	SO	ASK
Chosen	*Help each member of the family weigh alternatives and make free choices.*	Where and when did you get that idea?
		What other choices did you reject and why?
		What do you expect to happen?
Prized	*Encourage them to decide what they prize and cherish.*	How long have you wanted it?
		Do you feel glad about it?
		How would your life be different without it?
Affirmed	*Give them opportunities publicly to affirm their choices.*	Whom have you told about your decision?
		Will you stand up for what you feel?
		Would you tell everyone at school or work?
Acted	*Encourage them to behave and live by their convictions.*	What are you going to do about it?
		Who else will work with you?
		Can I help?

The introduction of future consciousness into education is the next wave of educational change, says Philip Werdell—but it has deep connections with the political and educational reform movements of the sixties. If educational futurism is to have any bite, it must go beyond conventional curricular reform. It must press for institutional restructuring, student rights to participate in decision-making, an action-based curriculum, and new linkages between learning and future forms of work. To this end, he makes radical suggestions for the creation of Work Support Groups, Intentional Work Experiments, and Future Assemblies.

CHAPTER SIXTEEN

Futurism and the Reform of Higher Education

by Philip Werdell

> Democratic nations care little for what has been, but are haunted by visions of what will be; in this direction their unbound imagination grows and dilates beyond all measure. . . . Democracy, which shuts the past against the poet, opens the future before him.
>
> —*Alexis de Tocqueville*

In recent years courses in the future have begun to proliferate on the college campus. Books like *The Meaning of the Twentieth Century, Future Shock, The Year 2000* and *Profiles of the Future* are seen everywhere. An educational movement, in fact, is emerging around the idea of futurism and is pressing for important curricular innovation. Yet the introduction of the future into our colleges and universities is not just a matter of adding the term "futuristics" to the catalog.

If all that was accomplished were the opening of a few additional electives, the educational futures movement could turn out to be even more past-oriented and limited in vision than most earlier reform efforts. For the introduction of the future into higher education involves not merely the curriculum, but the structure of the system as well. It involves not merely reading about the future, but the ways in which students experience and *create* change. In short, for the educational futures movement to succeed, it must become a movement for social change as well.

To see why, it is necessary to stand back for a moment and examine the ways in which the futures movement fits into the larger picture of educational reform and political action on the campus.

The first section of this paper, therefore, sketches the emergence of reform in higher education, the backdrop against which the futures movement has developed. The second section assesses the accomplishments of the reformers until now. The third argues that the precondition for introducing the future into higher education is effective student participation in the decision-making of the multiversity. The fourth presents ways in which higher education can build upon the lessons of the educational reform movement to assure that students learn the new skills needed in imagining possible futures, predicting probable futures and deciding preferable futures. The final section links learning and work, and offers four simple and practical models which can help us begin the process of discovering how to work for the future.

The Emergence of Reform

During the 1950s educators began heroic acts of self-analysis in American colleges and universities. Three major collections of research papers offered, at the end of the decade, a resounding indictment of higher education. By this time the United States had become the most powerful country in the world and had committed itself to increasing involvement in international affairs. Yet Bidwell's report, *Undergraduate Education in Foreign Affairs*, stated that "seniors emerge from . . . college with hardly more acquaintance with foreign affairs than when they entered as freshmen."[1]

In the latter half of the decade, it was becoming apparent that the technological revolution was rapidly creating new societal environments. Yet Philip E. Jacob could shock the educational community with his evidence that "the college student does not significantly change his view of himself or the society in which he lives as an undergraduate."[2]

Finally, many of the country's most distinguished educators offered well-documented findings, in Sanford's *The American College*, that, in essence, intellectual and personal development were inextricably intertwined, but that higher education was not dealing adequately with the former because it was not dealing at all with the latter.[3] The verdict was clear: Teaching and learning in American higher education were provincial, structurally stagnant, and psychologically simplistic.

The response of American colleges and universities to these early warnings was half-hearted. Vested interests were too strong. The Department of Defense, already spending over half the tax dollar and deeply intertwined with the growing corporate conglomerates, had become dependent on the specialized research facilities of the university. The conditions for crisis in most American cities—pollution, accelerating technological change, the exodus of the middle class to the temporary haven of the suburb, cycles of poverty and oppression in the inner city—had already been set, and the immediacy and magnitude of the problems drained what little creative energy educators might have devoted to reconceptualizing and reforming the university itself.[4]

Faculty members, trained in narrow fields of specialization and prepared with razor-sharp minds but underdeveloped emotional and social capabilities, had their hands full coping day to day with the growing number of students in their classes who did not find the traditional academic style stimulating or useful.[5]

Beginning off campus in the early 1960s with the civil-rights sit-ins in Greensboro and then the first antiwar march on Washington, student protest found its focus in the Free Speech Movement in 1965 at the ultimate multiversity itself, Berkeley. It was at this symbolic point that students began to understand that the multiversity had become a product and tool of the broader society, rather than a creative force for understanding and changing that society, and that, therefore, they would have to take on responsibility for their own education. It was no longer possible simply to rely on the university to furnish an adequate education.[6]

In the wake of protests which rocked campuses across the country, a wide range of experimental programs began to take hold. Most of these were started by students themselves, sometimes with the help of sympathetic faculty and administrators, more often in spite of roadblocks put in their way by those in power.

Although campus demonstrations were the most visible indication of student discontent, disruption was *not* the major concern of most student activists. In fact, with respect to education, the central arguments of protesting students were notable for their similarity to research findings of the previous decade.

Few students had read Sanford's *The American College*, yet, through the student community tutorial movement, more than 200,000 students at over 1,200 campuses volunteered 7,000,000 hours a year to carry into the primary and secondary schools of the ghetto reforms that Sanford had recommended for higher education. Jacob's *Changing Values in College* was hardly a campus best-seller, yet thousands of student veterans of the civil-rights movement took Robert Moses Paris of the Student Non-Violent Coordinating Committee (SNCC) seriously when he said, "Don't use Mississippi as a moral lightning rod. Use it as a looking glass. Look into it and see what it tells you about America—and yourself"—i.e., about values. Hardly any undergraduates had read Bidwell's *Undergraduate Education in Foreign Affairs*, yet the Vietnam War challenged students to create a social movement with papers, teach-ins, and strategies in mimeographed form moving swiftly from campus to campus.

In a statement of the kind that attracts more student commitment than newspaper coverage, the former president of the Students for a Democratic Society (SDS) explained:

By social movement, I mean more than marches, petitions and letters of protest or tacit support of dissident Congressmen; I mean people who are willing to change their lives, who are willing to challenge the system, to take the problem of change seriously. By social movement I mean an effort that is powerful enough to make the country understand that our problems are not in

Vietnam or China or Brazil or outer space or at the bottom of the ocean but here in the United States. What we must begin to do is build a democratic and humane society in which Vietnams are unthinkable.[7]

It was in this spirit that a growing number of students began to look critically at the multiversity.

Successes of the Sixties

At the center of the educational reform movement of the sixties were new, so-called *free universities*. Quickly taking up the example of the student Experimental College at San Francisco State College, free universities sprang up in or near almost half of the traditional colleges and universities in the United States.[8] Their creative principle was simple: Anyone could teach anything he or she wanted, in any form, and when a teacher was not available, a group of students could gather to begin learning how to learn on their own. Students would judge for themselves whether or not they could learn in each particular situation or course they entered.

Free-university courses ran the gamut from traditional academic lectures on Indochina, science and technology, and black history, to experiences in meditation, bicycle trips into the country and organic gardening; from reading courses on the world view of McLuhan, Marx or the alchemists, to highly personal and emotional encounter groups. Some courses were taught by faculty, others by students, still others by experienced craftsmen, lawyers and even policemen in the community. Some courses lasted the length of the academic semester; some were over in a few sessions when mutual interest was obviously lacking. Some never got started at all; some so caught the imaginations that people studying ecology or new architectural technology or theories of education decided to continue their learning through practical experimentation—action programs which often lasted for years.[9]

It was (and still is) an impressive demonstration of students' commitment to their own learning and social understanding. In courses for which they often receive neither grades nor credits, and which they prepare for and attend in addition to a heavy course load and/or a job, hundreds of students (at large multiversities, often thousands) continue to enroll regularly in free-university courses.

The free-university phenomenon was a second jolting indictment of traditional higher education and was not as easily filed away as the research reports of the fifties, and it was accompanied by many other efforts at reform.

By the end of the sixties *evaluations of courses and teachers by students*, some confidential but more and more published, began giving students, faculty and administrators some minimal yearly feedback on the quality of the formal curriculum.[10] Student leaders in regular weekend retreats with faculty and administrators began to break down barriers of communication, the stereotypes of roles, misinterpretations about intentions and values.[11] The Tussman Program at Berkeley, Justin Morril College at Michigan State, Bensalem College at Fordham, and Project #10 at the University of Massachusetts created relatively isolated total *living-and-learning residences* with faculty and classes living together in the dormitories and creating their own education together.[12] *Black studies programs*, then Chicano studies and women's studies, and most recently Appalachian studies programs began to be demanded and designed.[13]

Not all these experiments were successful, but enough were, and with varying degrees of speed and quality, they began to edge their way into the formal curriculum. This process accelerated as those who had been graduate students in the early sixties began, in turn, to move into faculty roles later on. Among the new courses they generated, those based on *sensitivity training* or encounter were, perhaps, the most popular, drawing on the work of Esalen Institute, the National Training Laboratories, Western Behavioral Sciences Institute and the Institute for the Study of the Person.[14] These process-oriented courses were complemented by further student experiments with communal living.[15]

Similar in flavor, but more outwardly directed, were the early experiments with *action curriculum*—experiments like that at Western Michigan University which integrated two years of Peace Corps service into a five-year B.A. program, or the award of credits for work in Appalachia by students at the University of Ohio at Athens, or the introduction of practical problems of pollution in courses at the California Institute of Technology. In some cases, whole academic departments—like the Department of Psychology at the University of Michigan or the School of Management at Case Western Reserve—recognized both personal growth and social action as complements to the traditional academic education.[16] Taken together there were hundreds of experiments, possibly thousands.

A parallel effort, initiated on dozens of campuses, from the University of Houston to the University of Minnesota, involved student development programs, beginning with freshman orientation and the organization of *"support groups"* to help students define their own educational objectives in terms of their own value systems. Student life is typically transient and often lonely and filled with anxiety.[17] These support groups provided a social network in which questions of personal values and the complexities of the modern world could be raised.

Another important innovation was achieved at hundreds of colleges by changing the academic calendar from two four-and-a-half-month semesters to what became known as the 4-1-4, in which an interim or *January Term* was opened up to be as free, at least ideally, as a free university.[18] Within the limits of what faculty would accredit (limits often sadly restrictive), the "free" month offered an opportunity for *all* students to win credit for self-initiated or individualized learning.

These scattered reforms were assisted on many campuses when students, faculty and administration worked together to reexamine the archaic grading policy. The *Pass-Fail option* was instituted on many campuses, first for one or two electives taken by upperclassmen, and then progressively broadened to include more and more courses. A majority of students—still needing numerical, if superficial, evaluation from teachers or else not trusting that they could get into graduate school or get jobs without competing for grades—still chose to be graded. But the opportunities for more self-directed learning, more cooperative styles of teaching, and more meaningful forms of evaluation were opened up. Although it still remains to create new, personally useful and socially effective forms of evaluation, some of the debilitating pressures of the traditional grading system were removed.[19]

Altogether, the reform movement of the sixties scored important gains on a number of fronts. While the future as such was seldom, if ever, an explicit concern in these programs, it *was* an implicit concern. Whether expressed in these terms or not, students engaged in the struggle for education reform were deeply worried about the directions of change in American life, and the inability of the traditional academic system to prepare the individual to cope with and shape change.

The Political Context

The educational reform movement of the sixties cannot be understood in isolation from parallel political developments. It proved to be no more or less successful than the complementary movements to stop the war, to stop oppression of the poor and people of color in America, and to stop the ecological rape of the planet.

The protests against the Vietnam War were successful in awakening a generation to the horrors of war, dumping Johnson and beginning to force the withdrawal of American fighting men, and stimulating new thought about a foreign policy not based on the Cold War; but American bombers continued interminably to drop the equivalent of two Hiroshima atom bombs a day on the already battered people of Indochina.

Through their protests, blacks, Chicanos and native Americans (most recently, poor whites) gained a new sense of personal dignity, caught glimpses of potential political power, and established footholds in the dominant American institutions. Yet the struggle has clearly only begun.

A wider range of people have become concerned about ecology. Pressures have mounted for a nonpolluting car. Some recycling of such things as pop bottles and beer cans has begun and initial efforts are under way to begin organic farming and stop the spread of oil slicks on our beaches. Nonetheless, no serious breakthrough has occurred. Nothing significant has yet begun to stop the catastrophic death of the ocean floor or to right the imbalanced exploitation of the world resources, mostly for quickly obsolescent products of war, by the industrial nations.

Similarly with the educational reform movement in our nation's colleges and universities: The recognition that something root-deep is wrong with the traditional teaching and learning process is still spreading rapidly. Led by some of the brightest and most capable students, the option of dropping out of the system has become increasingly legitimate. Even with the experimental programs, undergraduate education for *most* students continues to be no more than a further extension of the goals, requirements and methods developed for a different and smaller group of people a century ago in response to the industrial revolution.

Today some of the excitement and creative energy within the educational reform movement has begun to wane along with the political ferment of the 1970s. Many free universities have developed as far as they can go. Some, like the University for Man at Kansas State University which enrolls about a thousand students each semester, have become important, established parts of the multiversity. Others, like the large Mid-Peninsula Free University which broke completely with Stanford University, have become, in effect, community night schools for those identifying themselves with the counterculture in various urban centers. Others have died away.

Course and teacher evaluations are better at suggesting problems than at offering alternatives. Integrated living and learning programs, while providing excellent experiences for students and faculty, place high demands on faculty who are less free than students to drop out of the formal classroom and departmental system for extended periods. Moreover, the usual method of financing these special programs by adding a new item in the overall university budget is limited, especially with state legislatures responding to the middle-class antistudent backlash.

Tighter money within the university and tighter job markets due to the growing surplus of Ph.D.s also put personal and political pressure upon young faculty and administrators involved in or thinking about experimental programs, constraining their capacity to innovate.

These pressures also work on students. Most students now in college, especially the growing number from lower-income families and minority groups, come to college in response to the promise that an undergraduate degree is the ticket to a good job. It is understandable that a majority of students still hesitate to pursue their own learning inclinations. It is with some justice that the majority of honest middle-class and lower-middle-class Americans and their career-oriented, upwardly aspiring children now in college view the experimental programs in colleges and universities with skepticism. These may be excellent models for personal growth, but will they get me a job? And will the learning in such programs help me in the job that I do get? If they do not, what will they do to my future?

This, then, is where the educational reform movement is as the futures movement begins to take hold, and it suggests that one priority issue must now become the question of work. If it is true that the old industrial society is breaking down and a new society is beginning to form, education must address itself to the new ways of work that must emerge.

What work is relevant to the survival and growth of the people of the world? How does an individual or group find, create and sustain work that is not only economically productive, but *feels* good? How do we build upon the advances in industrial technology without being slaves to the obsolete or unhealthy manifestations of technology which now overwhelm us? How do we, during this vast transition in society, change the nature of work from an onerous duty to a simultaneous fulfillment of personal and social needs?

Students learning to take responsibility for their own education are, at the same time, citizens preparing to take personal and political responsibility for their own lives. It is for this reason, and in this context, that we must now begin to introduce the future into higher education as the next stage of education reform.

For the many young people already committed to experimenting with their own lives (and this is the essential process/product of the educational reform movement), we must construct a path beyond the campus to the longer-range problems of "learning a living." We need to find a way for the majority of white, middle-aged, middle-class American working people (all too glibly labeled the "silent majority") to share their experience, their successes, failures, dreams and frustrations with the young in the process of conceptualizing constructive alternatives for the future.

On the campus itself, the majority of students and faculty, still hesitant about the new teaching and learning models (and the risks and burdens of taking responsibility for their own education), must be challenged to join in the creation of truly democratic educational institutions. This is nothing less than a call to make the multiversity, indeed all of our nation's colleges and universities, the focus of an ongoing search for possible, probable and preferable futures.

The Roots of Tomorrow

All education is commonly regarded as education for the future. However, it is only in the last few years that higher education has even begun to catch up with the present.

The first university in Bologna, Italy, began in the 1500s when a group of young aristocrats organized themselves to employ learned people to teach them about their heritage. As colleges and universities took root across Europe, classical scholars aligning themselves with at least part of the ruling aristocracy gained control of the institutions. The dominant subject matter was the Christian Bible and the classics of Greek and Roman civilization. The primary methods: rote memorization and the private scholasticism of the monastery.

For centuries this medieval form of higher education flourished for small groups of the European elite, and the early universities in America—Harvard, Yale, William and Mary—were founded to perform a similar function in the New World. Indeed, well into the nineteenth century in America, colleges organized on the medieval model continued to serve an elite fraction of one per cent of the citizenry. The formal curriculum continued to be limited to Latin, Greek, the Bible (sometimes in Hebrew) and a few essays with theological and social interpretations of the world. These few writings and the "dead" classical languages were still taught almost exclusively by rote, the teacher calling out what students should repeat or directing students through memorized recitations and translations. University education was primarily learning about, and in the style of, the past.

It was only in the period 1850–1870, under the pressure of the Industrial Revolution, that higher education as most know it today began to take shape. Much of the change was initiated by students themselves who, dissatisfied with the educational diet, created their own literary societies on campus. At one point there were more books in the libraries of student societies at Yale than in the university's own library. Moreover, student book collections included the contemporary and heretical: the new Biblical criticism, the scientific writings of Darwin, the social theories of Smith and Spencer, along with novels.

Within their own societies, students presented papers, argued the accuracy of analysis, and discussed the moral and social worth of these new ideas. The subject matter in these literary societies foreshadowed the academic disciplines we know today. The form of presentation and discussion came to be the lecture and seminar, radical new methods for teaching and learning as compared with the pure rote of the traditional class.

As students from these literary societies moved on to become faculty (and as alumnae, part of the leadership of the new industrial society), the study of scientific and contemporary problems was introduced into the mainstream of higher education. Broad political support developed for the creation of public land-grant institutions in each state to offer education to an expanded minority of the populace, and colleges and universities began educating about and for the present.[20]

During the century of industrial revolution, roughly 1850 to 1950, colleges and universities focused on the goal of turning out a new professional and managerial class. The university began to model itself after the factory, producing each year, in assembly-line manner, hundreds of students with the latest accumulation of new knowledge and the intellectual skills to process and evaluate it. College became the primary vehicle of upward mobility for the growing middle class.

By the end of this period, the number of people going to college increased to 5, then 10 and then 15 per cent of the citizenry. The classical subject matter of the medieval university was squeezed into a corner, sometimes abandoned completely. The scholastic pedagogy of rote memorization and recitation was replaced with an academic style that placed high value on the collection of new empirical data and the rigor of scientific method. Higher education became a sophisticated social process for channeling highly trained human resources into the higher reaches of the industrial system.

The multiversities of today are straight-line projections of the machine-model colleges and universities of the industrial era. However, through its own technology and its techniques for accelerating technological innovation, the industrial system has begun to transform itself. A new cultural system is emerging. The new electronic technologies (and soon new biological, nuclear and solar technologies) are not only dramatically altering society, but further accelerating the rate at which new changes come about. In less than a half-century, the airplane changed the rules of warfare, politics and business. The time from Rutherford's discoveries about the atom to Los Alamos and Hiroshima was only thirty-five years. The first landing on the moon occurred less than a decade after the test-run of solid-fuel missiles. How far away is the fusion of man and machine, now that artificial organs, hormone producers and transistorized brain supplements are a reality in the laboratory?

The impact of this accelerative process began to be felt in the fifties precisely at the time that more and more students began to enter college. Information—whole bodies of knowledge—became more and more perishable. Purely intellectual skills, without equally developed intuitive, social and practical skills, became less and less useful and masses of students, increasingly articulate about the irrelevancy of their own education, began to rebel.[21]

It is now clear that the recent upheavals in higher education are part of the larger revolution that is transforming the advanced technological nations from industrial to superindustrial powers. This vast historic transition is moving very rapidly, based on the new technologies and on cultural and social innovations. Yet higher education is neither changing rapidly enough to keep pace, nor producing students capable of moderating and shaping the forces of change.

The formal curriculum continues to be based solely on a search for increasingly abstract truth. A problem is solved when the "true," correct, or reasonable answer is discovered and verified. Knowledge is thought to be transmitted when the intellectual analysis of a problem is organized into a lecture, paper or book.

The primary goals of teaching are still to transmit an organized body of knowledge to the student and to help him develop critical judgment. It is assumed that when a student has amassed a large body of knowledge and acquired a highly developed analytic ability, he is prepared to deal with the problems of society and to pursue his own learning. Yet he and/or she finds it harder and harder to cope with the complexity and rapid change that surrounds us. He is left to solve for himself, without institutional support, the formidable problem of imagining or creating alternative futures, of deciding what learning and work are worthy of pursuit, and of integrating his learning, work and life in practical action.[22]

The silent alienation of students in the fifties and the surge of protests in the sixties were undeniable proof that the psyches and bodies of the young could no longer cope with the demands of the world in the context of educational institutions that were simple extensions of the industrial era; that to meet the present with integrity, students had to begin creating the institutions of the future.

Until the emergence of the educational reform movement, serious criticism of higher education tended to polarize. On the one hand were those, both educators and students, who maintained that higher education consistently failed to meet important *social* needs. On the other hand were those, again both students and educators, who maintained that higher education must first pay attention to the development of the *individual* student, and that it did not.

The experience of the educational reform movement demonstrated that one criticism cannot be met without meeting the other.

It takes a *whole* person to deal with whole-earth problems, and without a realistic world view an individual cannot for long attend to his own personal growth. Teaching and learning models for the future must integrate learning and living, the personal and the political.

The future of higher education is best seen as a continuous evolution of new and self-conscious experimental forms, each attempting at once to support the individual growth of those directly involved and to create the new social understandings, skills and goals necessary for the evolution of democracy.

Preconditions of the Future

The precondition for introducing the future into higher education is effective student participation in decision-making in the university—in policy formation and implementation, not just in the extracurricular life of the student, but also in the classroom and the institution as a whole.

The greatest public service higher education can perform is to develop people prepared to help solve society's emerging problems—who can articulate their own needs, who can understand the needs of others, and who can thus go on to create new goals and develop new forms of learning and doing. Only people so trained will be able to assume new roles as old ones become obsolete. Only those who have gained confidence in their own identity and direction can create healthy future goals for society. The challenge is to develop future-oriented self-directed learners.

The development of a self-directed learner is subjective and not to be forced. But if the student lacks the power to change the objective conditions in which he lives, learns and works, such development is all but impossible. For most students, the sense of powerlessness is felt on many levels: in the simple desire of two young human beings to express love for each other without fear of punishment or interference from a bureaucracy; in the desire of many students to obtain credit for learning which at present lies outside the narrow definitions of academic legitimacy; in the desire for effective student representation on policy bodies as decisive as departmental policy committees, faculty senates and boards of trustees.

At stake is not just the introduction of the future into higher education but the possibility for an evolution of functional democratic institutions within our lifetimes. For students this issue is central because it touches the proper use of power in a mass institution—that it serve the personal growth of those who live and work in it as well as the general social goals for which it was created.

Most arriving freshmen experience these as conflicting demands. Students often find themselves in college because their parents feel they should be there. Society demands a degree as an entrance requirement into any established job or career. Students are caught in a dilemma: Is their education for some externally defined social purpose which they do not feel to be wholly relevant to human needs at this time? Or is it for themselves?

Most institutions underestimate the importance of the questions: What do you want to learn? What needs to be done? What work is worth doing? For most students, college is four years of mounting recognition that higher education leaves inadequate time and space for individual development. Sitting in large classrooms, listening to an elaborate pattern of words from a distant faculty member, students seldom find the way to even ask a question. Even in the prized small seminar class, a heady and competitive academic style so dominates discussion that real feelings and the ideas implicit in them are rarely developed.

Under the pressure of regular tests and papers to be graded, few students ever enjoy the exhilarating experience of following an intellectual problem wherever it may lead. Out of class. Across disciplines. Off campus. Into practical experimentation and action. Similarly missing in the classroom is the consideration of values, personal and political feelings, much less the opportunity to test and apply them in the here and now. With the interminable deferment of gratification and immediate learning needs comes the repression of interpersonal and social values, the essential context in which people make decisions about their own lives and the world. The relationship of present decisions and actions to the future is seldom deeply explored.

For many, the choice quickly narrows to either learning how to beat the system or dropping out. Even the student in a slightly experimental classroom and the student leader sitting on the most recently conceived student-faculty-administration committee face similar problems. Given a role, however small, in planning the direction of a class or the future of the university itself, he begins to ask: Should higher education meet the needs of a society of which he does not wholly approve? The choices narrow down quickly to participating almost impotently in a severely limited discussion or organizing, formally or informally, a demonstration of frustration. When a small circle of educators by themselves set the norms for "good academic behavior" and the limits of "relevant participation in policy," students everywhere are removed from the possibility of meaningful community.

Why community? A new consciousness is emerging. It derives from the world in which students grow up. The Bomb and the possibility of total war. The rapid growth of technology and the visions of automation. TV, paperbacks, jet youth-fare. Increasingly visible inequalities which draw lines between races in

America and between the rich and poor of the world. A revolutionary environment in which all known political-economic forms —fascism, communism, capitalism—seem to be inadequate in meeting human needs. And a diverse youth culture sustained locally through rituals like the pot party and disseminated worldwide through the evolution of rock music and the antiwar movement. Parents of the Depression and World War II generations find it difficult to comprehend their children's world. A world in which one swims in the ambience of uncontrolled media and dislocation of explosively changing technology. A world in which survival requires the spiritual strength to move through and beyond alienation.

The Experience of the Student

The experience of students varies widely. In fact, the deep pluralism of the emerging student culture is among its least understood and most dynamic elements. The soul of the new student consciousness is a sense of new personal possibilities and alternative futures for society. The catalytic events come at different times and in different ways for each individual student. A confrontation with parents over life-style or the uses of money. Suffering a sarcastic put-down one too many times for expressing new feelings or experimenting with new dress. Slowly recognizing that it is not just the Selective Service System, but the whole educational system that serves as a powerful channeling mechanism, and sensing the possibilities of real freedom if the mechanism can be eluded. Suddenly being caught up in a political campaign and seeing fellow students beaten by police. A fleeting feeling of resonance with young people in new communities, the black in the American ghetto, even the Vietnamese people in "their own" country. The examples are endless, unique for each individual student. Most recently Watergate—each of yesterday's paranoid flashes becoming tomorrow's realities.

If there is one common experience forging the student consciousness, it might be feeling the profound contradictions between the latest underground LP, which speaks to the needs of the young, and the network news on TV, which somehow misses the point, time after time. And through all these strands, a nagging question remains: Can the elders commit themselves to learn from the young as they demand that the young learn from them.

Student participation in decision-making must thus be understood in the context from which it springs, a heightened sense of the need for educational reform and change in the larger community as well. The central problem is to find ways to help students take responsibility for their own education. If there is a first-step goal, it is to encourage student leadership that can help *other* students organize and make effective decisions about student interests.

This is not a painless process. Its essence is the willingness of faculty and administrators to abdicate real responsibility to students as a way of building trust. Students realize that adults offer significant opportunity only to those with whom they agree. Yet many faculty and administrators are finding that before they can accomplish *their* purposes they must first regain trust, not with more words but with new actions. If the thought of facing this problem anew with each generation of students is frightening, the educator must choose between escalating the risks he is willing to take and losing touch with students finding their own direction, and thus with the possibility of creating constructive social change.

The problem is *not* finding the right words. Not even finding the correct structural solutions. There are models for making classrooms less authoritarian, even for decentralizing power within the vast multiversity. But these are not packages that can be transferred from one classroom to the next, from one institution to another. Where serious efforts to change have taken place, the near successes are understood by those responsible as first approximations to be learned from rather than replicated. It is just this judgment which offers hope. The goal is self-trained people. The process is as important as the product. Thus, the best guideline for student participation in decision-making: Does a particular educational form or institutional process move toward real responsibility, toward community, for those directly involved, and toward a world view responsive to other such communities?

Colleges and universities are now mass institutions. Creating institutional democracy on such a large scale has never been done before, but it is the obvious and necessary condition for moving into the future with continuing devotion to the dreams and ideals of democracy.

Where Education Reform Left Off

The futurist movement in higher education must learn from the lessons of the educational reform movement. While cognitive learning should continue to have high priority, the problem of integrating learning and living for the future clearly demands new emphasis on other kinds and styles of learning, as well. Specifically, the curriculum must offer experiences in creative and speculative uses of the intellect as well as analytical uses. It must offer practice in dealing with people from diverse backgrounds of various styles of life with differing goals, as well as practice in understanding their problems from a distance. It must offer opportunities to *act* on the basis of what one understands as well as the opportunity to theorize about ideal solutions. In short, the curriculum must introduce students to a variety of styles of learning as well as a variety of bodies of knowledge. And taken together, these new styles of learning must prepare students for imagining possible futures, for predicting probable futures, and for deciding about preferable futures.

Imagining Possible Futures

The imagining of possible futures is now fundamental both to the process of personal growth and to the development of a world consciousness. The individual begins deciding who he can be and wants to be through internalizing role models from the existing culture. With new technologies rapidly and radically reshaping the entire society, however, role definitions are no longer stable. They are, on the contrary, changing along with whole social forms at an accelerating rate. Roles for young people and the very context in which roles are defined are likely to be more different than the same in the future. Increasing numbers of people need to learn to create their own roles. This demands both imagination and an orientation toward the future.

From the social perspective, it is becoming difficult even to anticipate scientific and technological advances, let alone to understand their social implications.[23] Yet our emerging ecological consciousness suggests there is probably no greater social need to which higher education must respond. Every student needs to recognize that the future is a field of multiple possibilities and that these demand imaginative exploration. Every student thus needs to learn and rigorously practice the skills of creative speculation and synthesis.

Even the best academic seminar seldom encourages free creative speculation and synthesis; rather, it is designed to further the analysis of existing information. The communication is discursive, the tone argumentative. The teacher is assumed to be an authority for whose approval there tends to be informal competition, and the grading system reinforces informal sanctions against playing a hunch or speculating about the implications of observations. There is a strong implication that students cannot be trusted. Though often proposed as an improvement over the lecture, few social forms are *less* suited for the cultivation and development of imaginative skills.[24]

The challenge to higher education is to expose every student to learning experiences more conducive to developing his creative capacities, including highly personal free association and more rigorous development of scenarios about the future of our society.

If a group is involved, the tone should be gentle and open, the attitude mutually reinforcing. There should be rewards for the risks of intimacy and for daring articulation of experiences and theories. Confrontation and encounters should focus on helping individuals trust their own feelings. The operating principle should be that of suspended judgment. The social goal should be creating a non-zero-sum game, that is, a situation in which everyone can win.[25] This is the essence of educational research on this matter to date.

So rare are such experiences in the traditional educational environment that their absence may be related to the widespread use of marijuana among students. The rituals, norms and expectations surrounding its use—not to mention the influence of the psychedelic drugs themselves—shift the user out of the mode of critical analysis and into the mode of creative speculation and synthesis.[26] It becomes possible to express ideas, associations, insights and feelings that might invite ridicule or retribution if expressed in the traditional classroom in which judgment is almost never suspended.

A variety of more formal teaching and learning models to foster highly sophisticated creative thinking have been developed within the educational-reform movement. The Institute for Creative Education at the University of Buffalo has developed a basic course on applied imagination, and the techniques have been applied in a variety of subject fields including aeronautics (San Jose State College), agriculture (Purdue), architecture (University of Illinois), business management (University of Illinois), chemistry (Graceland College), economics (University of Chattanooga), educational research (University of Colorado), English (Findlay College), engineering (University of Maryland), geography (University of Oregon), group discussion (University of Minnesota), human relations (University of Montreal), industrial design (Georgia Tech), journalism (University of Washington), marketing (Harvard University), physics (Long Beach State College), teacher training (Reed College).[27]

The University Christian Movement pioneered a format using essays called "Dialog Focusers" to initiate free discussions about new approaches to the problems of education, poverty and technology.[28] A technique called the "Facilitator," beginning with open one-to-one interviews about what each person wants to learn and followed by feedback of this data into the whole group, has been used equally well in free universities, traditional classrooms and temporary learning environments such as conferences, to help small and large groups define their own learning needs and create imaginative approaches to meeting these needs.[29] The multidisciplinary group working on the World Resources Inventory at Southern Illinois University has created an ongoing "World Game" in which participants attempt to anticipate new technologies and invent future scenarios which make the most efficient use of the planet's physical resources for all the people of the world.[30] As Billy Rojas tells us in an earlier chapter of this volume, many other future-focused games and simulations have been developed that encourage the use of the student's creative abilities in the definition of possible futures. Dennis Livingston suggests the ways in which science fiction can be used to broaden our conception of these possibilities.

Forecasting Probable Futures

Because forecasting probable futures in one's own life and for the world is becoming more difficult, it is increasingly important for young people to learn to be able to do just that. The process of developing internal discipline in one's life is dependent upon understanding the slower rhythms in one's life as well as those aspects of the social environment that are most likely to recur. To the degree that change, itself, becomes a major constant in people's lives, it is important for students to learn more about their own limits, to anticipate problems of adjustments and transmutation, and to be able to relate to other people struggling with the process of transition.

The pace of change intensifies the need for large technologically dependent organizations to plan for three- to five-year periods of time or more. A certain minimum time is needed, for example, for a large corporation to move from research to production of a new technology or service.[31] If technology is to be placed more effectively at the service of individuals, masses of people will need to acquire some of the predictive and planning skills now practiced only by managerial elites.

With financial support from the federal government, especially the Department of Defense, and big business, a new group of academic futurists are struggling to legitimize the application of systems theory and social-science techniques to the problem of delineating probable futures. This new work of the futurists often provides useful information, and it is important that this information be made available to all students for general discussion and the debate of probable futures. Yet the academic and business approaches are often limited to a severely linear method of verification and projection.

By analogy, while linear futurists become more sophisticated at predicting the path of a caterpillar as it crawls across the lawn, they tend to forget that a single misplaced step by the gardener might cut its trajectory short—or, conversely, that, left alone, the caterpillar might some day turn into a butterfly and soar away. While serious futurists consistently make qualifications about such possibilities, this does not provide students (or, for that matter, the futurists' own clients) with the experience, the attitude or skills required to deal with such revolutionary mutations in their own lives.[32]

Forecasting—especially the kind we require in our personal lives—cannot rely on conscious, explicit or linear methods alone. However useful it might indeed be for students to be familiar with the methods and premises of professional futurists, they also need a wholly different kind of sophistication. They need exposure to people from diverse cultural backgrounds, of various styles of life, and with radically different goals. The skills needed are those of articulating one's own deepest feelings and ideas, and of listening, even if not with empathy, to conflicting opinions and aspirations of others. The ability to identify and define the values of others is a critical tool in forecasting their responses to our behavior. The tendency of the multiversity to create youth ghettos and the effects of the traditional classroom in establishing norms of distant, "objective" discussion among people both work strongly against the development of these important personal and social skills.[33]

Thus, whatever cognitive skills the university provides with respect to forecasting—a grasp of probability theory, for example, or experience in the use of Delphi, or participation in the construction of mathematical models—they need to be supported with wholly different kinds of experiences. The growing student practice of hitchhiking or driving around the country—and even the world—is better suited to the long development of personal predictive skills than many of the formal and informal skills presently legitimized as higher learning in the multiversity. Rather than discouraging touring, the multiversity might be wise to turn some of its dorm space (usually obsolete before it is paid for and seldom used to capacity during vacation periods) into giant, inexpensive hostels for student travelers. Educators ought to encourage traveling students to look for and evaluate the emergent social future—the directions of change—in the communities visited and to search for the emergent future—the directions of personal change—in the people with whom they interact.[34]

In fact, academic credit for learning pursued and evaluated on such trips would legitimize this important social experience and encourage students to focus, evaluate and integrate this experiential and future-oriented learning with the subject matter and styles of learning offered in the classroom.

Elements of the traditional curriculum must also change. Again, it is important to build upon the successes of the educational reform movement. Encounter groups and sensitivity training may be useful in cultivating listening and interpersonal skills.[35] The growing literature on possible and preferable futures emanating both from industrial think tanks[36] and from the underground press[37] offers highly accessible curricular materials that can be used to integrate complex personal feelings and rigorous intellectual development through the discussion and analysis of alternative tomorrows.

The challenge is to incorporate these new materials, new styles of learning and future-oriented subject matter into every class in the multiversity without negating the material each teacher already wants to make accessible to students and without allowing T-groups or future-gaming to become the tools of a new conformity.

Similarly, material on possible and preferable futures can be introduced whenever appropriate. At a minimum, the faculty member or whoever is in a position of authority in the classroom ought to make it clear that this is a legitimate option. Some obvious examples: The scenarios in the packet *Peace Education* issued by the Student Forum for Peace and World Order might be used in a political science course; articles projecting the death of the oceans or science fiction speculating about microscopic life on other planets might be used in a biology course;[38] the plethora of material on communal living and alternative life-styles might be used in sociology and psychology courses;[39] utopian fantasies of major inventors like Buckminster Fuller might be used in engineering courses;[40] the platform of the Black Panther Party might be used in an economics course.[41]

Fascinating and crucial questions can be pursued—open-endedly—to their limits. Where is science taking us? How can tomorrow's communication technologies be used more democratically? What is the future of religion or friendship? What is the economic future of the developing world? What political structures will be needed in an increasingly transnational world? Will basic resources be exhausted by the year 2000? What transportation options ought to be developed over the next fifteen years? What is the likely future of the English language? The novel? What will be the central questions in physics or biology in fifteen or twenty years?

The essential goal is to introduce a wide range of material on possible and preferable futures into the classroom so that students, in the process of learning how to relate to this material themselves, also learn the reaction of a variety of different types of people, and thus gain perspective on what futures really are probable—assuming that everyone else's needs and dreams will play a critical part in determining the society that will actually evolve.

Deciding on Preferable Futures

Making a decision about one's own values and world view is becoming the most difficult problem in modern society. Students today pursue education longer, know more, and have more opportunities upon graduation than any previous generation, but the systems within which students develop have become so vast, so complex and so awesome that most students feel only a profound sense of powerlessness. With 15,000 journals published every year, with the body of knowledge doubling every ten years, the student is at a loss to decide where he should begin, much less what he should pursue. With organizations becoming larger, with the prerequisite time for advancement becoming longer, the student often feels that he is locked into an inevitable pattern. With material advancement no longer the sole or dominant personal challenge for most students, with the number of possible roles one can adopt or create presenting a bewildering variety of options, the student is often numbed by "overchoice"—so overwhelmed he finds it difficult to make any choices at all.[42]

A similar predicament is found in the world situation. American students today have lived since birth under the threat of nuclear annihilation, have been continually bombarded by television coverage of world crises, and increasingly have been able to travel abroad while still in college. They are gaining a new concern for, and knowledge of, world affairs. Yet, the complexity of political or international problems leads most students to believe that little they learn or do can matter. A student may become highly involved in the plight of the inner city or the war through intimate, on-the-spot television coverage, but frustration and indignation mount when he finds he can take no comparably involving action. Thus a fatalistic resignation sets in.[43]

Today's is a mass, technological society in which it is difficult to develop a sense of personal power. Yet, it is only through self-renewal of the individual that the society itself can be renewed. Higher education cannot reform the entire society. But the multiversity can prepare students to deal with other institutions by making itself—or at least part of itself—into a laboratory of institutional change. Students need to develop a realistic sense of personal power based on knowledge gained by practice of what one understands, especially when it has been contrary to the formal and informal rules of the society in which one grew up. The skills needed are those of organizing: not just organizing facts and ideas in one's head, but also organizing social situations which help one reality-test the consequences of one's concepts.

The traditional curriculum is itself an institutional system. It prescribes rules and procedures that encourage passive learning, not action based on a student's own ideas. To introduce the future into higher education means to offer every student an action curriculum—learning experiences in which he can test the implications and practicality of ideas, in which he can see for himself which subjects and styles of learning are relevant, in which he can generate his own ideas, select the problems he will pursue, and examine the future consequences of present action. The first action needed is that of students' organizing themselves to gain legitimacy for their own paths of learning within the institutional system of the traditional curriculum.[44]

One laboratory of action learning is found in the alternative or counterculture communities that have sprung up within and around most of the nation's multiversities. Here a person has the opportunity and support to experience alternative personal lifestyles and to build from scratch alternatives to existing institutions: to experiment with the effects of different foods and styles of eating, with alternative forms of growing, distributing and buying food; to try living in different physical environments; to build with the low-cost, ecologically sound techniques of the new architectural technologies; to start one's own school; to participate as learner and/or teacher in a community crisis center, free clinic or legal assistance program; to create new and participatory forms of art and entertainment; to reformulate notions of self-defense and the social functions of police; to begin explorations for ways in which the technology of the telephone, television and computer can be decentralized and put to the better service of the individual.[45]

Whether all or any of these experiments are lasting is not the point. They are opportunities for people to test out their ideas on a small and manageable scale, to gain practical experience in solving problems that affect their own lives, and to learn, in a highly critical environment, how to plan and act upon future alternatives they value as whole people.

But action-learning models *within* the formal curriculum are also plentiful. In the Antioch College work-study program, students alternate academic study with work every three or six months; the Dearborn program at the University of Michigan integrates internships in business with technical training; a five-year B.A. at Yale allows a growing number of students to undertake independent projects at home and abroad between their sophomore and junior years; The College for Human Services in New York City has developed a unique work-study curriculum for low-income adults aspiring to the professions. Within any single course, an action curriculum is possible.[46]

It is important in concluding this section on the lessons learned from the educational reform movement to stress that research on these new teaching and learning models indicates that they need not displace or even disrupt the traditional concern of students, faculty and parents with developing the *analytical* abilities of students. Every indication is that experiences designed to help a student develop his creative ability, social skills, and ability to act, support and stimulate cognitive learning as much as the traditional curriculum.

The creative-education models developed by the University of Buffalo Institute for Creative Education have been shown to produce large gains in practical problem-solving and to stimulate further reading and study.[47] The group-dynamics and sensitivity-training models of the National Training Laboratories and

Western Training Laboratories have been shown not only to facilitate dealing with other people, to further understanding of oneself, but to stimulate purely intellectual pursuits as well.[48] Students in action curricula have consistently fared at least as well on standard academic tests as those who have participated in traditional programs.[49]

In short, the introduction of new teaching and learning techniques in higher education would give students more opportunity to pursue personal development, would help assure society a supply of college-educated people better able to cope with new and complex problems, and would not downgrade the quality of a student's pursuit of knowledge and traditional analytical skills. As we begin to build these lessons from the educational reform movement into every aspect of higher education, we are beginning to learn more effectively for the future.

Student Roles vs. Worker Roles

Our images of the future are linear extensions of the industrial era. The prophecies of Huxley's *Brave New World*, Orwell's *1984* and Vonnegut's *Player Piano* strike notes of truth and horror in our souls. Images of more centralized authority, larger and larger bureaucratic systems, deeper alienation from the supertechnology. Ideas that brought us economic efficiency and material comfort now plague us with the possibilities of eco-catastrophe, mass social impotence and the waste of human potential. This is possible, even probable, if we do not learn to create a preferable future.

Work for that preferable future begins with an understanding that our present images of ourselves, and of the world, are the greatest limits to personal development and social evolution. It is difficult to imagine that we can be different, much less better, than we are now or have been in the past. It is particularly difficult to imagine ourselves as more integrated and wholly developed people. Similarly, it is difficult to understand how the seemingly awesome powers of technology can be reshaped into more humane tools and brought more closely under the control of individual people. Believing this is impossible makes it so. It alienates us from our own power by alienating us from our imagination.

One of the ways we limit ourselves is in our everyday practice of classifying people and, in turn, seeking to live up to, or break out of, the classifications others impose on us. What is *your* major? What kind of *man* are you? What do you do? (usually meaning, What is your job classification?) What does your husband do? (usually meaning, Are you "just" his wife?) Are you some kind of *hippie*? What race are you? Aren't you an American? As helpful as these categories may sometimes be in helping us understand the world as it is (or, at least, as it was), the personal and social costs of trying to enforce, or trying to break out of, these classifications are staggering. Their assumption of stable, stereotypic character types and classes negates both personal growth and social change.

Social change is no longer easily denied, much less avoided. The critical question is how to create future-focused roles and social forms that meet both our individual needs and our world responsibilities. The obsolete ways in which we classify people and are classified by others are legion and the interrelationships incredibly complex. How do we start to think in terms of changing, rather than fixed, categories? How do we begin to piece together flexible future-focused role-images?

People can, in fact must, start where they are at. If a woman or a man feels the oppression of a static sexual role—the submissive female or the machismo male—this is where the possibilities of individual change and growth are greatest. It is the battle to reconceptualize oneself that helps clarify one's future-focused role-image. If racism in an institution bars social progress for a people and freezes one into a racial role, then building a movement to challenge that institution is a learning experience that forces the student to clarify his or her values and sense of future alternatives. If the distribution of wealth and power denies working people respect, then clearly their focus needs to be on the struggle to change that system. For any person or group, the process of personal and social liberation begins with a recognition of the imputed roles that negate feelings of self-worth.

The situation within the multiversity is a special one, for it is a place in which people have time to explore the personal and social limits of the various roles they have been born into and are still playing out. The multiversity is unique, moreover, for in addition to being a place in which people who are classified (and classify themselves) in different roles can join with their peers, it is also a place in which, at this point in time, *all* students share in a common alienation in their assigned roles as students.

This alienation arises not from the generation gap, but rather from the separate personal and social roles that in industrialized nations have been assigned to young people and older people. In short, younger people are supposedly learners, and older people workers.

Highest status goes to young people who limit themselves to the role of student for a third to a half of their lives. Many do not finish grinding out the cherished Ph.D. until they are well into their thirties. On the other hand, older people are locked into jobs and the very limited role of worker from whatever time they may have finished their education until the age of retirement, usually no more than a few years before death. And finished with their education they certainly are; the golden pot of retirement at the end of the corporate rainbow serves as the worker's substitute for involvement with social problems and personal growth during the years he occupies his role as worker.

The idea of a working person struggling to become a whole person and actively pursuing learning about the whole world is as much a heresy as the idea of a student attempting to engage in relevant work. The working person is separated from the learning process and from the decision process that determines what work is, in fact, relevant. The student is separated from any opportunity to test the consequences of his or her learning through work.

In this situation, the future-focused role-image that emerges in most young people is one that is dominated by work and that virtually excludes further or continued learning. As though young people could not work and older people could not learn.

In a stable society this alienation of learners and workers would be wasteful and oppressive, but in a society rushing headlong toward the future it creates acute social crisis. We have examined the ways in which the young respond to accelerating change, but not the response of their working parents. Why the middle-class backlash to campus protests? Why the reluctance of a majority of students to demand, as a growing minority are doing, the new teaching and learning models in which they can take responsibility for their own education? Why the qualitatively new difficulties faced by the educational reform movement?

The fundamental reason for all these problems is that the major economic institutions of the society are not yet prepared to support the human needs of the people who work within them to continue their learning. Some progress has been marked in creating conditions for people in the higher places of management in large organizations to pursue personal growth, often by going back to the multiversity to keep in touch with rapid changes and new concepts about the world. For the masses of working people, however, blue collar *and* white collar, the role of worker cuts them off from control over their own learning: It delegitimizes profound questions of personal growth and separates them from the process of defining what work is socially relevant.

Without influence over the social decisions which affect their lives, without access to the new understandings about man and the world upon which such decisions are often made, people in the traditional roles of workers are understandably threatened by students who are struggling to extend the possibilities for personal growth by breaking out of the traditional roles of learners. Similarly, the majority of students sense, quite realistically, that most of the jobs offered them upon graduation, if indeed there are jobs, offer them roles as workers no less limiting than the traditional roles of learners.

To break out of these obsolete and increasingly socially dangerous roles, students must not only assume responsibility for their own education, but fight later on to create working situations in which they may continue the process of learning. The problem is momentous, never faced before on the mass scale now necessary. It demands nothing less than a change in the nature of work itself from an onerous duty to a gratifying fulfillment of personal and social needs—nothing less than a reformulation of the priorities of all our economic institutions to combine concern for the personal development of people working within them and social responsibility for the world effects of their products and services.

Only this transformation in work, itself, can, in the end, open the way for realistic future-focused role-images that beckon the student to a wholesome future and thereby provide both motivation and life-direction.

To address these challenges, we must begin to define the personal and political conditions needed for a healthy work process and ways in which today's industrial-era economic institutions limit this process. This must include self-criticism and research as heroic as the learning-process studies done in institutions of higher education in the fifties. The reform of work must be built upon a broad-based movement of workers, themselves committed to experimenting with their own lives. The initial theory in this direction, like John Gardner's thought on self-renewal and Warren Bennis' work on temporary societies, must be extended and more concretely developed.[50] Many corporations and large organizations are doing pioneering work today in decentralization, personalization and democratization of the work process. This work must be extended and made more accessible to the masses of working people themselves.

This paper is limited in content to the subject of higher education, to the creation of new future-focused teaching and learning models within the multiversity. How, then, can we simultaneously deal with the problems of education and work?

I would like to conclude by suggesting four models through which traditional elements of the multiversity can be focused on learning, work and the future. They are simple, practical and inexpensive, and some of the experience accumulated by the education-reform movement can be applied to them. They are transitional forms—a beginning. We might begin in our own lives and within (and without) the institutions which have control over our lives to create (1) work support groups; (2) intentional work experiments; (3) experiments toward humanizing technology; and (4) future assemblies.

Work Support Groups

One of the central problems faced by students in the multiversity is a sense of isolation, loneliness or superficiality in personal relationships. As human ties in our society grow more transient, many young people, despite outward signs of participation in class and social activities, feel that they have no one they can truly level with, trust, and count on for psychological and other support in case of need.

The work support group is meant, among other things, to address this problem.

Students in the various movements during the sixties banded together, forming close personal relationships and learning, after a time, to offer each other needed support—psychological and otherwise. The combination of an external goal—social change—and a psychologically supportive group helped many to define appropriate future-focused role-images. The women's liberation movement best developed this support feature in what were called "consciousness-raising" groups. These helped participants sharpen their own individual and work objectives.[51]

Today we can extend this idea by creating work support groups in which students can experiment together with the concept of work, examining such issues as, How do we find jobs linked to both our own personal growth and social values? How do we get money and resources for work we need and want to pursue, but which is not yet seen as legitimate in the formal economic structure? How do we create, step by step, changes in our working situations, inside and outside the established system, to help us gain both personal gratification and social satisfaction from our efforts?[52]

At many campuses such as Oberlin, San Diego State and Queens College, students have set up alternatives to the traditional vocational-counseling offices. These groups help students get together to talk about alternative life-styles, help them look for new types of jobs in the community, and are general think tanks about what new work is needed. These groups are linked together through Vocations for Social Change, a national organization which publishes a monthly newsletter, *Work Force*, cataloging existing jobs for those who seek socially meaningful work. In Boston, New York, Manhattan (Kansas), and elsewhere, local VSC organizations produce "People's Yellow Pages"—in effect, job exchanges through which those who want work done and those who want personally or socially meaningful work communicate.[53]

Eventually the integration of learning and work will require that students and working people come to know one another and to support each other. The functional resources of students, free time and fresh energy, can become very useful to working people. Similarly, the functional resources of working people, stable income and rich experience, can become very useful to students. Students can teach and learn at the same time.

Recently, young working people have begun to demand changes in the nature of work, forcing new consideration of issues such as boredom, lack of individual responsibility, pacing, etc. These young workers in auto plants and other factories can, with the help of students, be drawn to learning as an important, continuing component of their lives and work. Conversely, students shut off in the multiversities emerge from the educational cocoon innocent not merely of practical work skills, but of the ordinary realities of the world of work. Students can learn much from the young workers—who tend, generally, to take on responsibilities for their own lives earlier.

The goal of the Work Support Group thus is an in-depth sharing between students and working people in which the traditional roles of the isolated learner and the isolated worker begin to break down.

Students should be encouraged to participate in action learning —especially through holding down actual jobs in the off-campus community. Work Support Groups in which the problems of work and learning are discussed can make the experience of work itself far more valuable, and can help the members of these groups shape future trajectories that combine continued personal development with socially valuable output. In this way, Work Support Groups can feed important considerations about the future into the present education of their members.

Intentional Work Experiments

We also need experiments with new forms of work. Today, dissatisfaction with the standard job and work setting has led many to search out new ways of making a living or surviving, while still doing work that they find rewarding. For example, opening a storefront "drop-in" center represents a form of useful entrepreneurship in which the organizers help a population of young people, addicts, women, or older citizens define their needs.

PHILIP WERDELL

Serving these needs, whatever they may be, then becomes the "work." This can and often does lead to drug counseling, day-care centers, medical or legal-aid services.[54]

Another form of intentional work is organization around major national or global issues, so that a group springs up around Ralph Nader, providing real and eminently useful work for young lawyers and researchers,[55] or around such organizations as Environmental Action, which draws on the energies of students, scientists, and others.[56]

Yet another form of work is to be found in the free schools in which young people, disillusioned by the established educational system, organize their own schools and then work as teachers, administrators, fund raisers, curriculum designers, etc.[57]

Today a number of small new businesses, spun off from large corporations or from government programs like VISTA and the Peace Corps, are also, in fact, intentional work experiments carried on within the framework of the traditional economic system. Thus in Washington a group of former Office of Economic Opportunity employees have started their own consulting group offering services to various poverty groups and agencies. Another variant is to be found in the numerous health-food stores whose operators see themselves as educators as well as businessmen.

The nature of work is also affected by the development in many professional organizations—and now, indeed, in commercial organizations like educational publishers—of "caucuses" or groups whose members come together on their own to help each other deal with the day-to-day problems they face in their work, and at the same time, to reexamine the values and goals of the association or corporation. They are, in effect, saying that the work does not define the person; the person has a right to define the work.

At present, both in the traditional economy and outside it, the intentional work experiments are largely participated in by white upper-middle-class males—precisely those people who, in American society, would have the highest probability of achieving success by traditional standards. We need to open these experiments to many more lower- and lower-middle-class young people as well.

The multiversity, if it is interested in the future development of its students, must support those engaged in Intentional Work Experiments. One possibility is through increasing the legitimacy rewards—including perhaps course credits—for people who volunteer to live at lower than ordinary standards of living to pursue self-chosen paths of personal and vocational growth. Another is to create income-sharing clusters, groups of students trading off time spent in traditional jobs and time spent pursuing more holistic concepts of work.

Such approaches parallel recent experiments in the United States and other countries having to do with "job enlargement" or "job enrichment"—attempts to restructure work so as to involve more of the individual's capacities and to provide a greater sense of responsibility and accomplishment. An additional path toward support of Intentional Work Experiments may lie through a broadened concept of the guaranteed annual wage that would include not merely those unable to find traditional employment, but also those who chose, on their own, to risk the creation of work integrating their own personal needs with what might be called a "planetary perspective."

Experiments Toward Humanizing Technology

Special emphasis upon technology is needed in learning to work for the future not just because the accelerating rates of change in technology are producing social and educational discontinuities, but also because there is a pervasive need to make technology work more directly for the individual. For example, the computer is invading education, and almost universally it is used to store information (memory banks full of students' scores), centralize (multiple IBM cards to be filled out at each registration), and standardize (already through cruder uses of teaching machines) the individual student.

The computer *can* be used to decentralize and individualize, instead. Yet it was introduced into education in this way because this is the way it was first introduced in business—and used by and on workers. While the individual may receive certain secondary benefits from these uses of the computer, indeed benefits which might be unobtainable in any other way, the social environment this creates leaves masses of individuals with feelings of powerlessness and provokes blind hostility toward technology itself.

The standardization, centralization and control of other major technologies by small managerial elites (television, modular architecture,[58] nuclear and solar energy[59] are four obvious examples) have similar effects. Since the use of technology in this way has been a central cause both of accelerating rates of change and of increasing alienation, it is imperative that we decentralize its uses and give the individual more control over these uses as it becomes an increasingly integral part of every learning and working process.

For some, this might begin with experiments in deconditioning—exploring ways of life that are less dependent on modern technology than our own, and thereby providing a better perspective from which to rethink the ways in which technology can best be made a tool for human uses rather than vice versa. For others, this might begin with attempts to build democratic controls on technology—creating uses which support pluralism, fantasizing new forms based on effective citizen feedback. Still others might begin by trying to free up the technological knowledge that remains inaccessible to the majority of people because of secrecy imposed by the military and/or private corporations.

Here are just a few work-related technological questions that need to be explored for the future: How much technology is enough? What technological products and services are really necessary to one's life? What is it like to live on a fair share of the world's resources? To fast? To live with only a couple of changes of clothes? To use only the average amount of electricity available to all the people in the world?

Educationally useful experiments aimed at making technology more susceptible to democratic control might include building from the crude beginnings of computer match-dating to find more sophisticated ways in which questionnaires and automated feedback might help people to find other people they could learn from or work with; using audio-visual tape recorders, as was successfully done by the Canadian National Film Board, to help people in common or conflicting circumstances get to know each other to organize themselves and work out their problems; constructing living, learning and working space with the new lightweight, inexpensive and modular architectural technologies like the dome, space frame, and foam; trying to use solar energy or other alternative sources of energy for a part of one's daily energy requirements.

Declassifying or opening access to the incredible amounts of technological know-how hoarded by the military-industrial complex might begin with in-depth fantasies about how advances in weaponry, the space program and the organization of corporate conglomerates might be applied to the survival problems of a majority of people in the world. It might include challenging outmoded copyright laws (which stand in the way of everyone having all material in print and on film in supermicrofilmed libraries with computer-retrieval systems); outmoded building codes (which are holding back the construction of ecologically sound and *really* low-cost housing); outmoded professional standards and licensing procedures (which discourage the training of paraprofessionals and drive up the price of "professional" services); outmoded security regulations (which are used to build a powerful and semiautonomous empire within the military as much as to maintain an effective system of defense); and patents (which are increasingly bought by large corporations to control and keep products off the market). And, of course, there are more direct approaches, which because of their present illegality could only be regarded as acts of civil disobedience, to challenge laws that keep information critical to world survival out of public domain. Campaigns of this kind could not only help focus attention on the dangerous long-term consequences of these policies, but, by so doing, introduce a serious futural component into the education process.

Future Assemblies

The idea of a "future assembly" derives from conferences created by groups as diverse as the U.S. Student Press Association, the University for Man in Manhattan, Kansas, and the state government of Hawaii, each of which has taken explicit steps to open up the subject of alternative futures.

The Hawaii 2000 conference, for example, was an experiment in "anticipatory democracy" in which hundreds of citizens, ranging in background from truck drivers and housewives to students, professors and specialists in various fields, came together under sponsorship of the governor of the state to consider such questions as the appropriate urban/rural balance for the state in the next thirty years, or the desired mix of tourism and other industries, or the future of race relations in the islands. The Hawaii 2000 conference, reported on by an enthusiastic press, aroused so much constructive energy that is is now being carried out on county and township levels in Hawaii. Other states, including Washington and Iowa, are conducting or contemplating similar exercises.

At a minimum, these events expose participants to new thought about possible, probable and preferable futures. At their best, they are action-learning experiences in which all those involved are confronted with opportunities to focus their imaginations, social skills and decision-making abilities on the future. Multimedia presentations and participatory celebrations are used to catalyze imaginations. Small group sessions and learning games provide opportunities for people to explore in depth some of the implications of new ideas encountered. People actively involved in creating alternative life-styles and institutions are encouraged to use the conference as a theater for creating microenvironments—dramatizations of their own preferable futures—and to offer participants ways of working with them after the conference.

The alternative-futures conference can be seen as a transitional form, a way of using the innovations of the educational-reform movement to revitalize existing organizations and institutions through experiential contact with the future. The idea of future assemblies attempts to extend this experience one step further by introducing fundamental questions about work: What should people be working with, or relating to, in the process of defining work? What needs of these people and of our own should we focus upon in the future? Should not future assemblies of media groups, for example, include participants from groups considered newsworthy, and, even more important, include representatives of various readership or viewing audiences? Should not future assemblies of students include a voice from each of a wide variety of workers? Should not future assemblies of state organizations involve those in the citizenry who pay for and are served by their programs?

The creation of future assemblies might well be thought of as a two-step process: first, the holding of alternative futures conferences *within* the formal structures of existing institutions such as universities or governments; and second, the calling of voluntary ad hoc gatherings of people from diverse backgrounds who may or may not be attached to existing institutions, but who share the desire to learn how to work together for the future.

In the first stage, such future assemblies could be held within the framework of the multiversity itself, giving students, faculty, administration, nonprofessional employees and others an opportunity to explore alternative futures for the university itself, or for the various schools or departments within it. What are the appropriate goals of the institution? What should they be? Such assemblies, in which alternative futures might be displayed and their consequences examined, could lead to clearer understanding of where the university should be going, and what it should be doing today. At the same time it can help students clarify their own personal goals and define their own future-focused role-images.

The second stage, in which such assemblies are held across institutional lines, could help those working within institutions to see more clearly how the future of their institutions relates to the future of the larger communities, local and global, of which they are necessarily a part. Out of such meetings can come not merely a clearer set of individual and institutional goals but close personal relationships built around small groups interested in pursuing similar futures.[60]

These are a few of the ways in which the multiversity might begin to build on the limited successes of the education-reform movement as it reorients itself toward the future. The introduction of futurism, therefore, must be seen not merely as a new curricular category, but as a new dimension of the essentially political process of redefining education itself. The imaginative introduction of the future into the life of the multiversity, combined with an emphasis on action curricula and work opportunities, can save the institution of the multiversity from lapsing into scholasticism and meaninglessness at a moment when the society as a whole is moving beyond industrialism toward a new and dramatically different form of society.

Notes

CHAPTER ONE / TOFFLER

1. POLAK, Fred, *The Image of the Future* (Jossey-Bass Publishers, San Francisco, 1973), offers a discussion of the role of the image of the future in past societies. This is a worthwhile abridgment of his two-volume work published in the United States by Oceana.
2. GORDON, Theodore J., "The Current Methods of Futures Research," in TOFFLER, Alvin (ed.), *The Futurists* (Random House, New York, 1972), presents a simplified summary of various forecasting methods now in use. A growing technical literature is available. See also issues of the journal *Futures*.
3. Results of this "experiment" have not been published elsewhere.
4. The University Without Walls is a program of the Union for Experimenting Colleges and Universities, a consortium of twenty-five United States educational institutions. It is headquartered at Antioch College, Yellow Springs, Ohio. It is funded by grants from the U.S. Office of Education and the Ford Foundation. UNESCO has contributed funds to begin plans for UWW programs outside the United States.
5. *U.S. Statistical Abstract*, 1972 edition, table 156, p. 106.
6. BREMER, Arthur, "An Assassin's Diary," *Harper's* (January 1973), by the man who shot George Wallace, offers extraordinary evidence of the power of this psychological pressure to "make a mark."

CHAPTER TWO / SINGER

1. KLUCKHOHN, Florence R., "Dominant and Variant Value Orientations," in KLUCKHOHN, Clyde, and MURRAY, Henry A. (eds.), *Personality in Nature, Society and Culture*, 2nd ed. (Knopf, New York, 1964), p. 348.

2. FINCH, Robert, "The Question of Relevancy," *The School and the Democratic Environment* (Danforth-Ford Foundations, Columbia University Press, New York, 1970), p. 21.

3. WHITROW, G. J., *The Natural Philosophy of Time* (Harper Torchbooks, New York, 1961), p. 114.

4. ERIKSON, Erik H., *Identity, Youth and Crisis* (W. W. Norton, New York, 1968), p. 116.

5. MILLER, Walter B., "Lower Class Culture as a Generating Milieu of Gang Delinquency," in WOLFGANG, Marvin E., SAVITZ, L., and JOHNSTON, N., *The Sociology of Crime and Delinquency* (John Wiley, New York, 1962), p. 271.

6. ERIKSON, *op. cit.*, p. 159.

7. ALLPORT, Gordon, *Becoming* (Yale University Press, New Haven, 1955), p. 36.

8. GORDON, Chad, and GERGEN, Kenneth, *The Self in Social Interaction* (John Wiley, New York, 1968), p. 29.

9. RADIN, Norma, and SONQUIST, Hanne, *The Gale Preschool Program Final Report* (Ypsilanti Public Schools, Michigan, 1968), p. 16.

10. SIMMONS, Roberta G., and ROSENBERG, Morris, "Functions of Children's Perception of the Stratification System," *American Sociological Review*, 36, 2 (1971), p. 237.

11. GREENBERG, Bradley S., and DERVIN, Brenda, *Use of the Mass Media by the Urban Poor* (Praeger, New York, 1970), p. 295.

12. DeFLEUR, Melvin L., and DeFLEUR, Lois B., "The Relative Contribution of Television as a Learning Source for Children's Occupational Knowledge," *American Sociological Review*, 32, 5 (1967), pp. 777–789.

13. LeSHAN, Lawrence L., "Time Orientation and Social Class," *Journal of Abnormal and Social Psychology*, vol. 47, 1952, p. 592.

14. FRANK, Lawrence K., *Society as the Patient* (Rutgers University Press, New Brunswick, N.J., 1948), p. 344.

15. TEAHAN, John E., "Future Time Perspective, Optimism and Academic Achievement," *Journal of Abnormal and Social Psychology*, vol. 57, 1958, pp. 379–380.

16. ROSEN, Bernard C., "The Achievement Syndrome: A Psychocultural Dimension of Social Stratification," *American Sociological Review*, 21, 2 (1956), pp. 203–211.

17. BERNSTEIN, Basil, cited in LIPSET, Seymour M., "Working Class Authoritarianism," STOODLEY, Bartlet H. (ed.), *Society and Self* (Free Press, New York, 1962), p. 527.

18. LEVINE, M., and SPIVACK, George, "Incentive, Time Conception

and Self Control in a Group of Emotionally Disturbed Male Adolescents," *American Psychologist*, vol. 12, 1957, p. 377.

19. BARNDT, Robert J., and JOHNSON, Donald M., "Time Orientation in Delinquents," *Journal of Abnormal and Social Psychology*, vol. 51, 1955, pp. 343–345.
20. SCHNEIDER, Louis, and LYSGAARD, Sverre, "The Deferred Gratification Pattern: A Preliminary Study," *American Sociological Review*, 18, 2 (1953), pp. 142–149, for example.
21. ZYTKOSKEE, Adrian, STRICKLAND, Bonnie R., and WATSON, James, "Delay of Gratification and Internal Versus External Control Among Adolescents of Low Socioeconomic Status" (paper delivered at the Southeastern Psychological Meeting, New Orleans, March 1969).
22. ROSEN, *op. cit.*
23. MOWRER, O. H., and ULLMAN, A. D., "Time as a Determinant in Integrative Learning," *Psychological Review*, vol. 52, 1945, pp. 61–90.
24. GURIN, Gerald, and GURIN, Patricia, "Expectancy Theory in the Study of Poverty," *Journal of Social Issues*, 26, 2 (1970), pp. 83–104.
25. Cited in SLOCUM, Walter L., *Occupational Careers* (Aldine, Chicago, 1966), p. 202.
26. HOLLINGSHEAD, August, *Elmtown's Youth* (Science Editions, New York, 1961), p. 286.
27. LERNER, Daniel, *The Passing of Traditional Society* (Free Press, Glencoe, Ill., 1957), p. 24.
28. ROSENBERG, Morris, *Occupations and Values* (Free Press, Glencoe, Ill., 1957), p. 24.
29. SMITH, William L., "Cleveland's Experiment in Mutual Respect," *The School and the Democratic Environment* (Columbia University Press, New York, 1970), p. 91.

CHAPTER THREE / BART

In addition to those writers whose works have been cited, I would like to thank Neena Schwartz, Barbara Seaman, Anne Seiden and Jack Maidman for their expertise and support in revising this paper, particularly with reference to the place of the biogenetic factors in futurism.

1. MONEY, John, "Determinants of Human Sexual Behavior," in FREEDMAN, A. M., KAPLAN, H. I., and KAPLAN, H. S. (eds.),

Comprehensive Textbook of Psychiatry, 2nd ed. (Williams and Wilkins, Baltimore, n.d.), mimeographed, p. 8. John Money and his colleagues at Johns Hopkins have been studying sex and gender anomalies, that is, hermaphrodites and individuals who, because of some abnormality, appear to be and are, therefore, raised in a sex different from their biological or endocrinological or chromosomal sex. Gender usually refers to role in the sociological sense, so that one can speak of one's sex as being different from one's gender.

2. *Ibid.*
3. WEITZMAN, Lenore J., EIFLER, Deborah, HAKODA, Elizabeth, and ROSS, Catherine, *Sex Role Socialization in Children's Picture Books* (paper presented at the meetings of the American Sociological Association, September, 1971).
4. *Ibid.*
5. *Ibid.*
6. *Ibid.*
7. U'REN, Marjorie B., "The Image of Women in Textbooks," *Women in Sexist Society* (Basic Books, New York, 1971), p. 218.
8. *Ibid.*, p. 221.
9. *Ibid.*, p. 225.
10. TRECKER, Janice Law, "Woman's Place Is in the Curriculum," *Saturday Review* (Oct. 16, 1971), pp. 83–86, cont. pp. 92–94. The entire issue, entitled "Educating Women: No More Sugar and Spice," is excellent.
11. BOWLES, Cheryl, "One Aspect of Female Role Socialization: Literature Given to Students in a High School Health Class" (unpublished paper, 1971, available from The Research Center on Women, Alverno College, Milwaukee, Wisc. 53215).
12. BOWLES, *ibid.*, p. 4, quoting *Growing Up and Liking It* (Personal Products Company, N.J., 1970).
13. BOWLES, *ibid.*, p. 13. The quote is from NEUGARTEN, Bernice, *Becoming Men and Women* (Science Research Associates, Inc., Chicago, 1955), p. 29. Dr. Neugarten is presently chairperson of the Committee on Human Development of the University of Chicago, and a full professor.
14. MACCOBY, Eleanor, "Sex Difference in Intellectual Functioning," *The Development of Sex Differences* (Stanford University Press, Stanford, 1966), p. 40.
15. LEONE, Juan Pascual, personal communication.
16. SILVERMAN, Albert J., lecture at Northwestern Medical School, Nov. 15, 1972, reported that he did not find women more field

dependent than men at the University of Michigan, but found these differences at Washtenaw Community College.

17. CAREY, Gloria L., *Reduction of Sex Differences in Problem Solving by Improvement of Attitude Through Group Discussion*, dissertation, Stanford, 1955, cited in MACCOBY, *op. cit.*, p. 51.

18. MACCOBY, *op. cit.* She notes that "the same environmental input affects the two sexes differently. . . . The brighter girls tend to be the ones who have not been tied closely to their mothers' apron strings, but have been allowed and encouraged to fend for themselves. The brighter boys, on the other hand, have had high maternal warmth and protection in early childhood."

19. HORNER, Matina S., "Femininity and Successful Achievement: A Basic Inconsistency," *Feminine Personality and Conflict* (Brooks/ Cole, Belmont, Calif., 1970), p. 58.

20. MURRAY, Dr. Marian, personal communication, Oct. 31, 1972. The danger of psychosurgery as "The Final Solution to the Woman Problem" (in *The Radical Therapist*, 3, 1 [Sept., 1972], pp. 16–17 [reprinted from *The Second Wave*, 2, 1]) was reported by Barbara Roberts, Ph.D. The largest target group, over 70 per cent who were operated on, were women. Peter Breggin, M.D., was so concerned he inserted information on the return of the lobotomy into *The Congressional Record*. These lobotomies will also be used on homosexuals, children and prisoners.

21. CHESLER, Phyllis, *Women and Madness* (Doubleday, New York, 1972).

22. FIRESTONE, Shulamith, *The Dialectic of Sex: The Case for Feminist Revolution* (Bantam Books, New York, 1971).

23. SCULLY, Diana, and BART, Pauline B., "A Funny Thing Happened on the Way to the Orifice: Women in Gynecology Textbooks," *American Journal of Sociology*, 79, 1 (January 1973); and SEAMAN, Barbara, *Free and Female* (Coward, McCann & Geoghegan, New York, 1972).

24. ROSSI, Alice, "The Beginning of Ideology," *The Humanist* (Fall 1969). I called it "ironic" because sociologists (male) referred to the *end* of ideology in the fifties.

25. ROSSI, Alice, "Family Development in a Changing World," *American Journal of Psychiatry*, 128, 9 (March 1972), pp. 1057–1080.

26. Men and women do view the future differently, as is apparent when the work of a male futurist, Robert T. Francoeur, is compared with the three women discussed above. What are the differences between these male and female images of the future? First, Francoeur wants to maintain, or is interested in the possibility

of maintaining, genealogical lines through artificial insemination; while Firestone wants to abolish such lines and their implied ownership of children, and neither Chesler nor Rossi shares his concern. Second, Francoeur makes no mention of homosexuality, lesbianism or bisexuality, but discusses trans-sexual surgery; Chesler and Firestone dwell at length on the benefits of the former, Rossi mentions it, Firestone discusses breaking incest taboos and taboos on childhood sexuality generally, and speaks of the return and legitimacy of "polymorphous perversity." Francoeur, Chesler and Firestone discuss the possibility and imply the advantages of non-biological motherhood. Firestone speaks of artificial placentas, Chesler of men having babies; Rossi does not believe people will opt for such biogenetic possibilities. All the women are radical. They do not accept the current economic system as a given, and believe that the economic institutions must and will change, bringing about changes in the sex roles. Francoeur believes in the strong influence of heredity on personality and cites the work of eugenicists, including the racists among them, such as Shockley. Chesler, Firestone and Rossi (and Suzanne Langer, whom we will quote later) believe in the primacy of sociocultural factors in determining personality and behavior.

FRANCOEUR, ROBERT T., *Eve's New Rib* (Harcourt Brace Jovanovich, New York, 1972); also *Utopian Motherhood: New Trends in Human Reproduction* (Doubleday, Garden City, New York, 1970).

27. BERNARD, Jessie, "The Paradox of the Happy Marriage," in GORNICK, Vivian, and MORAN, B. K., *Woman in Sexist Society* (Signet, New American Library, New York, 1972), pp. 145–162.
28. MEAD, Margaret, "Future Family," *Trans Action* (Sept. 1971), pp. 50–53.
29. HAUSER, Philip M., *The Future of the Family* (Family Service Association of America, New York, 1969).
30. PIERCY, Marge, *Dance the Eagle to Sleep* (Doubleday, New York, 1970).
31. ROSSI, Alice, "The Beginning of Ideology."
32. GORDON, Linda, *Families* (New England Free Press, Boston, 1970).
33. BART, Pauline B., "Depression in Middle-Aged Women," in GORNICK and MORAN, *op. cit.* For a longer version, see BART, Pauline B., *Portnoy's Mother's Complaint* (forthcoming).
34. MILMAN, Marcia, "Observations on Sex Role Research," *Journal of Marriage and the Family*, 33, 4 (Nov. 1971), pp. 772–776.

35. This suggestion was made by Dr. Joan Roberts of the Center for Educational Policy of the University of Wisconsin, Madison, at a conference on women held at the University of Wisconsin at Oshkosh, April 1972.

36. KELLER, Suzanne, "Looking Ahead in the 1970s," presented at Radcliffe Institution Conference, "Women: Resource for a Changing World," April 1972.

CHAPTER FOUR / POUSSAINT

The author is grateful for the assistance of Carolyn Atkinson Thornell and Marie Lindahl in the preparation of this paper.

1. MEAD, George H., *Mind, Self and Society* (University of Chicago Press, Chicago, 1934), Part III.

2. COOLEY, Charles H., *Human Nature and the Social Order* (Free Press, Glencoe, Ill., 1956).

3. *Sociological Quarterly* (entire issue), 7, 3 (1966).

4. MEAD, *op. cit.*

5. COOLEY, *op. cit.*, p. 184.

6. SINGER, Benjamin, "The Future-Focused Role-Image," supra, pp. 19–32.

7. CLARK, Kenneth, *Dark Ghetto: Dilemmas of Social Power* (Harper & Row, New York, 1965); KARDINER, Abraham, and OVESEY, Lionel, *The Mark of Oppression: Explorations in the Personality of the American Negro* (Norton, New York, 1951); PETTIGREW, Thomas F., *A Profile of the Negro American* (Van Nostrand, Princeton, N.J., 1964).

8. ERIKSON, Erik H., "The Concept of Identity in Race Relations: Notes and Queries," *Daedalus* 95 (Winter 1966), pp. 145–171.

9. DEUTSCH, Martin, "Minority Groups and Class Status as Related to Social and Personality Factors in Scholastic Achievement," in DEUTSCH, Martin, et al., *The Disadvantaged Child* (Basic Books, New York, 1967), p. 106.

10. *Ibid.*, p. 107.

11. COOMBS, R. H., and DAVIES, V., "Self-Conception and the Relationship between High School and College Scholastic Achievement," *Sociology and Social Research,* 50 (July 1966), pp. 468–469.

12. DAVIDSON, Helen H., and GREENBERG, Judith W., *Traits of School Achievers from a Deprived Background* (City College of the City University of New York, May 1967), pp. 133–134.

13. KATZ, Irwin, "Academic Motivation and Equal Educational Opportunity," *Harvard Educational Review*, 38 (Winter 1968), pp. 57–65.
14. *Ibid.*, pp. 61–62.
15. CLARK, Kenneth B., and CLARK, Mamie P., "Racial Identification and Preference in Negro Children," in MACCOBY, Eleanor E., et al. (eds.), *Readings in Social Psychology* (Holt, Rinehart & Winston, New York, 1958), pp. 602–611.
16. GOODMAN, Mary Ellen, *Race Awareness in Young Children* (Wellesley, Cambridge, Mass., 1965); COLES, Robert, *Children of Crisis* (Little, Brown, Boston, 1966); GREENWALD, H. J., and OPPENHEIM, D. B., "Reported Magnitude of Self-Misidentification among Negro Children—Artifact?" *Journal of Personality and Social Psychology*, 8 (1968), pp. 49–52; PORTER, Judith R., *Black Child, White Child: The Development of Racial Attitudes* (Harvard University Press, Cambridge, 1971).
17. McCARTHY, John D., and YANCEY, William L., "Uncle Tom and Mr. Charles: Metaphysical Pathos in the Study of Racism and Personal Disorganization," *American Journal of Sociology*, vol. 76, no. 4 (1971), pp. 648–672.
18. *Ibid.*, p. 26.
19. GREENWALD and OPPENHEIM, *op. cit.*, pp. 49–52.
20. COLES, Robert, *Children of Crisis* (Little, Brown, Boston, 1966).
21. COLEMAN, James S., et al., *Equality of Education Opportunity* (U.S. Office of Education, Govt. Printing Office, Washington, D.C., 1966).
22. *Ibid.*, p. 3201.
23. BAUGHMAN, E. Early, and DAHLSTROM, W. Grant, *Negro and White Children* (Academic Press, New York, 1968).
24. *Ibid.*, p. 462.
25. COLEMAN, *op. cit.*, pp. 278–280.
26. KATZ, *op. cit.*, p. 64.
27. *Ibid.*, pp. 63–65.
28. GORDON, Joan, *The Poor of Harlem: Social Functioning in the Underclass*, Report to the Welfare Administration, Washington, D.C., July 1965.
29. COLEMAN, *op. cit.*, p. 281; KATZ, *op. cit.*, p. 63; GORDON, *op. cit.*, pp. 155, 160–161.
30. AUSUBEL, David P., and AUSUBEL, Pearl, "Ego Development Among Segregated Negro Children," in PASSOW, A. Harry (ed.), *Education in Depressed Areas* (Teachers College Press, New York, 1963), p. 135.

31. GORDON, *op. cit.*, pp. 115, 161.
32. KATZ, *op. cit.*, p. 63.
33. DAVIDSON and GREENBERG, *op. cit.*, p. 58.
34. COLEMAN, *op. cit.*, p. 319.
35. *Ibid.*, p. 289.
36. *Ibid.*, pp. 323–324.
37. DAVIDSON and GREENBERG, *op. cit.*, p. 54.
38. DEUTSCH, *op. cit.*, p. 108.
39. POUSSAINT, Alvin, "A Negro Psychiatrist Explains the Negro Psyche," *New York Times Magazine* (August 20, 1967), pp. 58–80.
40. DAVIDSON and GREENBERG, *op. cit.*, p. 61.
41. KATZ, *op. cit.*, p. 57.
42. *Ibid.*
43. GORDON, Edmund W., and WILKERSON, Doxey A., *Compensatory Education for the Disadvantaged* (College Entrance Examination Board, New York, 1966), p. 18.
44. GORDON and WILKERSON, *op. cit.*, p. 18.
45. DEUTSCH, *op. cit.*, p. 102.
46. DOUVAN, Elizabeth, "Social Status and Success Striving," cited in RIESSMAN, Frank, *The Culturally Deprived Child* (Harper & Row, New York, 1962), p. 53.
47. MERTON, Robert K., *Social Theory and Social Structure* (Free Press, Glencoe, Ill., 1957), ch. 4.
48. GORDON, *op. cit.*, p. 164.
49. CLARK, Kenneth B., *Dark Ghetto*, pp. 139–148.

CHAPTER FIVE / BELL

The author wishes to thank James W. Fesler, Bettina J. Huber, Arvin W. Murch, Bruce M. Russett, R. Stephen Warner, and Francine Blau Weisskoff for their comments on an early draft of this chapter.

1. CLARKE, Arthur C., *Profiles of the Future* (Harper & Row, New York, 1958); JUNGK, Robert, and GALTUNG, Johan (eds.), *Mankind 2000* (Allen & Unwin, London, 1969); and KAHN, Herman, and WIENER, Anthony J., et al., *The Year 2000* (Macmillan, New York, 1967), for lists of "coming events."
2. MANUEL, Frank E., *The Prophets of Paris* (Harvard University Press, Cambridge, 1962), p. 6.
3. BARNES, Harry Elmer (ed.), *An Introduction to the History of Sociology* (University of Chicago Press, Chicago, 1948), p. 72.

4. BRUMBAUGH, Robert S., "Applied Metaphysics: Truth and Passing Time," *Review of Metaphysics*, 19 (June 1966), pp. 649, 651.

5. STINCHCOMBE, Arthur L., *Rebellion in a High School* (Quadrangle Books, Chicago, 1964).

6. HUBER, Bettina J., and BELL, Wendell, "Sociology and the Emergent Study of the Future," *American Sociologist*, 6 (November 1971), pp. 287–295.

7. POLAK, Frederik L., *The Image of the Future*, vol. 1 (Oceana, New York, 1961), p. 56.

8. CLARKE, *op. cit.*, p. 11.

9. American Anthropological Association, Cultural Futurology Symposium, Pre-Conference Volume, 1970, mimeographed. The author is indebted here and elsewhere to this excellent collection of papers and has drawn especially on chapters by Elise Boulding, Richard D. Jones, and Magoroh Maruyama.

10. TOFFLER, Alvin, *Future Shock* (Random House, New York, 1970).

11. EULAU, Heinz, "H. D. Lasswell's Developmental Analysis," *Western Political Quarterly*, 11 (June 1958), pp. 229–242.

12. SWEEZY, Paul M., "Toward a Critique of Economics," *Review of Radical Political Economics*, 2 (Spring 1970), pp. 1–8.

13. LASSWELL, Harold D., *The Future of Political Science* (Atherton, Prentice-Hall, New York, 1963), pp. 3–4.

14. RUSSETT, Bruce M., *Trends in World Politics* (Macmillan, New York, 1963).

15. EULAU, *op. cit.*, for an excellent summary of developmental analysis.

16. BELL, Wendell, and OXAAL, Ivar, *Decisions of Nationhood* (Social Science Foundation, University of Denver, 1964); and BELL, *Jamaican Leaders* (University of California Press, Berkeley, 1964), and (ed.), *The Democratic Revolution in the West Indies* (Schenkman, Cambridge, Mass., 1967).

17. MOSKOS, Charles C., Jr., and BELL, Wendell, "Emerging Nations and Ideologies of American Social Scientists," *American Sociologist*, 2 (May 1967), pp. 67–72, for a discussion of ideologies that American social scientists smuggle into their studies of political and social change in emerging nations.

18. MORGENTHAU, Hans J., "The Purpose of Political Science," in CHARLESWORTH, James C. (ed.), *A Design for Political Science* (American Academy of Political and Social Science, Philadelphia, 1966), p. 71.

19. *Ibid.*, p. 72.

20. ISRAELI, Nathan, "Some Aspects of the Social Psychology of Futurism," *Journal of Abnormal and Social Psychology*, 25 (July 1930), pp. 121–132.
21. McGREGOR, Douglas, "The Major Determinants of the Prediction of Social Events," *Journal of Abnormal and Social Psychology*, 33 (April 1938), pp. 179–204.
22. TOCH, Hans H., "The Perception of Future Events: Case Studies in Social Prediction," *Public Opinion Quarterly*, 2 (Spring 1958), pp. 57–66.
23. CANTRIL, Hadley, *The Pattern of Human Concerns* (Rutgers University Press, New Brunswick, N.J., 1965).
24. *Ibid.*
25. BART, Pauline B., "The Myth of a Value-Free Psychotherapy," in BELL, Wendell, and MAU, James A. (eds.), *The Sociology of the Future* (Russell Sage Foundation, New York, 1971), p. 113.
26. SKINNER, B. F., *Walden Two* (Macmillan, New York, 1962).
27. BART, *op. cit.*, p. 142.
28. SIMON, Herbert A., *The Sciences of the Artificial* (M.I.T. Press, Cambridge, 1969), has made important progress in this direction and has proposed a science of design.
29. SCHULTZ, Duane P., *A History of Modern Psychology* (Academic Press, New York, 1969), p. 325.
30. HYMAN, Herbert H., and WRIGHT, Charles R., "Evaluating Social Action Programs," in LAZARSFELD, Paul F., SEWELL, William H., and WILENSKY, Harold L. (eds.), *The Uses of Sociology* (Basic Books, New York, 1967), pp. 741–782.
31. LUCHTERHAND, Elmer, "Research and Dilemmas in Developing Social Programs," in LAZARSFELD, et al., *ibid.*, p. 507.
32. PARSONS, Talcott, *The Social System* (Free Press, Glencoe, Ill., 1951), for example.
33. DAHRENDORF, Ralf, "European Sociology and the American Self-Image," *Archives Européenes de Sociologie*, vol. II (1961), pp. 324–366.
34. REID, Sue Titus, and BATES, Alan P., "Undergraduate Sociology Programs in Accredited Colleges and Universities," *American Sociologist*, 6 (May 1971), pp. 165–175. It is only fair to add that 60.1 per cent offered courses in social welfare and reform. But one suspects that these are largely service or cross-listed courses for social-welfare training programs.
35. GOULDNER, Alvin W., *The Coming Crisis of Western Sociology* (Basic Books, New York, 1970), p. 332.

36. FRIEDRICHS, Robert W., *A Sociology of Sociology* (Free Press, New York, 1970).

37. BELL and MAU, *op. cit.*

38. POLAK, *op. cit.*, pp. 36–37.

39. LASSWELL, *op. cit.*, p. 157.

40. MOORE, Wilbert E., "The Utility of Utopias," *American Sociological Review*, 31 (December 1966), pp. 765–772.

41. CANTRIL, *op. cit.*, pp. 145–146.

CHAPTER SIX / MCDANIELD

1. Creativity Session held at Synectics, Inc., Cambridge, Massachusetts, October 16–20, 1972.

2. TOFFLER, Alvin, *Future Shock* (Random House, New York, 1970), p. 234.

3. *Ibid.*, p. 353.

4. COSER, Lewis A., *The Functions of Social Conflict* (Free Press of Glencoe, Inc., New York, 1955), from the preface.

5. HOMANS, George C., *The Nature of Social Science* (Harcourt, Brace, and World, Inc., New York, 1967), pp. 8, 13.

6. POSTMAN, Neil, and WEINGARTNER, Charles, *Teaching as a Subversive Activity* (Delacorte Press, New York, 1969).

7. MAYER, Martin, *The Social Studies in American Schools* (Harper & Row Publishers, Inc., New York, 1964), pp. 12–13.

8. BOULDING, Kenneth E., in MORRISSETT, Irving, and STEVENS, W. William, Jr. (eds.), *Social Science in the Schools: A Search for a Rationale* (Holt, Rinehart, and Winston, Inc., New York, 1971), p. 151.

9. HOMANS, *op. cit.*, p. 3.

10. BEER, Stafford, *Decision and Control: The Meaning of Operational Research and Management Cybernetics* (John Wiley and Sons, Inc., New York, 1966), p. 242.

11. KROEBER, Alfred L., and KLUCKHOHN, Clyde, *Culture: A Critical Review of Concepts and Definitions* (Random House, New York; originally published in 1952 as vol. XLVII, no. 1, of the Papers of the Peabody Museum of American Archaeology and Ethnology, Harvard University), p. 357.

12. BOULDING, Kenneth E., *Economics as a Science* (McGraw-Hill Book Company, New York, 1970), pp. 11–17.

13. KROEBER and KLUCKHOHN, *op. cit.*, pp. 335–336.

14. *Ibid.*, p. 374.

15. CENTER FOR ADAPTIVE LEARNING, Paper #3, October 26, 1971.

The C.A.L. Project is still in the process of developing student materials, and substantive changes may be made from the discussion in this paper. The definitions given here of Information-Idea Shifts and Cultural Diffusion are C.A.L. modifications of those shown in the working paper.

16. CLARKE, Arthur C., *Profiles of the Future* (Harper & Row Publishers, Inc., New York, 1963), p. 14.

17. NADER, Ralph, and ROSS, Donald, *Action for a Change: A Student Manual for Public Interest Organizing* (Grossman Publishing Company, New York, 1971), pp. 3, 7.

CHAPTER EIGHT / EURICH

1. POLAK, Frederik L., *The Image of the Future* (Oceana, New York, 1961), 2 vols.

2. KEPES, Gyorgy, "Toward Civic Art," *Leonardo, International Journal of the Contemporary Artist*, 4, 1 (1971), p. 69.

3. THIELICKE, Helmut, *Time* Magazine (April 19, 1971), pp. 48, 51.

4. SKINNER, B. F., "Beyond Freedom and Dignity," *Psychology Today* (August 1971), p. 37 (article prior to publication in book of same name by Alfred A. Knopf, Inc., New York).

5. CLARKE, Arthur C., *Profiles of the Future* (Harper & Row, New York, 1958), p. 14 [italics mine].

6. EURICH, Nell, *Science in Utopia* (Harvard University Press, Cambridge, 1967). See especially chap. IX, "Utopias in Perspective," pp. 259–274.

7. *Ibid.*, p. 271.

CHAPTER NINE / WREN-LEWIS

1. SNOW, C. P., "The Two Cultures and the Scientific Revolution," in *Public Affairs* (Charles Scribner's, New York, 1971), reprints the original lecture, with the author's later thoughts and replies to some of his critics.

2. PURVER, Marjorie, *The Royal Society: Concept and Creation* (Rutledge & Kegan Paul, London, 1971), is one of the best recent studies of the seventeenth-century pioneers who put Bacon's philosophy into practice.

3. Box, Stephen, and FORD, Julienne, *Sociology*, vol. 1, no. 3. See also the studies of Bernice EIDUSON in *Scientists: Their Psychological World* (Basic Books, New York, 1962).

4. ROSZAK, Theodore, *The Making of a Counter Culture* (Doubleday, New York, 1971).

5. COX, C. B., and DYSON, A. E. (eds.), *The Twentieth Century Mind* (Oxford University Press, Oxford, 1972), vols. 1 and 2, contains my own story which relates these two events in more detail, and in which I have made my own attempt to prove that scientific ideas can be expressed in terms any layman can understand.

6. FRIEDAN, Betty, *The Feminine Mystique* (W. W. Norton, New York, 1963), for studies quoted. The plea of the overcrowded timetable is often, I suspect, an excuse for laziness, akin to that made by housewives who have no other occupation, but find their homes occupy all their time, while their sisters who have jobs outside the home cope with the same amount of work at home and are actually less tired at the end of the day.

7. ROSZAK, Theodore, *Where the Wasteland Ends* (Doubleday, New York, 1972).

8. TOFFLER, Alvin (ed.), *The Futurists* (Random House, New York, 1972), has an essay, "Can We Transform into a Post-Industrial Society?" by leading Indian futurist, M. S. Iyengar, who puts in a plea for "leapfrog." In the same volume, Arthur C. Clarke, in "Hazards of Prophecy," recounts some notable examples of scientists' failure to be sufficiently imaginative about the future of their own subjects.

9. SNOW, C. P., *Science and Government* (Harvard University Press, Cambridge, 1961). The lecture is also reprinted in *Public Affairs*, with the author's afterthoughts.

10. SNOW, C. P., "The Moral Un-neutrality of Science," *Public Affairs*.

11. SCHULTZ, William, *Here Comes Everybody* (Harper & Row, New York, 1971), has one of the best accounts of techniques for bringing out hidden emotions underlying economic, technical, and political discussions. See also FARADAY, Ann, *Dream Power* (Coward, McCann & Geoghegan, New York, 1972), in which the British psychologist-author goes as far as to suggest that dream-analysis meetings can profitably be made a regular part of business decision-making; I have recently seen this done with some success in "think tanks."

CHAPTER ELEVEN / SHANE & SHANE

1. CLARK, Henry B., "Psycho-chemical Control of the Mind," *The Futurist*, 5:160–165 (August 1971).

2. ETZIONI, Amitai, *The Active Society* (The Free Press, New York, 1968).

3. THOMPSON, William Irwin, *At the Edge of History* (Harper Colophon Books, New York, 1971), cf. chapter VI, "The Re-Visioning of History."

4. For more detailed discussion of the FFRI and its educational implications, cf. chapter XV, "Prospects and Prerequisites for the Improvement of Elementary Education: 1973–1985" in GOOD-LAD, John I., and SHANE, Harold G., *The Elementary School in the U.S.* Seventy-second Yearbook, Part I, The National Society for the Study of Education (University of Chicago Press, Chicago, 1973).

5. For a comprehensive 12,000-word treatment of future-oriented education and its emerging goals, cf. SHANE, Harold G. "Looking to the Future: Reassessment of Educational Issues of the 1970's," *Phi Delta Kappan* 54:326–337 (January 1973).

6. As used here "instrumental" skills are those which are useful instruments in the exercise of one's social duties or obligations to contribute to society.

7. "Expressive" skills are cultivated talents that bring personal-creative satisfactions and, as in the case of artists, that sometimes bring pleasure to others.

8. A more detailed review of the direction of curriculum change may be found in SHANE, June Grant, SHANE, Harold G., GIBSON, Robert L., and MUNGER, Paul F., *Guiding Human Development* (Charles A. Jones Publishing Company, Worthington, Ohio, 1971), cf. pp. 137–151.

9. Cf. GALLAGHER, James J., and BRADLEY, Robert H., "Early Identification of Developmental Differences" in GORDON, Ira J. (ed.), *Early Childhood Education.* Seventy-first Yearbook of the National Society for the Study of Education, Part II (University of Chicago Press, Chicago, 1972).

10. The glacial slowness of change is reflected in the fact that Professor Harold O. Rugg wrote in 1923 that the curriculum was clotted with ". . . the rise and fall of kings, and the policies of prime ministers" rather than enriched with useful information.

11. Again, sad to relate, change has been slow. In 1936, Paul Hanna was advocating that children do "socially useful work" in his book, *Youth Serves the Community.*

12. An excellent treatment of the implications of education for better settings for learning is *Educational Change and Architectural Consequences* (Educational Facilities Laboratory, New York,

1968). Another stimulating report from the same source (EFL) dealing with environmental management for youth is *High School: The Process and the Place* (1972).

13. Children also are exposed to massive doses of carnage on TV. An American Academy of Pediatrics speaker says, "By age 14, a child has seen 18,000 human beings killed on television." Cf. "This World of English," *English Journal* (November 1972), p. 1248.

14. Thoughtful approaches to improved learning are presented succinctly in the twenty-five-page Occasional Paper, *Toward a More Relevant Curriculum*, sponsored by the Danforth Foundation, Institute for Development of Educational Activities (IDEA), and the National Association of Secondary School Principals (1972).

15. Many attempts nonetheless have been made to group young learners. One of the writers identified over thirty forms of grouping for instruction back in 1960. Well over forty exist today. Cf. SHANE, Harold G., "Grouping in the Elementary School," *Phi Delta Kappan*, 41:313–319 (April 1960).

16. A measure of the complexity of the task, even in early childhood, was well presented last year by David R. FENDRICK. See his commentary on "The Issues," pp. 8–9 in "What's Happening to Early Childhood Development?" *Notes on the Future of Education*, 3:7–9 (Summer 1972). (A publication of the Educational Policy Research Center at Syracuse, 1206 Harrison Street, Syracuse, New York, 13210.)

CHAPTER TWELVE / GRIFFITH

1. POSTMAN, Neil, and WEINGARTNER, Charles, *Teaching as a Subversive Activity* (Dial Press, New York, 1969).

2. TOFFLER, Alvin, "The Future as a Way of Life," *Horizon*, 7 (Summer 1965), pp. 108–115.

3. ———, "The World of 1984," *Playboy* (July, August, 1963), panel.

4. CLARKE, Arthur C., *Profiles of the Future* (Harper & Row, New York, 1958).

5. BELLAMY, Edward, *Looking Backward* (Harvard University Press, Cambridge, 1967).

6. TOFFLER, "The World of 1984."

7. TOFFLER, Alvin, "Can We Cope with Tomorrow?" *Redbook* (January 1966).

8. CLARKE, *op. cit.*
9. *The Futurist*, World Future Society, P.O. Box 30369, Bethesda Branch, Washington, D.C. 20014. $10.00 per year.
10. HUXLEY, Thomas H., "The Method of Scientific Investigation," in RAPPORT, Samuel, and WRIGHT, Helen (eds.), *Science: Method and Meaning* (Washington Square Press, New York, 1964).
11. GEORGE, Peter, *Dr. Strangelove* (Bantam Books, New York, 1964).
12. CLARK, Grenville, and SOHN, Louis, *Introduction to World Peace Through World Law* (World Law Fund, 11 West 42nd Street, New York, N.Y. 10036).
13. BRADBURY, Ray, "The Other Foot," *The Illustrated Man* (Bantam Books, New York, 1952).
14. WHEELER, Harvey, *South Africa's Racial Troubles*, Center for the Study of Democratic Institutions, Santa Barbara, Calif. 93108 (tape).
15. ———, "Uses and Abuses of the New Leisure," *Playboy* (March 1965).
16. BELLAMY, *op. cit.*
17. PIEL, Gerald, *Caught on the Horn of Plenty* (Center for the Study of Democratic Institutions, Santa Barbara, Calif. 93108).
18. ASBELL, Bernard, *The New Improved American* (McGraw-Hill, New York, 1965).
19. HALL, Edward T., *The Silent Language* (Doubleday, New York, 1959).
20. ORWELL, George, *1984* (New American Library, New York, 1949).
21. SCHNEIDER, John G., *The Golden Kazoo* (Signet, New York, 1964).
22. BURDICK, Eugene, *The 480* (McGraw-Hill, New York, 1964).
23. BURDICK, Eugene, and LEDERER, William J., *The Ugly American* (Fawcett, New York, 1970).
24. MEAD, Margaret, *New Lives for Old* (New American Library, New York, 1956).
25. McGINNIS, Joe, *The Selling of the President* (Trident, New York, 1968).
26. HUXLEY, Sir Julian, "Age of Overbreed," *Playboy* (January 1965).
27. JACOBS, Jane, *Death and Life of Great American Cities* (Random House, New York, 1961).
28. ROSENFIELD, Alfred, "The Control of Life," *Life* (October 1, 1965).
29. ČAPEK, Karel, *The Makropoulos Secret* (Branden Press, Boston, 1925).

30. VAN DYKE, Jon, "Guiltmakers, Farewell," *The Center Magazine*, 4, 4 (1971), p. 47.

CHAPTER THIRTEEN / ROJAS

1. LÖWITH, Karl, *Meaning in History* (University of Chicago Press, Chicago, 1949), p. 103.
2. The best available descriptions of the cross-impact forecasting method are contained in two Institute for the Future (IFF) papers:
   ENZER, Selwyn, *Delphi and Cross-Impact Techniques: An Effective Combination for Systematic Futures Analysis* (IFF, Middletown, Conn., 1970), WP-8; also
   ROCHBERG, Richard, GORDON, Theodore J., and HELMER, Olaf (IFF, Middletown, Conn., 1970), R-10.
3. In *Monopoly,* courses of action are severely limited by several factors. Dice determine exactly where a player's token lands, and one has minimal control over the outcome. Dice as a means for movement need not be so fatal, however. Players can be given the choice of rolling one, two or three dice, for example. And someone else besides the "owner" may be able to affect the fate of some "property." Indeed, spaces do not need to be properties at all. In *Futuristics*, a simulation designed by the author, squares represent future events. Player #1 can land on a space and invest money to bring about the development of selective memory-erasing drugs. Player #2 may also land on the same space and may also—because the impact of these drugs on learning technology is positive—decide to invest cash to facilitate the occurrence of the event. Player #1 might reap all of the direct profits, but Player #2 would also obtain rewards. Player #3, however, may find the event distasteful and decide to invest negatively when he lands on the space in question. His or her financial finesse would be the equivalent of stock-market manipulation or behind-the-scenes wire-pulling. Game interaction is maximized, regardless of how this is justified.

   A square might also be programed to serve as a leading indicator of future events. A card, face down, could be positioned on top of a space. The first player to land on the card would be able to examine it without cost ("American Indian rock music fad becomes popular in California") and invest in Columbia records at the first opportunity. The second player to land on the square might need to pay $1,000 to see the card. The third player to reach the space might automatically turn the card over so that the information it contains becomes public domain. Which, incidentally, is an example of an escalation clause in game rules. The value of an event—landing on a square, playing a card, constructing a shopping center, inventing some new technology— may increase or decrease during each round of play. This makes the development of an effective strategy for winning the game future-oriented. The same move, one turn later, is not identical in importance, just as the same event, one year later, does not mean the same thing in real life.

CHAPTER FOURTEEN / LIVINGSTON

1. For discussions on the task of defining science fiction, see
   WOLLHEIM, Donald A., *The Universe Makers: Science Fiction Today* (Harper & Row, New York, 1971), pp. 10–16;
   MERRILL, Judith, "What Do You Mean: Science? Fiction?" in CLARESON, Thomas (ed.), *SF: The Other Side of Realism* (Bowling Green University Popular Press, Bowling Green, Ohio, 1971), pp. 53–90; and
   ALLEN, Dick, "Science, Space, Speculative, Fantasy, Fiction," *Yale Alumni Magazine* (January 1971), pp. 7–11.

2. On reading SF as preparation for the future, see TOFFLER, Alvin, *Future Shock* (Random House, New York, 1970), pp. 364–365.

3. It should be noted that while "anything is possible" is an implicit concept in much of SF, there are also many stories which explore the opposite notion, that events in time are either entirely pre-determined or more or less affected by recurring historical cycles.

4. For an analysis of the characteristics of SF heroes, see KELLEY, R. Gordon, "Ideology in Some Modern Science Fiction Novels," *Journal of Popular Culture* (Fall 1968), pp. 211–227.

5. For a survey of SF predictions related to war and military technology, see CLARKE, I. F., *Voices Prophesying War: 1963–1984* (Oxford University Press, Oxford, 1967). Clarke also writes a column in *Futures* magazine on "The Pattern of Prediction."

6. Particularly relevant Institute for the Future surveys using the Delphi technique include
   GORDON, Theodore J., and AMENT, Robert H., "Forecasts of Some Technological and Scientific Developments and Their Societal Consequences," Report R-6 (1969); and
   de BRIGARD, Raul, and HELMER, Olaf, "Some Potential Societal Developments: 1970–2000," Report R-7 (1970).

7. For general surveys of futuristic fictional societies, see
   ARMYTAGE, W. H. G., *Yesterday's Tomorrows: A Historical Survey of Future Societies* (Toronto University Press, Toronto, 1968);
   LEWIS, Joan, *Utopias as Alternative Futures* (Stanford Research Institute, Menlo Park, Calif., 1970); and
   POLAK, Fred L., *The Image of the Future* (Oceana, New York, 1961), 2 vols.
8. BLOCH, Robert, "Imagination and Modern Social Criticism," in DAVENPORT, Basil (ed.), *The Science Fiction Novel: Imagination and Modern Social Criticism* (Advent, Chicago, 1964), pp. 126–155. Other critiques of contemporary SF include
   AMIS, Kingsley, *New Maps of Hell: A Survey of Science Fiction* (Harcourt, Brace, New York, 1960);
   ATHELING, William, Jr., *The Issue at Hand* and *More Issues at Hand* (Advent, Chicago, 1964 and 1970);
   BAXTER, John, *Science Fiction in the Cinema* (Paperback Library, New York, 1970);
   BRETNOR, Reginald (ed.), *Modern Science Fiction: Its Meaning and Its Future* (Coward-McCann, New York, 1953);
   CLARESON, Thomas, *op. cit.*;
   DAVENPORT, Basil, *op. cit.*;
   KNIGHT, Damon, *In Search of Wonder* (Advent, Chicago, 1967);
   LUNDWALL, Sam J., *Science Fiction: What It's All About* (Ace, New York, 1971);
   MOSKOWITZ, Sam, *Seekers of Tomorrow: Masters of Modern Science Fiction* (Ballantine, New York, 1967);
   PLANK, Robert, *The Emotional Significance of Imaginary Beings: A Study of the Interaction between Psychopathology, Literature, and Reality in the Modern World* (Charles C Thomas, Springfield, Ill., 1968);
   ROSE, Stephen, and ROSE, Lois, *The Shattered Ring: Science Fiction and the Quest for Meaning* (John Knox Press, Richmond, Va., 1970);
   WOLLHEIM, *op. cit.*;
   JONAS, Gerald, "Onward and Upward with the Arts: S.F.," *The New Yorker* (July 29, 1972), pp. 33–52;
   LANDRUM, Larry (ed.), "In-Depth: Science Fiction," *Journal of Popular Culture* (Spring 1972), pp. 839–996;
   ALDISS, Brian, *The Billion Year Spree* (Doubleday, New York, 1973);
   BAILEY, J. O., *Pilgrims Through Space and Time: Trends and*

Patterns in Scientific and Utopian Fiction (Greenwood Press, Westport, Conn., 1972);

PANSHIN, Alexei, and PANSHIN, Corey, *The World Beyond the Hill* (Scribner's, New York, 1973);

KETTERER, David, *New Worlds for Old: The Apocalyptic Imagination, Science Fiction, and American Literature* (Doubleday, New York, 1973; and

GUNN, James, *Alternate Worlds* (Prentice-Hall, Englewood Cliffs, N.J., 1973).

9. For an analysis of H. G. Wells's influence on SF, see
WILLIAMSON, Jack, *H. G. Wells: Critic of Progress* (Mirage Press, Baltimore, 1973).

10. On self-actualizing or "transcendental" utopias, see LEWIS, *op. cit.*, pp. 32–47.

11. On the role of women in SF, see LUNDWALL, *op. cit.*, pp. 143–162.

12. For a more detailed study of SF's international futures, see LIVINGSTON, Dennis, "Science Fiction Models of Future World Order Systems," *International Organization* (Spring 1971), pp. 254–270.

13. On SF and science policy, see NAKABAYASHI, Ray, "Science, Technology, and Public Policy in Science Fiction," paper delivered to the Secondary Universe IV Conference, Toronto, 1971.

14. One stimulating course that uses the SF framework to mingle cognitive and affective education is that developed by Aaron Hillman (P.O. Box 30592, Santa Barbara, Calif. 93105) as "Speculative Fiction: Trips into Inner and Outer Space (A Course in Science Fiction and the Quest for Meaning)."

15. For additional examples of SF games in the context of elementary and junior high schools, see
BURKE, Patricia, "Designing Your Future Body: A Futuristic Project for Elementary School Children";
DRIESSEL, Judi, "Science Fiction for Sixth Graders"; and
GAUGHAN, Jane, "Futuristics As a Subversive Activity," all in *Trend* (Spring 1971), pp. 11–13, 18–19, 22–23, 28. See also
RUSS, Joanna, "Communique from the Front: Teaching and the State of the Art," and
MARSHALL, David F., "That Great Curriculum in the Sky," in *Colloquy* (May 1971), pp. 28–33; and
LIVINGSTON, Dennis, "Science Fiction: Scripts for Games?" *Simulation/Gaming/News* (September 1972), pp. 7–8.

16. I believe the first attempt at this kind of exercise came from

MIT: ARNOLD, John E., "SF on the Drawing Board," *Science* (September 1953), pp. 39–43. The course referred to in the text is described by its teacher in BURGESS, Andrew J., "Teaching Religion Through Science Fiction," *Extrapolation* (May 1972), pp. 112–115.

BIBLIOGRAPHIC ADDENDUM

For teachers and students who plan to use SF in their educational experiences, the following remarks may serve as a general guideline.

A list of SF college courses taught in 1970–1971 has been collected by Jack Williamson, "Science Fiction Comes to College," *Extrapolation* (May 1971), pp. 67–78. Teachers starting new courses should inform Mr. Williamson (Dept. of English, Eastern New Mexico University, Portales, N.M. 88130).

A film series consisting of interviews with SF authors about their work and SF in general is now available from Audio-Visual Center, 6 Bailey Hall, University of Kansas, Lawrence, Kansas 66044. A catalog of SF radio plays on tape is available from Morris Scott Dollens, 4372 Coolidge Avenue, Los Angeles, Calif. 90066.

Classes with funds available may wish to rent an SF author to speak to the class or the school. For a brochure on SF authors so available, write Harvey L. Bilker, Science Fiction Writers Speaking Bureau, 4 Sylvan Bldg., Candlewood, Lakewood, N.J. 08701.

A Science Fiction Research Association has been formed to promote teaching and research in SF; its president is Thomas D. Clareson, Box 3186, College of Wooster, Wooster, Ohio 44691. SFRA holds an annual meeting, called the Secondary Universe Conference, open to those interested in the analysis of SF and fantasy. The Modern Language Association also holds an annual Seminar on Science Fiction as part of its general meeting. The official journal of both SFRA and the MLA seminar is *Extrapolation*, whose editor is Mr. Clareson.

The sources of most of the short stories referred to in the chapter "Science Fiction as an Educational Tool" that have been anthologized may be found in

LIVINGSTON, Dennis, "Science Fiction Taught as Futurology," 14 *Extrapolation*, 152–156 (May 1973);

SIEMON, Frederick, *Science Fiction Story Index: 1950–1968* (American Library Association, Chicago, 1971).

Other indexes include

BLEILER, Everett F., *The Checklist of Fantastic Literature* (Shasta, Chicago, 1948);

DAY, Don, *Index to the Science Fiction Magazines (1926–1950)* (Perri Press, 1952);

STRAUSS, Edwin S., *Index to the Science Fiction Magazines: 1951–1965* (New England Science Fiction Association, Cambridge, Mass., 1966); vol. II, *1966–1970, ibid.* (1971);

PFEIFFER, John R., *Fantasy and Science Fiction: A Critical Guide* (Filter Press, Palmer Lake, Colorado, 1971);

LERNER, Fred, *An Annotated Checklist of Science Fiction Bibliographical Works* (The Editor, 7 Amsterdam Avenue, Teaneck, N.J. 07666, 1969);

BRINEY, Robert E., and WOOD, Edward, *SF Bibliographies: An Annotated Bibliography of Bibliographical Works on Science Fiction and Fantasy Fiction* (Advent, Chicago, 1972);

OWINGS, Mark, *A Guide to Science-Fantasy Reference Works* (Mirage Press, Baltimore, 1973);

HALL, Hal W., *Science Fiction Book Review Index* (The Editor, 3608 Meadow Oaks Lane, Bryan, Texas 77801, annually since 1970); and

CLARKE, I. F., *The Tale of the Future from the Beginning to the Present Day* (The Library Association, London, 1972).

The definitive reference work on critical literature about SF is

CLARESON, Thomas D. (ed.), *Science Fiction Criticism: An Annotated Bibliography* (Kent State University Press, Kent, Ohio, 1972).

Several lists of SF for school use are available:

PANSHIN, Alexei, "Books in the Field: Science Fiction," *Wilson Library Bulletin* (February 1970), pp. 616–620;

———, "A Basic Science Fiction Collection," *Library Journal* (June 15, 1970);

ALM, Richard S. (ed.), *Books for You: A Reading List for Senior High School Students* (Washington Square Press, New York, 1964), pp. 146–152;

SOLOMON, Doris (ed.), *Best Books for Children* (R. R. Bowker, New York, 1970), pp. 71–72, 119–120, 170.

In addition, every year the SF fans in their world convention award the Hugo for best SF stories, which have been collected in two volumes: ASIMOV, Isaac (ed.), *The Hugo Winners* (Doubleday, New York, 1962 and 1971).

The Science Fiction Writers of American similarly award the Nebula; winning short stories are collected annually in *Nebula Award Stories* (Doubleday, New York). The SFWA is also compiling its own list of all-time best SF, published under the general title *The Science*

Fiction Hall of Fame: The Greatest Science Fiction Stories of All Time Chosen by the Science Fiction Writers of America by Doubleday: SILVERBERG, Robert (ed.), Vol. I [short stories and novelettes], 1970; BOVA, Ben (ed.), Vol. IIA [novellas], 1973.

Other collections of each year's best SF include

HARRISON, Harry, and ALDISS, Brian W. (eds.), *Best SF* (Putnam, New York);

CARR, Terry (ed.), *The Best Science Fiction of the Year* (Ballantine, New York);

POHL, Frederik (ed.), *Best Science Fiction For* [year] (Ace Books, New York);

WOLLHEIM, Donald (ed.) with SAHA, Arthur W., *The* [year] *Annual World's Best SF* (DAW Books, New York); and

REY, Lester del (ed.), *Best Science Fiction Stories of the Year* (Dutton, New York).

The leading SF magazines also issue annual collections of their best stories.

Several guidebooks and collections of stories specifically oriented to classroom use of SF are now available:

ALLEN, Dick (ed.), *Science Fiction: The Future* (Harcourt, New York, 1971);

HARRISON, Harry, and PUGNER, Carol (eds.), *Science Fiction Reader* (Scribner's, New York, 1973);

MCGHAN, Barry, and CALKINS, Elizabeth, *Teaching Tomorrow—A Handbook of Science Fiction for Teachers* (Pflaum/Standard, Dayton, Ohio, 1972);

OFSHE, Richard (ed.), *The Sociology of the Possible* (Prentice-Hall, Englewood Cliffs, N.J., 1970);

SANDERS, Thomas E. (ed.), *Speculations: Fantasy/Science Fiction* (Glencoe Press, Beverly Hills, Calif., 1973);

MCNELLY, Willis, and STOVER, Leon (eds.), *Above the Human Landscape: An Anthology of Social Science Fiction* (Goodyear Publishing, Pacific Palisades, Calif., 1972).

There are also available several general SF anthologies that emphasize stories describing alternative social possibilities:

DOZOIS, Gardner (ed.), *A Day in the Life* (Harper & Row, New York, 1972);

ELLISON, Harlan (ed.), *Dangerous Visions* and *Again, Dangerous Visions* (Doubleday, New York, 1967 and 1972);

HARRISON, Harry (ed.), *The Year 2000: An Anthology* (Doubleday, New York, 1970);

STOVER, Leon E., and HARRISON, Harry (eds.), *Apeman, Spaceman:*

Anthropological Science Fiction (Doubleday, New York, 1968, and revised edition, 1973);

MOHS, Mayo (ed.), *Other Worlds, Other Gods: Adventures in Religious Science Fiction* (Doubleday, New York, 1971);

DISCH, Thomas M. (ed.), *The Ruins of Earth: An Anthology of Stories of the Immediate Future* (Putnam, New York, 1971); and

MOSKOWITZ, Sam (ed.), *When Women Rule* (Walker, New York, 1972).

A project to produce microforms of all SF magazines is being planned by Greenwood Press (51 Riverside Avenue, Westport, Conn. 06880) under the direction of Thomas Clareson. In the tentative stage, as I write this, are plans by Indiana University Press to reissue a series of classic SF novels with critical introductions for classroom textbooks, also with Thomas Clareson as general editor, and by Prentice-Hall Spectrum paperbacks to publish a series of SF anthologies on social issues for the classroom, under my own general editorship.

CHAPTER FIFTEEN / KIRSCHENBAUM & SIMON

1. RATHS, Louis E., HARMIN, Merrill, and SIMON, Sidney B., *Values and Teaching* (Charles E. Merrill, Columbus, Ohio, 1966).
2. KIRSCHENBAUM, Howard, SIMON, Sidney B., and NAPIER, Rodney W., *WAD-JA-GET? The Grading Game in American Education* (Hart, New York, 1971).
3. SIMON, Sidney B., HOWE, Leland, and KIRSCHENBAUM, Howard, *Values Clarification: A Handbook of Practical Strategies for Teachers and Students* (Hart, New York, 1972). HARMIN, Merrill, SIMON, Sidney B., and KIRSCHENBAUM, Howard, *Clarifying Values Through Subject Matter* (Winston Press, Minneapolis, Minn., 1973).
4. KIRSCHENBAUM, SIMON, and NAPIER, *op. cit.*
5. KOHL, Herbert, *The Open Classroom* (Vintage Books, New York, 1969).
6. ROGERS, Carl R., *Freedom to Learn* (Charles E. Merrill, Columbus, Ohio, 1969).
7. WEINSTEIN, Gerald, and FANTINI, Mario D., *Making Urban Schools Work* (Holt, Rinehart and Winston, New York, 1968).

CHAPTER SIXTEEN / WERDELL

This essay has evolved over the past several years; hopefully, it will continue to change and grow. Based upon the thought and practice of a very large number of people, only a few of whom are noted here, the writing has been deeply collaborative. In particular, I want to recognize the help of Carol Thorpe, Edward Joseph Shoben, Michael Vozick, Rick Kean, Patricia O'Bryan, Stephen Sunderland, Elizabeth Sunderland, Mark Cheren, and Alvin Toffler. While I worked with each separately, they have, as a group, contributed as much or more than I have in bringing this writing to its present stage. Final responsibility lies with me, but this essay could not have been written without a deep effort of cooperation with each of these people. I feel it important that in the future we move further toward cooperative writing and make shared authorship at least as common as individual.

1. BIDWELL, Percy W., *Undergraduate Education in Foreign Affairs* (Columbia University Press, New York, 1962).
2. JACOB, Philip E., *Changing Values in College: An Exploratory Study of the Impact of College Teaching* (Harper, New York, 1957).
3. SANFORD, Nevitt (ed.), *The American College: A Psychological and Social Interpretation of Higher Learning* (John Wiley, New York, 1962).
4. KERR, Clark, *The Uses of the University* (Harvard University Press, Cambridge, 1963), is the classic description and rationalization of colleges and universities as holding actions among the pressures of interest groups.
5. KATZ, Joseph, "The Classroom: Personality and Interpersonal Relations," in SANFORD, *op. cit.*; and
    WILSON, Logan, *The Academic Man* [sic] (Octagon, New York, 1964), for documentation.
    GOODMAN, Paul, *Community of Scholars* (Random House, New York, 1962), the first comprehensive diagnosis of this situation to have wide circulation.
    ROGERS, Carl, "A Passionate Statement: Graduate Education in Psychology," unpublished manuscript, Western Behavioral Science Institute, La Jolla, Calif., documented and stated simply the implicit assumptions and their disastrous consequences limiting the traditional academic department;
    CHOMSKY, Noam, *The Mandarins* (Vintage, New York, 1968), attempts an overview of the traditional academic standards.
6. ROSSMAN, Michael, *The Wedding in the War* (Doubleday, New York, 1971), for a good description of the Free Speech Movement by a participant conscious of the context from which the event emerged.
7. POTTER, Paul, untitled address, Students for a Democratic Society

march in protest of the Vietnam War, Washington, D.C., April 7, 1965.

8. TAYLOR, Harold, *Students Without Teachers* (McGraw-Hill, New York, 1969), for good descriptions and analysis of the program. The statement of principles and policy of the student Experimental College at San Francisco State, along with its first major course listing, can be found in *Moderator* (Philadelphia), November 1966.

9. An internal description and several past catalogs from one of the most successful free universities can be obtained from University for Man, 615 Fairchild Terrace, Manhattan, Kansas. See also *EdCentric: A Journal of Educational Reform*, 2115 "S" Street, N.W., Washington, D.C. 20008.

10. WERDELL, Philip, *Student Course and Teacher Evaluation* (U.S. National Student Association, Washington, D.C., 1966), for an analysis and practical handbook.

11. SHOBEN, Edward Joseph, *Report of the National Conference on Student Stress in the College Experience* (U.S. National Student Association, Washington, D.C., 1966), has one particularly useful model.

12. TUSSMAN, Joseph, *Experiment at Berkeley* (University of California Press, Berkeley, 1966); and
ROSSMAN, Michael, *On Learning and Social Change* (Random House, New York, 1972), offer two conflicting descriptions and viewpoints by leading participants in one such program.
JEROME, Judson, *Culture Out of Anarchy: The Reconstruction of American Higher Learning* (Scribner, New York, 1968), has a description of several such programs by an outside observer.

13. For information about black studies, write Martin Luther King College, Atlanta, Georgia.
For information about women's studies, write *Female Studies*, Commission on the Status of Women, Modern Language Association, New York, N.Y.

14. ROGERS, Carl, *On Becoming a Person* (John Wiley, New York, 1963); and
PEARLS, Fritz, and GOODMAN, Paul, *Gestalt Therapy* (Real People's Press, San Francisco, 1970), are two classic books on this approach to learning.
RUNKLE, Philip, HARRISON, Roger, and RUNKLE, Margaret (eds.), *The Changing College Classroom* (Jossey Bass, San Francisco, 1969), for a description of specific applications of

some of these principles integrated with traditional subject matter.

15. KANTOR, Rose Beth, *The Utopian Communities* (Harvard University Press, Cambridge, 1971), for a description of current communal experiments and their relationship to intentional communities in American history.

    One source of information on communes is the Alternatives Foundation, P.O. Drawer A, Diamond Heights Station, San Francisco, Calif. 94131.

16. DUNCAN, Karen, *Directory of Action Curriculum* (U.S. National Student Association, Washington, D.C., 1967), is a dated but useful description of a wide variety of such programs.

    More up-to-date information can be found through the National Field Study Conference, coordinated from Hofstra University, Hempstead, N.Y.

17. WERDELL, Philip, "Teaching and Learning: The Basic Function," in LEE, Calvin (ed.), *Whose Goals for Higher Education?* (American Council on Education, Washington, D.C., 1968), has a basic model for such support or reference groups.

    CHEREN, Mark, "Learning Skill Laboratory," unpublished manuscript, School of Education, University of Massachusetts, Amherst, Mass., is a practical guide for those involved in such groups.

18. The clearinghouse for 4-1-4 or "January Programs" is The 4-1-4 Conference, P.O. Box 12560, St. Petersburg, Florida 33733.

19. KEAN, Richard, *Rumors of Change* (U.S. National Student Association, Washington, D.C., 1967), has a short and conclusive indictment of the numerical or letter-grading system.

20. RUDOLPH, Fredrick, *The American Colleges and Universities* (Knopf, New York, 1962), is a good history of American higher education to the 1960s.

21. TOFFLER, Alvin, *Future Shock* (Random House, New York, 1970), elaborates in great detail on the forces at work here.

22. BRUNER, Jerome, *Towards a Theory of Instruction* (Belknap, Cambridge, Mass., 1966);

    ROSSMAN, *On Learning and Social Change*; and

    KEAN, *op. cit.*, have critiques of traditional teaching and learning assumptions and notes toward alternative theories; also

    TAYLOR, Harold, *How to Change Colleges: Notes on Radical Reform* (Holt, Rinehart, New York, 1971).

23. TOFFLER, *op. cit.*

24. ROGERS, "A Passionate Statement."

25. OSBORN, Alex F., *Applied Imagination* (Charles Scribner's, New York, 1957).

26. JAFFE, Dennis, and CLARK, Ted, *Drugs and the Youth Culture: A Pilot Consumer Evaluation*, unpublished manuscript, Office of Special Concerns, Dept. of Health, Education and Welfare, Washington, D.C., 1972.

27. OSBORN, *op. cit.*

28. KEAN, Richard (ed.), *Dialogue on Education* (Bobbs-Merrill, New York, 1967).

29. WERDELL, Philip, *Introduction to the Facilitator* (U.S. National Student Association, Washington, D.C., 1967).

30. BRAND, Stewart (ed.), *Whole Earth Catalog* (Random House, New York, 1971), for a description, or write directly to World Resources Inventory, Southern Illinois University, Carbondale, Ill.

31. GALBRAITH, John Kenneth, *The New Industrial State* (Signet, New York, 1967).

32. Summarized from FULLER, Buckminster, untitled lecture, Alternatives Conference, U.S. Student Press Association, Washington, D.C., 1967.

33. ROSSMAN, *On Learning and Social Change*.

34. DEWEY, John, *Democracy and Education* (Free Press, New York, 1966), develops some criteria for the evaluation of educational experience.

35. BRADFORD, Leland, GIBB, Jack, and BENNE, Kenneth (eds.), *T-Group Theory and Laboratory Method: Innovation in Re-education* (John Wiley, New York, 1964), is an early introduction to encounter groups. Sources of trainers for such groups include campus counseling programs, people with several years' experience in communes, the National Training Laboratories, and Esalen Institute.

36. KAHN, Herman, and WIENER, Anthony J., *The Year 2000* (Macmillan, New York, 1967), is a classic futurist work. There are many more.

37. If local libraries do not keep back issues of the underground press, they can often be obtained in the resource rooms of large alternative institutions, such as free universities, crisis centers, and Vocations for Social Change offices.

38. PARKER, Patsy, and SHEEHAN, William, *Peace Education* (Student Forum for Peace and World Order, 1865 Broadway, New York, N.Y., 1970). [For sources of science fiction, see Dennis Livingston's chapter in this volume.]

39. Alternatives Foundation: see n. 15.

40. FULLER, Buckminster, *Operating Manual for SpaceShip Earth* (Pocket Books, New York, 1969).
41. *Black Panther* newspaper, Oakland, Calif., 1969–1972 (any copy).
42. TOFFLER, *op. cit.*
43. WERDELL, Philip, *Student Participation in University Decision Making*, unpublished manuscript, Urban Coalition, Washington, D.C., 1970.
44. WERDELL, in LEE, *op. cit.*
45. BRAND, *op. cit.*, is a major source for such explorations.
46. ABRAMS, Irwin, "The Student Abroad," in BASKIN, Samuel (ed.), *Higher Education: Some Newer Developments* (McGraw-Hill, New York, 1965).
47. OSBORN, *op. cit.*
48. SCHUTZ, William C., and ALLEN, Vernon L., "The Effects of a T-Group Laboratory on Interpersonal Behavior," *Journal of Applied Behavioral Science* (June-Aug.-Sept., 1966).
49. STICKLER, W. Hugh (ed.), *Experimental Colleges: Their Role in American Higher Education* (Florida State University Press, Tallahassee, 1964).
50. GARDNER, John, *Self-Renewal* (Harper & Row, New York, 1967); BENNIS, Warren, and SLATER, Philip, *Temporary Society* (John Wiley, New York, 1966). See also RASKIN, Marcus, *Being and Doing* (Random House, New York, 1971).
51. Literature and people to talk with about consciousness-raising groups, and women's liberation as a whole, can be found by contacting the women's group or center in most local communities. If a contact is not obvious, check out a nearby large university campus, or write: National Organization for Women, Box 643, Ansonia Station, New York, N.Y. 10023.
52. New Vocations Project, STEINBERG, David, et al. (eds.), *Working Loose* (American Friends Service Committee, Random House, San Francisco, 1971), is an especially helpful book dealing with these subjects.
53. For a copy of *Work Force*, back issues of the *Vocations for Social Change Newsletter*, and addresses of local contacts, write: Vocations for Social Change, Box 13, Canyon, Calif. It would be helpful to make a small contribution appropriate to the service requested.
54. Stopping in to talk with people who have started such organizations locally is the best way to learn. Literature about such efforts, examples of projects around the country, and addresses of infor-

mation clearinghouses in each area can be found in the *Vocations for Social Change Newsletter* (see note 53).

55. A central clearinghouse for the Nader-related work is Public Interest Research Group, P.O. Box 2808, Central Station, Washington, D.C. See also NADER, Ralph, and ROSS, Donald, *Action For a Change: A Student Manual for Public Interest Organizations* (Grossman, New York, 1971).

56. The address of Environmental Action is 1346 Connecticut Avenue, N.W., Room 731, Washington, D.C. 20036.

57. One of the many information sources for the growing free-school movement is *New Schools Exchange Newsletter*, 301 E. Conon Peudo, Santa Barbara, Calif. 93101. See also NEILL, A. S., *Summerhill: A Radical Approach to Child Rearing* (Hart, New York, 1964), and ARONS, Steven, SENTERFITT, Walton, MILMED, Alice, STEINBERG, David, SENTERFITT, Pamela, STONEMAN, Dorothy, "The Great Atlantic and Pacific School Conspiracy," *Doing Your Own School: A Practical Guide to Starting and Operating a Community School* (Beacon Press, Boston, 1972).

58. One example of a new architectural projection is an alternative high school in California whose participants built their own campus. Their experience is usefully recorded in Pacific Domes, *Domebook Two* (Random House, San Francisco, 1971).

59. Many such experiments in new and more appropriate uses of energy are described in *Alternative Sources of Energy*, Route 1, Box 36B, Monong, Wisc. 54859.

60. Those interested in organizing future assemblies may contact me c/o 10 Prospect Place, Brooklyn, N.Y. 11217; I will pass on a list of people either experienced or interested in such efforts as I hear of them.

Appendix
Status Report: Sample Syllabi and Directory of Futures Studies

By Billy Rojas and H. Wentworth Eldredge

The pages below provide those interested in the design of future-oriented curricula with materials, resources, ideas and contacts that may be helpful.

Section One *reports the findings of several informal surveys conducted by us, providing data on the history, number, geographical distribution and nature of futurist courses and activities in educational institutions in North America. The report is partial rather than exhaustive, but it gives some sense of the variety of approaches being used and the ways in which these activities are organized.*

Section Two *presents a sampling of actual course syllabi. It covers fifteen college-level and four precollege courses, as well as three "learning modules" designed for futurist activities lasting one to three weeks. It also includes a description of the rather ambitious program now under way at Fairleigh Dickinson University. These items were chosen (with difficulty) to reflect variety and novelty of approach.*

Those wishing to design new curricula or materials may find, in these pages, syllabi or parts of syllabi that can be modified to suit their needs, or combined with other materials to form new wholes. Whether or not this proves to be the case, the syllabi will almost certainly spark useful ideas.

Section Three *consists of a listing of approximately 200 courses offered at approximately 140 institutions. These are classified so that students and/or faculty may locate courses of interest to them and make direct contact with others in the field.*

Section Four *provides a reading list consisting of the seventy-five books most frequently used in futures courses.*

Section Five *consists of the names and addresses of several organizations or institutions with special interest in the field of educational futuristics.*

Section One: Survey of Educational Futuristics

The *Future Studies Syllabus* was written as a resource for teachers who are interested in utilizing futures research in the classroom. While designed primarily for college educators, a special section on pre-college futuristics is also included to illustrate the kind of activities that have been successfully carried out in public schools in the United States.

C. P. Snow once talked about the "two cultures," the sciences and the arts, and noted the gulf that separates professionals in one from those working in the other. Since then, the "discovery" of the future by both contemporary humanists and scientists has begun to provide one of the few channels of mutually satisfactory communication between the two groups. This is only one of the benefits of the new educational interest in the future. Indeed, futures research, it turns out, is a vehicle for academic change in rather unexpected ways. It has been from its own earliest days.

I

In the early 1960s the future became subject matter in the classroom of Richard Meier at the University of Michigan and at the University of California after his move to Berkeley. Other professors took similar initiatives following the publication of Herman Kahn's *On Thermonuclear War* at the beginning of the decade. Special units of the future of Soviet-American relations or the coming impact of automation were included in a number of courses. However, as closely as can be determined, interest in alternative futures as a focus for scholarship did not take hold at this time. The notion that coherent academic programs could be future-oriented had to wait.

The first university class in futuristics was the brainchild of Alvin Toffler and was offered at the New School for Social Research in Fall 1966. Although the early courses developed elsewhere soon afterward were, as a rule, conceived without direct knowledge of that pioneering class, it turns out that the New School course contained many of the elements still present in introductory future-studies seminars.*

Thus, the New School students who signed up for "Social Change and the Future" discussed general aspects of social and technological change that could be expected to make their lives ten or twenty years hence quite different from their existence in the era of Vietnam. Moreover, ". . . the spread of urbanization, the advances in biological and behavioral sciences, and other fields will," the catalog description said, "have deep impact upon work-leisure, education, family, divorce, intergenerational conflict, bureaucratic organization, the arts, the psychology of affluence, and on our values."

The broad outlines of educational futuristics can be seen at this early date; it is an interdisciplinary activity, the province of generalists in the social sciences. It focuses on broad social problems, rather than specialized bodies of knowledge. In one respect, however, the New School course can be considered atypical as a model. Although students in it played a variation of *Future*, a game based on Delphi forecasting, the course devoted relatively little attention to scientific forecasting methodology—one of the notable omissions in *Future Shock* as well. Today most courses in futuristics include units devoted to techniques for "predicting" alternative futures.

"Social Change and the Future" (which was also taught in the Spring and Fall semesters of 1967) was soon followed by three additional courses at Illinois Wesleyan, at the University of California at Berkeley, and at Santa Clara. Successive surveys conducted by Professor Eldredge and/or me indicate that by 1968 the number had risen by sixteen; an additional thirty-one could be counted in 1969.

* Just as the early wave of pioneers were generally unaware of each other's work, Toffler, at the time, had not yet discovered the essay written two decades earlier by Ossip Flechtheim in which such courses were first proposed.

During these years at least seventeen courses which incorporated units centered around futures concepts could also be counted. By 1970, assuming a rather low attrition rate from the first classroom experiments, about sixty futuristics courses were being offered at American and Canadian universities. The hard count of all futures seminars, discussions, lectures, etc., given through the end of the 1970–1971 school year was 129, although the figure was undoubtedly incomplete.

A reasonable "guesstimate" of courses taught through June 1971 would be 150 to 175. For the 1971–1972 academic year the number increases by approximately 100. Some classes have been discontinued, some teachers have lost interest, some have died, and—in at least two cases—some have been fired. Since 1967 approximately 125 futures courses may have come and gone. Nevertheless, currently, according to the information gathered by Professor Eldredge, there are some 350 to 400 futures courses being taught in North America.

II

Today a small number of colleges retain "resident futurists" on their faculties, although the usual pattern is for an instructor of, say, political science or humanities to teach a single futures course per semester. Because of the difficult academic job market, few new futurists are being recruited for teaching positions, but large numbers are encouraged to add futures research to their professional repertoires. There is some likelihood that a new academic discipline will emerge from the futures "boom" now going on.

The success of best sellers like *Future Shock*—and, to a lesser extent, *At the Edge of History*, *The Biological Time Bomb* and *The Limits to Growth*—has made speculating about the future topical. Copious journal literature discussing the future has also contributed to making futuristics courses academically respectable.

Another trend, however, should also be reported. A growing number of schools are trying to "futurize" their programs without developing new classes in future studies. The most well-known exponent of this position is John McHale of the State University of New York at Binghamton, New York. Those who resist the establishment of special courses devoted to the future argue that *every* discipline needs to incorporate a futures perspective and that to departmentalize futuristics would be inconsistent with its interdisciplinary character. This difference in approach is best handled, perhaps, by the Office of Applied Social Science and the Future at the University of Minnesota. There, a serious effort is under way to "futurize" various academic departments. Simultaneously, however, a limited number of futures classes are also available for students wishing to undertake a closer study of futures literature and wishing to learn to "think futuristically." Other writers, like Harold Strudler in this volume, argue that futures courses are one phase in the process of curriculum futurization.

Most futurists prefer to remain active in their original professions as urban planners, biologists, sociologists or whatever. This phenomenon is due, no doubt, to the fact that, except for the few graduates now in school who are majoring in futures research, virtually all the teachers of the subject were trained as specialists in something else. Today's futurists are ex-political scientists, ex-design theorists, ex-historians, ex-theologians, ex-anthropologists, ex-computer analysts, ex-one-thing-or-another. Indeed, even the "ex" is not an altogether accurate prefix. Future-studies teachers usually are still members in good standing of nonfuturist departments.

Thus, among respondents to our latest survey, the single largest contingent are political scientists, some twenty-five altogether, followed by twenty-two sociologists and twenty educators. Those drawn from other fields include

Business Administration and Management	12
Engineering and Technological Forecasting	9
City Planning and Architecture	8
History	7
Theology	6
Physical Science	5
Psychology	4
Biological Science	4
Computer Science	3

Also represented are philosophy, anthropology, English, economics, humanities, geography and home economics. Timothy Weaver reports that there is some future-oriented classwork in various medical schools around the country as well. And at least five futures teachers hold interdisciplinary appointments.

The social sciences dominate the identified sample (46 per cent), but this may reflect researcher bias. There may be dozens of courses in the natural sciences, engineering and business of which neither Dr. Eldredge nor I am aware simply because our associates most often are fellow liberal-arts pundits. Some disciplines, in fact, are not represented at all, i.e., law, agriculture, astronomy and library science. Whether this is because no futures teaching has occurred in those areas or because we simply don't know about work that is being done is impossible for us to assess.

III

Futures classes have begun in no less than twenty-eight states and three Canadian provinces. Three states were overrepresented from the start. California had fifteen futuristics courses before 1970 and has developed twenty since; New York has developed ten since 1970 and had sixteen before that date. Six futures courses were taught in Illinois through the end of 1969, another eleven since then. Between April 15, 1971—the publication date for the previous edition of our *Syllabus* —and November 15, 1972, Ohio had become another "overrepresented" state with at least a dozen classes reported as well as several workshops and conferences. Other states which have hosted these courses are

Massachusetts	10 (7 since 1970)
New Jersey	6
New Hampshire	5
Connecticut	5 (none before 1970)
Florida	5
Washington	5
Texas	4
North Carolina	4
Minnesota	3 (none before 1971)
Missouri	3 (all since 1970)
Indiana	3
Georgia	3 (all since 1970)
Rhode Island	3
Colorado	3

The remaining states in which college-level classes in the subject have been offered are Arizona, Hawaii, Kentucky, Louisiana, Maryland, Michigan, Nebraska, Oregon, Pennsylvania, Utah, Vermont, Virginia and Wisconsin.

Interestingly, this geographical distribution does not match that of futures-research work. Research and education are not necessarily occurring in the same places. Thus, according to findings by Magda Cordell and John McHale, Washington, D.C., and Pennsylvania both show concentrations of research work pertaining to the future. In the academic field, very little of note is occurring in either place. By contrast, little in the way of futures research is being conducted in the South. The present survey shows, however, that while Dixie may be underrepresented, there are courses in futurism at a number of educational institutions in the region.

Some of our findings, however, are nearly identical to those reported by Cordell and McHale. They report, for example, that about 90 per cent of futures researchers are male and that better than 43 per cent belong to a single age cohort: thirty to thirty-nine years. It should be added that nearly 100 per cent are white. These conditions have been deplored by some futurists, including Toffler.

IV

Futuristics, in so many words, has already developed a history. At least a few changes—some outlined above—are evident over the past four years. A greater variety of disciplines are now represented among futures teachers now than was formerly the case. The *kind* of futures courses taught has also changed.

Before 1970 the great majority of classes in futuristics were introductions of one kind or another. These still constitute the single largest group, but most futures courses in 1972 specialize in some subject matter, e.g., "The Future of Appalachia" or even "Futurontology"— dealing with metaphysical, linguistic, psychological and axiological issues and future-time perspective. What seems to be happening is that, after teaching a general futures course for a year or more, professors begin to specialize in aspects of the future that appeal to them for professional reasons.

At the same time, growing numbers of institutions are making major commitments to futuristics work. In 1969 only one institution, the School of Education at the University of Massachusetts, had a full-fledged program permitting students to major in future studies. Now there are at least eight, scattered from coast to coast, and several more in the planning stages. While the finishing touches were being put on this report, a telephone call was received from Stevens College in Columbia, Missouri. The Graduate School of Business Administration at the University of Southern California also sent a last-minute report on their Center for Futures Research. These eight centers are listed in *Section Three* below.

One feature of futures courses that has remained remarkably constant from the beginning has been objectives. An analysis of educational futuristics objectives in 1969 looks pretty much like the story in 1972. The most common goals are

1. Help students to anticipate change, i.e., make better career choices, develop future-oriented attitudes, contribute to personal growth, etc.
2. Survey forecasting methods.

3. Develop ability to relate ideas and information between disciplines.
4. Facilitate student-student and student-teacher group interaction (curiously, few courses designed since 1971 have this purpose).
5. Recognize the continuing impact of technology upon society.
6. Develop ability to evaluate forecasts and utilize feedback in doing so.
7. Study major trends shaping the future.
8. Explore ideas, images, models of the future.
9. Examine case-study forecasts in specific problem areas.
10. Develop alternative scenarios of the future.

Also mentioned frequently as goals were developing futuristic curricular materials, finding intervention-points that can influence policy discussions, and stimulating creativity. In the latest survey, a number of new objectives cropped up. These include, for example, facilitating communication between institutions. Almost no professors were concerned, however, with developing specific skills in their students even though interviewing, computer programming, or forecasting techniques, for instance, might be learned in a futures course or sequence.

V

Futuristic subject matter can be structured to suit a number of needs and purposes. However, it is fairly typical to divide courses into two sections: background themes and alternative futures. The most common background topics include

> Population
> Ecology and Environment
> Education
> International Relations
> Historic Conceptions of the Future
> Urbanization
> Privacy
> Automation, Computers, Cybernetics
> Systems Thinking
> Science Fantasies and Utopias
> Creativity
> Concepts of Time

Curriculum units, often treated during one- or two-week periods, frequently cover the following subjects:

Forecasting Methods
Biomedical Developments
Global Changes
New Values
Impact of Technology on Society
Rate of Change
Economic Change
The Future of Sex and Marriage
Technological Change
Planning
Social Control
Post-Industrial Society
Transportation and Communication in the Future
Theories of Futuristics
Life and Influences of Individual Futurists
Prospects for War and Peace

What is interesting to note is the lack of attention paid to subjects that education-watchers would normally expect to see accorded a reasonably high priority ranking. Few futures classes have dealt with trends in women's role in society, racial and ethnic groups, religion, the arts, and space travel. (This may reflect the fact that most futurists are white and male, as noted earlier.) Other subjects discussed in classes were weather control, influencing public policy, future crimes, and the rate of natural-resource depletion.

While futuristics lends itself to holistic, global issues, and most courses are oriented outward, some focus on the intensely personal— the student's own future. Thus, William H. Brickner's 1967 class at Santa Clara, for instance, required a term paper from each student which instructed him or her to "outline a plan for your life as you see it now." The plan was to include

A. Long-term objectives (e.g., ask yourself "What am I in life for?").
B. Strategy to achieve these objectives (include an analysis of strengths and weaknesses).
C. Intermediate-term (three to five years) goals.
D. Specific action programs to achieve goals with timing and allocation of existing resources.

VI

There are various approaches to teaching futuristics at the precollege level. Several programs are listed in the sections that follow. However, one of the most promising is the program at Wallings Road Elementary School in Brecksville, Ohio. Philip G. Hastings, the principal, was instrumental in organizing the school's teachers into committees which redesigned components of the curriculum to include futures units and a general futuristic orientation. Objectives of the project are

(1) To prepare children to accept coming changes in communication, transportation, health, careers, lesiure.
(2) To help children adjust to changes.
(3) To help them take advantage of new opportunities.
(4) To develop alternative methods for coping with change-induced problems.
(5) To learn how to influence predictable changes.

Learning activities at Wallings Road feature role-playing, science-fiction reading, media utilization, future fairs, music and art experiments, simulation, guest speakers, and interviews with people who may have insight into the future. The means for infusing futuristics into the school are individual pupil projects, mini-courses, and large group experiences. If the "experiment" is successful, District Curriculum Director Richard M. Strajford believes that the program can be expanded to other schools in the system for the 1973–1974 academic year.

Although our survey was primarily aimed at higher education, judging from unsolicited correspondence received by ourselves and others, we believe that interest in futuristics in elementary and secondary schools is spreading rapidly. The program described earlier in this volume in the chapter by Michael McDanield is likely to further accelerate this process. Elementary and secondary schools offering courses will be found in *Section Three.*

Much had to be deleted from this Syllabus; the present version is abbreviated from 134 pages of manuscript text. And there are shortcomings which have nothing to do with length. This said, it is hoped that the usefulness of the document can compensate for its questionable features or omissions. It provides strong evidence that educational futuristics is more than a passing fancy.

I extend special thanks to my collaborator H. Wentworth Eldredge. The two of us have been working in tandem on similar research for almost four years now. Professor Eldredge's comments and criticisms during this time have made life more interesting for me.

Futuristics teachers are creating the means for looking forward into time and shaping the time into which we are all moving. Which is fitting. Max Pape, one of the first to teach this genre, said it best: "If you don't invent the future, it will invent you."

Section Two: Selected Futuristics Syllabi

1. THE BEHAVIORAL SCIENCES AND THE STUDY OF THE FUTURE

Course designation: Behavioral Science Foundations 427
Institution: Simon Fraser University (Canada)
Faculty: W. Basil McDermott

This course has been taught since 1968, and during this time its form and content have changed considerably. BSF 427 may be thought of as a cybernetic futuristics course, since it is modified each term as new issues are incorporated into the organization of the class. The syllabus for the course has the distinction of being the most readable seen by this reviewer; from it students can learn a good deal, one suspects, about this futuristics class—and about the professor.

A quotation from Joseph Heller's *Catch 22* starts the 1972 syllabus off on the left foot.

"I have bad news for you. Are you man enough to take it?"

"God, no!" screamed Yossarian. "I'll go right to pieces."

Then comes the professor's remarks.

". . . Men have grown used to the prospects of famine, disease, riots, and racism in the international sphere. And when it comes to war, or rumors of war, they would be genuinely shocked if peace broke out tomorrow. Even in the most advanced and richest parts of the world there has been no concerted effort to deal with problems of crime, slums, mental disease, traffic congestion, pollution, unemployment, agricultural malaise, racism. And if you listen carefully you can hear the song, 'We Shall Overcome,' being slowly, imperceptibly transformed into 'Trust and Obey.'

"We shall not overcome our social problems for four principal reasons. The first concerns the role of psychological denial in human affairs. This is the principle that states, No problem is so large and threatening that it cannot be ignored indefinitely. The second reason is that we lack sufficient knowledge about both the kinds of future we want to create and how we might go about implementing any given dream. A third reason deals with the way societies and political systems are organized and structured. . . . Fourthly, the future is not ours for the making due to demon change. We simply cannot deal with the rate of change. Problems grow geometrically; the time with which to deal with them, arithmetically.

"There is no decent exit from our crisis-ridden present. We are now at a point in human history where we must devise new kinds of control systems for the problems facing our world. The real issue is not whether we ought to control human behavior or leave it uncontrolled. . . . This is a course about control systems."

What follows is a list of topics for discussion, such as

> Tomorrow As Tragedy.
> What are you doing . . . AFTER THE FUTURE?
> Big Bad Problems—On getting your enemies straight . . .
> How do you ask the right questions?
> How the Post-Industrial Society Exercises Control.
> How Science and Technology Might Organize the Future.
> But It's Always the Eleventh Hour!
> Beyond Everything—The Vision of Arthur Clarke.
> How John Platt Thinks About Change.
> What Do Social Inventions Look Like?
> One World—More Or Less.
> On the Limits of Prediction.
> Too Late, My Brother . . . the day the counterculture took over
>   the Department of Defense, and other such improbables . . .
> Walk on the grass—or smoke it. Pick the Flowers. Loiter
>   anytime. Welcome. Free Parking.

Clear explanations of student responsibilities are included:

I. The first essay. Discuss the following questions in as organized a manner as you can:
"In what kind of society would you like to live twenty years from the present? What means, methods, or routes would you like to use in order to move from the present society to this future society? What would you anticipate the major problems of your desired society to be? What kinds of alternative controls do you think you would find acceptable to deal with these major problems?"

II. The second essay . . .
"The first seven weeks of the course provide a framework for identifying and evaluating the major problems threatening the survival of mankind. Rewrite your first essay in light of the

analysis provided in the lectures and readings during this time, including your own evaluation of the arguments put forth."

III.   The third essay . . .

"What major objections would Clarke, Reich, and Huxley raise to your second essay? Discuss and evaluate these objections."

Professor McDermott also teaches a graduate seminar, BSF 829, with the cryptic title "Can the World be Saved?"

2. FUTURISM AND LONG-RANGE PLANNING

Course designations: Sociology 80S
Institution: Dartmouth College
Faculty: H. Wentworth Eldredge

The course is devided into four sections. The first part, "Intellectual Roots of Futurism," considers what might be termed the ideological or disciplinary system for futuristics.

Among the materials discussed for this part of the course are utopian works like B. F. Skinner's *Walden Two* and science-fiction books such as Arthur C. Clarke's *The City and the Stars*. The second section of the course is called "Futurism Techniques" and considers the work of R. Buckminster Fuller, the Hudson Institute and other future forecasters. Part three is called "Futurism and Planning." During the last, and fourth, section of the course, students deliver reports that are evaluated by the teacher. Among the possible topics for futuristics research papers Professor Eldredge suggests

Communist Long-Range Planning
Holistic Planning with Twenty-Five Years' or Longer Lead Times
Utopian Communities
Five-Year Plans for America
French "Indicative" Planning
Demography and Long-Range Projections
Design Utopias
Tropic, Undersea or Arctic Futures
Megastructures
Methods of Long-Range Prediction

Students alternate as reporters; each is required to discuss some self-selected reading before the class. A list of topics is distributed at the start of the term and students sign up for the subject and date they desire. Everyone in class is expected to review the paper being reported on "as a reasonable basis for an ongoing discussion." In addition, materials are assigned from Kahn and Wiener's *The Year 2000*.

3. EDUCATION IN CORPORATE FUTURISM

Course designation: Seminar in Business Administration
Institution: Wayne State University
Faculty: Harvey Nussbaum

Professor Nussbaum has been teaching a series of courses dealing
with the theme of business futures since 1969. The purpose of these
seminars is "to give students the best preparation for their long-term
careers as managers." In effect, such a course is not unlike the training
programs given to "managerial employees prior to their being sent to
various overseas assignments." Goals for the course are threefold: (1)
to help M.B.A. majors learn to cope with corporate future shock, (2)
to allow them to utilize technological forecasting methods in order to
predict alternatives for business firms, and (3) to provide students with
the experience of utilizing pertinent educational media—such as computer time-sharing systems.

Nussbaum reports on the process by which he developed his class
in a paper presented to the American Meeting of the Institute of Management Sciences in 1971; it is entitled "Futurism: A New Direction
in Management Science Education." At first he experienced difficulty
introducing the idea of thinking futuristically to his students. "I had
begun class one day," he writes, "with the simple question: 'What will
you be doing in the year 2000?' I received, besides an array of answers
about early retirement, a series of responses which indicated that most
M.B.A. management-science types could not project themselves into
a distant time period." "There is," he says, "a kind of 'trained incapacity' which produces tunnel vision, i.e., students tend to perceive
solutions to problems 'in narrow terms and simple stereotyped models.' "

In previous classes Dr. Nussbaum had tried teaching by means of
analogy to stretch thinking habits. The firm was treated as a biological
organism, a physical system, an ecological network, a personality.
However, his utilitarian students sometimes reacted negatively to thinking about business in cross-disciplinary terms. They "felt that my
excursions," Nussbaum says, "into fields foreign to their own work or
job duties had little bearing on their future careers, and perhaps they
were right." At this point he encountered the nascent futures movement; when their minds were pulled toward the twenty-first century
they received the desired stretching. At the same time, no relevance
was sacrificed.

The course as it is presently structured features

Long-range forecasts regarding the future of American society
The future business firm and its environment

Corporate futures: new management, information, organizational
developments
Forecasting methods: Delphi, Cross-Impact, Trend Extrapolation,
Scenarios

Student reports, based upon forecasting research, have already
shown a number of useful approaches to corporate futuristics. Some
selected papers dealt with

Business education in the future
Today's youth and tomorrow's corporation
Minorities and the future of the private enterprise system
Multinational business firms in 2000 A.D.
The future business corporation and its influence on business edu-
cation

Nussbaum uses brainstorming methods and the Delphi technique to
generate ideas about business futures. The basic question that this
course seeks is "How does what we learn today apply to what we will
be doing twenty or thirty years from now?" Plans for further modification in the class include creation of a "game simulator" which will
"incorporate events pertinent to the corporation of the future. Plays
would work through several iterations of the game to bring them up
timewise to an environment most nearly like that projected for the
year 2000. The simulation exercise would permit the student to develop
his capacities over a time dimension while learning to plan for and
cope with the future events."

4.   CALIFORNIA AS THE WAVE OF THE FUTURE

Course designation: SIDS 923
Institution: Case Western Reserve University
Faculty: Dennis Livingston

A number of schools have begun to modify their academic calendars
in order to accommodate the large proportion of students who enter
or leave college throughout the year, who transfer into an institution
or transfer out. The difficulty that is encountered regularly is that
many schools have conflicting schedules. One solution to the problem
is to change the calendar so that the schedule of course activity during
the year becomes compatible with as many institutions as possible.
This usually means ending the September term before the Christmas
recess and using the month of January as a short, intensive term.
During that time students enroll in one course only.
The one-month term has more justification than scheduling con-

venience. Things can be done with classes in which students devote full attention that cannot be accomplished in the traditional five-course-at-a-time system. Dennis Livingston's class devoted to the futuristics of California illustrates the point.

This class meets in California, i.e., it is probably the first field course in futuristics. Students choose their own mode of transportation to the Golden Gate state and are responsible for their costs—but once there they tour as a group. Places to visit include

1. Planning groups oriented toward science and technology like the Rand Corporation, Stanford Research Institute, etc.
2. Free universities and other "human awareness" institutions like Esalen Institute, Amanda Meditation Retreat and Topanga Center.
3. Communes and other alternative life-style groups such as the Whole Earth Truck Store, the Wheeler Sheep Ranch, etc.

California, it has been said, is a model of tomorrow's society; i.e., the things that transpire in Los Angeles, San Francisco and elsewhere now may become normative for the rest of American society in the decades ahead. Accordingly, since students are required to record their impressions of the trip in a journal, they are asked to "think about the following possibilities":

You can't find anything in California that you can't find in Ohio
    (except an ocean);
You have seen the future and it doesn't work;
You have seen the future and it's groovy;
California girls are better;
Etc.

Before leaving for the West Coast the class meets with their teacher to explore some pertinent issues. The purpose here is to iron out problems about itinerary, mutual responsibilities and the like, beforehand. Students should read before leaving. Recommended texts are

Rasa Gustaitis, *Turning On*;
Curt Gentry, *The Last Days of the Late, Great State of California*;
Stuart Chase, *The Most Probable World*;
Michael Frady, "California: The Rending of the Veil" in *Harper's*,
    December 1969.

The goal of the course, as explained in the syllabus, "is for students to develop, as a result of their experience, some knowledge of the variety of ways in which important patterns affecting their future are being determined in the present.

"It is presumed that leaving the student with a mere jumble of unorganized impressions would have little educational value; therefore, while the course is free-form in style, it has been structured to some degree as to content so that the student may take advantage of a variety of learning spaces that will be made available to him, from self-reflection to formal seminars."

5. ALTERNATIVE IMAGES OF THE FUTURE

Course designation: Humanistic Studies—University College
Institution: Syracuse University
Faculty: Michael Marien

This was one of the first adult-education classes to consider the futures theme. The guiding concept of the course was a question: How can we understand the future world we are moving into? A number of phrases such as "technetronic society," "post-industrial society," and "age of discontinuity" have been used to describe these transitional times, but which are accurate? Which assist our understanding and which impede it?

What is happening? Where are we going? Where could we go? The course is designed to survey "the major facets of our unfolding future, with emphasis on alternative views, concept lag, future shock, forecasting bias and error, cross-impacts, and—above all—an appreciation of future-study as a serious enterprise. For, although we cannot know the future, we can develop some plausible approximations, as well as an appreciation for the necessity of inventing a viable future, if we are to have one."

Tentative weekly discussion topics:

The Age of Extending Horizons vs. The Unprepared Society: Why we look at the future and how.

The Effluent Society vs. Anthropolis: Ecology, urbanization, and population

The Garrison State vs. The Age of Aquarius: Science, technology, and love

The Medicated Society vs. Nature's Way: Health and happiness in the biofuture

The Global Village vs. World Superculture: Mobiletics (communication and transportation) in the world society

The Organized Society vs. Noetic Society: Social organization in the superindustrial age

The Ignorant Society vs. The Learning Society: Who learns what, where, and how?

The Innovative Society vs. The Alternative Society: What can we
do to invent the future?

Most of these societal images have served as a major theme or title
of a recent book or article. Although reading will not be required, it
will be encouraged, in order to stimulate independent inquiry into the
broad and lifelong concern of survival.

6. THE USE OF SCIENCE IN ENVIRONMENTAL AND SOCIAL CHANGE

> Course designation: Psychology 293
> Institution: University of Illinois (Urbana)
> Faculty: Stuart Umpleby

Stuart Umpleby is responsible for this class although Charles E.
Osgood from the Department of Psychology, Richard L. Merritt of
Political Science, and Cameron Satterthwaite in Physics are also involved. The varied background these men bring to the course seems
to have been deliberately arranged in order to make the ecumenical
content of the semester intelligible to students. And although two
assigned papers are vital to the program, members of the class are
able to select topics, and may elect to do group work in lieu of individual essays. Students are also encouraged to redesign the itinerary
for the term that their teacher provided. A novel feature of this course,
furthermore, is the fact that it is not structured sequentially. Since
students learn randomly, rather than in linear order, the following
schedule is easily justifiable:

Futures research: The work of Daniel Bell, Olaf Helmer, Herman
     Kahn, et al.
Systems theory: Discussion of the Dustin Hoffman film *The
     Graduate*; readings include cybernetics literature.
Systems analysis in engineering: The Manned Orbital Laboratory.
Systems theory for social problems solving: i.e., R. Boguslaw's
     The New Utopians.
Demonstration of PLATO and Delphi Exploration.
How to get things done: The "technological fix" and attitude
     change.
Technological forecasting.
The impact of technology on society.
The future of the international system.
Understanding American society: A case study—the assassination
     of President Kennedy.

Other approaches to futures research: The humanists and the activists.

The future of interpersonal relations and the dialogue-focuser methodology; readings include Robert Rimmer's *The Harrad Experiment* and Robert Theobald's *Dialogue on Women*.

Scientists and scientific revolutions.

Macroengineering or "playing God."

Utopias and anti-utopias.

Much of the fame of futures investigation at the University of Illinois is due to the computerized future game that students can play in this class. A description of this system is available from Dr. Umpleby; it is entitled *The Delphi Exploration, A Computer-Based System for Obtaining Subjective Judgments on Alternative Futures*. This contains an outline of the PLATO (Programmed Logic for Automated Teaching Operations) computer systems.

At selected times students play a game making use of a computer terminal outfitted with a viewing apparatus; this operates on a time-sharing basis so that a number of keyboards may operate simultaneously in communicating with the machine. The Delphi Exploration is based on three basic assumptions:

1. The future can be described in terms of short descriptive statements with probabilities attached to them.
2. People influence what the future will be like by making investments (i.e., the student's own time, energy, wealth).
3. The occurrence of one development may increase or decrease the probability of occurrence of other developments (i.e., factors operating in the world are interrelated).

In the Delphi Exploration the student has an opportunity to make events "happen" and to witness their consequences. In working to make his or her desired future come into being, the player has an opportunity to observe the effects of chance and/or undesired secondary consequences of his or her choices.

Background information is provided so that they can choose courses of action with a fund of knowledge about tomorrow's world. Among the titles of these "background paragraphs" are Nationless Corporations, Tooth Decay Eliminated, Air Cushion Vehicles, etc. The information presented assumes the continued existence of one or more current trends. One paragraph reads as follows:

THE PASSING OF RELIGION

"By the twenty-first century, religious believers may be found only in rural communities and in small sects, huddled together to resist a worldwide, secular, technological culture. Churches in industrial centers increasingly take consumer preferences into account in marketing their wares. Some people see each of the major religions as offering only one of many religious commodities in the religious marketplace. Thus the churches are secularizing themselves from within in order to attract members. Protestantism, being the most advanced, has been said to have almost reached the stage of self-liquidation."

"Oracle messages" also flash before the student's eyes every so often to announce the latest trends. For example, the player might be told that, by 2000 A.D., food synthesized from inorganic ingredients will be commercially available. Such information is likely to affect the choices made.

The actions of players are "interpreted" by the computer. For example, while increased armaments might seem like a step in the direction of military security to a student, the machine might be programmed to view such a hostile act as increasing the probability of war.

At the conclusion of the game, the machine tabulates the likely outcome of the student's desires. The player might be informed that, because of what he or she did or didn't do, the probability of intelligence-stimulating drugs has been raised or lowered to 90 per cent.

The Delphi game is also being further developed at this time so that it can deal with several input factors at once. And a more focused game dealing with the future of the university is also being created.

7. INQUIRY INTO EDUCATION ADMINISTRATION: FUTURE COGNITION

> Course designation: Education 353
> Institution: University of Vermont
> Faculty: Charles Case, Robert Larsen

"The primary purpose of this seminar," to quote the instructors, "is to examine alternative futures for our society and its . . . educational subsystem. Class interaction will utilize the Delphi process for predicting alternative futures. . . . As a group and as individuals we will examine our knowledge, attitudes, values, and feelings regarding future cognition and the relationship between these variables and individual inquiry processes." Case reports that the value-clarification aspect of Ed. 353 has been a crucial feature of the seminar because many of the students, when their assumptions are examined, are often predestinarian, and that the concept of an open-ended future is threatening to many egos.

During the year-long course students are asked to focus upon four questions and to carry out value-clarification exercises for each. The Vermont syllabus reads (somewhat paraphrased) like this:

What will the world be like in 2000 A.D.? Derive and rank-order alternative futures.

What kind of educational system will be needed to prepare people to live in the most desirable future society? Rank-order the educational implications of the establishment of such a society.

For what kind of world does our present educational system prepare people? What will need to be changed the most to achieve the most desirable educational system?

How do we get from here to there?

The larger class meets in smaller groups to discuss strategies for answering these questions, and in the process of answering, works to achieve consensus among the members. Individuals are expected to contribute to a group position paper; each group reads and analyzes the writing of each member in it. In order to reach agreement a process of "Consensual validation" is used which, in essence, involves four steps. First, much like creativity workshops, all problems are approached in an unbiased manner "and every conceivable variety of evidence is examined to maximize a solution." Second, students are asked to facilitate communication by only dealing with "here and now" perceptions. Third, Kahn's technique of exploring all the alternatives is followed, and fourth, agreements are repeatedly tested.

Each student is required to write one brief paper, in addition to group activity, "outlining his or her objectives" for the seminar. In the process of the course it is hoped that class participants will become better able to

1. Identify logically consistent ends;
2. Select means by which to achieve these ends;
3. Recognize ethically consistent means and ends;
4. Select means and ends that are consistent with "social-self realization";
5. Think in terms of future cognition, i.e., considering all alternatives to a problem, creating new alternatives;
6. Analyze futures literature critically (through one-page abstracts);
7. Function in a group.

A bibliography is provided so that students can locate relevant documents. No textbook is used for the course, however. The one-page abstracts generated by class members provide a working, convenient "data bank" that all students can draw on for research purposes.

At the end of each semester the students are asked to write a course evaluation.

8.   ADVOCACY DESIGN STUDIO

Course designation: School of Architecture
Institution: University of Minnesota
Faculty: Scott Helmes

Strictly speaking, the following is not a course description; instead, it is a collection of ideas that Helmes has developed for independent study with graduate students. However, some of these learning techniques have been adapted for use at the high-school level. Furthermore they include media work as well as drafting and art activities. Credit should also go to Tom Bender for some of these ideas.

Urban Design Problem. What is your conception of an ideal city? What kinds of structures would it include? Draw an outline map of your city; all class designs will be mounted on the walls and the ideas of various city plans will be discussed.

Media Day. Using only portable video-tape recording units, Polaroid cameras, tape recorders, etc., communicate abstract ideas to other members of the class. What are your classmates saying? Why did they choose the media they did to get their ideas across?

Movement Day. Tour your community by any convenient means of transportation: bicycle, bus, car, subway, boat. Symbolize what you saw using the Doxiadis visual-shorthand system. What is the city visually organized to accomplish? Even if there is no master plan for the town, what would the objectives of a hypothetical plan be, based on street layout, population densities, expansion areas and the like?

Climate Modification. If rain or sunshine can be procured when desired, what impact would this have on urban development? (In a paper prepared for an environmental design course, Bender says: "If we can de-mosquito Minnesota, we could perhaps make it habitable.")

City Building Experience. Use geodesic dome kits and other architectural modules to construct spaces to live in. Why did you choose the form and style eventually selected? What effects does enclosed space have on values and attitudes?

Alternative Futures Day. Redesign the world; what human purposes do you want to facilitate? How will new urban systems, communications networks, political boundaries, expedite these goals? What will the world of the future look like?

There is yet another way to create visual interest and awareness of the effects of architecture—color, decoration, design, structure—on the individual: Redesign your classroom. Needless to say, some practical problems must be confronted first, such as permission from one's administration to undertake modifications to school property, but academic objectives may be sufficient justification in many cases and "lab fees" may cover the costs involved. But what would be the appearance of the ideal classroom of the future? After debating the issue, submitting alternative designs, etc., a student jury can decide on a plan and the class can do the work needed to change the immediate environment. After several weeks new designs might be considered, selected and carried out.

9. TECHNOLOGICAL FORECASTING

Course designation: Business Administration
Institution: Stanford University
Faculty: Robert D. Berkowitz (Institute for Defense Analysis, Arlington, Virginia)

This Fall 1969 lecture series covered the subject of forecasting technological change in an extensive manner. During the section of the class devoted to trend analysis, a *trend extrapolation exercise* was presented to the students. The following series of questions was asked in this regard:

1. What is the objective of the forecast?
2. What are the measurable parameters?
3. Where can you find data on these parameters?
4. What does the tabulated information show?
5. After points have been plotted and trends established, do you observe any natural limits?
6. How can the performance trends be explained? I.e., What factors have a bearing on the technology in question?
   A. economics (cost effectiveness; competition for resources)
   B. demography (How many need it?)
   C. psychology (How do people feel about it?)
   D. sociology (Who benefits and who loses?)
   E. politics (Who has the power?)

Berkowitz also asked the class to check and see if any of these factors (or the effects of the technology) could be changed; if "precursor events" could be located in which one could foresee effects of the technology; whether or not the change in question was constrained by envelope curves; and, finally, if models for the growth of a new technology could be predicted by analogy to some other growth pattern.

Normative forecasting was also discussed in the course. Of concern here was the matter of "goal or need identification." The question is, What technology will be required to satisfy future needs? The mission-oriented relevance tree forecasting method was also studied. The "levels" of the tree are tied together in the following manner:

We accomplish the	OBJECTIVE
by upgrading the	TASKS
using an	APPROACH
to deal with a	SYSTEM
containing a	SUBSYSTEM
by measuring a	FACTOR
pointing out a	TECHNICAL DEFICIENCY.

Solution trees were also examined in the class, a solution tree being a systematic breakdown of a complex problem in such a way that the exact cause of a technological inadequacy can be identified. The course ended with consideration of Delphi and Cross-Impact Matrix Analysis methods.

10. CHRISTIANITY AND CULTURE

Course designation: 402
Institution: St. Andrew's Presbyterian College
Faculty: William M. Alexander, George Fouke,
                      and Douglas Hick

The theme of William M. Alexander's senior seminar is "Thinking for the Future." Its purpose is to look at many of the diverse factors that can operate upon a student's life in the years after college. Members of the class are required to present—and defend—two papers before the class during the term.

The first should be a research paper that is basically predictive in nature. It is to be judged according to its relative objectivity, its imaginativeness and its ability to anticipate the criticisms of the student's peers. Suggested topics include

What will be the future of the national economy?
What models predict the future of the city?

What is the future for democracy?
In what direction is the teaching profession headed?
Is peace possible?
Will belief in God continue to be a possibility for man?
How will the United States deal with revolutions?

The second paper is to be a position paper in which the student takes a moral stand. The likelihood of desired events coming true should have been dealt with in the earlier essay; the position paper "should be prescriptive and recommendatory."

Work is not purely individualized in Alexander's classes. Each pupil is responsible for meeting with a faculty adviser prior to distributing copies of the paper to the class for the independent critiques of each student—a one-page evaluation due before discussion of the paper takes place. Also, the seminar will "adopt by majority vote an agreement about what assumptions, factors and trends will condition models of the future." After all papers have been presented during the term, an elected board from the seminar will select "a total program for the future, including priorities, budgets and plans for finance. This program shall be debated and voted upon. Finally, the seminar should say what shall be done to or for the minority who lost in the voting."

Texts for the course were as follows:

Stuart Chase, *The Most Probable World*.
Kahn & Wiener, *The Year 2000*.
Henry Still, *Man: The Next Thirty Years*.
David Bell, ed., "Toward the Year 2000: Work in Progress,"
    Daedalus (Summer 1967).

Probably the most interesting feature of the seminar is the written critiques that students are¹ asked to write of each other's papers. "Special critics" are appointed from among the class so that each position paper and each research paper is examined in a thoroughgoing manner. Professor Alexander's suggestions for doing so can be found below.

Critiques are to be four or five pages in length and should answer a number of questions that bear on content and expression. There are too many questions to repeat in their entirety here, but a representative selection is stated below:

CRITIQUE OF RESEARCH PAPER

1. Introduction
    —Is the background information in the introduction adequate?
    —Are terms clearly and adequately defined? Explain.

2. Factors, trends and assumptions
   —Did the author analyze the degree and rapidity of diffusion of trends?
   —Do you agree with this analysis? Explain.
3. Models
   —Are the models distinct from one another?
   —Should some models be eliminated?
   —Should some models be combined to form a larger and more distinct model?
   —Why?
   —Did the author establish feasibility for each model?
   —Are the major desirable and undesirable consequences of each model presented?
4. Footnotes and Bibliography
   —Are the footnotes adequate and in proper form? Cite specific examples.
   —Check . . . references at least on a spot-check basis . . . [and] see if you can find any major references that the author has overlooked.
   —[Are] . . . the references in the bibliography . . . merely padding?
   —Are quotes and conclusions from references accurate?
   —Were references up-to-date?
5. Technical criticism and summary, i.e., critic's evaluation.

CRITIQUE OF POSITION PAPER

1. Defense of model
   —Did the author omit any major arguments for his model?
   —Is the major argument clearly explained and logically presented?
   —Did the author recognize the difference between major and minor arguments?
   —Did the author recognize and deal with all major opposing arguments?
   —Did he take a definite stand on a real issue? . . .
   —Did the author present his own thinking or did he merely hide behind a smoke screen of references?
2. Taking responsibility for practical consequences of model
   —Did the author reiterate . . . practical steps for bringing about this model?
   —Did the author take specific moral responsibility for specific steps? . . .

—If the author opted for increased centralized power for survival, did he assume any responsibility for loss of freedom?

—If he opted for increased freedom, did he assume any responsibility for compromising chances of survival?

—Did the author assume responsibility for solving any financial problems?

3. Technical criticism and summary

—Comment specifically on . . . organization, spelling, grammar and style.

—Do you feel that the quality of writing is up to the standards one would expect from a college senior?

The class was first offered during the Fall, 1968. Guest lecturers have been a part of the program. Herman Kahn spoke to the Laurinburg students in 1969.

11. SOCIOLOGY OF THE FUTURE

Course designation: Sociology 170
Institution: St. Louis University
Faculty: Clement S. Mihanovich

Undoubtedly the most ambitious class syllabus compiled to date is Professor Mihanovich's 122-page opus. Most of this collection is not descriptive or instructional, needless to say; a number of important futurist articles are reproduced (with permission), and the tome also contains an extensive bibliography. One very useful feature of the syllabus is a listing of "Twelve Ways to Predict Social Trends." These are

1. Extend past trends into the future.
2. Identify long-run trends in public opinion; postulate that public concerns will become objects of scientific research, law-making, etc.
3. Identify differences in opinion between experts and laymen; what experts advocate today usually becomes socially normative.
4. Study differences between backward and advanced countries and predict that the backward will steadily become more like the advanced.
5. Identify efficient practices in organizations; these will replace less efficient arrangements in other institutions.
6. Note consumption habits of rich and poor in a given country; as average real incomes rise, the life-style of the poor will increasingly come to resemble the rich.

7. Similar to #6, except that in this case the tendency is for the less educated to adopt the habits of the better educated.

8. Locate "successful pioneer social reforms" and predict their adoption in other areas.

9. Nearly all distinctive old customs and institutions . . . peculiar to a single region and not justified by geography will gradually be replaced by more universal ones. For instance, the custom of wearing a distinctive local dress will continue to weaken.

10. Anticipate the social consequences of new technological innovations.

11. Select the most plausible predictions from various works of utopian and science-fiction literature; those supported by the methods listed here have some possibility of coming true.

12. Develop new predictions based . . . on these premises: Men are partly rational and hedonistic and will eventually adopt nearly all major social reforms which would enhance their welfare.

The problem of forecasting methods is dealt with at the outset of the class with a series of lectures dealing specifically with predictive techniques. With some knowledge of methods, students are then exposed to the "new worlds" of futures speculation. A number of guest speakers began the semester with considerations of these subjects.

12. INTRODUCTION TO INTELLECTUAL HISTORY: THE FUTURE
    OF AMERICAN CULTURE

> Course designation: History 221
> Institution: Alice Lloyd College
> Faculty: Billy Rojas

The purpose of this course is to introduce students to sources of value change in American society. Needless to say, there are many dimensions of attitude modification, and this class is made up of modules that can be included or excluded at will.

These units are

1. The changing establishment—what do new organizational metaphors tell us about the values of business and government during the coming ten or twenty years? What values will people need to survive in a temporary, post-bureaucratic, post-industrial, cybernetic, self-renewing, discontinuous society?

2. What is "human nature" *now* and how can it be expected to change? Robert Heilbroner has pointed out that the phrase "human nature" obviously refers to a condition, not to a substance. The "human nature" of red-skinned, American Indians and the "human nature" of the Chinese are quite dissimilar. In recent years a new, critical literature has appeared appraising our most cherished beliefs; it may be that love is pathological and that every person has many identities, for example. New models for sexual roles, new forms of marriage, and new means of dealing with problem areas within personality can be studied.

3. Human liberation—who is trying to liberate whom? And why? With what chances for success? Focus in this unit will be on women and the women's movement. Its implications for marriage will be studied.

4. Communes—what types of life-styles are emerging from social experiments that may become large-scale alternatives for Americans in the future?

5. New directions for the mind—religious developments in the past decade and their possible meaning for the next ten years. What accounts for the interest in Oriental religious systems, occult phenomena and the revival of sectarian images? What do Jesus Freaks and Hare Krishna devotees tell us about our future?

6. New directions in the arts—what does our taste in music and visual art tell us about our values in the future? What next for rock? What next after rock?

7. Drugs and drug culture—an examination of the hippie movement and the effect of drugs in influencing value changes. A look at youth culture after marijuana is legalized.

8. The debate on radical strategy—what can be expected from American Marxists, anarchists, etc., during the next several years? What about "counterrevolution"? How will radical-reactionary political struggle shape our values?

9. The Future of Appalachian Culture—in what ways are mountain values developing independently of mainstream America? Where is the greatest accommodation? Where is Appalachian culture exerting influence upon the tastes of other Americans?

10. Prescriptions for the future—putting it all together: Reich, Goodman, Theobald, Toffler, et al.

Class activities can include future marriage contracts, writing a constitution for a commune, future television commercials, writing songs to be sung in the future, simulated marriage ca. 1984, and simulated divorce court ca. 1984. Various games can also be played, encounter sessions held, and debates staged. Final class project consists of putting together a time capsule supposedly collected in A.D. 2000. Each student will open someone else's capsule and is then expected to interpret the artifacts to the class as if he or she were a twenty-third-century archaeologist. Group activities that are optional include script-writing to illustrate family life in 1991, a future dada-surrealist art festival, "you-are-there" video-tape dramatizations of hypothetical events a decade hence, and a future-foods potluck supper.

13. INTRODUCTION TO PHILOSOPHY: DEVELOPING A PHILOSOPHY
    OF LIFE FOR THE FUTURE

> Course designation: Philosophy 105
> Institution: Alice Lloyd College
> Faculty: Billy Rojas

The goal of this course is to introduce students to classical philosophical problems that bear directly upon how individuals think about their future and make decisions affecting their future lives. Almost any classical and modern philosophers can be studied to reach these objectives.

As presently structured, the class begins by reading Lawrence Casler's piece "This Thing Called Love is Pathological" which appeared in the December 1969 issue of *Psychology Today*. Ostensibly an analytic article, college students soon discover that Casler's argument rests on debatable assumptions. Questions are raised: Can the evidence presented in the essay lead to other conclusions? Does the original conclusion require more evidence than Casler provides?

Since the point of view is controversial and the subject is love and sexual behavior, student interest in studying something as abstract as reasoning processes can be obtained from the start. Sexuality also serves as a motif when ethical problems are brought up later in the assigned readings and when thinking about one's possible life-styles in the next century.

The classical philosophers are also studied and hopefully brought to life. Six or eight of the *Fragments* of Herakleitos can be rearranged by the student so that he or she, in effect, composes a paragraph of his or her own without ever developing a single phrase or sentence. By rewriting other ancient literature, something of its spirit can be resurrected. Setting Act 15 in 1973 or Chapter 19 in the year 2000 presents students with the problem of translating meanings from one time idiom to a completely different historical orientation.

Debates can be staged between long-dead philosophers; students role-playing St. Paul and Socrates might dispute the nature of the good life, or the correct way to make decisions. Another pairing could feature Marx and Nietzsche. The Orient can also be consulted by inviting Buddha to talk things over with Abdu'l-Baha. Perhaps different Buddhas might talk things over: say, the Buddha of historic Tantra tradition could discuss the meaning of sexuality, honesty, and the future with Gotama, the modern psychotherapist that A. J. Bahm understands. Two contemporary futurists can debate such issues: Harvey Cox meets Herman Kahn.

The community can also be a class resource. What two or three people on the campus would you like to talk to about *their* philosophy of life?

Next the class moves on to the study of a contemporary philosopher —Wittgenstein, Russell, Sartre, Korzybski—or whoever seems appropriate. I have found it extremely useful to consider questions relating to the nature of language, the game qualities of human communication, and the like. Instead of merely considering these things symbolically, one can and should convert thoughts into deeds. The student has more to think about when he or she has taken part in classroom theater than if his or her only activity was sitting. At any rate, when the class recognizes that the English language creates an intellectual environment in which some kinds of thinking, but not other types, are possible, it is time to investigate an epistemological issue of some weight: Is truth autobiographical? The philosophy textbook for this part of the course might be *The Autobiography of Mark Twain* for Appalachian students; urban black students would probably find more relevance in *The Autobiography of Malcolm X*, while white collegians could review a book like Robert Rimmer's *Proposition 31*. The topic of drugs can be explored through a text like *The Teachings of Don Juan: A Yaqui Way of Knowledge*. Women's liberation can be considered by reading one of Simone de Beauvoir's autobiographical volumes. What is true, after all, depends upon what different people want to be true.

Finally, students consider their tomorrows. A provocative journalistic essay, Barry Cunningham's "Life in the Year 2000," which appeared in *Cosmopolitan* magazine, makes the twenty-first century seem very close indeed. Harlan Ellison's "The Very Last Day of a Good Woman" also makes the future uncomfortably real. Other science-fiction scenarios can be read to stimulate thinking about the post-1980 world, the world in which today's twenty-year-olds become thirty, forty, fifty . . .

The final paper required of students is a future autobiography. Homework assignments are designed to facilitate writing the speculative life-story. Early in the term the class is asked to write a list of "twenty things I would like to do before the year 2000." These can be discussed in their own right or can be part of an assignment in which the "twenty most important things that I have ever lived through" are treated.

Another written paper is required: "Two questions that a philosophy of life should seek to answer—and how I might go about answering them."

At the end of the term, the *Age Game*, a simulation based upon the child's game of London Bridge, is played (it was designed by students). The objective of the simulation is to create the illusion of growing old; each round brings a participant further away from the present as 1975, 1979, 1986, 1992 are reached. During play the nature of decision-making is age-relevant.

There are many questions that this kind of course can never answer —How am I going to change when I respond to people that I have not even met? But there are other kinds of questions that it can. What rewards can I expect in return for my being an honest (or dishonest) person? Can I learn to use my own thinking-about-the-future as a resource in my here-and-now life? And the operational value of ideas can be made evident by creating classroom *situations* in which futures thinking or honest speaking has real-life "payoff." An example of the latter: The class is divided into two groups according to sex; the men retire to one room, the women to another. Each group now meets to put together a list of questions that they were always-afraid-to-ask of the other sex. Anonymity protects individuals from disclosures which they would rather not make both in creating questions and in answering them. The sexes are brought back together to talk about the answers—which are group replies. Honest questions, it turns out, can take a group beyond game relationships.

14. SEMINAR IN TECHNOLOGICAL FORECASTING

Course designation: Business Administration
Institution: University of Connecticut
Faculty: Jay Mendell

This course was offered during the Spring, 1970. The focus was upon "technological issues in the context of their full social, economic, and political implications." For instance, during one class session Dr.

Mendell asked a student to presume that he was a coal-mine owner. "After he had reflected on the state of the coal industry and the predicament of a mine owner, he was supposed to explain the nature of his business *as he perceived it.*" He identified his business quite simply . . . "I dig it up and ship it out." Couldn't he see his business in a broader context? . . . He couldn't. By introducing creativity-inducing techniques, however, other students began to take the issue away from the first class member. A second student thought that since coal was sought for its energy-producing properties that the owner might, as a possibility, consider generating and selling electricity. Another student suggested converting coal to chemical constituents and piping these chemicals to industrial customers. Next, after no new ideas were forthcoming, students were asked to list the attributes of coal, which, it turned out, included hard, black, carbon, heat, dense, etc. A new idea emerged at this point. "Can we eat coal?" a student asked. Then someone asked, "All the while we have been focusing on what comes out of the hole—the coal. But why can't we use the hole itself?"

Businessmen need futurists to help determine the value of the forecasts they use because corporate planners often overlook the possibilities of creating the future, as outlined above. Also, Mendell points out: "Forecasters often pay insufficient attention to easily available information on events and trends outside their own company and industry. Furthermore, they often overlook work unfolding in the early stages of research and development because they cannot imaginatively perceive its long-range consequences." This was the rationale for the class which dealt with a standard range of interests (trend analysis, envelope curves, scientific research)—but in a nonstandard way.

15. INTRODUCTION TO EDUCATIONAL FUTURISTICS

Course designation: Education 686
Institution: University of Massachusetts
Faculty: Chris Dede, Jim Thomann

This class is open to both undergraduates and graduates; it seeks to give students the means for applying futures-research methods to educational problems. Discussions are held which deal with the subject-matter potential of futuristics. Books studied range from Edward Kormondy's *Concepts of Ecology* to Nigel Calder's *The World in 1984.*

A number of guest speakers make presentations to the class. Their topics include futuristics methodology, "the psychological time bomb," Buckminster Fuller, artificial intelligence, value theory, global sociology and future shock. Class-led discussions are also held; among the topics considered are sex-roles in the future, future school media and technological man.

At the conclusion of the term, projects are submitted by the class members. Examples from previous classes include a workshop using humanistic skills to delineate the distinction between determinative and normative forecasting; a paper outlining the design of a high-school curriculum based on altered states of consciousness; a research study focusing on the thoughts and attitudes of children aged five to nine toward possible changes in our physical bodies (c.f. *The Biological Time Bomb*); using a Delphi-like survey, a scenario and simulation on the university in 1980; a paper-seminar exploring ways of changing the roles of administrators in the public-school system; a "futuristic media" experience in creative expression; and so on.

A follow-up course is also offered; this is called "Advanced Educational Futuristics." It is a student-led class which concentrates on "the development of curriculum materials for use in the classroom and for teacher training."

16. FUTURE VALUES LABORATORY (Course module)

Course designation: Design and Environmental Analysis 400
Institution: Cornell University
Faculty: José Villegas

An example of a game unit played as *part* of a course is the "Future Values Game" developed by José Villegas and Alvin Toffler and their students at Cornell in 1969. The game involves two players at a time who, through the use of "Value Cards," negotiate their future. The Value Cards each contain a statement describing some state of affairs. Each player reacts to the state of affairs positively or negatively, indicating the intensity of response by rating it as 1 (weak intensity), 2 (medium intensity), or 3 (strong intensity). Thus the state of affairs might be "Vietnam War" and a hawkish player might respond "Positive 3." The player, however, must go beyond simply registering a pro or con attitude, and must assess the effect of the state of affairs on some valued thing, person or institution. Thus a player might respond by saying that she is "Negative 3" toward the war because it represents a danger to her boyfriend (valued person). By registering her attitude and the impact of perceived consequences deriving from the state of affairs, she has made a complete value statement.

The "trick" in the game comes with the introduction of "Technological Event" cards. Each card introduces a technological event that forces revaluation of the various states of affairs and of consequences that are presumed to flow from them.

In a more complex game involving the whole class, each technological event was presumed to have triggered certain changes in the "Life Situation" of the player—i.e., changes in his or her job, education, community, recreational patterns, etc. In turn these changes in life situation were presumed to generate changes in the values held by the players, and these, then, in turn, led to changes in the sequence of technological events in the game.

Work on these games continued the following year with the help of the Institute for the Study of Science in Human Affairs at Columbia University.

17. DIVORCE COURT 1999 A.D. (Course module)

Course designation: The Future of American Culture
Institution: Alice Lloyd College
Faculty: Billy Rojas

The assumption is made that adversary procedures are still in effect as the century draws to a close. Students are coached in roles as defense attorney, prosecuting attorney, recorder, etc. The situation acted out in class in 1972 can serve as an example of the procedure involved. A Rimmer-style group marriage was the unit involved. Some of the group wanted to end their marriage—theoretically legalized by that date. The two men wanted to stay married to their wives; the women were asking for the divorce. Plaintiffs and defendants were responsible for finding witnesses to testify on their behalf, who were then cross-examined by the lawyers. A jury was selected from among the remaining students in the class. Beforehand, students held workshop sessions to draft laws regulating group marriage and stipulating grounds for divorce and determining matters such as custody of children, division of property and the like.

This procedure can also be modified. The courtroom of the future may not, after all, be conducted in adversary fashion. And the parties to the divorce case can be a couple with twenty-first-century difficulties instead of a future group marriage. Either before or after the trial, the parties might play out a simulated session with a marriage counselor.

18. 1984 NEWS PRESENTATION (Course module)

Course designation: The Future of American Culture
Institution: Alice Lloyd College
Faculty: Billy Rojas

Students prepare a news program for television or radio ca. 1984. This activity utilizes video-tape equipment (or tape recorders, if none is available). Considerable background preparation is required as students prepare news stories describing events in 1984; this homework consists of selected futuristic readings and examination of the latest issues in journalistic, television, and broadcast media. In-class activities should include group brainstorming to open the class to considering the shape of things to come, followed by a critical evaluation of hypothetical events (Which are mutually exclusive? Which are premature? Which are highly unlikely?). Roles are assigned: anchorman, various reporters, camera personnel, etc. Students meet to plan the order of presentation for the newscast and then carry it out. Interspersed between elements of the news, however, are futuristic advertisements. Props for the ads as well as news items are suggested. At the conclusion of the taping, the program is viewed by the class and evaluated.

A variation of this activity consists of developing a future newspaper. Roles involved are business manager, editors, reporters, photographers, and the like. If circumstances permit, the paper can be duplicated and distributed on campus.

19. SECONDARY-SCHOOL COURSE

Course designation: English, Seventh and Ninth Grades
Institution: Central Junior High School (Quincy, Mass.)
Faculty: Jane Gaughan

Week I.   Why are we going to look into the future?
            Who else has looked into the future?
            A. The prophets in the Bible
            B. Utopians and anti-utopians
            C. Science-fiction writers
            D. Clairvoyants
            E. Philosophers
            F. Weather forecasters
            G. Futurists
Week II.   What is the path of man's evolution?
            What is man's future biology?
            A. Evolution
            B. Self-modified man
            C. Genetic engineering
            D. Population control
            E. Medicine in the future
            F. Future implications for drugs, alcohol, tobacco
Week III.   How will man's primary and secondary needs be met?
            A. Shelter
            B. The environment

C. Transportation

D. Communication

E. Education

Week IV. Options for man: Where else could man satisfy his needs if present trends continue?

A. Outer space

B. Under the sea

Week V. Extension of man. How will man relate to new technologies?

A. Computers

B. Automation

Week VI. Future social relationships—microcosmic and macrocosmic.

A. Influence of the young on family structures

B. Changing roles—Women ask "Why?"

C. Community life

D. National and international relationships

Week VII. Things to Come—science-fiction literature.

This final part of the unit involved both reading and writing of science fiction. Field trips to science-fiction movies would fit in nicely.

Week VIII. Future Fair

Student projects: designs, displays, games, etc.

Gaughan devised "class inquiry sessions" as a technique of working together on the assumption that students who investigate the future as a group can develop a sense of community. These sessions were also based on the premise that complex future problems such as "What path will human biological evolution follow?" should be treated as a series of shorter questions. Accordingly the following procedure was adopted:

1. At the start of a class session an "inquiry sheet" is passed out to all students. This sheet contains possible questions to be considered and areas that might be explored during the forty-minute session. For example, if man's future biology were the topic under discussion, one of the groups would perhaps decide that the problem could be stated as, "What effect will our future evolution have on us?" Each student would then read the information sheet and either decide on a suggested topic related to the question or propose one of his own. (This process usually took about ten minutes.)

2. Next, class members break into groups according to expressed interests. Each group receives information related to its chosen field. This material includes newspaper clippings, tape recordings, marked

books, filmstrips, and the like. A group secretary extracts pertinent ideas from both the sources and the ensuing discussions. The small groups plan a two-minute presentation suggesting a problem or question related to their area of concern as well as offering comments or possible solutions. For example, one of the future biology groups was concerned with genetic manipulation and control. By reviewing pertinent articles or a source like Chapter Six of *The Biological Time Bomb*, they formulated the question "Who will control the genetic engineers?" They then noted pertinent points and possible methods of solving the expressed problem. Thus new questions are written on the board under the main problem. (This process usually lasts fifteen minutes.)

3. Each secretary, at this stage, orally communicates the findings and viewpoint of his group. Often five two-minute reports were given.

4. The findings of the entire class are then related to the major problem of the day. If the class is satisfied that the issue is exhausted, the same process will be repeated the next meeting. When students are obviously concerned with the set of questions they have begun to survey, subsequent class sessions could be set aside in order to treat an alternative future in more depth. This is done independently or in groups. Role-playing, dramatization, use of media, are all used by the class groups at different times.

20. SECONDARY-SCHOOL CLASS

Course designation: Humanities
Institution: The Consortium School (Utica, New York)
Faculty: Angela M. Elefante

In various classes at the Consortium School pupils are introduced to futuristic ideas. Among the topics considered:

What Will the Twenty-First Century Call Art?
    Students are asked to borrow ten slides from the local media library which, in their opinion, may be typical of artwork fifty years or so hence. Accompanying each slide the student prepares a brief tape-recorded talk discussing the artist, the artist's life-style, and personal impressions of the artwork.
Twenty-First-Century Technology—The Computer.
    A preselected filmstrip is viewed to gain the following information: how a computer is programmed; how a problem is flow-charted; how the binary system works; and how the machine operates. The facts learned are applied to a written

report dealing with future medicine; a movie, "Medical Electronics," supplies additional data.

The City in the Future.

After reading and viewing film materials, students discuss three questions: What are the city's major problems? What origin do these problems have? What possible solutions can be conceived for these problems? The unit concludes with a written paper on one of these topics—"Science in City and Suburb" or "Our Polluted World."

Men and Women for the Twenty-First Century.

In this unit more-or-less traditional materials (books, films) on the lives of selected famous people are examined from a futuristic vantage point. In what way are Shakespeare, Dickens, Luther, Queen Victoria, Mary Queen of Scots, Einstein, etc., twenty-first-century people? Dickens, for example, can be considered (partially) as an urban ecologist, sociologist, psychologist, moral critic, and as a sophisticated individual. The descriptions of Victorian rooms found in different Dickens books can be used for comparison purposes between his time, ours, and the furnishings expected in the next millennium. Another comparison which can be handled in a paper might be Uriah Heep in *David Copperfield* with Richard Nixon.

Other subjects explored in the twenty-first-century humanities program include photography in the future, poetry, films, drama in tomorrow's world. Improvised class theater productions can be carried out to depict life in the future. Also used are panel discussions, architectural planning work, required notebook for records of class assignments, lectures, etc., review of futuristic articles in magazines, and an individual portfolio for each pupil.

21. SECONDARY-SCHOOL COURSE

Course designation: Social Studies
Institution: Lewiston-Porter Central School
                      (Youngstown, New York)
Faculty: Jerry Kaiser

The Social Studies Department at Lewiston-Porter has assembled a program of study called "The Real World"; this includes a series of mini-courses and full-fledged courses focusing upon subjects that are relevant in today's and tomorrow's society. Among the courses that students can take are these:

Election, 1972
Courts and the Law
Political Parties
Geopolitics
Peace Studies—Alternatives to War
War Studies
American Women Today—Free or Frustrated
The Sociology of Rock Music
Moral Reasoning—Clarifying Value Conflicts
Changing Trends in the Family
Population Control—Whose Right to Live
Your Career: A survey of occupational trends and problems
Creative Problem-Solving
The Occult: Fact or Fancy
Sunshine: A simulation of current racial problems in a typical
    American city.

Futuristic Studies is one of the courses in "The Real World" program. According to the catalog description, the class focuses upon the coming post-science-fiction era when many of the speculations of that literature will be history. Subjects dealt with include tomorrow's society, the shape of the economy in the future, the promise and peril of science, world management, and alternative life-styles of the future, from communes to consumer cooperatives. Students were asked to examine relevant historical trends, identify major influences on the future of their topic, and project forward in time to A.D. 2000. While most papers were ordinary, "One student wanted to research the idea of a universal language and decided on a projected UN conference where the world would decide on one language. He researched the important languages, had representatives debate on the merits of their tongue, and then ran through fourteen ballots until one was chosen. The paper read like *The Andromeda Strain* and I refrain from giving away the ending. . . ." Topics for other papers were concerned with the future of cities, sports, religion, social control, etc.

22. SECONDARY-SCHOOL COURSE

Course designation: (Planning in Process)
Institution: Maple Heights High School (Cleveland, Ohio)
Faculty: Betty Franks

The Greater Cleveland Council for the Social Studies is in the midst of preparations for a large-scale futures program to begin in the Fall of 1973. Ultimately, Maple Heights and other area high schools will offer a three-credit interdisciplinary course for seniors in future studies. Tomorrow's world will be examined through the medium of several academic disciplines all focusing on the same subject, possibly natural science, social studies and English, although another combination might be selected instead.

To date the futures class has not been designed, but the background work is proceeding. What the reader might like to know is *how* the planning is being conducted.

Almost one and a half years before the future-studies course was scheduled to begin, the services of a consultant were obtained. Lois Lequyea, Betty Franks and other teachers secured permission from their school principal to spend time doing preliminary planning before the consultant arrived; they then used the information they obtained to draft a proposal which would get enough funds together to start a futuristics workshop.

The initial meeting of the workshop was held at John Carroll University in June 1972. All the teachers who were interested in working in futuristics from the Cleveland Council Schools met with futurists who specialized in various aspects of the field: curriculum design, classroom simulations, media, science fiction, etc. Together with students from the schools involved, participants met in small groups to design units of study. Religion, the family, and the city were among the topics considered. Workshop members experienced an introduction by immersion to the idea of futuristics for the three days they lived together.

The next step in the process of planning was a series of five Saturday morning workshops held in the early Spring of 1973. On the agenda for three meetings were seminars with famous futurists, followed by a "think tank" comprised of Cleveland-area futuristics teachers and a futuristics media fair. Just before the academic program starts, a five-week institute will be held in the summer. Already, however, several teachers have introduced short futures modules into their existing courses.

23. DIVISION OF THE FUTURE—DREYFUS COLLEGE

Institution: Fairleigh Dickinson University
Faculty: Irving Buchen

In its first phase, the Division of the Future will serve to generate intercollege courses and perspectives that will cut across traditional college and department lines. Students from Liberal Arts, Business, Education, and Science and Engineering will be admitted and mixed together in courses designed not to replace but to support traditional majors in traditional colleges.

A series of basic futuristic courses will be offered as a fundamental orientation. They include

1. *Communiculture with Multimedia Lab*
   This course explores all aspects of communication including cross-cultural, and focuses on the concept of communication as a measure of culture. Also includes a Lab which, among other things, will make use of Future Drills (specific ways of living in the future now).
2. *History of Futurism with Time-Machine Lab*
   A historical survey in all cultures of the prophetic and apocalyptic traditions up to the present preoccupation with horoscopes and futurists. Time-Machine Lab will be used for controlled dislocation of notions of time and space.
3. *Future Styles: Learning, Loving and Working*
   An attempt to project future images of men and women along future lines by breaking down the false split between living and working, private and public lives. In the process, what will be put forth is a new notion of career training, that of career-conversion training.

Three general clusters of courses have been designed as central areas of activity: Global Futures; Regional and National Planning; and Information, Communication and Control Skills and Systems. From the cluster of courses available in each area, students will elect those that provide maximum support and amplification of their majors.

Some of the course titles by cluster are as follows:

Global Futures:

        Peace Studies (Models of World Law Fund)
        Multinational Companies
        Futuristic Planning and Policy Sciences
        Global Planning Council
        Global Electronic System
        Models of Inequity and Equity
        Global Distribution Centers and Systems

Planning:

        Planning Ethics
        Advocacy Planning
        Participatory-Anticipatory Model: Citizens
          and Community Planning

Home Rule-National Sovereignties: The Trade-
   Off Negotiation
Ecology and Planning
Minorities and Planning

Communications:
   The Future of Leisure Learning Centers
   Design of Communications Nets for Communities
   The Pathmark Model: Part-Time Education and Work
   Nonverbal Communications
   Mind-Expansion and Consciousness-Raising

Section Three: Directory of Futuristics Courses

Note: Courses described in *Section Two: Selected Syllabi*, are not double-entered here. Dates given are those of the most recent verified time that a class was offered. Courses are grouped into ten categories:

Introductory
Futuristics and Education
Futuristics and Forecasting
Futuristics and Systems
Futuristics and Technology
Head Trips
Overseas Futuristics Education
Futuristics Programs
Futuristics K–12
Futuristics Post-College

INTRODUCTORY COURSES

British Columbia, University of (Canada): Zoology 500—Ecology of the Future; Julius Kane (1970).
Brooklyn, Polytechnic Institute of: IE-941—Issues in Science and Technology; Anthony J. Wiener (1969).
California State University: CS-204—Future Studies Surveys; David C. Miller and Ronald L. Hunt (1972).
Drexel Institute of Technology: futuristic sociology; Arthur Shostak (1971).
Illinois Wesleyan University: Sociology 314—Sociology of the Future; Max A. Pape (1967–1972), the second futures course ever taught.
La Verne College: Ahmed S. Ispahani (1971).

Long Island University (Southampton College): N.S. 299—Search for Long-Range Goals for Mankind; Radh Achuthau (1972).

Massachusetts Institute of Technology: futuristic political science; Ithiel de Sola Pool (1969).

New York, State University of (Buffalo): Bases for Futures; C. H. Waddington and Robert Underwood (1971).

North Dakota, University of: Futuristics; Douglas Irving (1973).

Phoenix College: FT 101—Perimeters of the Future; Maxwell H. Norman (1972).

Pittsburgh, University of: Sociology 27—Social Change; R. C. Bricston (1972).

Pomona College: Government/Politics in the Year 2000; Franklyn Tugwell (1972).

Prince Edward Island, University of (Canada): futuristic political science; Saul N. Silverman (1969).

Princeton University: Sociology 348—Sociology of the Future; Suzanne Keller (1969).

St. Clair Community College: Futuristics; Robert E. Tansky (1973).

San Diego State College: Studies of the Future; Willis H. Thompson (1970).

Sangamon State University: PAC K-20—Futurism; Cullom Davis (1972).

Southern Connecticut State College: I. D. 5xx—Alternative Pathways to the Future; Jere W. Clark (1972), and other related courses.

South Florida, University of: Interdisciplinary Social Science/Human Relations and Productivity; Henry Winthrop (1972), and other related courses.

Texas, University of (Austin): The Year 2000; David V. Edwards (1969).

Trinity College (Burlington, Vermont): The Future of Man; Sister Rose Rowan (1973).

Upsala College: Sociology 440-02—Seminar in Social Futuristics; Robert Johansen (1973).

Valdosta State College: The Sociology of the Future; Bernard J. Cosneck (1972).

Virginia, University of: political futures; Paul David (1971).

Washington University (St. Louis, Missouri): A Critical Approach to the Future; Thomas V. Cahill (1969).

West Georgia College: The Future; Newt Gingrich (1972).

Yale University: Sociology 84 b (undergraduate), Sociology 185 a (graduate)—The Sociology of the Future; Wendell Bell (1972).

FUTURISTICS AND EDUCATION

Adelphi University: Edu. 702—Futures in Education; Julian Wilder (1973).

Andover Newton Theological School: The Future as a Theological Problem; Joseph C. Williamson (1969).

California at Los Angeles, University of: Futures Research and Education; Charles N. Ehler, Marv Adelson, and Harvey S. Perloff (1971).

Connecticut, University of: Ed. 406—Seminar Using Modern Theories of Education to Invent the Future; Frank A. Stone (1971).

Great Neck Teachers Association: Teaching the Future; Wes Thomas (1973).

Heidelberg College (Tiffin, Ohio): Future Studies; Bruce A. Lohof (1972).

Illinois, University of (Urbana): Future Studies and Educational Policy; Ralph A. Smith (1971).

Indiana University: J 670—Current Educational Thought and the Curriculum; Harold G. Shane (1972).

LeMoyne College (Syracuse, New York): Theology and the Future; Fr. Ed. Zogby (1969).

Livingston College (Rutgers University): Alternative Futures in Education; Al Record (1972).

Loyola College (Canada): Futurontology; John G. McGraw (1972).

Mankato State: R. Barnes (1971).

New York, State University of (Rensselaerville, New York): The University at the Year 2000; Samuel B. Gould (1968).

Ontario Institute for Studies in Education: 3012 X—The Future Context of Education; David Livingstone and Melvyn Robbins (1972).

San Francisco State College: futures in English; Edward Coletti (1971).

Syracuse University: numerous futures courses under Thomas F. Green since 1968.

Western Ontario, University of (Althouse College of Education, Canada): History of Education E 195/Contemporary Trends in Education; D. W. Ray and H. A. Stevenson (1973).

FUTURISTICS AND FORECASTING

Antioch College: Futuristics; Magoroh Maruyama (1972).

California, University of (Berkeley): Bus. Admin. 205—Industrial Research and Industrial Change; Richard L. Sander (1969).

————: Forecasting the Future, Concepts, Problems, and Methods; Allen Griffiths (1972).

California at Los Angeles, University of: Technological and Social Forecasting X 403; Albert G. Wilson (1970).

Columbia University: Problems of Long-Range Forecasting; Daniel Bell (1969).

Drexel Institute of Technology: F 225—Engineering, Technology, and Society; A. J. Pennington (1969).

Fontbonne College: Forecasting and Planning Techniques; Jayne B. Burks (1972).

Lowell Technological Institute: The Technological Future—Technical Aspects (1968), Social and Political Aspects (1969); William S. Harrison.

New Hampshire, University of: Ed. 897—Designing the Future of Education, An Approach to Long-Range Planning; Timothy Weaver (1970).

New York, State University of (Albany): science and technology studies; Jack J. Bulloff (1973).

Ohio University: Technological Forecasting; Paul Anton (1970).

Purdue University: Industrial Administration 690 J—Seminar in Strategic Planning; Arnold Cooper with D. E. Schendel (1968).

Southern California, University of: Engineering 685—Technological Forecasting; Harold A. Linston (1969).

Utah, University of: Futurist Methodologies and Techniques; Gerald W. Smith (1973).

Washington, University of (Seattle): Forecasting Methods in Urban Planning; J. B. Schneider (no date).

Wayne State University: The Future of Information Systems; Martin Pfaff (1969).

Wright State University: Technological Forecasting Methodologies; H. W. Lanford (1972).

FUTURISTICS AND SYSTEMS

Brown University: VC 101-02—World Game Design Studio; C. P. Wolf (1972).

California, University of (Berkeley): CP 227—Futures of Urbanism and the City; Richard L. Meier (1972).

California at Los Angeles, University of: Conflict Research; Jiri Mehnevajsa and R. C. Brictson (1967).

Cornell University: gaming courses—Ghetto 1984; Peru 2000; New York City School Decentralization; Introduction to the Society of the Future and the City of the Future; Squatter Settlement in Latin America in the Year 2000; Future Values Laboratory—José Villegas (1971).

Dayton, University of: The Future: An Interdisciplinary Approach; Fr. Frank Maloney and Bro. Larry Cada (1970).

Denver, University of: Technology and Public Policy; John S. Gilmore (1970).

————: Technology and Society; A. J. Pennington (1969).

————: Engineering—Technology and Public Policy; John S. Gilmore (1969).

Kendall College: Technology and Modern Civilization/Creating Your Own Space; Noel McInnis (1968).

New School for Social Research: Nuclear War—its anatomy, pathology, etiology, and prevention; Tom Stomer (1968).

Northwestern University: Global Society; P. Smoker, C. F. Alger, and L. F. Anderson (1970).

Pennsylvania State University: Geography 412—The Geography of the Future; Ronald Abler (1972).

Rhode Island School of Design: Designing Alternative Futures/Future Games: Adventure in the Arts; Thomas Carleton and Russ Kolton (1972).

St. Francis College (Brooklyn): Planning for the Future; Clement Jedrzejewski (1969).

San Jose State College: Cybernation and Man; Ralph Parkman (1969).

Virginia, University of: Computers, Society, and the Future; Craig Decker (1972).

Wesleyan University (Connecticut): Urban Simulation—The Future of Middletown; Dennis Little and Raul de Brigard (1970).

FUTURISTICS AND TECHNOLOGY

California, University of (Berkeley): Political Science H 190—Science, Technology, and Future World Politics; Ernst B. Haas and John G. Ruggie (1971).

———— (Davis): Fred E. Case.

Harvard University: Man in an Age of Machines; J. M. Porte (1969).

————: Legal Process and Technological Change; Tribe (1969).

Illinois, University of (Urbana): The Long-Range Goals of Man; Sidney Rosen (1971).

———— (Chicago Circle): Management 366—Technological Forecasting; Management 367—The Impact of Technological Change; Ronald E. Jablonski (1972).

Kennedy, John F., University: Harry L. Morrison.

Loyola University of the South: Bus. Admin. 550—Business Administration in the 21st Century; Irving A. Fosberg (1971).

Santa Clara, University of: Engineering and the Technological Society; Richard C. Dorf (1969).

Stanford University: Engineering Seminar on the Future; Willis Harman (1969).

Syracuse University: Marketing 756—Current Problems in Marketing; Robert F. Bundy (1970).

Washington, University of (Seattle): Urban Planning and Political Science, P. S. 553/586—Environmental Change and Urban Policy; P. S. 580—Environmental and Technological Change and Urban Policy; Robert Warren (1971).

HEAD TRIPS

Alfred University: History 160—Survey of the Future; Lawrence Bell (1972).

Burlington County College (New Jersey): Futuristics—A Study of the Next 30 Years; Harlan Douglas (1972).

California, University of (Berkeley): Environmental Design 100 AX— Design of Alternative Futures; Jon Dieges (1969).

Canisius College: The History of Future Studies; James A. Duran (1972).

Case Western Reserve University: SCPP 347—Alternative World Futures (1971); SCPP 380—Science Fiction and Social Policy (1970); SIDS 301—Utopias (1972); Dennis Livingston.

Colorado State: Sociology 340—The Family (anticipated futures); Thomas Harblin (1971).

Drew University: Anthropology 140—Man's Future Social and Cultural Development; Roger W. Wescott (1972).

Indiana University: Experimental Course J 219—1980 and Beyond; Keith Jepsen (1972).

Marin, College of: Inventing the Future; Maryjane Dunstan (1972).

New School for Social Research: Sociology 513—Social Change and the Future; Alvin Toffler (1966–1967).

Oakland, University of: Rebels, Reformers, and Other Human Hatpins —Strategies for Planned Change; William F. Sturner (1972).

Rollins College: Sociology 320—Social Change and the Future; Thomas Harblin (1972).

Santa Cruz College: Future Environments of America; Jerry M. Yudelson (1971).

Southern Illinois University: Futuristic Design Science; Edwin Schlos-
berg and Jon Dieges (1968).

OVERSEAS FUTURISTICS EDUCATION

New Delhi (India): Marianne Hook-Butalia (1970).
Prague, Economic University of: Futurology; Otto Sulc (1970).
Technische Univeritaet (Vienna): Technological Forecasting and Com-
parative Methodology in Futures Research; Robert Jungk (1968).

FUTURISTICS PROGRAMS

Alice Lloyd College: Futuristics Curriculum Project/Appalachian Futuristics Project; directed by Billy Rojas. Education 101—Alternative Futures in Education (1971); Sociology 231—The Year
2000 (1973), continued; Sociology 239—Urban Appalachia
(1973), continued; History 243—The Future of Appalachia
(1973), continued; History 245—Space Exploration in the Future
(1972); Political Science 210—The Future of American Government (1972); Political Science 215—Spaceship Earth (1972).
Massachusetts, University of—School of Education (Amherst): Program for the Study of the Future for Education; directed by Chris
Dede. Ed. 785—The Future of Higher Education: Billy Rojas
(1970); Ed. 386—Methods for Predicting the Future: Billy Rojas
(1971); E-60—Teaching for the Future: Paul Burnim and Ken
Hoagland (1972); E-66—Development in Educational Futuristics: Chris Dede (1972); Seminar in the Ideas of Marshall Mc-
Luhan and Buckminster Fuller: Art France (1969); Films and
the Future: teacher not identified (1972). *Proposed courses—and
modular mini-courses*: Futuristics Curriculum Research; The Lit-
erature of Futuristics; Alternative Life-Styles; Synergetics and
Technology; The Future of Higher Education; The Countercul-
ture, Media, and the Future; Drugs, Education, and the Future;
Computers, Education, and the Future.
Minnesota, University of: Office for Applied Social Science and the
Future; co-directors: Arthur M. Harkins and Richard G. Woods.
Basic requirement: SS 3-981—Societies of the Future (1972).
Related courses: Agricultural Econ. 5630—Regional Development
Systems; Economics 5611—The Economics of Environmental
Control; H. Education 5211—Social Planning and Education;
H. Education 5212—Education and Societies of the Future; So-
cial Science 5991/2/3—Seminars in Alternative Futures; Social

Science 5101—Steady State Earth: Goals, Constraints; Sociology
5551—World Population Problems; Sociology 5506—New Forms
in the Family; Biology 3051—Biology, Future of Man; EBB 1003
—The Final Crisis; Humanities 3006—Imagination in the 20th
Century; Music 3971—Electronic Music Literature.

Newark State College: Collateral Program for the Study of the Future;
Howard F. Didsbury, executive director. History 4082—Philoso-
phy, Science, and Civilization II: The Modern Scientific and
Technological Impact on Culture (1972); History 3870—Dreams
and Nightmares: Utopias and History; History 5810—Impact of
Science and Technology on Culture; Interdisciplinary Seminar on
Futurism.

Stanford University: summer science-fiction colloquia; director not
noted. U.S. 125—Sociology of the Possible: Richard Ofshe; U.S.
132—Science Fiction as the History of the Future: David Mc-
Neil; U.S. 190—Studies in Science Fiction: Arthur Hastings; U.S.
192—Technology and the Future: Samuel McIntosh; U.S. 203—
Views of the Future in 20th Century Art and Drama: Wendell
Cole; S.C. 17—Utopias: Arthur Hastings; S.C. 12—Explorations
in Science Fiction: A. Berkley Driessel—"What can be regarded
as human? What are the psychological functions of myth, cere-
mony, and fantasy?" are considered in this class; English 279—
Science Fiction: H. Bruce Franklin—This course is described as
a "Marxist approach to the science fiction of both socialist and
capitalist countries."

OTHER PROGRAMS

Fairleigh Dickinson University: See Item 23, *Section Two.*

Hawaii, University of: The Commission on the Year 2000; Program for
Futures Research directed by James Dator. Political Science 4114
—Political Futuristics: James Dator (1972); Tune to the Future—
Educational television extension course (1972). Also: Educational Foundations 684—Education and World Order; Engineering 203—Technology and Society; New College 202—The World's
Future; Political Science 335—Applied Futuristics; Political Science 670—Advanced Futuristics; Science 124—Technology, Ecology and Man; Speech/Communication 387—Communication and
the Future.

Prescott College: futuristics concentration; director not known. Contemporary Visions of the Future: Draper Kauffman (1971); Independent studies options.

University Without Walls at Roger Williams College: Futures Lab, directed by Thomas Carleton. Offers multi-disciplinary, learner-centered alternative to traditional education. Students learn about and prepare for alternative futures. The process curriculum, "Designing Alternative Futures," consists of training seminars, group projects, and individual study. Seminars, "The Design Process" and "Applied Futuristics," develop skills in decision-making, problem-solving, and forecasting applied to self-directed projects. Major projects now under way include the "Earthrise World Model," an assessment of present and future global conditions, and "Rhode Island 2000," a proposal for community participation in seeking long-term solutions to longstanding problems toward the year 2000. The Futures Lab is coordinated by Earthrise Inc., a nonprofit educational organization developing a comprehensive approach to futures research, education and design.

FUTURISTICS K–12

Priscilla Griffith apparently taught the first precollege futuristics course in the United States at *Melbourne* (Florida) *High School*, during the school years 1967–1968, 1968–1970. Other public and private institutions:

Baldwin School, New York, New York.
Choate School, Wallingford, Connecticut; Tom Colvin.
Columbus Elementary School, Berkeley, California.
Fox School, Belmont, California; Judi Driessel.
Glenn, John, High School, Long Island, New York; George Ostrander (1972).
Harwood School, Harwood, Vermont; John Weil.
Jericho High School, Long Island, New York; Bob Hoffman (1972).
Kailua High School, Hawaii.
Licking County Public Schools, Newark, Ohio; Bob Mentzer.
Maryknoll High School, Hawaii.
Minneapolis Public Schools, Minneapolis, Minnesota; Tom Bender.
Montachusett Region Vocational Technical High School, Fitchburg, Massachusetts: 21st Century; Wilbur H. Carter (1972).
O'Farrell Jr. High School, San Diego, California; Geraldine Rickman.
Pacific Domes, Los Gatos, California; Lloyd Kahn.
Peninsula Elementary School, Menlo Park, California.
Ravenswood High School, East Palo Alto, California; Jack Fasman.
Tacoma Park Jr. High School, Silver Spring, Maryland; Manford W. Smith.
Wasson High School, Colorado Springs, Colorado; Robert Peck.

FUTURISTICS POST-COLLEGE

William Bradshaw directed the L.S.U. 2067 project, perhaps the first adult-education futures program when it was staged in 1967. "The World of 2067" was featured in the August 1967 issue of *The Futurist*. Other continuing futures-learning classes:

Miami, University of, Division of Continuing Education (Florida): Introduction to Comprehensive Anticipatory Design Science; Bennett Shapiro (1971). Also, Utopia or Oblivion: The Prospects for Man on Earth; Bennett Shapiro (1971).

New School for Social Research: Our Options for the Future; Thomas E. Jones (1972).

Syracuse University, University College of, Humanistic Studies Center: The Future of American Politics; Robert McClure (1971).

U. S. Department of Agriculture, The Graduate School (Washington, D.C.): The Future; Charles William (1969–1971).

Section Four: Readings

So broad a variety of books and materials are now used in futures studies that it is impossible to summarize them adequately. It is likely that learning materials in the futures field are more eclectic than in perhaps any other educational field. Faced with this impossibility, we have prepared a list of seventy-five frequently mentioned titles. With rare exception, the list limits itself to books. Moreover, it excludes one category of books that are widely used—science fiction—because a detailed bibliography of science-fiction materials appears in this volume at the end of the notes to Dennis Livingston's chapter.

Starred items are the ten most frequently used according to our latest survey, November 1972.

AYERS, ROBERT U. *Technological Forecasting and Long-Range Planning*. McGraw-Hill, 1969.

BAIER, KURT and NICHOLAS RESCHER (eds.). *Values and the Future*. Free Press, 1969.

BANFIELD, EDWARD C. *The Unheavenly City—The Nature and the Future of Our Urban Crisis*. Little, Brown, 1970.

BECKWITH, BURNHAM P. *The Next 500 Years*. Exposition, 1968.

*BELL, DANIEL (ed.). *Toward the Year 2000*. Beacon, 1969.

———. "Twelve Modes of Predictions—A Preliminary Sorting of Approaches in the Social Sciences." *Daedalus*, Summer 1964.

BELL, WENDELL, *The Sociology of the Future*. Russell Sage Foundation, 1971.

BENNIS, WARREN G. and PHILIP E. SLATER. *The Temporary Society*. Harper Colophon, 1968.

BERNARD, JESSIE. *The Future of Marriage*. World, 1972.

BOOCOCK, SARANE S. and E. O. SCHILD. *Simulation Games in Learning*. Sage, 1968.

BOULDING, KENNETH. *The Meaning of the Twentieth Century*. Harper Colophon, 1965.

BRIGHT, JAMES R. (ed.). *Technological Forecasting for Industry and Government: Methods and Applications*. Prentice-Hall, 1968.

BROWN, HARRISON. *The Challenge of Man's Future*. Viking, 1964.

BURNS, JIM. *Arthropods—New Design Futures*. Praeger, 1972.

BUTLER, W. F. *How Business Economists Forecast*. Prentice-Hall, 1966.

CALDER, NIGEL. *Technopolis*. Simon and Schuster, 1970.

——— (ed.). *Unless Peace Comes, A Scientific Forecast of New Weapons*. Viking Compass, 1968.

CHASE, STUART. *The Most Probable World*. Harper and Row, 1968.

*CLARKE, ARTHUR C. *Profiles of the Future*. Bantam, 1964.

DICKSON, PAUL. *Think Tanks*. Atheneum, 1971.

DRUCKER, PETER F. *The Age of Discontinuity*. Harper & Row, 1969.

DUNSTAN, MARYJANE and PATRICIA GARLAN. *Worlds in the Making*. Prentice-Hall, 1970.

EBON, MARTIN. *Prophecy in Our Time*. New American Library, 1968.

EHRLICH, PAUL. *The Population Bomb*. Ballantine, 1968.

EURICH, ALVIN C. (ed.). *Campus 1980*. Delta, 1968.

———. *High School 1980*. Pitman, 1970.

EWALD, WILLIAM R., JR. (ed.). *Environment and Change*. Indiana University Press, 1968.

*FABUN, DON. *Dynamics of Change*. Prentice-Hall, 1967.

FORRESTER, JAY W. *World Dynamics*. Wright-Allen Press, 1971.

FRIEDMAN, WOLFGANG. *The Future of the Oceans*. Braziller, 1971.

FULLER, R. BUCKMINSTER. *Education Automation*. Arcturus Books, 1962.

GABOR, DENNIS, *Innovations: Scientific, Technological and Social*. Oxford University Press, 1970.

GALBRAITH, JOHN KENNETH. *The New Industrial State*. Houghton Mifflin, 1967.

GENERAL ELECTRIC. *Our Future Business Environment: Developing Trends and Changing Institutions*. G.E., 1968.

GORDON, THEODORE. *The Future.* St. Martin's Press, 1965.

GREEN, THOMAS (ed.). *Educational Planning in Perspective.* I.P.C. Science and Technology Press, 1971.

GREER, GERMAINE. *The Female Eunuch.* Paladin, 1971.

HACK, WALTER G. and others. *Educational Futurism 1985.* McCutchan, 1971.

*HEILBRONER, ROBERT. *The Future as History.* Grove Press, 1961.

HELMER, OLAF, THEODORE GORDON and B. BROWN. *Social Technology.* Basic Books, 1966.

HETMAN, FRANÇOIS. *The Language of Forecasting.* Paris: SEDEIS, 1969.

ILLICH, IVAN. *Deschooling Society.* Harper & Row, 1970.

*DE JOUVENEL, BERTRAND. *The Art of Conjecture.* Basic Books, 1967.

KAHN, HERMAN. *Thinking About the Unthinkable.* Avon, 1962.

*——— and ANTHONY J. WIENER. *The Year 2000.* Macmillan, 1967.

——— and B. BRUCE-BIGGS. *Things to Come: Thinking About the 70's and 80's.* Macmillan, 1972.

LEONARD, GEORGE B. *Education and Ecstasy.* Delacorte, 1968.

LIEBERMAN, MYRON. *The Future of Public Education.* University of Chicago Press, 1960.

*McHALE, JOHN. *The Future of the Future.* Braziller, 1969.

MARGOLIN, JOSEPH B. and MARION R. MISCH (eds.). *Computers in the Classroom.* Spartan Books, 1970.

MARIEN, MICHAEL and WARREN L. ZIEGLER (eds.). *The Potential of Educational Futures.* National Society for the Study of Education, 1972.

MARTIN, JAMES and ADRIAN R. D. NORMAN. *The Computerized Society.* Prentice-Hall, 1970.

*MEADOWS, DENNIS, et al. *The Limits to Growth.* Universe Books, 1972.

OETTINGER, ANTHONY G. with SEMA MARKS. *Run, Computer Run: The Mythology of Educational Innovation.* Collier, 1969.

PADDOCK, WILLIAM and PAUL. *Famine 1975! America's Decision: Who Will Survive?* Little, Brown, 1967.

PLATT, JOHN. *The Step to Man.* John Wiley, 1966.

POLAK, FRED. *The Image of the Future.* Elsevier, 1972.

PRINCE, GEORGE M. *The Practice of Creativity.* Cambridge, Massachusetts: Synectics, Inc., 1969.

RIMMER, ROBERT. *The Harrad Experiment.* Bantam, 1967.

RUZIC, NEIL P. *Where the Winds Sleep—Man's Future on the Moon: A Projected History.* Doubleday, 1970.

SKINNER, B. F. *Beyond Freedom and Dignity.* Bantam, 1972.

SMITH, RALPH A. (ed.). "Special Issue: The Future and Aesthetic Education." *The Journal of Aesthetic Education*, January 1970.

SOLOMON R. GUGGENHEIM MUSEUM. *On the Future of Art*. Viking, 1970.

SULLIVAN, WALTER. *We Are Not Alone*. McGraw-Hill, 1964.

*TAYLOR, GORDON RATTRAY. *The Biological Time Bomb*. World, 1968.

TAYLOR, JOHN G. *The Shape of Minds to Come*. Weybright and Talley, 1971.

TEICH, ALBERT H. (ed.). *Technology and Men's Future*. St. Martin's, 1972.

THEOBALD, ROBERT (ed.). *The Guaranteed Income, Next Step in Socioeconomic Evolution?* Anchor, 1967.

————. *An Alternative Future for America II*. Swallow, 1969.

*TOFFLER, ALVIN. *Future Shock*. Bantam, 1971.

———— (ed.). *The Futurists*. Random House, 1972.

WEAVER, W. TIMOTHY. *The Delphi Method*. Syracuse: Educational Policy Research Center, 1970 (mimeo.).

YOUNGBLOOD, GENE. *Expanded Cinema*. Dutton, 1970.

Final item: For a thorough, annotated bibliography of the literature in this field, one is well advised to see Michael Marien's *Essential Reading for the Future of Education*, Revised, Educational Policy Research Center, Syracuse, 1971; his "hot list" Delphi brings the titles up-to-date.

Section Five: Centers for Research or General Information about Educational Futuristics

Center for Adaptive Learning, Inc.
34 West 13th Street
New York, N.Y. 10011

Educational Policy Research Center
1206 Harrison Street
Syracuse, N.Y. 13210

Futuremics, Inc.
2850 Connecticut Avenue
Washington, D.C. 20008

World Future Society
P.O. Box 19285
20th Street Station
Washington, D.C. 20036

Index